FRANCES MAYES
ALWAYS ITALY

FRANCES MAYES
ALWAYS ITALY

WITH **ONDINE COHANE**

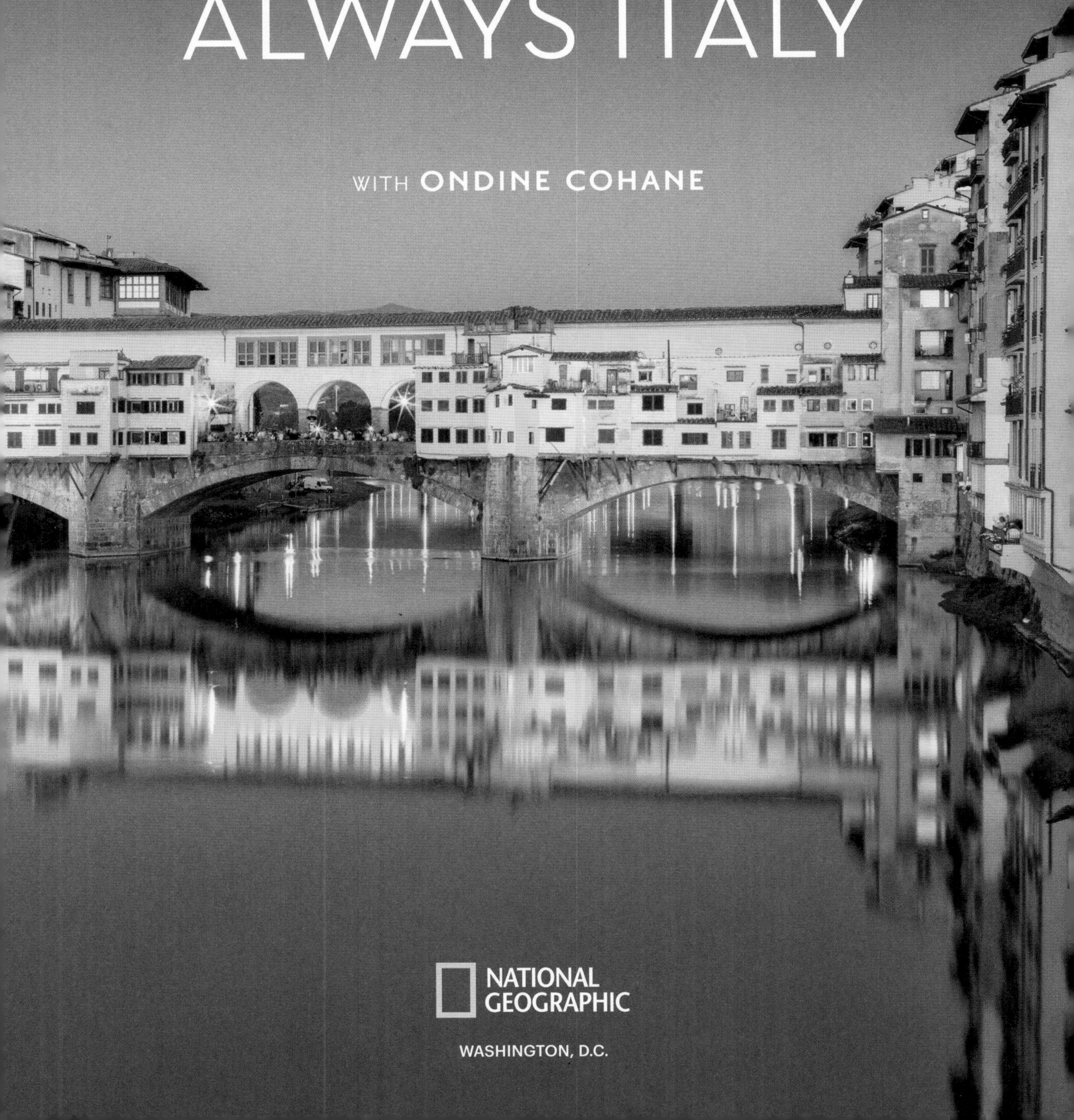

NATIONAL
GEOGRAPHIC

WASHINGTON, D.C.

CONTENTS

PAGE 1: A quiet stairway runs behind Gelateria del Teatro in Rome.
PAGES 2–3: Shops line the Ponte Vecchio over the Arno River in Florence. **LEFT:** *Trullo* architecture made of limestone masonry is well preserved in small towns of the Puglia region in southern Italy.

Introduction

The journeys I took for this book were exhilarating because, finally, I could stop at Greek ruins in Calabria; order the rustic pastas of Sardinia; stand under waterfalls in Trentino–Alto Adige; watch water buffalo milk turn into mozzarella in Puglia; and hike the sublime trails of Valle d'Aosta. I scoured the sights in all 20 regions. *At last,* I thought. *I am beginning to know this country.* Still, much remains for as many future trips as I can plan.

What a grand quest! My sense of adventure multiplied. Lost-in-time *borghi* (villages) of the Abruzzo and Molise; peak dining experiences in Emilia-Romagna; the joyous Sicilian Baroque churches that seem to have whipped cream as a building material; Le Marche's turquoise waters and beaches, which looked to my Southern eyes like white grits. Finding the far reaches of Lombardy's lake country: bliss. Those eagle-nest mountain retreats around Bolzano and Merano for curative mineral waters and robust mountain food. I especially liked the little castle strongholds in Piedmont, with undulating vineyards neat as rows of knitting.

Getting to know the north was the big surprise. I thought that as I began to hear German and the terrain neared Austria and Switzerland, some Italianness would erode. Not so; the cultural mix near the borders was, instead, stimulating. I learned a new word: *ecotone,* the zone between two places with characteristics of each. The cross-fertilization of histories enlarged my love for Italy.

How glorious, too, discovering each region's food traditions: vastly different, passionately maintained. I'm sure you can find a bad meal in Italy—but if you follow your good instincts, where might that be? Even freeway Autogrills serve tempting panini and often feature cafeterias with pasta, grilled meats, and fresh vegetables. At the gas station! How is this possible? The simple answer: Italians won't put up with bad food. My idea of heaven is to walk into a town around noon on Sunday and locate, usually by aromas drifting from the doorway, where the locals will be having their *pranzo* (lunch) on this *buona domenica.*

I followed several food—especially cheese—and wine quests, wanting to try everything. It was fun tracking how the all-important daily bread varies. From the unsalted, hard-crusted loaves of Tuscany to Puglia's cakelike rounds weighing in at six pounds (3 kg) or more to Liguria's tender focaccias and Sardinia's savory flatbreads, all taste of the place itself.

So ancient, Italy is actually quite young. Previously fragmented, it became a unified country in 1861. The heritage: settlers, invaders, and power grabbers, all spreading their languages and customs. Rugged mountains cut off egress, creating isolated villages within the craggy Apennine and Dolomite ranges. The *mezzadria* (sharecropping) system, a

Italy is roughly the size of Arizona. Imagine that state studded with Rome, Venice, Milan, Florence, and a few dozen other fascinating cities.

feudal tenant-farming arrangement, was essentially serfdom: nobody going anywhere. For dwellers in the Papal States, the church prohibited movement outside their boundaries without a passport. All this resulted in self-contained small worlds, highly individualistic. Broken into Papal States, House of Savoy rulers, the Kingdom of Two Sicilies, and the Bourbon reign, the governments up and down the peninsula held sway in their territories, but no central power prevailed.

The fiery nationalist Giuseppe Garibaldi, with his ragtag army, first conquered Sicily, then moved onto the mainland, sweeping his volunteer Redshirts north, some armed with farm implements. Unification! Today, almost every town in Italy has a Piazza Garibaldi.

But guess what? Unification never totally worked. The country refused to blend into a harmonious whole. The particular patchwork of dialects, cuisines, architecture, and art remained intact. Therefore, Italy endures as the most diverse country in the world.

A quick hit of context. Italy is roughly the size of Arizona. Imagine that southwestern state studded with Rome, Venice, Milan, Florence, Turin, Siena, Palermo, and a few dozen fascinating cities. Imagine 5,600 museums and archaeological sites. And that's not all. Italy possesses more UNESCO World Heritage sites than any other country in the world.

Amid so much beauty and humanism, you feel confirmed. The glittering, otherworldly Orvieto cathedral. Majestic Marcus Aurelius on horseback in Roma's Piazza del Campidoglio. The frescoed palazzi of Trento look like medieval board games. Not a thing apart, art exists as naturally as air.

On your way to buy bread in Venice, pass Palladio's white-white church, Il Rendentore. Breathe in. Your sense of the possible expands. In Puglia, when I look up from my cappuc-

The elliptical canal in Padua's Prato della Valle piazza is lined with statues of notable intellectuals and Renaissance leaders.

cino at Troia's 12th-century duomo's stone rose window—delicate as a paper doily—I realize that, like me, locals over the centuries have glanced at this marvel daily. On my way through the park each morning in Cortona, I greet the dolphins and nymphs cavorting in the fountain. How this lifts you.

Diverse as Italy is, one quality unites: the spirit of Italians. I'll generalize. In all my trips for this book, I met only one rude person, a hotel receptionist. She wasn't awful, just abrupt and distant. Immune to friendly overtures.

But the norm prevails. Chefs come out to talk, the museum guard wants to express his opinion about Giotto, the priest wanders around the church with you, the cheesemonger offers tastes, the innkeeper gives a jar of jam, the driver detours to show you his favorite hill town. There's a palpable generosity. After you've tasted two gelatos, the maker sends over his pistachio. You must try! After-dinner herbal concoctions—specialty of the house—appear after the check: a gift. Those old monks kneeling on cold stone floors devised liqueurs to warm them, using any old plant at hand: pine needles, fennel seeds, olive leaves, angelica roots, and bark. And they work, these *digestivi*. Evenings end on a prolonged, mellow note.

The other quality that seems to traverse the regions—the *battuto,* the back-and-forth banter—is key to understanding Italy. (How brilliantly Ernest Hemingway captures this in *A Farewell to Arms.*) Everywhere I travel, people love the play, the one-up, the fun to be had from encountering *you.* Make a clever comeback, initiate a joke, and you're in. It's part of the exuberance of daily contact. I always notice that I may say *buon giorno,* but the Italian I'm meeting says *BUON GIORNO,* louder, arms extended, drawing emphasis on the *"gior-,"* as though you are the *one* person most desirable to see on this incredible morning.

You have only to reach out to be brought into a circle of warmth, even if momentarily. This causes you to remember *that* barista in *that* tiny village, the signora who cut your hair in Bologna, the dentist in the Veneto who joked as he saved your cracked crown. (I remember them well!)

Travel is always a leap of faith into new worlds: 20 of them in Italy. Isn't that exciting? Each region remains unique. What's not yet known lies shimmering before you.

HOW TO USE THIS BOOK

To create *Always Italy,* my co-author, Ondine, and I traversed the entire country, zigzagging north to south, east to west. We're both profoundly in love with this place. Though we've each lived for years in Tuscany and traveled extensively, we are thrilled to have visited many brand-new places for this collaboration. We dove in with a big sense of adventure.

We were also seeking something we hadn't found elsewhere: a fresh look at the country's vibrant present. What we know from living here is that contemporary Italy is always in fast-forward motion. We've found one-of-a-kind hotels, forward-thinking chefs, artful shops, new vineyard architecture, up-and-coming neighborhoods, secrets of well-known cities, writers not to miss, the most pristine beaches—even the new generation of cocktail bars.

Ondine, a hotel designer, style maven, and world traveler, is naturally up on all the latest. Also a marathon runner, she is especially keen on outdoor activities, a part of Italian travel often overlooked. Our interests proved to be complementary. I love finding surprising art in less traveled areas, exercising my sommelier tendencies, reveling in the beauty of each region—and tasting along the way.

This is our very personal take on Italy today. All recommendations are searchable online, though we have included information for more obscure suggestions.

Most towns have tourist offices that offer maps, the latest information on local sights, boat rentals, trail and lift schedules, and special events. For wide context, we recommend the Blue Guide series. Also inspiring for discovery travel, check out the websites for *I Borghi più belli d'Italia,* the Most Beautiful Villages in Italy, and the Touring Club of Italy's *Bandiere Arancioni* (Orange Flags), which list exceptional villages of cultural and historic interest. A good app such as Vivino can be invaluable when facing a wine list in unfamiliar territory. We constantly use the handy annual Gambero Rosso guide *Italian Wines.*

I have written the introductions to each region—my impressions and discoveries in each. My wine recommendations and other finds can be found in "In Your Glass" and "Frances's Favorites." Ondine writes all the information you need to plan the perfect trip: "Hot Spots," "Insider's Guides," "In the Know," "Checking In," and the "Best Of" each region.

Ondine and I have had great fun meeting to compare notes as we dined in a trattoria off her hometown Pienza's grand piazza or sipped something dazzling on my Cortona terrace under the linden trees. We hope the spirited fun of the collaboration inspires you to take off for adventures in Cogne, Lake Trasimeno, Alghero, or dozens of other alluring places.

Ci vediamo in Italia—see you in Italy!

Part One
Northern Italy

Come fall, the vineyards and land-scapes of Piedmont's Langhe Valley turn red, gold, and deep brown.

Get lost in the mountains or in some of the country's most suggestive cities. From fashion to wine, northern Italy has the stars.

Welcome to Italy's richest area—in both economic output and geographical diversity. Mountains draw outdoorsy types. Cities like Milan pull in bankers and fashionistas, and Venice offers some of the most beautiful tableaux in Italy. Italians in the far north remain deeply influenced by other cultures—for example, those of Austria and Slovenia.

Come spring, temperatures tend to be cooler; the fall shoulder season (September to November) is great for eating and drinking; and winter and summer are fine for those who enjoy nature. Spa culture also abounds for wellness seekers.

The rest of the region beckons with equally appealing pursuits. Smaller towns like Mantua and Udine remain dazzling without too many tourists, while the coastline of Liguria and the Italian Riviera still shine despite legions of fans. Cerulean lakes that have attracted visitors for centuries are reinventing themselves for 21st-century travelers who like luxury mixed in with the pristine scenery. And when it comes to soccer, this is the land of some of Italy's most famous teams—not to mention sleek automobiles (think Fiat, Lamborghini, and Ferrari).

Here too a veritable treasure trove of some of the country's treasured wines. DOC, a denomination to protect products from specific terroirs, and Italian ingredients like prosciutto, truffles, Parmesan, chocolate, coffee, and balsamic vinegar all speak to the north's fertility.

It's no wonder that with all of these riches—literal and figurative—the north also has a reputation for being a bit snobby. This is especially true in its attitude toward its southernmost cousins, who are often largely blamed for the economic problems of the country. Southerners, on the other hand, feel that northerners are cold. There is some truth to this stereotype: You are unlikely to get as warm a welcome in Milan, for example, as you would in Naples or Palermo. But who cares? You will be too busy choosing how to enjoy its treasures.

CLOCKWISE FROM TOP LEFT: Quintessential gondolas on Venice's rightly named Grand Canal; a sublime dish at Milan's tiny 10 Posto restaurant; the majestic San Fruttuoso abbey sits right on the sea on the Ligurian coast; writing up the tasty daily specials at Udine's L'Alimentare.

Chapter One

TRENTINO-ALTO ADIGE

My favorite book when I was eight was Johanna Spyri's classic novel *Heidi*. Although the story is a little vague from this distance, I remember no pesky parents or schools. Heidi was sent to live with her curmudgeonly grandfather in the Swiss Alps, not far from the Trentino-Alto Adige region. What I recall from my flat south Georgia, U.S.A., perspective is pure air, cheese, goats, and yodels echoing across the valley. A rural

idyll at a high altitude imprinted in my mind; I was smitten with Heidi's lucky place in the Alps.

Today I'm smitten again among the pastel Italian peaks of the Trentino-Alto Adige: the hay fields, grassy upland meadows, and the feeling of deep contentment rising from the landscape.

The upper part of the region is named for the River Adige, and is still sometimes referred to as Südtirol, from when it belonged to the Austrian Tirol. The lower area takes its name from the historic town of Trento. The Brenta Alps of the western edge change dramatically into the majestic Dolomites as the range sweeps east.

What sets these mountains apart? The crags are mesmerizing because of the dreamy play of colors on pale limestone calcareous rock faces. The sun moving over the surfaces shifts from pink to rose to lavender, gold, and white. Fairy-tale castles with imprisoned princesses? Probably.

Breathtaking may be overused, but English doesn't have a better word to describe the Dolomites. These massive, rugged stone upheavals are like no other mountains on the planet. Formed over 200 million years ago, they still have dynamic eruptive energy.

Through them runs one of the great scenic drives in the world: The 68-mile (110 km) Strada delle Dolomiti starts at Cardano, near Bolzano, ending at Cortina d'Ampezzo, the

chic resort town over the border into the Veneto. The road traverses a landscape of peaks and verdant pastures abutting avalanches of rock. I was afraid of the drive (oh, carsick!) but soon trusted the skills that Italian engineers inherited from their ancient Roman predecessors. The current *strada*, constructed in 1901, took 2,500 workers eight years to build. How easy now to cross this formidable terrain! Along the way, many dramatic observation points overlook different clusters of peaks. A thousand photo ops!

Trentino-Alto Adige is known for world-class skiing, which also includes extensive cross-country trails (see *outdooractive.com*), blissful hiking through high meadows, and stupefying panoramas reached by *funivie,* cable cars. In the Marmolada zone, Punta Penia juts up against the sky for 10,100 feet (3,343 m); dozens of others are almost as lofty.

WHAT YOU NEED TO KNOW...

- **BEST TIME TO VISIT:** December to March for Alpine sports; May to October for hiking, rock climbing, and enjoying the region's hundreds of wildflowers. Many hotels and restaurants are closed in November and after Easter, so check availability before you go.

- **TOP SPOTS:** Bolzano, Merano, Sella Ronda, San Cassiano, Trento

- **GETTING THERE:** Fly into Milan or Venice and then rent a car or take a picturesque train ride north to Bolzano.

The Dolomite peaks loom over Lake Carezza.

It's fascinating to observe the cross-fertilization of cultures in this border region, which was part of the Austro-Hungarian Empire from 1814 until 1919.

All nine distinct areas of the Dolomites are UNESCO World Heritage sites and the UNESCO Dolomites Foundation sponsors TrekFinder, a helpful website for locating your ideal trail, from strolling through the wildflowers to drastic vertical climbs.

This region is more than just picturesque, more than snow fun and trekking the great outdoors. The waters, from the hurling, jade River Adige to the lakes—Braies, Misurina, Tovel, Carezza, and many others—are profound pleasures. The mountains are even more beautiful in their pellucid reflections on clear green-as-a-lime waters. And waterfalls! A fine hike at Campo Tures leads you up, up, up to three levels of cascades plunging into ferny, primeval woods.

Off piste (ski runs) and hiking trails, what is there to see and do? The options are many: thermal baths, remote mountain *rifugi* (inns or restaurants along the trails), cable car rides up to panoramic views, elegant spa towns, exquisite remote hotels that have perfected comfort, a wealth of museums, and perching castles.

It's fascinating to observe the cross-fertilization of cultures in this border region, which was part of the Austro-Hungarian Empire from 1814 until 1919. Cuisine, language, and architecture reflect that heritage. Italian, the main language in Trento, the region's capital, yields in the nearby spa town of Merano and farther north to German, and tourists are likely to be Austrian or German. (I must say I prefer being called "Signora," rather than "Frau," which sounds dowdy!) So close to Austria and Switzerland, raclette and fondue appear on the menus, and you're as likely to see spätzle as pasta. My husband grew fond of tasty herb dumplings!

Trento, my favorite town of the region, was put on the map by the momentous Council of Trent. Lasting from 1545 to 1563, the series of meetings convened so that Roman Catholic bishops could devise ways to stop the spread of Protestantism.

I could live in this city of about 118,000. Ringed by snow-topped mountains and apple orchards—best apples in the world?—the town centers on a grand piazza, with a fountain of Neptune and a compelling duomo. Radiating streets, lined with frescoed palazzi, transport you back to the era of the Council. The newer part of town is attractive too: pedestrian streets lined with bookstores, mountain gear shops, juice bars, gelato parlors, and restaurants.

Absolutely essential to see: MUSE, Museo delle Scienze, the science museum designed by Renzo Piano. The history of the Dolomites is displayed through fauna and flora, as well as geology, avalanches, and weather. The sharply angled glass structure echoes the nearby mountains' silhouettes. Inside, six floors spiral around an open atrium center where animals and birds suspend on clear wire at different heights. Taxidermy raised to art! Start at the top, and circle down through the interactive displays; see different animals up close as you descend—certainly the most imaginative natural history museum I've ever visited.

In nearby Rovereto, MART, Museo di

The soaring roof of Rovereto's Museum of Modern and Contemporary Art (MART)

The lovely fountain of Neptune, a city centerpiece in Trento's Piazza Duomo, is surrounded by stately buildings in golden and terra-cotta tones.

Arte Moderna e Contemporanea, is another significant attraction. The star architect, Mario Botta, is known for, among many projects, the San Francisco Museum of Modern Art. What a coup for this small town!

Just 66 miles (107 km) away, you'll reach Merano, an old spa mecca favored by Habsburg royalty. The elegant town sits on the banks of the pretty River Passirio. Grand promenades allow you to walk in the steps of Elisabeth, known as Sissi, the Austrian empress who brought her entourage to partake of the curative waters. Her delicate touch is all about in the creamy yellow and white belle epoque buildings.

In the *centro* is another major contemporary architectural moment: the marvelous Hotel Terme Merano, designed by Matteo Thun. I would like to go back there in winter and sit in one of the steaming outdoor pools surrounded by snow. There's not a bad time to visit; the area basks under 300 days of sunshine a year.

I feel healthy and strong just thinking of hiking in the Dolomites. Friends of mine know how to do it right. For a week every July, they meet other friends either at *pensione* Garni Ingrid or at the Hotel Villa Monica, both in the village of Dobbiaco in Val Pusteria. Each morning they take a different hike to a *rifugio* for a hearty lunch. Sometimes they rent bikes and ride up to Lienz in Austria on the bucolic Drava cycle path, mostly downhill. After lunch, a shuttle brings them and the bikes back. Their favorite hikes include the rigorous Giro delle Tre Cime, which they describe as the "hike of hikes," and Monte Croce, with lunch at Rifugio Malga Nemes, where the owner plays the accordion. They come home toned and raving over views, sweet-smelling air, and fir and larch forests tinged with wild rhododendrons.

My family's favorite remains the serene Vigilius Mountain Resort, also a work of Matteo Thun. Reachable only by cable car, the hotel reinvents the definition of quiet. The minute I step off the *funivia*, I feel relaxed. Several trails start from the inn, and we take a chairlift up higher for other options. Tired after hiking? Spa treatments and the stone-bottomed pool lured me at least twice a day, and just lying in the wildflower meadow looking up at the stars seems enchanting enough.

In the Know

You Say Latin, I Say Ladin

The history of the Trentino–Alto Adige region makes for a confusing lesson. This northernmost part of Italy was under the rule of the Austro-Hungarian Empire until the end of World War I, when it passed into the hands of the Italians. Mussolini actively Italianized his new citizens through a mix of cajolery and dictates (Italian became the official language in 1922, for example). After a period of unrest, the area became a semiautonomous region in 1972. This unique history shaped its culture, combining Austrian, Italian, and indigenous people into a very rich mix and shaped a population that is proud of their particular past.

But the scars of World War I remain. Bullet holes in the majestic pines testify to the fact that this place was once an active front. Remote caves were the hiding places of soldiers trying to outrun the enemy and seek shelter from the bitter nights. Mountain passes became passages to safety. Even a casual hiker can appreciate how difficult their march was, loaded down with supplies and arms. For more than three years, Austrian and Italian soldiers faced each other on these craggy peaks, gaining only inches for the front; the cruel price was hundreds of thousands of lives, many from hypothermia or starvation. The Italian casualties alone numbered more than 600,000.

Still, there were settlers who had roots here even before the Austrian rule—well before. A contingent of Roman soldiers were given land as a reward for their loyal service; they were collectively known as the Ladin because they spoke Latin. The small, insular group kept their distinctive language, culture, and customs through generations of rulers, despite being treated almost like third-class citizens. Today, they comprise one of the region's cultural treasures. At San Cassiano's **Ladin Museum,** you can learn more about their history, which shows how they persisted in safeguarding their traditions through community festivals and by passing down the Ladin language within families. ◾

A hiker pauses on the trail from Passo di Rolle up to the Rifugio Rosetta.

Hot Spot

The Dolomites

The Dolomites, an Italian stretch of the Alps, have sculptural, imposing peaks that run from Trentino and Alto Adige before spilling into the Veneto. In spring and summer, visitors flock to the region for hiking and mountaineering among the wildflowers and pink sunsets; in winter, they enjoy downhill skiing and other Alpine sports. But many just come to admire the mountains, each with its own shape and fairy tale attached. It's no wonder that this was one of the places that inspired J. R. R. Tolkien's *Lord of the Rings*.

One of the mountain musts is a visit to the **Messner Mountain Museum Corones,** part of a network of museums in honor of one of the world's most famous living climbers, Reinhold Messner, and one of the final and most spectacular of star architect Zaha Hadid's projects. Located at 7,464 feet (2,275 m), it is reachable only by cable car. Well worth the ride, it offers views of the peaks and gentle valleys below that are as inspiring as the collection inside: the objects that the world's greatest mountaineers took with them on their ascents.

At over 17,000 acres (6,879 ha), the gorgeous **Sciliar-Cantinaccio Nature Park** offers epic views of the impressive massif of the same name, as well as miles of forest, lakes, and verdant pastures. With the Marmolada, the Dolomites' highest peak at 10,967 feet (3,343 m); Cantinaccio, a famous ridge that glows red at sunset; and a mix of gentle meadows and picturesque villages with domed churches, this is one of the most striking places in Italy.

If you are in the region in winter, make sure to grab a pass for the **Dolomiti Superski.** The 850-mile (1,200 km) route through the Dolomites is one of the largest ski areas in Europe; it's also a UNESCO World Heritage site. Among the highlights is the Sellaronda, a 30-mile (about 40 km) route through four mountain passes—Alto Adige's Val Gardena, Alta Badia, Arabba (in the Veneto region), and Trentino's Val di Fassa—that runs through every level of trail, and delicious mountain restaurants also worth the journey. ■

The Odle mountains tower above St. Magdalena church.

The spa at Miramonti Boutique Hotel, overlooking the town of Merano and the Alps, is one of the highlights of the property.

Insider's Guide

Dolomite Spa Culture: An Alpine Surprise

Boasting postcard-worthy mountains covered in snow and fairy-tale towns, the Dolomite region is a natural draw for visitors around the world. But the fact that the area is also home to dozens of cutting-edge spas, many housed in modern architectural showstoppers, has made it an excellent, and burgeoning, wellness destination.

To Italians, the flourishing spa culture here is no secret. Pomades and remedies were traditionally made from local mountain roots and trees; that custom morphed into a lifestyle that

accentuated beauty and relaxation. From treatments for aging and aching muscles to personal training and nutritional advice, the region's offerings are particularly focused on seasonal and local products. In fact, many sybarites enjoy as much time spa-side here as on the slopes or hiking trails—or spend their après-ski time lolling poolside in steaming therapeutic water. That these spas are also aesthetically stunning only adds to the allure.

The beauty of these wellness institutes stems largely from the fact that architecture here is a little more exper-

imental than in other parts of the country—and visiting them has become one of the region's main draws. Matteo Thun, a "starchitect" from the city of Bolzano, near the Austrian border, began the trend of building large, state-of-the-art spas in the area. One of his most striking structures houses **Terme Merano,** a complex of 13 indoor pools set within a floor-to-ceiling glass cube (there are another 12 pools outside for summer use). It's a cathedral-like setting for wellness. The airy interiors draw the sun's rays as you float in the healing thermal water that helps sore muscles and purifies skin. Steam rooms come alive with changing ambient light.

At Thun's other main attraction, the **Vigilius Mountain Resort,** the effect is just as inventive. It's sexy sleek with Alpine chic. Cowhide rugs, fluffy duvets, and indoor fireplaces keep things cozy. Glass-fronted saunas overlook a pine forest, and a suggestive lap pool gives the surroundings a frisson of excitement. Treatments include hay baths using local herbs and massages using oil from nearby wildflowers. But beware the naked Germans in the wet area (Italians prefer a bathing suit!).

Family-generated projects have also taken full advantage of the area's natural beauty—but with a twist. The owners of the **Miramonti Boutique Hotel,** for example, took an existing hotel (parts of the James Bond movie *The Spy Who*

Before or after treatments, guests at Rosa Alpina's spa relax on double beds with views onto the indoor pool or pine forest outside.

Loved Me were filmed here) and added a photogenic glass-fronted spa. The showstopper is the heated outdoor infinity pool that hangs over the town of Merano, facing the surrounding mountain peaks. Guests can snag a body scrub-down using the cult product Juvenate, followed by a massage with essential oils. It isn't unusual for visitors to stay on site all weekend, thanks to the three restaurants and a varied, extensive treatment menu. ∎

CHECKING IN

The Dolomite region has an extensive choice of lodging options, from modern masterpieces to cozy Alpine spots.

SAN LUIS HOTEL: Near Merano, this is a newcomer to the Italian spa-hotel game. Set within 98 acres (40 ha) of virgin forest, the resort's centerpiece is the spa housed in a restored barn—with a huge indoor pool and hot tub that sit in the middle of the resort's lake. Barefoot walking in the woods, warm compresses with local herbs, and a diverse menu of treatments draw Italians and visitors from elsewhere in search of a complete unplug. For outdoorsy types, hiking, mountain biking, and long swims in the lake are all available without even leaving the confines of the resort.

ROSA ALPINA: This family-owned hotel, complete with a three-Michelin-starred restaurant, continues to expand and evolve. Chef Norbert Niederkofler started with more international dishes that called for imported ingredients like foie gras or lobster; he then realized there was absolutely no reason to look outside his own environs. Locality became his mission, and Michelin noticed; the restaurant received its coveted Michelin stars in 2018. With a new spa and indoor

pool, loft-like rooms, and a *baita*—a slopeside farmhouse in the nearby mountains for retreats—Rosa Alpina may be a splurge, but one that's well worth it.

SAN LORENZO LODGE: Consider this spot for an important occasion. The 10-room 16th-century hunting lodge was lovingly restored by the former CEO of the fashion house Escada. It's maintained a sense of Alpine coziness with additions that are decadent indeed. The master bedroom has its own spa, and the antique bunk beds for kids are carved from local wood. The helipad and high-altitude golf course are designed for exhausted CEOs looking to commune with nature.

HOTEL ADLER DOLOMITI: The original property of this expanding franchise (which also has an outpost in Tuscany's Val d'Orcia), this family-oriented resort mixes northern no-nonsense service with Italian charm. Part of its appeal is the easy access to both slopes and hiking trails (there's a kids' club too).

Frances's Favorites

In Your Glass

In wine stores, if I see "Alto Adige" on the label, I tend to grab the bottle. You hardly can go wrong in this exceptional wine region known especially for sauvignon blancs. How many cases of Lafoa Colterenzio and St. Michael-Eppan Sanct Valentin have we poured for friends?

The Adige, most unforgettable of rivers. I would like to follow it from its northern source at the Resia Pass to its release into the Adriatic near Chioggia, a 255-mile (410 km) run. Barely contained within its banks, the river surges alongside the main road through this sweet wineland. The twists and plunges of foamy aqua water, castles looking down on the river, grazing sheep, and steep, well-tended patchwork vineyards are a thrilling backdrop to road trips in this region.

All over Italy, the designations DOC (*denominazione di origine controllata*) and DOCG (*denominazione di origine controllata e garantita*) displayed on wine labels are guarantees of inspection and quality. DOCG signifies an additional level of scrutiny from government inspectors. Good to watch for in unfamiliar territories.

From these hills, a few other favorite wines, among many:

- Elena Walch's *Schiava,* an indigenous red wine grape, and also her Pinot Grigio. (Yes, I know that Pinot Grigio is a bar drink and usually innocuous, but in the Alto Adige, give the grape its moment.)
- Hofstätter Pinot Noir, and also their gewürztraminer and riesling.
- Castelfeder Pinot Grigio, another chance to experience this grape at prime. Summer in a glass.
- Abbazia di Novacella, pinot grigio and *lagrein,* the most up-and-coming of the indigenous grape threesome: *schiava, teroldego,* and *lagrein.*
- Alois Lageder, another terrific *lagrein* wine, with a forward taste, assertive but soft, and hints of tannin seeped in ripe fruit tastes.

Each sip of these wines recalls the thunderous and joyful Fiume Adige on its way to the sea. ∎

ABOVE: Varna's spectacular Novacella Abbey dating from 1142 is surrounded by gentle vineyards. **OPPOSITE:** Harvesting the grapes at the Elena Walch winery, a wonderful spot in the Alto Adige, which produces vintages like gewürztraminer and pinot noir

Local Flavors: From Rustic to Michelin

A perfectly creamy cauliflower soup, served in a hollowed-out loaf of freshly baked bread. Fresh river trout just caught from a cold mountain spring. A *krapfen* (the northern equivalent of a dough-nut) stuffed with fresh cream, straight from the oven. A flaky strudel or grilled local *wurtzel.* A *tris di pasta*.

In the Dolomites, forget dreary slope-side cafeterias. Here, the food is no afterthought; instead, it's one of the main reasons Italians return to the region season after season.

Ingredients and tradition make the food of this region exemplary. The soft green meadows tinkle with the sound of cow and goats' bells; their milk makes delicious varied cheeses. Slopes dotted with flowers and herbs make foraging a sport for innovative chefs. And because of the area's complicated cultural history, its palate skews Austrian one moment, Italian another, and then revels in flavors very particularly its own. (Though technically in the Veneto, nearby Cortina is included here.)

The great pleasure here is the variety. One can eat lunch in a simple *rifugio,* one of the mountain refuges that also happens to have an epic view of the rose-hued Alpine peaks, and, then, dinner at a three-Michelin-starred spot. Wine lists become works of art, but a home-brewed draft beer might be just as appealing.

This "0 *kilometro*" approach to cuisine, the burgeoning idea that ingredients should be gotten from as close to home as possible, was a mainstay in these parts long before it was trendy. Locally sourced dishes are a genera-tions-old tradition.

In winter and summer, plates of *canederli,* a type of bread dumpling, make their way to the table in excellent local *rifugi.* Close to the slopes or hiking trails, these huts come with a roaring fireplace in winter and terraces for enjoying the sun on warmer days. Some of the best of them include **Rifugio Scotoni,** where highlights include grilled pork sausages and crispy polenta. At **Rifugio Lagazuoi,** where hikers also bed down for the night, the orzo soup and tagliatelle with mushrooms are as compelling as the *Lord of the Rings*–like setting. The family-owned and -run **Rifugio Scoiattoli** offers a dramatic view of the Cinque Torri (five towers) mountain range, along with *violetta ai sapori di mirtilli,* an unusual pasta with blueberries.

Outside Cortina in the tiny village of San Vito di Cadore, **Aga** has become a destination restaurant for good reason. Oliver Piras worked at Copenhagen's legendary restaurant Noma, and his dishes reflect chef René Redzepi's obsession with using local ingredients foraged and hunted in the area. On the menu are dishes including a cappuccino of pumpkin chestnuts in a foam of porcini and freshly made linguini with venison and sweet carrots from the restaurant's vegetable garden.

In Cortina, **LP 26** is one of the fashionable spots for *aperitivo* (alongside plates of prosciutto and cheese), while **Panificio Alverà** draws townsfolk and visitors for a morning espresso alongside melt-in-your-mouth *krapfen,* raspberry tarts, *puccia* (a type of bread with speck), macarons, and strudel. ∎

OPPOSITE: Three-Michelin-starred restaurant St. Hubertus, in the Rosa Alpina hotel, uses local ingredients like these edible wildflowers in an innovative way. **ABOVE:** Rifugio Scotoni, embraced by the Dolomites

Chapter Two

PIEDMONT

Let's eat. What first? In Piedmont, the answer is always chocolate. Dark, unctuous cherry-scented truffles melting in your mouth, crunchy cocoa pralines, thin candies filled with syrupy fruit liqueur, and pretty foil-wrapped boats called *gianduja* (john-DU-ya), allegedly named after a commedia dell'arte character's tricorn hat. Addictive, these creamy chocolates with *nocciole*, ground hazelnuts.

(I keep a stash in my desk drawer for inspiration while writing.)

In Piedmont's Barolo and Barbaresco wine-growing districts, vintners aren't allowed to plant the sacred *nebbiolo* grape on north-facing hillsides, so hazelnut trees often fill those slopes. That most nutty of nuts, blended with rich chocolate, is a marriage of true minds, although the wedding was originally one of convenience. In the early 19th century, when trade embargoes and the Napoleonic Wars caused chocolate imports to shrink, nuts extended the quantity. What a lucky match! Every Italian schoolchild is raised on Nutella. Smeared on bread, it's the equivalent of the American peanut butter and jelly snack. But we're not after Nutella—not when artisan chocolates are available in Turin.

I devote mornings here to chocolate appreciation, starting in one of the atmospheric historic cafés along the arcaded streets: Baratti & Milano, Caffè Torino, Caffè San Carlo, or Caffè Mulassano. They're rich with old-world paneling, gilded ceilings, and marble tables. All venerate the famous *bicerin*, a traditional hot drink served in a small glass filled with layered hot chocolate, espresso, and cream. Cocoa entered Turin as a hot drink in the 16th century; by the 18th, they were pouring the same *bicerin* at Caffè al Bicerin that they're pouring today.

Next, I proceed to the master confectioners Guido Castagna, and my favorite, Guido Gobino. Send a few gifts;

then pick and choose a tidy box to take along with you while exploring the undulating roads of this unique wine, cheese, and truffle destination.

Note to self: Attend the city's annual chocolate bash in March.

Turin, gateway to the castle-topped, hummocky hills of Piedmont, is one of the primo food cities in Europe. It's regal, thanks to the palaces, ballrooms, libraries, and gardens of the Savoy rulers, who also infused the cuisine with French influences. Vintage and new trams run around the *centro*. The tree-lined streets, shady river walks, and numerous parks keep this the greenest city in Italy. Turin is home to the second largest Egyptian museum in the world. There's

WHAT YOU NEED TO KNOW...

- **BEST TIME TO VISIT:** Piedmont has lots going on throughout the year, with wine tastings across the seasons and culinary treats galore. But fall might be the best time of all to visit, with recent vintages uncorked, vines turning gold and red, and truffles—those heavenly truffles—being unearthed. Book your restaurants early, as returning foodies and oenophiles tend to come in October and November as well.

- **TOP SPOTS:** Alba, Turin, Langhe Valley

- **GETTING THERE:** Fly into Turin Caselle Airport.

The town of Cannobio, the last Italian village before the Swiss border, sits right on the shores of Piedmont's Lake Maggiore.

Cocoa entered Turin as a hot drink in the 16th century; by the 18th, they were pouring the same *bicerin* at Caffè al Bicerin that they're pouring today.

also the surprise of the Museo Nazionale del Cinema, with interactive displays, a lounging area for viewing film clips, and a dizzying elevator ride up to the top of the Mole Antonelliana tower. On clear days, you see how close the Alps are.

Anyone who's ever longed for a vintage Italian car will love MAUTO, the Museo Nazionale dell'Automobile. And I'm dazzled at the Porta Palazzo covered and also sprawling open-air market, the largest in Europe. One-stop shopping—everything from umbrellas to white truffles. The produce is astounding. On sale are vibrant greens I hadn't known existed, every egg from quail to goose, a rainbow of peppers, and flowers—so cheap. On the same piazza, visit Mercato Centrale, a fabulous event space, cooking school, and emporium of food *bottegas* representing many of the city's most renowned tastemakers. A favorite stop is Davide Scabin's, he of Ristorante Combal.Zero fame. At the market, he's serving forth egg dishes, soups, and grilled meats.

With such *favoloso* produce, the chefs in Turin are inspired. In four trips, I've not made a dent in my restaurant list. So far, I can vouch for three deep-tradition cuisine temples: Ristorante del Circolo dei Lettori, Tre Galline, and Del Cambio. At these, you'll taste the heights of the Piemontese cuisine in deeply old-world atmospheres. I love Del Cambio's

Bicerin comes with espresso, melted chocolate, and frothy cream.

resplendent elegance: wavery mirrors, velvet, plus unimpeachable food and service.

Those with adventurous palates may try the quintessential dish of Piedmont, *finanziera*. Some of the ingredients are marrow, brains, cockscomb, wattle, veal testicles, even rooster testicles. (Who even knew roosters have testicles?) Said to be delicious. I wouldn't know.

Moving on to the contemporary, the minimalist Consorzio also is making whoopee with new ideas. Try sweetbreads with bergamot and shallots, and the venison with red fruits and purple cabbage. Worth the 20-minute drive out of town, Combal.Zero's high-concept menu certainly widened my horizons. Super cool: the intimate Chiodi Latini. Angelo Chiodi Latini with wit and a genius palate raises vegetarian cooking to an art form.

Wherever you dine, close the meal with a board of irresistible local cheeses. You've probably tasted the Gorgonzola and taleggio of Piedmont. Move on to goat milk robiola—especially robiola di Roccaverano or Montebore, composed of three tiers arranged like a wonky cake. (I serve robiola with arugula leaves wrapped in bresaola as an antipasto.) Crumbly Castelmango's pungent taste is easy to love, as are the pillowy *tomini, toma di Murazzano,* and the *Bra duro,* which is soft when young and granular when aged. Piedmont is the *primo* cheese region in Italy, producing more than 50 types.

Heading into manicured vineyards just south of Turin—every leaf tweaked—you come to Barolo, a village where at all hours of the day, a cork pops from an inimitable bottle of wine. The WiMu-Museo del Vino gets you oriented with its displays and dioramas. In the cellar, the whole panoply of exceptional local wines is available to taste in the Enoteca Regionale del Barolo.

Gentle rises climb to La Morra. The medieval village makes a choice base for exploring. If you're staying over, try UVE Rooms & Wine Bar for a little glam. Our svelte room was decorated in wine colors. Ristorante Bovio, just outside town, is memorable for exemplary food and a dining terrace

The castle of Serralunga d'Alba peeks out of the mist in Piedmont's Langhe Valley surrounded by gentle vineyards in signature autumnal colors.

overlooking the sweet countryside. Notable too is chef Massimo Camia; try his variation on the revered *vitello tonnato,* veal with a tuna sauce. Both restaurants have formidable wine lists and a knowledgeable staff to help you pair well.

Alba, what a lovely name: dawn. Hordes flock here for fall truffle madness. During the rest of the year, the sloweddown city is a meander of streets radiating off a large piazza into an old town of intriguing shops. And again, let's eat: Piazza Duomo is the premier restaurant (three Michelin stars)—but at lunch, I like the owner's more casual La Piola. Both hew to high standards and enhance your pleasure with plates designed by Kiki Smith and whimsical art by Francesco Clemente and others.

I've made a big loop around Piedmont. Two favorites are the towns of Cherasco and Néive.

Up north, I adore Orta San Giulio on beautiful Lake Orta. Just offshore, a small island with church and castle seems precisely placed for a painterly view. The idyllic town's macaron-colored shops and palazzi border a squared U-shape piazza facing the water.

From here, it's a short drive to Lake Maggiore, one of the most dazzling of the northern Italian lakes. The waterfront town of Stresa, pastel and blooming, has a parade of grand hotels with lush gardens, fanciful Edwardian architecture, and ample grounds for strolling among fragrant jasmine and mammoth hydrangeas. Think string quartet and tea. At Villa e Palazzo Aminta, you can dine at Ristorante Le Isole or the more casual I Mori, both overlooking the lake; at least stop in for a drink and absorb the belle epoque atmosphere.

From Stresa, it's easy to hire a small boat for exploring the pleasant waters and for a visit to the hermitage of Santa Caterina del Sasso, nestled in the face of a rock cliff. Step off into unparalleled beauty on the Isole Borromee, three dreamy islands. If you have time for only one, stop at Isola Bella for its evocative gardens.

On the quay at Stresa, you can find various navigation programs for lake excursions. One might be to Cannobio. The last town before Switzerland, it's a beauty. Bell tower, palazzi, and churches, yes—but the main draw is strolling along the curved harbor, cobbled streets, and lakefront. It's all about beauty, as is much of Piedmont. Beauty, and, oh yes, the wine!

In the Know
Hallowed Bottles: Specialty Wines of Piedmont

Just an hour outside Turin, the area called the Langhe Valley, known for its gentle, vine-draped hills, claims two of Piedmont's (and arguably some of the world's) best wines: Barolo and Barbaresco. Made solely of *nebbiolo* grapes, a Barolo needs to be aged at least 36 months, and a reserve, 62 months, before it can be released for sale. If you want to make a wine lover (and your bank account) swoon, check out the Barolos of Giacomo Conterno. A family-run operation since 1908, it follows traditional winemaking methods to the letter, passing from patriarch Giacomo to his son Giovanni and now to Giovanni's visionary son Roberto. Their Monfortino Riserva costs over $1,000—but if you're seeking a once-in-a-lifetime Barolo experience, this might be the one for you. The vintage spends at least seven years in a *botte,* a large barrel that stops the wine from becoming too oaky and tames the tannins associated with this kind of wine.

While Giacomo Conterno's family relied on tradition to create the rule book on Barolos, Roberto Voerzio, another famed Piedmont producer, strove for rock star modernity and has become a cult darling for his winemaking practices. With some of the smallest yields in the region, Voerzio uses tiny vineyards to give the grapes special attention: green harvesting, pruning, leaf thinning, and discarding about 50 percent of the fruit early in the season to cultivate extra flavor in the grapes that remain. Try the Sarmassa, aged at least 20 years, for a taste that's powerful and intense. The bottle comes only as a magnum, so it's perfect for a feast-like scenario.

Gaja is another masterpiece to have on your tasting list. Many consider Angelo Gaja to be the winemaker who brought these Piedmont wines onto the global stage, and the family name, Gaja, on its labels is a simple but effective way of showing its importance internationally.

One of the most exciting aspects of the wine scene in Piedmont is the way that even the most traditional vintner families allow their children the freedom to experiment with new techniques. The Conterno Fantino vineyard exemplifies this kind of cooperation, with the youngest members of the family spearheading environmental changes like solar panels, a geothermal system, and using their wetlands for water purification. The atmosphere at the winery is light and fun, even while the wines are seriously good. And the "Barolo Boys" team jerseys show that in Italy, football is always top of mind.

Despite their proximity to one another, Barolos and Barbarescos taste different because of the difference in soil quality. The more fertile land used for Barbaresco means less tannin than the former. And Barbaresco is an even older wine of the region, dating back to Roman times. The aging requirement ranges from a minimum of two years for a normal vintage to a minimum of four for the reserve. Try the Dante Rivetti Bricco di Néive; it transports even armchair travelers to the heart of the region. ∎

OPPOSITE: The estate of Conterno Fantino outside Monforte d'Alba is run by generations of the same family. ABOVE: The barrels of Dante Rivetti, an esteemed producer

Frances's Favorites

In Your Glass

Barolo. Barbaresco. Or should I say Barbaresco and then Barolo? Both are made with *nebbiolo* grapes. Both take to aging gracefully. Both show big love; some may argue about which ranks first. But really, we don't have to choose. Let's take both.

Piedmont is rivaled only by Tuscany as wine heaven. These coddled hills are so beautiful that you want to drive all day, soaking in the lilting greens and the idea of order. Many of the castle towns have cooperative tasting rooms where you can quite pleasantly educate yourself in the subtleties of terroir and vintages. Waitstaff and sommeliers at every restaurant seem to have DNA-based wine knowledge. Trust them. Even so, let me mention a few wines to seek out: Vietti Rocche di Castiglione Barolo, Ceretto Bricco Rocche Barolo, Gaja Sperss Barolo and their Sorì Tildin Barbaresco, and Castello di Neive Barbaresco Albesani S. Stefano. Spoiler: Limber up your credit card.

Other notable makers of *nebbiolo* grown outside the legal districts of Barolo and Barbaresco include Travaglini, Mamete Prevostini, and Abbona. I'm especially impressed with the affordable Barbaresco Montestefano.

Barolo and Barbaresco are almost all you need to know. But some outliers appreciate the region's potential for white—and they're attaining high marks. I like many vintages pressed from the *arneis* grape. Watch the sunset over the vineyards with a glass of Monchiero Carbone Roero Arneis Cecu d'la Biunda. Another white grape, *cortese,* is grown around Gavi, near Liguria. At home, we often drink these sunny and affordable whites. Villa Rosa Gavi di Gavi—ah, that's an easy choice. At the superb vegetarian restaurant Chiodi Latini in Turin, our waiter brought us the lively, fresh Terre di Maté Regaldina, an inspired choice. La Smilla makes several show-offs with nice minerals and pear and almond perfumes. ■

ABOVE: Tanaro, one of Italy's longest rivers, is a water artery to Piedmont's Langhe vines. OPPOSITE: The region is full of excellent restaurants like this one in Asti, a culinary hub for slow food.

Best Of
Medieval Hill Towns

Whether you are in the region for wine, excellent food, or active adventure, Piedmont is full of picturesque villages amid the rolling hills.

Monforte d'Alba: Sitting in the hills near Alba, this tiny gem of a town makes the perfect launchpad for wine and truffles. Don't miss an *aperitivo* at Le Case Della Saracca, a restored tower with a ridiculous number of prizewinning vintages on offer. Begin with a tour of the building and its many staircases before starting to taste. Bed down at the Hotel Villa Beccaris with its beautiful views from the breakfast room, spreading over the UNESCO-protected Langhe Valley.

Serralunga d'Alba: Surrounded by some of the most famous vineyards in the country, this lovely little town draws both wine lovers and the producers that make the exceptional vintages. Join them at Vinoteca Centro Storico, below the town's castle, for a glass of Barolo and a plate of *affettati* (sliced meat) and cheese. Right outside the village, the boutique hotel Il Boscareto Resort & Spa has an indoor pool overlooking the vineyards and offers treatments to counteract all the eating and drinking you will be doing in the region.

Saluzzo: Located in Cuneo, this town, filled with well-preserved palazzi and delightful little churches, is considered one of the most authentic in all Italy. Don't miss the duomo at the heart of the medieval downtown and the botanical gardens at the Villa Bricherasio, open on Tuesdays and Sundays. The Gallina Bianca di Saluzzo is a famously delicious breed of chicken; try it at Terra Gemella.

Cherasco: This village of quiet streets and pretty churches is worth a trip just for its pleasant atmosphere. But chocolate lovers are in for more when they step into the Riccardi shop here. Think Nutella is delicious? A taste of Riccardi's heavenly hazelnut spread, with his use of handpicked nuts, renders the bigger name's version almost tasteless. ∎

Monforte d'Alba is a beautiful village in the heart of the wine region.

In the Know
Truffles: Better Than Sex?

Leaves cover the forest floor: wine red, banana yellow, ombré brown. Golden shafts of sunlight peek through the bare branches; the only sounds are the snaps of twigs under waterproof boots. A fluffy white dog bounds ahead, flitting back and forth over the path at top speed. "*Vai, va*"—go, go—calls her owner. She stops suddenly, pausing for a second, before starting to dig frantically. "*Brava, brava*"—excellent, excellent—he encourages her. She puts her nose into the ground, and he pulls her back by the collar, slipping her a piece of bread. Then, gently, he continues to excavate the earth with a tiny spade, past tree roots and small pieces of rock. "*Ma siiii!*" He pulls a white truffle from the dirt with a delighted smile, takes it lovingly to his nose, then examines its size on his palm. This is the moment of victory.

The truffle is one of Italy's true treasures, and its crown jewels reside in Piedmont, particularly in the area around Alba. There is a reason that many of the world's best chefs come here for their expensive loot. And Alba is also where the famous truffle fair, the International Alba White Truffle Fair, takes place on weekends in October and November.

What's all the fuss about? Just a few shavings of truffle can make an ordinary plate of pasta sublime. They are a delicacy and, supposedly, an aphrodisiac. They are a status symbol too; judged by their ounce-by-ounce price, they are the most expensive food in the world. A few years back, at an auction in Macau, a three-pound (1.4 kg) white truffle went for $330,000. But in part because of climate change, the truffle supply is plummeting, which has led to the birth of a black market. As *60 Min-utes* put it: "They're being trafficked like drugs, stolen by thugs, and threatened by inferior imports from China." Truffles grown in China are being sold in the Italian markets—a bit like counterfeiting clothing or designer bags.

When it comes to truffle hunting, pigs generally used to do the honors. But they were too often successful at snarfing down thousands of dollars' worth of the stuff before their owners could pull them away. Dogs, specifically the beloved breed called Lagotto Romagnolo, are easier to train, and they are primed for their role from puppyhood. The ones with an excellent nose become prized animals, and the relationship between dog and hunter is incredibly close. In the increasing shadow side of the business, dogs have been known to be stolen or poisoned by competitors. Who would have thought that truffles could be the source of such subterfuge?

To experience one of the best truffle hunt experiences in the country, try an excursion with Giuseppe (Beppe) Marengo and Luna, his dog, at Il Profumo della Notte, their truffle excursion company based near Alba. Cichin, Beppe's grandfather, started things off back in 1899, and Beppe continues to use Cichin's "secret journal" to find the best truffles. Handsome and articulate, Beppe, with Luna, exemplifies what it takes to keep the hunt authentic, sportsmanlike, and high quality. ∎

OPPOSITE: Hunters like Giuseppe (Beppe) Marengo and his dog, Luna, head into the forest to forage for truffles along trails that his grandfather found. ABOVE: Piedmont's prized white truffles

The mix of architectural styles in Santuario della Consolata include a Romanesque bell tower, a baroque dome, and an ancient Roman wall.

Turin: The Industrial Revolution

Google *The Italian Job,* Michael Caine, and Turin. You'll find a chase scene where bright vintage Mini Coopers circle the city. They zoom around the former headquarters of the Fiat car manufacturer, with its iconic rooftop track (now home to a hotel, cinema, and shops like Eataly). They career past some of Turin's main sights, like the **Chiesa della Gran Madre di Dio,** an iconic neoclassical church flanked by columns, and bump down the steps as a wedding takes place. If you didn't know before that you needed to visit Turin, you'll be sold just by this clip.

This northern Italian city has long been known for its industry—particularly for making cars like Fiat and Alfa Romeo. But the metropolis became surprisingly trendy following a significant face-lift in advance of hosting the 2006 Winter Olympics, when warehouses were transformed into restaurants and art spaces and the surrounding ski areas got new facilities. It's a lovely place, with its art deco cafés and gentle pace—but it's vibrant too, with a sense of new purpose and importance (being home to Italy's best football team, Juventus Football Club, and superstar player Cristiano Ronaldo gives it extra bragging rights).

Start your visit at **Caffè al Bicerin** for a taste of Turin's signature drink, made of espresso, melted chocolate, and perfectly executed frothy cream, or **Baratti & Milano,** a city institution with gilded mirrors and light-as-air Chantilly cream-filled pastries. Next up is the **Santuario della Consolata** with its raucous rococo interiors set against an architectural mix of a backdrop that includes a Roman wall and a baroque set of domes. Movie buffs *must* go to the **Museo Nazionale del Cinema;** this vast complex hosts exhibits, film festivals, and screenings in their original language.

Not surprisingly for a city smack in the middle of a truffle, wine, and produce mecca, you'll find that you can eat incredibly well in Turin. Snacking through the **Porta Palazzo** street market gives a terrific overview of this region's vast ingredients. **Edit** offers a more modern concept with an overarching theme that incorporates a little culinary something for every type. Housed in a former factory, the structure now has a brewery for craft beers, a cocktail bar, a bakery, a restaurant from the Costardi brothers, Michelin-starred chefs, and professional kitchens available for rent that allow fledgling cooks a chance to shine.

Aperitivo is a religion all over Italy, but in Turin it's a cult. Among the hot spots? The beautiful restored pharmacy, the **Farmacia del Cambio,** and

Sitting alfresco at Il Bacaro in the pretty Piazza della Consolata

the **Bar Cavour,** a speakeasy-style lounge upstairs where reservations are recommended, especially on weekends. For a more traditional cocktail hour head to **Caffè Torino,** a 1903 mainstay known for its killer Negroni, a combo of Martini Rosso, Campari, and gin. Luckily there is also an expansive spread of snacks to soak up the alcohol. ■

FIAT AND AGNELLI
Perhaps no other brand better exemplifies Italy's great style and sense of fun than the vintage Fiat 500.

BUT THAT MODEL ISN'T THE ONLY BEAUTY: The 600 and the Spider were also heartthrobs. Fiat's CEO was Gianni Agnelli, one of Italy's richest and most powerful men: an inventor, a scion, and a notorious playboy (Jackie Kennedy was one of his lovers). In fact, in many ways, the Agnellis could be considered the Kennedys of Italy.

It's difficult to not pair the name Agnelli with Turin. The family's dominant business presence also made them a kind of Italian royalty, with members marrying into other European dynasties and with royals. Although the

company was already in the process of becoming powerful, it was Gianni (nicknamed "The Lawyer" because he went to law school in the city before taking over the company) who made Fiat the richest company in Italy, and him its wealthiest businessman.

Although the company has been plagued by various scandals and downturns (and tragic early deaths or suicides within the family, another reason for the comparison with the Kennedys), Fiat continues to be one of Italy's most important corporations.

In the Know

Local Flavors: Slow Food

Boasting a celebrated range of delectable products from wine to truffles, Piedmont's food scene is both gourmet and long-standing. The region happens to also be the birthplace of the slow food movement, an approach to making dishes that are authentic, traditional, and take time to prepare. The crusade started as a protest movement over the opening of a McDonald's at Rome's Spanish Steps and now has international chapters all over the world. The headquarters are located in the city of Bra near the University of Gastronomic Sciences and the restaurant **Guido,** a showcase for slow food dishes.

Starting your tour in Bra, **Osteria del Boccondivino,** a Michelin-starred restaurant, exemplifies the approach. Sitting in a pretty courtyard sipping wine, hopefully in the sunshine, try dishes like the mouthwatering *brasato di Barolo,* a beef stew slowly cooked in wine.

As one might expect with this kind of legacy, the restaurants in Piedmont include mom-and-pop gems as well as Michelin treats. For example, in Alba, **Piazza Duomo** serves an entire white truffle menu: truffles atop scallops, truffles on a consommé of mushrooms, and pheasant cooked in truffles (their Insalata 21.31.41.51, served with herbs, flowers, leaves, and other greens, is one of the best in the country). Another stop in Alba for just one dish is **Enoclub;** its *tajarin,* a pasta made from 30 egg yolks, is the perfect bed for truffles.

Trattoria della Posta, outside Monforte d'Alba, is another revered but more traditional choice. Situated in an old coach house dating from 1875, the restaurant offers extremely rich cuisine that is incredibly satisfying—for example, a veal shank stewed in Barolo and baked onion filled with local cheese. Insiders also love La Morra's **Bovio.** In addition to the epic views (La Morra is the highest of the Barolo villages), fans come just for the *battuta* (the veal tartare specialty) and the wine list. With miles of hairpin turns along the way, you might want to hire a driver to get you there safely. ▪

Bovio restaurant's cheese selection is a delicious introduction to Piedmont's signature varieties.

Frances's Favorites
Family Lexicon

Turin—food city, industrial hub, center of royal might—is also a major literary town.

Long before Elena Ferrante lit up Naples with her acclaimed quartet of novels about class and female friendship, Natalia Ginzburg wrote her autobiographical *Family Lexicon,* a master portrait of a Turin family from the 1920s through the 1950s.

Her family was brawling, chaotic, funny. The Jewish father, a professor at the University of Turin, would be labeled verbally abusive today; he criticizes constantly but comes off as lovable because his insults are often so hilarious. The Catholic mother sings, tells stories, flutters, and worries as her five children strike out into the rising fascist reality outside their home. They're well equipped; if you survive in that family, you're prepared for any-

thing. Daily there were "ferocious arguments over politics, which ended in tantrums, napkins hurled into the air, and doors slammed so hard the whole apartment shook."

As adults, the family scattered, but when they later meet, "one word, one phrase is enough . . . One of them would make us recognize each other, in the darkness of a cave or among a million people." Ginzburg brilliantly structures the book around repeated family sayings—those quick reminders of funny, cruel, or ironic stories known to all and a shorthand to shared experience.

In addition to Ginzburg's fearless writing style, what gives this book wonder is the intense force of everyday life that runs counter to the brutal political tide sweeping this family, Turin, and beyond to world war. Dark

times ensue. They are exiled to the south in the Abruzzi. Ginzburg's children must take their grandmother's gentile name. Her parents are heroic. Eventually her young husband is tortured by the Nazis and dies. That she does not linger long on these horrors makes them even more shocking when she does reveal, as an aside, something terrible.

I also recommend Ginzburg's *Manzoni Family, The Little Virtues, The Road to the City, The City and the House, Voices in the Evening,* and the many other essays, plays, and novels of this fierce and funny writer.

Turin's other literary giant, a great love of mine, Cesare Pavese, wrote *Lavorare Stanca.* (Published as *Hard Labor* in English, the direct translation is a little less catchy: "to work is tiring.") His poems are long, looping narratives full of sensory details from close to the land. Pavese's translations of Whitman, Joyce, Melville, Defoe, and others introduced American and English writers to an Italian audience. His poignant, harsh novels *The Harvesters, The Beautiful Summer, Dialogues With Leucò,* and especially *The Moon and the Bonfires,* furthered his deep inquiry into the meaning of place. At his childhood village in Santo Stefano Belbo, autumn bonfires are still lit in his memory. In Turin, I was lucky to stay in his home, now La Luna e il Falò, a B&B named for *The Moon and the Bonfires.*

Both writers' memories are forever in Turin. ∎

ABOVE: Italian author Natalia Ginzburg explored politics and relationships. **OPPOSITE:** Cesare Pavese, translator and writer, was born in a village southeast of Turin.

Best Of

Outdoor Activities in Piedmont

While most people head to Piedmont to eat and drink, the region is also a hidden getaway for outdoor pursuits such as mountain biking, skiing, and hiking. JayWay Travel offers tours all over the country, but Piedmont native Daniele Toniolo knows his home territory particularly well. You can choose to be active throughout your stay or combine those activities with one of JayWay's custom itineraries, from vineyard visits to city tours. Here are some of the pursuits to keep your adrenaline going.

Ski With the Pros: Turin was the site for the Winter Olympics in 2006, and its lifts, trails, and level of instructors still shine from the spotlight. La Val di Susa is one of the epicenters for the activity. Nicknamed "the Milky Way," the varied terrain offers runs for all levels, as well as 15 ski schools. In addition to Piedmont's own ski areas, you can use an international ski pass to venture into France and Switzerland. In the summer, these same spots become fantastic hiking trails and spots for rock climbing or mountain biking destinations.

Follow the Royals: Hiking through the UNESCO-protected vineyards of the Langhe Valley to the former palaces of Savoia is a true delight.

Sail the Lakes: Rent a boat or follow the shores of Lake Maggiore by foot. Lake Orta, way less crowded and expensive than Como, boasts treasures like the town of Orta San Giulio with its exquisite Piazza Mario Motta. From there, you can get on a little boat to the lake's main island, Isola San Giulio.

Climb Every Mountain: To get a real sense of the geography of the region, try an Alpine trek: a day trip to Monviso, a multiday journey to Gran Paradiso, or an expedition from Piedmont all the way into Switzerland.

Take Flight: Paragliding is quite popular on the gentle hills that form the landscape before the Alps, and seeing the Barolo vineyards from a hot air balloon is another option for those who don't have a fear of heights.

Ride the Wind: Motorbike and vintage Vespa enthusiasts often hit the region on wheels. Electric bikes are another popular option. ∎

OPPOSITE: The island of San Giulio on Lake Orta ABOVE: Mountains above the Gardone Riviera

Chapter Three
LOMBARDY

The northern Italian lakes! The air turns blue at evening, sending blessed calm over those gathered on a terrace for sunset toasts. By day, the mountains change colors as clouds wander over blissful waters, emerald and indigo. Start with one of the prettiest villages on Lake Como, Bellagio. Gardens, cruises, and peaceful walks provide doses of beauty, while the Rockefeller Foundation's Bellagio Center, a private

retreat for gifted researchers and writers, lends intellectual gravitas to the quaint town. That lady in the big hat sitting near you at the café may be translating Gnostic gospels. Cernobbio, close to the town of Como, is known for silk fabrics, and many honeymooners seek the romantic hotel Villa d'Este. This 16th-century palace is sure to start a marriage off with high expectations.

On Lake Garda, largest of the northern lakes, I chose well: the Grand Hotel Fasano. This elite watering hole of the 19th century vibrates with privilege. The lobby exudes lighthearted elegance, all cream and gold, accessorized with caged songbirds. Its excellent restaurant, Il Fagiano, revels in rich paneling, ritual flambéing in copper, and friendly formality.

Lake Garda is the spot to pamper your stressed-out self. Arrange a private boat to arrive at your hotel dock and whisk you around to Salò, Desenzano del Garda, Gardone Riviera, Sirmione, Limone del Garda, and Riva del Garda, the loveliest towns on the lake. Between the towns of Desenzano, at the south end of the lake, and Riva del Garda at the top, public boats run all year. You can hop off at all 16 pretty lake towns. But it's more relaxing to hire a captain to take you where you want, wait while you have lunch, or enjoy drinks on board.

Plying the lake by boat is optimal; otherwise, you can drive to the lakefront towns. Studded with cypresses, the road takes you to villages festooned with oleander, bougainvillea, palms, lemons, bananas, and tumbling plumbago. Sheltering mountain ranges ensure a Mediterranean climate, with snow-topped peaks in the near distance. How fun to round a bend and come upon bevies of windsurfers, their colorful crescent sails skimming in rhythmic motions across the silvery waters.

Once you are ensconced in a dreamy lake hotel, forget the sprawl just behind you. Find the prettiest spot on the lake. Check into the stupendous Villa Feltrinelli if you've come into a recent inheritance. (Spend Aunt Hazel's legacy. It's worth it.) Otherwise, Villa Fiordaliso or Grand Hotel Fasano will suffice nicely. Of course, every village has a range of accommodations.

The lake towns all face colorful harbors, have a *lungolago* (walking path along the lake), and sorbet-colored

WHAT YOU NEED TO KNOW...

- **BEST TIME TO VISIT:** Unlike some Italian cities that essentially close in summer, Milan stays open year-round following business travelers as opposed to just the leisure visitors. And with Alpine sports a close drive away in winter, it can be nice to combine the trip with a jaunt up into the mountains (or in spring, summer, and fall, the lake region). The fog here is legendary, so don't be surprised if you experience flight delays.

- **TOP SPOTS:** Milan, Lake Como, Mantua

- **GETTING THERE:** Linate and Malpensa Airports, both in Milan

---

Il Vittoriale degli Italiani is a complex of buildings, streets, and gardens built in the early 20th century and once home to Gabriele D'Annunzio.

> City of music, Cremona makes you wish you'd continued with those violin lessons.
> I imagine Monteverdi, born here, still composing at a small desk.

neoclassical buildings surrounding wide-open piazzas lined with cafés designed for coffee breaks after you've seen Roman ruins, archaeological museums, and local shops. And look up: Mountains rise protectively all around, especially at the north end of the lake.

In Gardone Riviera, the unexpected site—*wildly* unexpected—is the Priory. This quirky home, with grounds that have lake views, once belonged to the poet and novelist Gabriele D'Annunzio. War hero, lover of actress Eleonora Duse, and prolific writer, he is said to have "invented fascism one summer afternoon," empowering Mussolini, whom he later vilified.

D'Annunzio's is the weirdest, most fascinating house I've ever seen. Walls are crammed with books (33,000). He collected statues, rugs, Persian silk draperies, globes, and way too many military uniforms. His palazzo became a cabinet of curiosities, with D'Annunzio himself as exhibit A. One room was designated solely for his meditations on the meaning of death; in another, his housekeeper was expected to have sex with him several times a day. For more on this character, take a look at Lucy Hughes-Hallett's *Pike: Gabriele D'Annunzio—Poet, Seducer and Preacher of War,* a fascinating and revolting biography. What a colossal ego!

I recommend, with love, the two small cities of Cremona and Mantua.

City of music, Cremona makes you wish you'd continued with those violin lessons. The light glancing off golden brown buildings casts passersby in a pale bronze glow. From upstairs windows, music wafts over the streets. I imagine Monteverdi, born here, still composing at a small desk. All around town you see shop signs with the word *liutaio,* "maker of instruments." Windows display the craftsman's lutes, mandolins, and violins. Of course, there's the Museo del Violino. The musical city also appeals to me for its turret-topped bell tower with clock face and for an octagonal baptistry with a soaring dome made of tiny centrifugally laid bricks.

In Cremona, *mostarda* reigns supreme in the local cuisine. These fruits in sweet/mustard syrup accompany the rich meats of the area. Numerous shops, such as Sperlari, invite you to pick up a pretty ceramic or glass jar of these jewel-colored fruits—or perhaps a box of the local specialty *torrone,* chewy honey and nut candy (watch those fillings!).

At the end of a brilliant day in Cremona, how lucky to repair to the exquisite restaurant Antica Corte Pallavincina (actually just over the River Po into Emilia-Romagna) near the home of Giuseppe Verdi. Chef Massimo Spigaroli has a passion for *culatello,* hind legs of black pig (aged 37 months or more) and white pig (aged 18 to 27 months). His underground caverns hold more than 5,000 of these. Spigaroli defines his philosophy as "gastro-fluvial," acknowledging the Po's gifts of frog legs, catfish, and eels and its verdant soil for growing vegetables.

Everything sounds good. We fell onto tender golden scallops, guinea hen with *culatello* cooked in river clay. Spigaroli's refined but exuberant cooking and his 11-room hotel—formerly a family bastion for river control—make this a natural spot for visiting Parma and Mantua, as well as nearby Cremona.

A violin maker in Cremona, home of a museum to the instrument

Outdoor tables in the main piazza of Cremona are next to spectacular sand-colored arched buildings and an exquisite church.

Mantua, delicious Mantua. The human scale of the Renaissance and medieval palazzi makes you feel immediately content. Often pale fog rises from the three nearby lakes, contributing to a feeling that you've stepped inside time's misty story.

The Gonzaga family ruled this town for 400 years. Palazzo Ducale—all 500 rooms—was home. And there remains one of the top works of Renaissance art: "La Camera degli Sposi," "The Newlyweds' Chamber," by Andrea Mantegna. What appear to be architectural features of the room—molding, relief, oculus, vaulting—are skillful plays with painted perspective. You sense the artist's joy: Look at me performing all this clever foreshortening! His subject? Glorious everyday life at the Gonzaga court. The painter's brilliance shines in the faces—he saw what made each one *that one*—and in the clothing, the eminence of the patriarch, the court dwarf—even a bunch of dogs. Crowning the room, an oculus presents a different mood. A naughty woman is about to tip over a flowerpot from the edge. Here's Mantegna's glorious wit. Genius work—completely accomplished in depth perspective, blue sky over all.

Back down to earth, another reason to love Mantua: *sbrisolona*. This crumbly local dessert, loaded with hazelnuts and slivered almonds, connects to tradition. Did the Gonzagas

serve it at their feasts? Enjoy it after dinner at Ristorante Aquila Nigra.

Now I circle back to Milan, lifeblood of Lombardy. It's bouncing with design energy, dazzling restaurants (I adore Sadler), and galleries. But start at the Gothic duomo. Take the elevator to the top, where you can scramble along the roofs among the sculptures. The flamboyant fantasy figures, lacy towers, and gargoyles stun even the most blasé traveler. Nearby, you can have dinner at fancy Felix Lo Basso or a casual lunch at Rinascente (named best department store in the world) and look into the upper levels of the cathedral. Across the piazza, don't miss the Museo del Novecento. Twentieth-century Italian artists—Boccioni, Balla, Carrà, Severini—have long been underappreciated. Here, that's put that to rights.

You have to be awed by Galleria Vittorio Emanuele II, a soaring glass-roofed promenade of boutiques, designer enclaves, world-class pastries, and cafés for watching the parade of *bella figura* Milanese. The big treat: Ristorante Cracco, hushed and flawless, with a Richard Ginori china pattern emulating the great dome of the galleria. What fun to stalk the luxury shops along Via Montenapoleone! I don't regret the foolish red lizard shoes at all.

Director Wes Anderson designed the café at Milan's Fondazione Prada, including the games. The museum also has a contemporary art collection.

Milan: The City's New Spark

When you ask Italian insiders about this celebrated fashion capital in the north, it's unlikely to produce the same sighs of excitement and awe as, say, Florence or even Rome. But while it's true that Milan may have more of a businesslike attitude than some of its southern counterparts (it is home to Italy's stock exchange and many of the country's business headquarters), in recent years the metropolis has morphed into a more vibrant and multilayered town, with up-and-coming neighborhoods, new architectural relevance, and a reputation for forward-thinking culture. Milan remains a city on the cusp, whether in repurposing old industrial sites; hosting the 2015 World EXPO, a huge international fair that drew 22 million visitors; or allowing fledgling talent to flourish in cooperatives and galleries around the city. And while visitors will certainly want to hit the major sights, like the city's massive duomo, Leonardo da Vinci's block-buster painting "The Last Supper," or an opera at **La Scala,** there are also other new must-sees in town.

Opened in 2015, the **Fondazione Prada** has become one of the country's most important centers for contemporary art (Miuccia Prada and her husband, Patrizio Bertelli, are cultural patrons). Housed in a complex of buildings designed by star architect Rem Koolhaas and concentrated around a former gin distillery, the result is a striking interlocking of old and new structures. The space has already showcased such artists as Gerhard Richter, Robert Gober, and Louise Bourgeois and also features new films, another of the Pradas' passions. In fact, one of the foundation's centerpieces is **Bar Luce,** the café designed by *Royal Tenenbaums* director Wes Anderson. With its pinball machines and pink-hued wallpaper, it has become a popular hangout for locals and city visitors. And at a time when the government's budget for cultural offerings is in free-fall, the Pradas' literal and symbolic funding of both art and new architectural icons is especially meaningful.

The **Zona Tortona** exemplifies Milan's ability to repurpose and resuscitate derelict buildings in a neighborhood that was once home to the city's manufacturing industry. Silos, warehouses, and factories now pulse with new life and have become favorites of those seeking to reinvent the neighborhood with fashion and art. One of its most recent tenants is Giorgio Armani, who tapped architect Tadao Ando to transform the former Nestlé factory silos into a sleek, cavernous space to showcase his collections called **The Armani/Silos,** a 48,000-square-foot (4,500 sq m) space devoted to his career.

Nearby, the David Chipperfield–designed **Museo delle Culture,** opened in 2015, has emerged as another of Tortona's most successful reinventions. It features exhibits on Basquiat and Modigliani among other retrospectives, as well as a permanent anthropological collection. The museum joins forerunners like **Superstudio 13,** the country's largest photographic studio and exhibition space, which continues to be a cultural anchor of the area.

After spending some time here, insiders like to stop in at **Emporio 31** for Italian furniture design at a more palatable price, as well as shops like **Nonostante Marras,** featuring books and artwork alongside clothes and accessories. It's also fun to grab a cocktail at the **Botanical Club,** a chic microdistillery that offers cordials made with its own gin as well as small plates and a popular brunch.

The **Cascina Cuccagna,** located in the Porta Romana neighborhood, also exemplifies Milan's conversion of formerly abandoned buildings into multifunctional spaces. This former 17th-century farmhouse now draws local residents and visitors for its farmers markets and yoga classes. ■

CLOCKWISE FROM LEFT: Some of the alluring merchandise at Nonostante Marras, a shop that offers not only clothes but also books and furniture; MUDEC Museum in Milan's hip Tortona neighborhood; the city's Navigli canal area is home to bars, restaurants, and shops

In the Know

Franciacorta: More Than Bubbles

No disrespect to prosecco, but when Italian oenophiles turn their attention to bubbles, it's all about Franciacorta. Lombardy's DOCG is in fact produced much in the same way as champagne (the second fermentation process creates the similarity), resulting in a much drier taste than prosecco. In fact, Franciacorta literally means "short France," which implies that it's somehow less good. In truth, it should not play second fiddle to anything—at least, not anymore.

Unlike champagne, which has been produced for centuries, the first Franciacorta was bottled in 1961, making it a relatively new arrival in the wine world. As a result, visits to the estates here still feel unpretentious and organic. One of the main producers, **Ca' del Bosco,** is also one of the most celebrated; its particular bottle, wrapped in an orange-yellow covering, makes it easily recognizable for those who know their bubbles. **Bellavista** also garners attention for good reason. Try the rose blend—its color and taste make it a delightful standout.

CorteBianca is one of the most beautiful of the Franciacorta wineries, and the small organic producer creates a version of the elixir that continues to win over wine editors. **Fratelli Berlucchi** has a similar commitment to sustainable production (and the 15th-century estate creates the perfect setting for its outstanding bruts). **Barone Pizzini** and **Ferghettina** also get high marks for their biodynamic approach, not interfering in

the wine's natural processes, from picking to fermentation. Book a room at **L'Albereta,** the area's favored hotel. (It also has a renowned medical spa, so guests who participate in its programs will have to wait on the tastings, as the strict diet doesn't include alcohol.)

Franciacorta deserves to be on the map for more than its sparkles, however. Its centerpiece, Lake Iseo, is less touristy than Como and Garda and is arguably the fairest of them all too— which is why insiders are so desperate

to keep it a secret. Take a boat taxi to **Monte Isola,** an island at the lake's center that is car free (well, except for the priest's, naturally). Here, you'll find pretty fishing villages and quaint cafés, as well as quiet churches (in the village of Peschiera, fishermen's wives darn the nets as if they were couture). Even the celebrated installation artist Christo was bowled over by Iseo's charms; his yellow "Floating Piers" project in 2016 connected the lakeside to the island in a stunning, ethereal way. ▪

OPPOSITE: The vineyards of Franciacorta sit near Lake Iseo, one of Lombardy's underrated gems. ABOVE: The Franciacorta region produces spumante sparkling wine that is Italy's answer to champagne.

In the Know
Project Milan: Italy's Fashion Capital

Dolce & Gabbana. Versace. Miu Miu. These are only some of the A-list fashion labels that have chosen to make Milan their headquarters. Models strut the runway twice a year for the city's Fashion Weeks. This is a city that breathes fashion trends, and the energy of all things that go into creating a collection is palatable in its very DNA.

Many of the big shots (including Valentino and Loro Piana) have their stores along **Via Montenapoleone** (Montenapo for short), where luxury items from sunglasses to evening dresses vie for attention in floor-to-ceiling window displays. For more palatable prices, take a look at **D Magazine,** where designer duds come at 50 to 70 percent less than their normal retail price.

All fashionistas worth their Instagram feed make tracks to **10 Corso Como** when they are in town. To call this temple to fashion merely a store would give the complex short shrift. Opened 25 years ago by Carla Sozzani, it is more akin to a series of art installations. The curated collection doesn't feature only Italian brands, though; the international heavyweights include Lanvin and Comme des Garçons and encompass all wardrobe needs. The site isn't just for shoppers: There is also an art gallery and bookshop. Fashion editors and model types end their shopping spree here at the courtyard café over a glass of prosecco or even book a room at the store's hotel, **3 Rooms.**

In the neighborhood of **Navigli,** with its crisscross of canals, bohemian-feeling shops are the name of the game. Among them is standard-bearer **Biffi,** helmed by Rosy Biffi, who keeps Milanese women looking chic with her selection from local and international fashion stars, as well as an enviable jeans collection, while concept shop **WOK** slants toward hipsters looking for understated classics. **Frip** skews Scandinavian, and is a one-stop for Acne Studios, Henrik Vibskov staples, and statement-making pieces. Afterward, fuel up at **28 Posti,** one of the area's best restaurants with a menu that changes every two months. Or have a cocktail at the tiny gem **Mag Café**—just one example of how the lounge craze has taken root in this city.

Vintage hounds will want to check out Brera's unbeatable **Cavalli e Nastri** featuring designs from Yves Saint Laurent and Alaïa, among others. And for men who like Italian-style clothing, **Al Bazar,** a must since the 1960s, carries double-breasted suits and trousers in mustard and burgundy, a particular penchant in this country.

While in town, keep an eye out for the new clothing line Attico. Founded by former street-style stars Gilda Ambrosio and Giorgia Tordini, it exemplifies the new talent in town, with silk dresses and sexy camisoles. ∎

ABOVE: Milan's 10 Corso Como is a fashion lover's must. OPPOSITE: Vintage hounds make tracks to Cavalli e Nastri, where one can find collectibles from designers like Gucci and Missoni.

In the Know

Where to Stay in Milan

With its deep roots in fashion and design, Milan unsurprisingly does not lack for stylish hotels, from luxury five-stars to boutique bolt-holes.

Armani Hotel: With a sizable empire in town, from shops to a café to a new museum, Giorgio Armani upped his presence with the opening of a signature hotel a few years ago. Among the highlights is a 13,000-square-foot (1,200 sq m) spa with an indoor swimming pool.

Magna Pars Suites: Located in the charming neighborhood of Tortona, this former perfume factory has been transformed into a boutique hotel full of light and modern furniture, along with a hotspot bar. The gardens are a bonus; the flowers here are used as the foundation of many of the property's fragrances.

The Yard: Full of quirky memorabilia with an emphasis on the sporty (think vintage skis and framed boxing photos), this hotel in the Navigli canal neighborhood feels like the cozy pied-à-terre of an eccentric but stylish great-uncle. Don't miss a cocktail at the hotel's bar, the Doping Club.

Excelsior Hotel Gallia: One of the greatest assets of this recent entrant to the hotel scene is its location next to the city's train station (the best way to get in and out of town). Though some might find its marble and glittering chandeliered lobby a bit too blingy, the rooms are more subdued, and the on-site spa provides a lovely respite after business meetings or sightseeing.

Luxury Trio Bulgari, Four Seasons, and Mandarin Oriental: During fashion week, these five-star hotels are booked by fashion editors and models for their sizable rooms and amenities—from spas to chauffeured cars—but in a discreet way. Each has its particular draw: Bulgari, the indoor pool; Four Seasons, the 15th-century convent setting; the Mandarin, super-personalized service. And all come with the price tag to match.

Onefinestay: This apartment rental service—a nice step up from your average Airbnb—has some lovely residential properties in its inventory, including a stunning one-bedroom home in the Porta Ticinese neighborhood and a three-bedroom modernist pad on Corso Como.

The Gray: One of the first boutique properties in town located just a stone's throw from the duomo, this chic hotel still draws insiders who want a convenient central location along with elegant design details. Opt for a gallery unit for a great view of the iconic Galleria Vittorio Emanuele II.

Milan VU: With a rooftop pool looking over the city and eco-attitude, this property embodies the regeneration of the city's Chinatown neighborhood.

Vik Milano: The latest from the South American hotel group, it has taken the former Townhouse Galleria boutique hotel and reinvented it with its signature mix of luxury and collection of art and design. ◼

OPPOSITE: Magna Pars Suites is housed in a former perfume factory. ABOVE: One-of-a-kind design at Milan's The Yard hotel

Frances's Favorites
Mostarda

Worth jamming into checked luggage: ceramic jars of the historic *mostarda* of Cremona and Mantua. Renaissance cooks liked sweetness sharply undercut with savory acidic flavors, and the tradition survives. Whole just-cooked fruits, their syrup, and mustard flavoring become a spicy condiment for the cheese board, roasted meat, and sometimes a filling for pumpkin *tortelli*. Made in Italy with a few drops of highly potent mustard essence, *mostarda* also works well at home using prepared mustard and seeds. In *The Surprise of Cremona*, the eccentric mid-20th-century travel writer Edith Templeton describes *mostarda* in a bright tapestry of words:

It serves as sweet spice to the mild meats and sets them on fire, in a cool and lovely way, like moonlight burning on water. The fruit is luminously transparent like semi-precious stones . . .

There are several cherries, unevenly rounded like antique corals; a green pear of the size of a walnut, with the black pips shining like onyx; a larger pear of the colour of rose-quartz; a green fig clouded like a flawed emerald, a curved strip of pumpkin, reddish brown and veined like chrysopase, and the half of an apricot which could have been carved out of topaz. They are almost too splendid to be eaten. ▪

ABOVE: Vintage tins of *mostarda*, a particular northern condiment made from candied fruit and a mustard-flavored syrup **OPPOSITE:** The various fruits of the *mostarda*, such as ripe figs, suspended in the jar make the concoction look like an art piece.

Design Darlings: Made in Italy

Milan is known for its fashion and business centers. But design mavens also flock here for brands like B&B Italia, Capellini, Poltrona Frau, Cassini, Achille Castiglioni, Paola Navone, Gio Ponti, and many others. The annual design fair, **Salone del Mobile,** held each April, attracts an international following of interior decorators and design buffs who arrive in droves to see what's in the pipeline for the following season. Pop-up stores, designer collaborations, after-parties, and food trucks are also part of the scene, and give the city an extra dose of spring energy.

As the main fair gets bigger and more corporate, insiders craving a more intimate experience, and cutting-edge creations, turn to **Fuorisalone,** which tends to focus on younger designers and group-curated collectives. Some of the most successful themes have included a "Made in Italy" exhibit, where vendors showed off everything from jewelry to bookmaking using turn-of-the-20th-century techniques. (When planning your trip, look to *Elle Decor Italia* or *Wallpaper* online for the coming year's highlights.) Created by both homegrown and international stars, these installations focus on a different annual theme.

After the day's fairs, the designers move on for dinner at **Antica Trattoria della Pesa** for *risotto alla Milanese* and then to **Bar Basso,** known for its Negroni Sbagliato, and where the scene gets so raucous that the crowd spills out into the street, mingling until the wee hours.

The fairs also present an opportunity to visit some of the city's most beloved design showrooms, and **Rossana Orlandi** is a must. Oracle to a new generation of designers, Orlandi is a true visionary who has brought many young talents into the international spotlight; her 19,000-square-foot (1,765 m) gallery meets shop, in a former tie factory, provides visitors with a quick study in her impeccable, far-reaching, and sometimes experimental taste. **Nilufar Depot,** curated by Nina Yashar, one of Milan's most important design dealers, should also be on the itinerary. A massive warehouse based on the layout of La Scala, it's a veritable who's who of the design world: a place where you could easily spend your entire income on the perfect chair or mid-century vintage table. The **Six Gallery** is the new design store in town curated by rising stars David Lopez Quincoces and Fanny Bauer Grung, who also plan to open a boutique hotel.

In the neighborhood of Brera, home to many small shops, art galleries, and furniture stores, **Bottega Ghianda** displays the deep roots and artisanship that have made Italy famous. The family got its start in 1889 and became the standard for wood-making designers. Masters like Gio Ponti, de Padova, and Gae Aulenti all fulfilled their prototypes for furniture pieces at the company. After the last family member decided to sell the business, the company was bought by Romeo Sozzi, another renowned woodworker who uses the showroom to display the legendary history of the family and the designers they inspired. Look forward but honor the past, and innovate with respect. That's Milan design. ▪

OPPOSITE: Rossana Orlandi's collection of designers is museum worthy, and she is known as a visionary for new talent. **ABOVE:** Milan's Fuorisalone exhibition takes place during Design Week.

Twilight over the atmospheric town of Bellagio, one of the many beautiful villages on Lake Como, an alluring destination for centuries

Lake Como: Beyond Clooney

Silver-mirrored placid waters. Mountains framing gentle curves. Small towns with fragrant bakeries and little cafés. Sleek wood boats moving VIPs from one bank to another. The lakes region has long been high on the list for well-heeled Milanese and other visitors seeking a particularly beautiful natural setting. Lately, new openings have given the destination another round of buzzy interest.

Many now associate Lake Como with George Clooney, who has a compound here (although Italian headlines have him reportedly selling his estate as often as he is keeping it). His presence keeps tabloids happy with his high-wattage guests—but truth be told, this lake has been favored by the glitterati for centuries, with the Alps soaring overhead and wooded hillsides the counterpoints to picturesque homes and ancient towns. Virgil called Como the greatest Italian lake, and surely the poet knew a thing or two about Italian paradises!

Start your exploration in the main town of Como at its cathedral, unusual for its three architectural styles— Romanesque, Renaissance, and Gothic—topped by a rococo dome. It also features exquisite handwoven tapestries. On Saturdays, check out the antique market in front of the Basilica di San Fedele too. Afterward, take the funicular to **Brunate,** a small residential village about 1,600 feet (488 m) up with bird's-eye views down to the lake. If you are active, avoid the crowds with a hike away from the main viewing points to the Faro Voltiano, which offers vistas that sweep into Switzerland.

Not far from Como town, **Villa Olmo**

is only one of many 18th-century neo-classical icons built on the lakeside, but it's certainly among the most beautiful. If there's an exhibit going on, you'll be allowed in to view the stunning art nouveau interiors. But either way, you'll be wowed by the vast English and Italianate gardens. In the past few years, the area's gourmet quotient has received a new injection with the opening of Le Sereno's hotel restaurant, **Berton al Lago.** It joins other Michelin-starred locations like **I Tigli in Theoria,** as well as spots like **Market Place** with its seasonal and local focus, and chic design.

In Bellagio, tucked perfectly between the two southern branches of the lake, the cobblestoned streets urge you to go slowly, perhaps stopping in local shops for some porcini or biscotti before heading to **Bar Rossi** for an otherworldly espresso. If you've come for nightclubs or glitz or guided tours, you won't find them here. But fresh air, strudel, and orderly consistency (people actually following the rules in Italy) come in spades.

People will say the best way to see the lake is by boat, and it is—preferably a sexy wood Riva from the 1960s, one of Italy's star designs. Skippers point out the villa treasures, alternately

Berton al Lago is only one of Lake Como's Michelin-starred restaurants.

being discreet and then whispering conspiratorially. Berlusconi. Russian oligarchs. Clooney again.

Be sure to stop in at **Villa Carlotta** in Tremezzo, a 17th-century mansion turned museum and with one of the most dazzlingly botanical gardens in Italy. Twenty acres (8 ha) of flora and fauna will inspire even an amateur green thumb. ■

CHECKING IN

Lake Como boasts some of the more expensive lodgings in the country, so be prepared to splurge.

VILLA D'ESTE: The 16th-century former summer home of a cardinal, Como's grande dame property has old-school glamour and style in spades—not to mention 25 acres (10 ha) of gardens, an indoor pool, and an outdoor pool that floats on top of the lake itself.

IL SERENO: One of the newest and most contemporary arrivals on the hotel scene, with interiors by famed Milanese interior

designer Patricia Urquiola. Insiders rave that it gets sun most of the day, unlike some of the other lake choices, and the vertical garden is a beauty.

MANDARIN ORIENTAL COMO: The luxury bigwig just took over the former CastaDiva Resort, where a major refurbishment included creating the largest spa on the lake and a destination *aperitivo* bar.

Frances's Favorites

In Your Glass

Everyone toasts with prosecco. But have you tasted its lesser known rival Franciacorta? *Che bellissimo.* Its cult status is well deserved. This suave champagne-method DOCG sparkling wine is beloved by aficionados for a dry, smoky aroma and effervescent hit. Bellavista has been my stand-by-me party wine for years. I also favor Ca' del Bosco, super to pour for favorite friends. That vineyard also makes a divine chardonnay, Ca' del Bosco Curtefranca.

Seek out too the distinguished reds: matches made in *paradiso* for veal *cotolette alla Milanese,* and osso buco. Valtellina produces the languid, rich, and weirdly named Ar. Pe. Pe.; Valtellina Superiore; and Sassella Rocce Rosse Riserva, recently Gambero Rosso's red of the year. No way to go wrong there. Other consistently fabulous producers of the area: Mamete Prevostini and Nino Negri. ∎

Less well known than prosecco, Franciacorta has a cult status. This suave champagne-method DOCG sparkling wine is beloved by aficionados for a dry, smoky aroma and effervescent hit.

ABOVE: Albergo Ristorante Olivedo in Lake Como's Varenna **OPPOSITE:** Milan's Enoteca Colli, a wine shop, treats its bottles like art pieces.

Best Of

Lombardy's Other Charms

People tend to think of the region as merely Milan and the lakes region, but Lombardy is full of other gemlike towns and natural beauty.

Best for Nature Lovers: Get away from the gray at Cascina Caremma in Ticino Valley's Besate. The working farm comes with organic food, country-chic rooms, and a spa menu based on the seasons.

Best for Vatican Fans: Take a side trip to Mantua. This city, pretty much untouched by recent development, has beautiful sights like the Palazzo Ducale, one of the largest complexes of palaces, and museums, in Europe, and Castello di San Giorgio, its atmospheric castle. Bar Caravatti is the town's other epicenter, with excellent Negronis and a crowd that lingers until midnight.

ABOVE: The evocative entrance of Cornello dei Tasso in Camerata Cornello
OPPOSITE: The blooming gardens on Isola Madre provide a green oasis for visitors regardless of the season.

Best for Thrill Seekers: Considered one of Italy's most beautiful hill towns, Cornello dei Tasso is not for the faint of heart. It's suspended over a deep chasm, with only a 30-minute winding pathway and bridge as the entryway into the village. The destination in this case is very much worth the journey. After working up an appetite, try the polenta with hare at Trattoria Camozzi.

Best for Boating Buffs: Set sail to Lake Maggiore's Borromean islands, a picturesque collection of islets like Isola Bella with its baroque palace and Isola Madre with its botanical gardens.

Best for Cheesy Types: Try Gorgonzola in the stinky blue cheese's birthplace, a village of the same name within a metro ride of Milan. In September, there is a festival in its honor. Otherwise, try the wild black rice timbali with Gorgonzola and walnuts at restaurant Vecchia Pesa.

Best for Roman Aficionados: Go Roman in Brescia. The largest archaeological site in the region, the town's impressive UNESCO-protected amphitheater sits next to thermal baths and a temple.

Best for Film Lovers: Lombardy has to share Lake Garda with Veneto and Trentino–Alto Adige, but Sirmone, an exquisite peninsula that sticks out into the lake and has become a national park, is Lombardy's alone. Make sure to visit the Roman ruins, as well as the Grotte di Catullo with natural thermal baths (and a rocking beach bar). Get a pre-visit taste by viewing the 2017 art house gem *Call Me by Your Name,* and book a room at the Villa Eden, a new architectural showcase hotel on Lake Garda.

Best for Frescoes and Food Types: Head to Padua for Giotto's exquisite and unforgettable frescoes—but save time for a stop at Il Calandrino, an all-day spot for small dishes and ingredients dreamed up by Michelin-starred chef Massimiliano Aljamo. ∎

Chapter Four

VENETO

Venice: the most outrageously beautiful city in the world? By my lights, yes. A peak experience is a gondola ride late at night—especially into the small canals, where lamplight from the palazzi falls in silvery bars onto the water and you hear only the knocking of the oar and the small splash as it turns. If the gondolier sings, you know it's touristy, but your heart melts anyway. Glance up and see frescoed ceilings, heavy

silk draperies, and glittering chandeliers. Who are those who live here, and what are they dreaming inside the damp and resplendent palazzi?

Given all the canals and gondolas, Venice is unexpectedly fun for walking. Walk! Get lost. Turn down a hundred tiny streets, crossing humpbacked stone bridges, entering and exiting churches, and pausing for a tumbler of red at a *bacaro* (neighborhood wine bar), where you can enjoy *cicchetti* (typical bite-size snacks). Exploring on foot, you're soon away from crowds, and Venice becomes *your* watery world, where reflections double every glorious thing you see.

Is there a greater pleasure than looking into the green canals' shifting colors of facades turned to ribbon candy, concentric ripples of gold, and the doubled geraniums and plumbago in window boxes? How many evocative doorways and glimpses of hidden gardens?

Torcello is not to be missed. Today, there are only a handful of inhabitants on this little island, located on the northern end of the Venetian lagoon. The Basilica of Santa Maria Assunta, built in 639, preserves some of the most amazing mosaics in the world. Floor remnants date from the seventh century and magnificent wall mosaics from the 13th century. The development of the lagoon started on Torcello. Here you can sense the foundations of Venice's origin: how radical it was in the seventh century that early settlers drove piles into the ground,

cut water channels around low sandbars, and started building. I'm always stunned at the courage of those pioneers.

Happily, you can stay overnight on the island at the timeless Locanda Cipriani with a good restaurant. After the last boat leaves in late afternoon, an eerie quiet descends.

When in Venice, many travelers neglect to explore the rest of the Veneto. It too is a watery world, filled with architectural delights. For me, always house-mad, what a profusion of stupendous villas! Many were built in the 16th century by Andrea Palladio, who changed the history of architecture as he charged through the region, constructing monumental villas where in prior centuries, only plain farms existed. How he astonished the landscape with grand bulwarks modeled on the Pantheon and other classical treasures!

As Venice's world domination of trade began to fade in the

WHAT YOU NEED TO KNOW...

- **BEST TIME TO VISIT:** March to May, October to December. The summer months are overcrowded and hot, and January can be cold and gloomy.

- **TOP SPOTS:** Venice, Verona, Torcello

- **GETTING THERE:** Fly into Aeroporto Marco Polo, Venice International Airport.

Among Venice's maze of canals, visitors will find hundreds of signs for *ponte,* or "bridge."

The Veneto's village restaurants reflect their territory. Some of the starring dishes include polenta, often made with white corn. Risotto is an art form.

16th century, rich or noble Venetians turned to agriculture. As a result, country palazzi on the mainland became a trend. The well-to-do traveled out of the Venetian lagoon and along the reshaped Brenta River in luxurious, horse-pulled barges called *burchielli* to get to their homes, stepping ashore to some of the most astonishing real estate ever constructed. Their lavish estates—some say 4,000 used to exist—graced the landscape. Hundreds of builders scattered their designs throughout the vast holdings of Venetian landowners. Today, more than 50 remain but only six can be visited. Seeing them from the outside is still quite amazing.

Twenty-four of Palladio's villas survive in the Veneto countryside. The village of Mira, a half hour from Venice by boat, makes a good base for villa explorations. From the refined Hotel Villa Franceschi, short drives are easy to La Rotunda, Villa Foscari, Villa Pisani, and others. Or take the modern version of a *burchiello* (the tour company has the same name) along the Brenta Canal and see 30 villas, stopping for visits at three. Cyclists will love the Brenta Riviera trails.

Also within striking distance of Mira: the Veneto's conical Colli Euganei (or Euganean Hills) rife with thermal springs, especially at Abano Terme. The zone is home to luxury spas and enticing villages such as Arquà Petrarca, Montagnana, Monselice, Este, and Galzignano. The *colli* form a regional park of more than 200 inviting walks and bicycling trails among vineyards and villages.

Rough-hewn barrels serve as tabletops at Venice's Basegò.

The Veneto's village restaurants reflect their territory. Some of the starring dishes include polenta, often made with white corn. Risotto is an art form. Forget sticky arborio variety, so often called for in American recipes. *Carnaroli* behaves much better and becomes sublime when part of the risotto's liquid is prosecco or amarone, the great red wine of the region. I've recently started cooking *venere,* a black whole-grain rice with a firm texture and nutty taste. *Saor,* which you see frequently on menus, is an ancient marinade (vinegar, raisins, onion) for sardines, fish, even chicken. The famous dessert of the Veneto: *pinza,* a dense polenta cake, unsweetened except from natural flavors—fig, raisins, and other fruits. With all the fish of the Adriatic, the lagoons' tiny crabs and frog legs, and the inland game and grains, this terrain puts forth bountiful gifts.

"I could live here" is a common response to the city of Treviso, about a 40-minute drive from Venice. It's one of those friendly places that gives itself to you all at once. An upscale town with clean canals and flowery balconies, its beguiling specialty is lettuces—especially a crunchy and slightly bitter burgundy red radicchio with elongated leaves veined with white. (The better known tight-balled version comes from around Verona.) Increasingly popular, Treviso's *radicchio del Veneto* is milder, with pink and rose leaves and a light green base. (A couple of packets of seeds slide right into the luggage.) How lovely—a town famous for lettuce.

Padua, 40 minutes west of Venice, offers a profound reason to visit. Come to this busy industrial city for the Cappella degli Scrovegni, a small chapel that holds one of the most important works of art in the Italian patrimony. Giotto di Bondone completed his fresco cycle by the end of 1305. He boldly depicts scenes from the lives of Christ and the Virgin Mary, and of Anna and Joachim, the parents of Mary (never mentioned in the Bible). Giotto injects new techniques into painting: Faces are more realistic, when before they were stylized, and he's trailblazing out of flat perspective into a new sense of depth. You must reserve at least a day in advance, as access is limited to 25 visitors at a time.

The Veneto encompasses a sliver of the Italian Dolomites. A beautiful drive north from Venice is the picturesque valley of the Cadore.

Padua has other attractions. Among them, at its university, where Galileo once lectured, is the Palazzo del Bo, a fascinating theater for anatomical dissection. Built in 1594, it has six levels for viewers, all hand-carved from walnut; on the first level, the table for the cadaver still stands. Medical students read the Latin inscription: *Here is where the dead are happy to help the living.*

A short jaunt west of Venice, the dignified town of Vicenza draws architecture students from around the world. They walk the streets that Andrea Palladio once strolled, rolls of drawings under his arm. He left us his Teatro Olimpico, the oldest indoor theater in the world. Construction began in 1580; Palladio did not live to see it completed five years later. His inspiration came from amphitheaters; the stadium-like seating, wildly uncomfortable, looks like the outdoor arenas for Roman entertainment. There the austerity ends, and a fantasy of statues and reliefs begins. The stage is an idealized classical piazza, with a backdrop of arches, columns, and the illusion of five streets receding to a vanishing point. Performances still take place. Carry a cushion with you.

Jewel-like Verona is a favorite of mine. Though Shakespeare never visited, the city is forever associated with him—and with romance. People flock to Juliet's house, ersatz as it is, and leave behind forlorn and hopeful notes. The River Adige flows through, with walks along the banks especially poignant in autumn. One of the largest piazzas in Italy, Piazza Bra is open and sunny, with the surrounding cafés ideal people-watching perches. Without a doubt, the best time to go is summer for the outdoor opera season, right in the piazza's arena. Originally a Roman amphitheater, the fabulous performance space seats 15,000 in front of the stage. On a July night under the stars, hear the mesmerizing processional march from *Aïda*.

Piazza dei Signori, known as Piazza Dante for the statue of the poet, seems the most intimate. Once, at the end of an ill-fated romance in the United States, an old boyfriend said, "Meet me in Piazza Dante five years from today." I didn't, but now I like to sit there among the dazzling Renaissance buildings and think of Juliet, who was never here, of the Latin man, who probably never came, of Dante with a pigeon on his head, and of my blue notebook, where I'm lucky enough to record images of Verona.

Venice's former customshouse, the Punta della Dogana, has been reinvented as a contemporary art museum that offers sweeping views over the lagoon.

Venice: Getting Away From the Crowd

Venice. Who could miss this Italian jewel? From the visitor statistics available, pretty much no one. The figures stagger: On average, 25 million to 30 million tourists a year descend on the celebrated destination that houses only 55,000 full-time residents. Like its residents, travelers to the canaled wonderland would appreciate more space to fully enjoy the maze of streets and waterside palaces—and to be free of the massive cruise ships that make their way along the Giudecca Canal, despite ongoing opposition.

The good news? Many of the groups' itineraries and day-trippers stay to the same well-worn path: **Saint Mark's Square,** the **Rialto Bridge,** the **Grand Canal.** With the right timing and the willingness to head out of the fray, you too can have moments where the city is truly yours and understand why it is one of the world's most beautiful and treasured destinations (though sadly, one that's slowly sinking). A word to the wise: Get lost, which is part of the fun!

Head to neighborhoods like **Il Castello.** Although this area is the largest *sestiere,* or area, in the city, many visitors give it a miss because its treasures are less well known, so it manages to remain residential and away from the fray. Even when the Biennale, the world-famous art or architecture (they alternate years) fair, is on, there is enough space to get a sense of authentic life here: laundry hanging outside dilapidated but still beautiful palazzi, sun-filled squares where kids kick around a football, and quiet canals where elegant women shop for fish or artichokes from boats moored alongside.

Stop in to the Renaissance marvel **Chiesa di San Zaccaria,** with masterpieces from Tintoretto and Titian, among others, and the atmospheric **Chiesa di San Francesco della Vigna,** one of Venice's underrated highlights, which boasts Bellini's "Madonna and Saints" among its treasures. For a culinary treat, book into **CoVino,** which offers artisanal beers and creative takes on such dishes as *melanzane al saor* (eggplant in sweet and sour sauce). Or make a beeline to **Local,** a new city hot spot with ingredients sourced seasonally—for example, Morlacco cheese, girolles, and black truffles in the autumn.

Be sure to take in the smaller museums. **Fondazione Querini Stampalia** is one of the best examples of a small palazzo library and art complex within an intimate space. Insiders particularly love the modern touches by master architect Carlo Scarpa, who respected the antiquity of the spot while incorporating new features like a footbridge and peaceful garden (a great place for a quiet espresso while reading a book). The former home of designer Mariano Fortuny (he of the beautiful lamps) has become an exquisite small museum, **Palazzo Fortuny,** with the atelier, fabrics, and furnishings lovingly preserved within the Gothic-style palace. The museum often hosts visiting exhibitions as well. Peggy Guggenheim made Venice her home for many years, and after her death, her sizable contemporary art collection and palazzo became a museum: the **Peggy Guggenheim Collection.** Works from Picasso, Duchamp, Giacometti, and Kandinsky, among other greats, are mixed through the property, along

A NAME TO KNOW: MAURIZIO CATTELAN

Although he was born in Padua, famed artist Maurizio Cattelan has found his true following in Venice.

ONE OF ITALY'S most admired and most prolific artists, Cattelan started his career as a woodworker for Forlì, a celebrated Italian designer. He went on to blossom as a sculptor, known particularly for his wicked sense of humor and use of taxidermy. Now internationally revered, he has had retrospectives at museums including New York City's Guggenheim and London's Tate.

Cattelan's satirical sculptures are often on view in Venice, and site-specific installations showcase city themes and jokes. Back in 1997, at the Biennale, for example, he placed 2,000 stuffed pigeons on rafters throughout the central pavilion, looking like a mass of unruly hooligans, and cheekily entitled the work "The Tourists." (Pigeons are considered the scourge of the city, so Cattelan was ironically pointing out that tourists too could be considered unwelcome guests.)

To see one of his most famous works, head to the city's Punta della Dogana and Palazzo Grassi. Cattelan's headless stuffed horse from 2007 is mounted through the Dogana's first gallery and gives the impression that it is leaping right through the wall, a disorienting and fantastical spectacle.

Artist Maurizio Cattelan has many works on view in Venice.

ABOVE: As well as zipping visitors all over the city, Venetian water taxis are a must for their photo ops. OPPOSITE: Antiche Carampane is an excellent restaurant that draws many Venetians.

Don't miss the steamed spider crabs—and book in advance.

Get on a boat and go around and around. The *vaporetto* system may be crowded, but it's also one of the best and cheapest ways to get the lay of the land. It also makes for some wonderful photo ops (the HelloVenezia travel pass offers unlimited rides and discounts on museums). If you want something occasion worthy, give **Cruising Venice** a try. Its staffed fleet includes the *Eolo,* a traditional *bragozzo* boat from 1946 with a shallow bottom that allows for access throughout the Venetian waterways, even in places where other vessels can't get to. Services on board include cooking lessons.

And by all means, go sightseeing at night. Venice does not have a reputation for nightlife, and most visitors head off to bed right after dinner. This means that places like **Saint Mark's Square** become delightfully uncrowded and look particularly picturesque in the moonlight. A ride on the vaporetto number one up and down the **Grand Canal** becomes romantic after hours, rather than when it is jam-packed with tourists and their luggage.

And don't miss a side trip to **Giudecca,** only five minutes from the main island of Venice but a world away, with a Brooklyn outer borough vibe and the sense of continuing industry and design, as well as quiet residential streets. The views back to Saint Mark's and the Doge's Palace are breathtaking. Restaurants like **I Figli delle Stelle** have outdoor tables and dishes like eggplant gnocchi with anchovies that attract a young Venetian crowd. ∎

with black-and-white photos of the arts patron in her preferred city.

Mix your modern art with antique structures. A number of excellent contemporary art museums have sprung up in repurposed buildings in the past few years. One of the most impressive is the **Punta della Dogana,** Venice's former customshouse transformed by architect Tadao Ando into a home for luxury retail billionaire François Pinault's art collection. The views from outside are also breathtaking. Afterward, check out the **Palazzo Grassi,** another example of the duo's ability to merge centuries seamlessly into a single space: a masterly reinterpretation behind a perfect classical facade.

Eat with Venetians. With millions of tourists arriving every year, many restaurants don't make the effort they should because they have such an easy market. Not so with the spots that have a loyal Venetian following. **Antiche Carampane,** a small, family-run restaurant that's consistently top-notch, keeps a captive audience coming for its exemplary *crudi* (raw fish) and seafood. Even in a city where it's hard to find addresses, this place is almost impossible to find, which is how the local residents like it. Another hometown must is **Osteria alle Testiere,** a one-room temple run by chef Bruno Gavagnin and sommelier Luca di Vita, who have made it one of the top restaurants in the city.

The island Mazzorbo is on the same lagoon as the famous city of Venice —and is much quieter.

Hidden Islands on the Venetian Lagoon

For many, Venice often invokes simply the main island and the sights within. But there are still more attractions for those who are willing to venture a little farther afield. In fact, the lagoon's other islands have always been an important part of the city's tapestry, providing seasonal and local ingredients, homes for fishermen, warehouses and factories for industry, a beachside playground—and even a refuge from tourist barbarians. (We aren't suggesting that modern sightseers are a new incarnation of the invading masses. Well, sort of.)

Start your adventure in **Mazzorbo.** This quiet island—attached by bridge to **Burano,** with its pretty, colored houses—has become a destination for foodies and wine lovers with the opening of **Venissa.** This restaurant meets guesthouse, a walled green oasis, was the brainchild of the prosecco-producing family Bisol, which transformed the 16th-century estate back into a vineyard while introducing visitors to the island. The restaurant emphasizes ingredients sourced from the garden or nearby water, with dishes like red mullet with wild fennel, quail

with peach and elderflowers, and langoustine in plum gazpacho. After a meal, stroll the quiet walkways along the waterfront, or nap in one of the property's top-floor rooms with expansive views of the lagoon.

Most of Venice's produce comes from the island of **Sant'Erasmo,** a network of orchards and vegetable gardens that provide boatloads of organic staples to the city each day (the particularly beloved purple artichoke, Violetta di Chioggia, is a prized ingredient on Venetian menus from April to June). You can walk or bike around the island, or schedule a visit to **Orto di Venezia,** a picturesque estate that has brought white wine production back to its former heyday. Sant'Erasmo is about a 30-minute vaporetto ride away from the main island.

Even farther out, **Torcello** is one of the most charming spots in Italy: the place where mainlanders sought refuge when Attila the Hun was busy terrorizing the country after the end of the Roman Empire. After making the pleasant 45-minute vaporetto ride across the water, head to Santa Maria Assunta, the island's extraordinary 12th-century church, featuring Byzantine mosaic frescoes and pure tranquillity. Take a walk around the tiny island idyll before stopping for lunch at 1940s stalwart **Locanda Cipriani,** an island hotel hideaway where Ernest Hemingway penned parts of various novels. Lunch in the rose-filled garden is a pleasure, and a night in one of its rooms gives new meaning to the art of unplugging.

Lido in the summer months is a much more crowded affair and (with no disrespect to the lagoon) not really on a par with some of the other beach destinations in Italy. However, a jaunt to the island immortalized in Thomas Mann's *Death in Venice* during the shoulder months (April and May, September and October) provides the feeling of an island getaway within Venice. Among the highlights: a bike ride around the **Oasis di Alberoni,** a nature reserve with wild sand dunes, and a glass of Soave (contrary to its bad reputation, this vintage is making a comeback) at **Al Merca.** ∎

For many, Venice often invokes simply the main island. But there are still more attractions for those who are willing to venture farther afield. In fact, the lagoon's other islands have always been an important part of the city's tapestry.

CLOCKWISE FROM LEFT: Traditional *sarde in saor,* marinated sardines, at the Venissa resort on Mazzorbo; the distinctive purple artichokes called Violetta di Chioggia come from Venice's Sant'Erasmo island; the cloister at Lido's San Nicolò church dating from the 16th century

Frances's Favorites
In Your Glass

In a word, amarone. Allegrini, Lorenzo Begali, Roberto Anselmi, F.lli Tedeschi, Masi, Speri—these are some of the top conjurers of this royal red wine. Pour amarone on the night you propose or celebrate 50 anniversaries. Buy bottles in the years of your children's births and give them as gifts when they're 21. Amarone is with you for the long haul.

What makes this wine distinctive is that the grapes—*rondinella, molinara,* and primarily *corvina,* from "crow" because they're so dark—are partially dried on mats for up to three months before being pressed. *Amarone* means "big bitter." The wine is aged in oak at least two years before bottling. The result is the most *corposo* (large-bodied) wine imaginable. Some use the words "leather," "cherry," or "raisin"—but, really, the impression I have is of a deep-reaching taste of quintessential grape. A great amarone is mind-bending.

Somewhat opposite, the fabled sparkling proseccos of the Veneto come from the area around the village of Valdobbiadene. I was lucky to be at Ruggeri for the harvest and have poured their exalted Giustino B ever since. And after visiting Villa Sandi at the source, their Cartizze Brut Vigna La Rivetta also became a favorite. Other fine makers: Bortolomiol and Merotto.

Soave used to be branded as a cheapo white wine but has long since been redeemed. Dry and spicy Soaves come out of the Verona province trailing glory. Graziano Prà deservedly wins awards for its gently floral Soave Classico Staforte, and Agostino Vicentini's Soave Superiore Il Casale may become your favorite for a summer evening with fish on the grill. ■

Pour amarone on the night you propose. Buy bottles in the years of your children's births. Amarone is with you for the long haul.

ABOVE: Lines of vineyards in Treviso, which produces the region's famous prosecco, a bubbly Italian mainstay **OPPOSITE:** The process of *pica,* an ancient and traditional way of withering the grapes, not only is beautiful but also is fundamental to creating wines like amarone.

In the Know

Where to Stay in Venice

From grandes dames to boutique hotels to palazzi for rent, Venetian hotels tend to offer rooms at prices higher than those in the rest of the country. Blame it on high demand and Venice's romantic reputation.

Palazzo Venart: This newcomer to the hotel scene has already become a favorite because of its tucked-away location (while still being close to the city highlights) and intimate atmosphere in a palazzo that's been reimagined as an 18-room hotel. Glam, the restaurant from Michelin-starred chef Enrico Bartolini, is also a draw; try his signature beetroot risotto with Gorgonzola.

Gritti Palace: Following a $50 million restoration, this iconic hotel on the Grand Canal comes with impeccable views of the city, one-of-a-kind antiques, and a price tag to match (although the property just became a Marriott, so if you are a member, try using points instead).

Aman Venice: The Clooneys stayed at this property during their destination wedding, and that fact alone will fill it for years to come. But there are other reasons for the high-wattage attention: The common areas on the piano nobile (noble floor, that is, the principal floor) are 16th-century

perfect, and the property comes with extra-attentive service and exquisite original details like a real-deal Tiepolo fresco in one of the suites.

Bauer Palladio: This property on Giudecca is only a five-minute hop from Saint Mark's—but the maze of gardens and 16th-century buildings designed by Andrea Palladio make it feel both secluded and lost in time. Go for one of the garden-side buildings with terraces opening into a meadow; it's a literal breath of fresh air.

Casa Flora Venezia: This three-bedroom apartment rental is the sister property to the Novecento and Hotel Flora hotels. It's a chic pad that's a great option for an extended family or a group of friends, and it's sustainably minded too, from the wood floors to repurposed countertops. The property offers excellent customized events and city tours.

Palazzina Grassi: If you don't appreciate the sleek, nightclub-in-the-lobby atmosphere that Philippe Starck made a signature in his hotels, you are unlikely to book a room here. But for a nightlife scene (think post–film festival premiere parties) and modern design, this trendy hotel is just the ticket.

Casa Codussi: One of the villas rented by luxury agent Merrion Charles, this restored palazzo near the Arsenale sleeps 18 (with a fun attic room for kids). With its professional kitchen and handpicked details from the beds to artwork, it looks right out of a design magazine.

Ca Maria Adele: A 12-room boutique spot that's romantic in a boudoir way—think Murano chandeliers and damask textiles. The rooftop terrace has a breathtaking view.

San Clemente Palace Kempinski: On its own island and only a five-minute boat ride from Saint Mark's, this former monastery has plenty of space for new amenities like tennis courts, a pool, and a spa, alongside an old-school bar that seems like it's been there forever. ∎

ABOVE: The facade of Venice's Palazzo Venart hotel **OPPOSITE:** The noble floor of the Aman hotel, where Amal and George Clooney stayed

In the Know

Venice Biennale and Film Festival

Despite its deep roots in the artistic past and former treasures of the city, Venice has been savvy in adding cutting-edge installations and promoting new talent as well. No other festival has given the city more cultural relevance than its annual Biennale, which concentrates one year on art and the next on architecture. Each May, artists, collectors, and trend makers head into town for the event's opening week; the festival lasts until the end of November (one of the most pleasant times to be in town, as it is much less touristy).

Biennale events are concentrated in two major sites: the Biennale Gardens pavilions (each devoted to a certain country) and the Arsenale, Venice's former navy yard. They are also spread through various museums and palazzi across the city. If you want to hit the highlights, give yourself a couple of days, because even covering just the Arsenale can be an hours-long undertaking. Make sure to familiarize yourself with the artists representing their home country's pavilion; sometimes it's celebrated names like Tracey Emin or Ai Weiwei, whereas at others it's a virtual unknown who is making a breakthrough here.

Even if you aren't an architecture buff, the architectural years of the Biennale can be fascinating and illuminating, focusing on themes like sustainability. The 2018 one, "Freespace," contemplated the use of open and connected spaces that create human connection or improvisation.

At the end of August into early September, the city comes alive again after the summer for Venice's internationally renowned film festival. The event has been held for more than 75 years and is considered to be the most important in Italy. Lately it has also become a launchpad for Oscar contenders like *La La Land* and *The Shape of Water,* but film buffs will find many less commercial screenings as well. Most of the events and screenings are held on the Lido; it's actually quite easy to buy tickets through the Biennale website. The program includes some great classics too. ∎

A work by British artist Jeremy Deller, "A Good Day for Cyclists," on display in 2013 at the now annual Venice Biennale exhibit

A bird's-eye view over the spectacular city of Verona in the Veneto, including its majestic duomo and romantic Ponte Pietra pedestrian bridge

Verona: The Perfect Side Trip

Despite an abundance of exquisite architectural treasures and a peaceful but vibrant vibe, Verona often gets short shrift from many tourists who come to the Veneto only for Venice. And that's just fine for fans who like the authentic and local side of this underrated gem. The city heaves at the opening of the opera season in June and during VinItaly, the country's top-rated wine fair (which takes place in April). But outside of those events, it's easy to book a hotel or a table at one of the city's best restaurants. A complete renovation of **Palazzo Victoria,** one of the city's grandes dames, makes for a good place to stay overnight.

Start your tour with the city's famous amphitheater, **Arena di Verona,** a well-preserved Roman structure dating from A.D. 30, where today, opera singers, rather than gladiators, try to win over the crowd. Even if you aren't in town for a show, you'll want to see this impressive outdoor theater—the third largest in the world.

Next, walk along the pedestrian-only **Via Mazzini,** filled with high-end shops and well-dressed Veronese who treat it as a sort of local catwalk. In **Piazza delle Erbe,** the stalls of the former food market now sell trinkets instead of produce. But it's still the heart of the city, with the 14th-century **Torre del Gardello** as its architectural punctuation. Grab an *aperitivo* at **L'Osteria del Bugiardo,** where the owner, Alfredo Buglioni, showcases his Valpolicella wine alongside plates of salami and cheeses. It's a popular dining spot for local residents after work.

In the past few years, Verona's culinary reputation has grown exponentially. At one of the best of the new restaurant arrivals, **Locanda 4 Cuochi,** four chefs perform their craft in an open kitchen, periodically ducking into the dining room to suggest a special or wine pairing. The polenta ravioli, stuffed with spinach and snail ragù, is the kind of experimental and delicious dish they create daily.

In a town dripping with romance, the Ponte Pietra, a pedestrian-only stone bridge, is one of the most romantic spots. After taking the requisite photo, book a table at **Osteria Ponte Pietra** and sit at one of the outdoor tables with a view of the river and bridge. (Order the *risotto ama-rone.*) Next door, make sure to sample the gelato from **Gelateria Ponte Pietra.** Despite its rather grumpy owner, local residents line up for a cup of *bacio* (crushed hazelnuts in creamy chocolate) or one of his seasonal fruit concoctions.

To work off your meals (weather permitting), hop on a bike and discover other celebrated city landmarks like the **Duomo Cattedrale di Santa Maria Matricolare,** with its unusual Romanesque base that becomes Gothic as it ascends. Other churches worth a look include the **Santa Maria in Organo,** which houses what Vasari called the finest choir stall in Italy, and **San Giorgio in Braida,** with its Tintoretto masterpieces. Finally, a visit to the 16th-century **Giardini Palace** gardens offers a green refuge and a panoramic view of the city and river.

And what about Juliet's famous balcony? you may ask. Although the character is fictional and there is no real proof that this was the actual balcony that Shakespeare was speaking of, romantic types can nonetheless visit Via Capello, 23 to see what is billed as the lovers' spot where Juliet asked, "Romeo, Romeo, wherefore art thou Romeo?" ◼

Despite an abundance of exquisite architectural treasures and a peaceful but vibrant vibe, Verona often gets short shrift. And that's just fine for fans who like the authentic and local side of this underrated gem.

CLOCKWISE FROM LEFT: Going on errands under the arches of Verona's back streets; rolling out handmade *tortelli;* the Adige River snakes past the city.

Frances's Favorites

Asolo: Petite Kingdom

Maybe it's the traffic you leave behind or the coiling roads leading ever upward. But arriving in the main piazza of Asolo induces a surreal feeling of dislocation—as if you've landed in one of the imagined places Italo Calvino conjured in his book *Invisible Cities*. Has time warped? Is it real? The town is elegant: gushing fountain, cafés under awnings, a spread-winged palace, arcaded shops. But that's not what casts a spell. I won't even try to explain it; that might dissolve the airy, mythic feel of the place.

On my recent visit, I got out of the car and looked in a shop window. Dusty, closed. A necklace was displayed in the window. Old. Delicate tiers of thin-beaten gold. I thought I had to have it. In another window, four painted glass apothecary jars were lined up. They were surpassingly beautiful, with designs of pomegranates and *cedro,* huge yellow citrus, and flowering vines. I wanted them too. A strange lust for possession took over. The moist air smelled of jasmine, cedar, and cypresses.

I sat at Caffè Centrale and looked up Robert Browning's poems. He was enchanted by this town. His tribute, *Asolando,* was published on December 12, 1889, the day he died. Many of the nicest shops line Via Roberto Browning (somehow, he sounds less stuffy as Roberto). No awful art galleries for tourists, no junky shops with colored pasta and tooth-cracking bis-

cotti. The dim and rustic wine bar glitters with grandiose chandeliers, gorgeous local prosecco. This would be *my* hangout if I lived here. The owner is already my friend.

Asolare (etymology: to breathe gently) has been a local word since the 1500s when Cardinal Bembo, a literary man and a church dignitary, described the local way of living: indulgent sweet aimlessness, sort of a verb form of *dolce far niente*.

Many famous people have spent time here. Ernest Hemingway, Ezra Pound, Giosuè Carducci, Eleonora Duse—but the great travel writer Freya Stark intrigues me most. That's her villa

right at the end of Roberto's street. She traveled the Far East, writing about it before any other Western woman. From age 14, when she inherited the villa, she always loved Asolo. A brilliant writer, she lived to be 100. Now I want her life. Her garden with Roman remnants, her huge curved desk, her walks among the country villas, dinners in big leather chairs at the Cipriani, Sunday mornings browsing at the antiques market.

Strange, this wild desire to take on the attributes of the place! Then I realize: That's what travel sometimes can do. You land in a town, and a mysterious link clicks around your wrist, catching hold, never letting go. ■

ABOVE: Tucked into the mountainside and surrounding forest, the town of Asolo is one of the Veneto's gems. OPPOSITE: Asolo's Via Roberto Browning is named for the poet, who fell in love with the town.

Best Of

Cicchetti: The Venetian Answer to Tapas

Even the name is evocative: *cicchetti*. This uniquely Venetian take on tapas, or small plates, is best washed down with a good glass of wine at various *bàcari,* the small bars Venetians prefer. The beloved city tradition provides the excuse for the *giro d'ombra,* or "a stroll for *ombra,*" slang for a glass of wine; the expression is derived from a roving wine stand that moved around Saint Mark's Square to stay in the shadow of the Campanile during the course of the day. *Bàcari* are also incredibly well priced—a boon in a town where restaurants tend to be expensive. Some favorites to graze and drink:

Ca' d'Oro (Alla Vedova): Far from the tourist fray, this neighborhood favorite is best known for its *polpette,* or meatballs; the finely minced pork will become your new benchmark for this classic dish. A one-euro glass of local red from the Veneto provides the perfect pairing.

Do Mori: Dating back to 1463, this enchanting restaurant near the Rialto Bridge is one of the oldest of the *bàcari* (and is rumored to have been frequented by Casanova himself). The house specialty is the *francobollo:* postage stamp–size sandwiches filled with ingredients like lagoon crab.

OPPOSITE: *Cicchetti* are the Venetian answer to tapas. **ABOVE:** Small bites come in a colorful variety of fish, meat, and vegetarian options.

Cantina Do Spade: Another city institution dating back to the 15th century, its *cicchetti* concentrate on seafood, with little dishes of fried zucchini flowers filled with *baccala,* creamed cod, *polpette* with tuna, grilled shrimp, and Venetian-style sardines. Join the bustling crowd of locals bellied up to the bar.

Al Ponte: From 11 in the morning until 11 at night, regulars drop by this tiny institution for a glass of the house wine and little plates of fried fish. It's a cheap date, and on a sunny day, it's the perfect place to sit outside on the steps and watch the world go by.

La Cantina: "The cellar" takes the concept of *cicchetti* up a notch, featuring fresh oysters shucked while you wait and delicate tartares of salmon and sea bass that are melt-in-your-mouth good. Wine lovers will also appreciate the selection of almost 30 vintages by the glass. Ask the barman for recommendations, as the staff loves to compare tasting notes.

Cantinone già Schiavi: Located on a side canal in Dorsoduro, this small wine shop features an excellent selection of labels mostly from the Veneto; it also serves *cicchetti* on the side; try the cheese and fennel crostino. The scene here is raucous, in no small part because there are more than 10 wines by the glass at only two euros.

Al Arco: Open only for lunch, this small wine bottle–lined restaurant is where local residents gather after hitting the Rialto fish market to relax and compare seafood recipes for the next meal.

Acquastanca: On the island of Murano, known for its handblown glassworks, this recent arrival has given Venetians and visitors one of the best new bars and restaurants in town. Freshly baked desserts and an impressive wine list are among the treats. ▪

Chapter Five

LIGURIA

Menton—French city of lemon trees, *soupe au pistou,* and belle epoque architecture— is the gateway into Italy and soul sister of the Ligurian Riviera, the eyebrow-shaped coast that arches along 133 miles (215 km) from Ventimiglia around the Mediterranean and down to meet Sestri Levante, then on to the golden sands of Tuscany. I've long been enamored with this sunny region (third smallest in Italy). The old explorers

must have thought they'd landed in paradise when they came upon these shores.

Near the top of the curve stands the capital city of Genoa, once the prince of the seas and now one of Italy's secret treasures. Thousands of Italian schoolchildren clamber off buses to see the fabulous aquarium designed by local architect Renzo Piano, but otherwise Genoa is unruffled by tourist invasions. The city remains aloof: aristocratic enclaves, a rowdy port area, dazzling architecture, and a labyrinthine old town locked into its history of maritime ascendancy. Odd how some towns catch the traveler's eye, while others just as interesting, such as Genoa, Parma, Piacenza, Ferrara, Trento, and Catania, remain off the radar.

For a central location, we chose to stay at Locanda di Palazzo Cicala on the Piazza San Lorenzo, dominated by the city's major church. Genoa has a ridiculous number of grand palazzi stuffed with major art. And other attractions beckon: The city's indoor market is one of the largest in Europe, and Renzo Piano has transformed the harbor with warehouse conversions, restaurants, an Eataly outpost, museums, the famous aquarium, and more.

Every corner interests me in this complex city. The twisted medieval *centro* retains a funky bazaar atmosphere, while the grandiose Piazza de Ferrari opens up the city to buttery light and radiating shopping and dining streets. I didn't

expect Genoa to be an art center, but those powerful old robber baron shipping magnates brought back paintings when they loaded the boats with spices, fabrics, and other booty from northern Europe, India, Africa, and all over the Mediterranean trading routes. And I can think of few cities with more contemporary art galleries.

When it comes to Genovese cuisine, everyone's devoted to seafood, focaccia, and pesto. Due to the tangy but sweet variety of local basil, the pesto is brightly flavored, never bitter. But the passion is not limited to the classic pesto. Try those made of fava beans, olives, rucola, almonds, and walnuts. *Farinata* is addictive: chickpea batter seasoned with rosemary and poured onto a large, hot metal disk suspended

WHAT YOU NEED TO KNOW...

- **BEST TIME TO VISIT:** Easter to June, September to mid-November. Be clear about what you want. Crisp fall days are best for hiking, summer months for water sports and swimming—and really anytime for sitting and eating, drinking, and observing the gentle routines of daily life.

- **TOP SPOTS:** Cinque Terre, Camogli, Alassio, Verezzi, Santa Margarita Ligure, San Fruttuoso

- **BEST WAY IN AND OUT:** Train. Find the schedules at *Trenitalia.com.*

Camogli's Cenobio dei Dogi is the perfect Ligurian seaside hotel, with terraces for cocktails or quiet reading overlooking the Mediterranean.

A picnic of still-warm focaccia, an afternoon spent photographing reflections of boats in the water, intriguing doors, and colorful tile house names.

over a grill or shoved into a bread oven. Like flat pancakes *farinate* are slightly crisp, with a softer interior. Sliced and eaten hot, this is Genovese soul food and an ode to simplicity. Another on-the-go favorite: vegetable tortas with flaky crusts and a filling of greens and cheese.

I fell for the righteous trattoria La Forchetta Curiosa, where it could be 2020, 1950, or 1900. Timeless. But in the waterfront restaurant Il Marin, it could only be today in the smoothly sophisticated, high-concept, and creative seafood restaurant in the Eataly complex.

Inland, Liguria is also super appealing. Leaving Genoa and driving around for a couple of days in the mountains above the sea, you enter a different world of isolated and magical villages. The hills are sharply vertiginous—reaching 8,600 feet (2,630 m)—with dense evergreens and the surprise of

deer leaping onto the road. One of the most intriguing little *borghi* is the castle town of Apricale. Situated above Bordighera, the steeply layered village of *carrugi,* tiny twisting streets, showcases a striking piazza with a Gothic fountain and ancient houses. Farms around Apricale produce a particular oil from the *taggiasca* variety of olive, which yields a smooth taste: faintly sweet, nutty, and without the piquant punch of Tuscan oil. It pairs well with the seafood of Liguria.

Other excursions: the ancient walled towns of Castelvecchio di Rocca Barbena and Finalborgo, both located just above the beach town of Finale Ligure. The inland towns are good choices when visiting in high season. Find a comfortable farmhouse inn, stay above the fray, and dip down to nearby beach towns at your leisure.

Above all, Liguria is about the sea. When I think of the region, the vision of the dramatic coast rises immediately—

Designed by architect Renzo Piano, Genoa's aquarium is a must for kids.

Fragrant lemon trees scent the trails of the Ligurian coast before their lemons are sold at markets in the Cinque Terre.

especially the carless Cinque Terre ("five lands") villages, where after hiking from town to town, you can, if you're very brave, take a huge jump from a cliff into clear blue sea, and reward yourself afterward with a chilled bottle of crisp Cinque Terre white wine while feasting on big scampi and wild greens.

My favorite coastal village is Camogli, intimately set on the sea, only a half hour east of Genoa. I stayed three days at the old-world luxury hotel Cenobio dei Dogi. Liguria is known for its pretty facades of saffron, cream, and melon adorned with painted embellishments of trompe l'oeil windows and reliefs; the architectural details are especially striking, as the houses rise often to seven, even nine, stories high. In this famous tuna-fishing village, these tall buildings enabled the women left behind to look out for when their fishermen would return. Camogli is said to mean *ca'moglie*, wives' houses. It's a good base; the train makes frequent runs to Genoa and many other attractions. From here, it's easy to start hiking the coastal paths. I could have stayed quite happily another three days.

Another favored seaside spot: Noli, for the palm-lined coast and laid-back atmosphere. Memorable to dine on Il Vescovado's terrace overlooking the sea.

Endless other choices: Of course, of course, Portofino, the glamorous harbor full of astonishing yachts—one with a helipad and Smart car—but also simple rowboats and fishermen who will take you along the coves and to San Fruttuoso's enchanting abbey and beach. Take a walk up to Castello Brown, where *Enchanted April* was filmed. From the terrace, it seems that squeezed tubes of all the watercolors swirl blue, green, gold, and pearl out to sea. *Dolce far niente,* sweet to do nothing, kicks in. A picnic of still-warm focaccia, an afternoon spent photographing reflections of boats in the water, intriguing doors, and colorful tile house names. Then dinner at one of the romantic harborside restaurants.

Liguria, washed by the bluest sea, revels in color. Pastel houses rise from the water at Camogli, Cinque Terre's vibrant villages stack the hillsides, residences of Portovenere's Gulf of Poets are a riot of shades. The palette comes from the land: grape leaf green, burnished pomegranate, sunflower, lime, and especially lemon—peel, zest, and juice—the color of joy.

A rainbow of buildings cling to the bluffs of Manarola, one of the five villages that make up the protected riviera of Cinque Terre.

Cinque Terre: The Fishing Villages That Became Famous

It's hard to describe the first sighting of the five pastel-hued fishing villages of the Cinque Terre. Or that first walk along the sweeping trails that lead through the countryside above pristine coves. Each pathway links one small town to the next in the same way they have for generations. Buildings painted in a faded patina of yellows, reds, and pinks glow as the sun changes its course through the day. Fishing boats bob in the gently framed harbors as tan, wizened veterans repair their nets or exchange local gossip. The terraced vineyards and tucked-away lemon groves create a scent that's warm and familiar. Tiny churches and chiming bell towers invoke the slow passage of time. This is the Cinque Terre.

Each of the five towns has its own personality. **Monterosso al Mare** has the wide beach. **Vernazza** is arguably the most beautiful. Tiny **Corniglia** sits regally on a hill overlooking the sea. Some of the best wines of the region come from **Manarola. Riomaggiore** has the beautiful sanctuary of **Madonna di Montenero.** The towns have been called the Cinque Terre, "five lands," since the time that monks worked this land back in the 1700s but became officially protected in 1999. Each town is about a three-mile (5 km) rugged hike, one from the next, and draws visitors to do one part of the interlocking trails or the whole expedition, a 12-mile (20 km) spread.

The problem with all this great beauty? Word has gotten out. Day-trippers clog the trains and ferries between the towns. Many visitors alight from cruise ships moored in Livorno or Genoa. Some sweaty sorts are in town for a quick stop during a long hike and seem oblivious of the disapproving looks of residents who don't expect their water fountains to become impromptu showers. The relatively low cost of food and hotels compared with spots like the Amalfi Coast or Como makes this particular destination attractive to a wide audience. But by noon, the number of tourists makes the towns difficult to navigate, and residents are increasingly concerned as to whether the infrastructure—not to mention the ecosystem—can withstand this level of popularity. Luckily, it has been a UNESCO-designated and -protected area since 1997.

These five celebrated villages play a fundamental role in Italy's heritage. Perhaps nothing illustrates this more starkly than a destructive storm in October 2011 that caused widespread damage all over the region, almost destroying two of Cinque Terre's towns, Vernazza and Monterosso. Mud from the mountains behind them combined with driving rain to create raging rivers through the towns. Trails were washed out; buildings were flooded. But the event reminded its

One of the highlights of the Cinque Terre is hiking the trails that link one town to the next.

residents of their homes' irreplaceable legacy, and together they joined forces to bring life and business back to the region in a remarkably short amount of time. Organizations like Save Vernazza were founded; together with the architect Richard Rogers (who has been vacationing here for decades) it designed a drainage plan to stop the tragedy from happening again while also restoring damaged buildings, trails, and squares.

Like so many fans of the Cinque Terre, loyalists return again and again. In spite of, and regardless of, so many people, it is just that beautiful. Fans

CHECKING IN

Compared with some other parts of the coastline, the hotel offerings in the Cinque Terre tend toward the small and simple. Renting a local apartment is always a good alternative.

VERNAZZA SUL MARE: Owned by American insider Ruth Manfredi (who knows the region intimately after living here for more than 20 years), this portfolio of apartments includes the family-friendly Carattino 12 and Il Ciasso. Both offer sweeping sea views from the terraces and Manfredi's wonderful tips from restaurants to beaches.

AGRITURISMO BURANCO: Even if you don't stay over, make sure to have a wine tasting at the bucolic working farm and inn outside Monterosso. You'll adore its terraced vineyards and groves of lemon and olive trees.

LA TORRETTA: Cinque Terre insiders love this Manarola hotel for the great service, chic but simple rooms, and views from the terraces. A free *aperitivo* every evening and the free bag transfer from the nearby train station are other pluses.

LA MALÀ: This Vernazza hotel is one of Cinque Terre's gems, with large, pretty rooms with sea views, a private aerie after the crowds. But with only four rooms and an excellent reputation, you will have to book well in advance to secure a stay.

ABOVE: Walking the trails of the Cinque Terre means carbo-loading afterward. **OPPOSITE:** Intrepid swimmers jump off the rocks in front of Vernazza's little sand beach and main square.

za's pier, watching nut-brown locals dive from the boulders. Or admire the harbor and framed view of Manarola with a *limoncino* spritz at **Nessun Dorma,** a local version utilizing the garden's fragrant lemons. Or take a pesto-making class there (keeping in mind that without the local ingredients, the at-home version won't be nearly as delicious).

For a moment of solace, consider hiding yourself away in Vernazza's **Santa Margherita d'Antiochia** church. The quiet sanctuary overlooks the sea, and on July 20 every year, the town celebrates its saint day with a parade through the streets. Or try on the pretty dresses at **Katrina** on Via Roma for summer staples. And before you leave, make sure to pick up local olive oil and wine at **La Cantina del Molo di Basso Alberto** to take home a piece of the crisp coastline.

Eating is a main event here. Snag a front-row table at Vernazza's **Gianni Franzi** for lunch or dinner. Sitting under the red and yellow umbrellas on the main seaside piazza with a plate of *spaghetti alle vongole* (spaghetti with clams) or fresh anchovies is one of the great joys of town. Franzi also has a hotel with basic but clean rooms, as well as a rooftop terrace for cocktails. In Riomaggiore, **Rio Bistrot** is a relative newcomer to the culinary scene but already an insider favorite for its seafood and well-priced, well-curated wine list. Book ahead, as there are only 20 coveted seats on hand.

Another ritual to try: Once you've made it up the seemingly thousands of steps from Corniglia's train station, celebrate with a cone of tangy basil gelato at **Alberto Gelateria;** then watch the stupendous sunset. It is simple. It is unbearably lovely. ∎

who try to be eco-minded follow only designated trails and eat as locally and sustainably as possible, which is a treat here anyway. The insiders try to go off-season. They take advantage of the mornings before the ferries arrive—swimming laps alongside the buoys to keep them safe from moving boats, or getting weather updates at the bar, which prove more reliable than the internet. They emerge again at dusk, when the day-trippers depart, for an *aperitivo* mirrored in the placid sea.

Head up into the countryside to hide in the olive groves with a simple but perfect picnic, or rent a boat and move from cove to cove along the seaside, diving in as soon as your salt-drenched bodies are dry. Focus on the things that made people fall in love with this place from the start.

Days can be lazy or full of outdoor activities. Some of the hiking trails linking the towns are still washed out from the flood, but many are accessible. Try swimming in the clean water at Vernaz-

Hot Spot

San Fruttuoso: A Benedictine Showstopper

I taly has no shortage of spectacular abbeys; they are in fact one of the architectural magnets of the country. But San Fruttuoso, between Portofino and Camogli, was a place that offered monks a refuge for quiet contemplation and study overlooking the crystal clear Mediterranean Sea. It's one of the region's finest structures.

Accessible only by boat or by hiking along a craggy path that leads along a magical coastline, this quiet abbey is not to be missed. Stroll past sunlit windows, and imagine hearing monk's chants alongside the whisper of the sea. Afterward, indulge in a plate of pesto within a stone's throw of a 10th-century masterpiece.

The original church and its abbey, built in the eighth century, were destroyed by the Saracens and rebuilt by the Benedictines in its current incarnation. A statue of Christ sits on the bottom of the sea offshore and is said to protect the bay and the structure itself. Bring a mask and snorkel, because the water's full of fish too.

If the aesthetic and spiritual draw of the spot isn't enough, know that this destination of the abbey and beach is also home to one of Liguria's best restaurants, **Da Laura.** While there are a number of seaside eateries to choose from, insiders know to make a beeline here for the *lasagnette di pesto,* a dish of delicate homemade pasta sheets laced with the freshly made Ligurian specialty—basil, local olive oil, garlic, and pine nuts. Plates of fresh anchovies, crisp white wine, and *fritto misto* (mixed fried fish) are also required. The restaurant used to be right on the beach but now sits above it.

Afterward, stroll down to the beach and nap in the shade of the abbey before hiking or boating back home. If you are lucky, you have booked a nearby fisherman's cottage like **Casa de Mar,** owned, strangely, by England's Landmark Trust. You will be one of the few residents who gets to enjoy this stretch of coastline almost alone. ∎

Beach waves nearly lap against the Benedictine abbey San Fruttuoso.

World-famous Portofino still seduces visitors, but in its heyday of the 1950s it attracted, among others, Princess Grace and Liz Taylor.

The Forgotten Italian Riviera

Terra-cotta-colored buildings that seem to be lit from within. Craggy mountainsides that meet the sea. Pretty town churches. Sound like the Cinque Terre? You wouldn't be wrong. But as it happens, the Italian Riviera, just north of the Cinque Terre UNESCO site, has almost the same architecture and topography—but without the crowds.

Before Europeans turned their attention fully to France in the early 20th century, this region of the Ligurian coast became known as the Italian Riviera (savvy marketing). Nineteenth-century Brits in particular, in need of sun and (let's face it) good food, came to towns near Genoa to convalesce by walking on the palm-lined promenades (or, in the case of British poet Percy Bysshe Shelley, to die in a storm in the Bay of La Spezia).

One of the preferred hideaways for these holidaygoers was **Alassio,** a town where mosaiced domes punctuate the green-shuttered 19th-century town houses. A gentle, sandy beach is dotted with beach clubs, backed by the famous promenade on which locals take their dusk *passeggiata* with hardly a tourist among them. Up in the hills, **Villa della Pergola,** built in 1875 and the staging post for such visitors as Edward Lear, has been transformed into a hotel, where lush gardens hark back to a quieter time. And nearby **Laigueglia** seems a Monopoly-size version of Alassio. Make sure to gobble up a plate of grilled anchovies at **U Levantin,** staffed by people with disabilities and migrants in need of work.

Classified among Italy's most beautiful towns (and, yes, there is such a designation), **Borgio Verezzi** has fewer than 2,000 residents and epitomizes the kind of simple but beautiful atmosphere and architecture that insiders to Italy's coast crave. Arches and cobblestone streets lead from one pretty piazzetta to the next. At the central square, the summer theater program remains one of the most important in the country. If you're less culturally inclined, opt instead for a meal at **Osteria La Rosa dei Venti,** with a view of the two churches out front, and order the pesto. Nearby, the long beach of **Malpasso** with its soft white sand, limpid crystal sea, and boulders draws visitors almost year-round. And **Finalborgo,** also one of Italy's most beautiful hamlets, called *borghi,* remains a perfect example of medieval architecture while also drawing bikers and avid rock climbers for its varied terrain.

Santa Margherita Ligure makes a great launchpad to Cinque Terre and Portofino but remains much lesser known than its neighbors—more of a resort town for Italians who like its grande dame hotels and 19th-century feel. Neighboring **Camogli** has a gentle residential atmosphere with bakeries, cafés, and quiet streets lined with fruit shops and fishmongers. **Ostaia da o Sigu** is a tiny osteria along the main corso, with a few tables in a little cave looking right out to the sea. Book a room at **Villa Rosmarino,** a pastel-painted boutique hotel with an infinity pool, or **Stella Maris,** a resort that one can access only by boat taxi or a 40-minute hike. It's well priced, and the views are spectacular.

More or less forgotten now, **Noli** was once the base for one of the most powerful maritime republics (rivaling Pisa and Genoa for centuries) before being annexed by Napoleon in the 18th century. It's rare to see medieval towns right on a beach—but there it is, just one of the Italian Riviera's many surprises. ∎

A NAME TO KNOW: RENZO PIANO

One of the world's true superstar architects, Pritzker Prize–winning Renzo Piano has designed some of its most famous and recognizable edifices.

PIANO'S CREDITS include the New York Times Building, Paris's Pompidou museum, London's Shard skyscraper, and Berlin's iconic Potsdamer Platz, to name just a few. What you might not know is that this famed Italian hails from Genoa, Liguria's bustling port city of tangled backstreets and excellent seafood. He also designed its enormous and evocative aquarium, which draws children from all over the country.

Piano's hometown has shaped his interests and architecture in many ways. He recently observed that New York's Whitney Museum was inspired by the shape of one of the boats he fell in love with in Genoa's harbor. (When possible, he takes to the high seas with his own custom-made sailboat, a beautiful vessel designed to look like a giant sail.)

Recently, when the city's main bridge, the Ponte Morandi, tragically collapsed, Piano jumped into action with a promise to design the 202-million-euro structure—amazingly, for free. The new edifice, a showcase of slender steel reinforced by sturdy pier-like supports, will show how an international luminary still keeps home close to heart.

Architect Renzo Piano is one of Genoa's most famous exports.

Hot Spot
Portofino

Sitting on a clogged road waiting to get into Portofino on a summer's day, you would be forgiven for wanting to make a quick U-turn—or when presented with a bill at one of the chichi restaurants on the waterfront, to conclude this is a fake version of Italy. Portofino is the country's equivalent of Saint-Tropez (or Sardinia's Porto Cervo), a town that has become too tied to the swanky yachts that dock here or to the swanky VIPs who crave photo ops and the crowds of sycophants that follow close behind. In the summer, the number of residents here triples.

But consider a visit on a midweek day in October or May when the sun shines bright, a light breeze plays in the lines of the sailboats, and the *clink clink clink* of the families' cutlery at mealtimes is the only thing you hear. Without the crowds, the nautical stripes and pastel backdrop can still transport you back to the time when people fell in love here.

Clack clack clack. The easy sound of Ava Gardner's or Liz Taylor's sandals passing over the cobblestone backstreets. Grace Kelly sipped an *aperitivo* in the port in peace while watching the other yachters pass by. On the terrace of the **Hotel Splendido,** Winston Churchill enjoyed the **Dolce Vita** bar, an icon where a career pianist still plays on the tinkling keys as regulars sip on Negronis.

When it comes to lodging, there are still some gems in Portofino. The **Piccolo Hotel** remains a well-priced deal compared with its neighbors; the only downside is the road that splits the property from the beach. **Da Puny** is the restaurant harbor spot to see and be seen, and dishes like an unusual onion tart and the lasagna in pesto are remarkably good. Take a hike up to the **Chiesa di San Giorgio** with its hidden ancient chapel and views down to the piazzetta, or to **Castello Brown,** a 16th-century Genovese tower with its peaceful, flower-filled gardens. Town residents founded the organization Niasca Portofino to restore local traditions and cultivate growth in the surrounding countryside, and its guided tour is an authentic way to get a new perspective on what Portofino is beyond the clichés. ■

Portofino's Splendido hotel, with views over the coastline, is an Italian icon.

Frances's Favorites

In Your Glass

In other regions, I drink a variety of wines. But in Liguria, I cannot imagine choosing anything not local. After seeing vineyards scrawled across tight terraces like primordial writing above that marvelous sea, you sense that the grapes soak up sun and salty sea mist, holding tight to the precipitous hillsides. Some fields can be reached only by boat; there'll be no machinery, just the caretakers' hands, their baskets, their ancient work: terroir in extremis. Therefore, take a glass of Liguria.

Cinque Terre gives the wine its name. Unless you've been there, you might not have tried this wine (since most of the time, what's made in Cinque Terre stays in Cinque Terre). Often described as light, I'd say the rhyme better suited is "bright." *Bosco* grapes make up the largest percentage, blended with *albarola* and usually *vermentino.* An *agrumi* (citrus) flavor is the hallmark, along with a faint mineral back note, perhaps from salt-bearing fog. I always think I can smell the dry grasses of late summer and a whiff of wild thyme.

Cantina Cinque Terre, a co-op, produces about half of the area's white. Other notable makers: Cinqueterre Campogrande, Cheo Perciò, and Terenzuola.

Vintners in the other growing area, Riviera Ligure di Ponente, call their *vermentino pigato*—same DNA, but *pigato* meaning "spotted skin." Look for Bruna's stellar Riviera Ligure di Ponente Pigato U Baccan and Ottaviano Lambruschi's Colli di Luni Vermentino Costa Marina.

The Ponente's Ka'Manciné's Dolceacqua Beragna (*rossese* grape) proves that Liguria's reds can be up there with the best. Maccario Dringenberg's Rossese di Dolceacqua perfectly complemented the *buridda,* Ligurian fish stew, especially with the cakey bread to dip. ■

ABOVE: Terraced vineyards above the Cinque Terre town of Manarola OPPOSITE: Round ripe grapes provide the base for the coastline's refreshing, well-priced vintages.

Best Of

Outdoor Pursuits

With its many coves, well-tended trails, and secluded beaches, Liguria has no shortage of things to explore—and eating well looms large too. Some favorites:

Best for Nautical Types: Rent a boat through Vernazza's NordEst for an excursion to places like the beach of Guvano, a tiny cove with crystal clear water and smooth pebbles that seem almost artificial in their perfection. The company organizes tours of differing lengths and with different types of boats. Its skippers are friendly and professional.

Best for Beachside Fashionistas: Book a table and beach lounger alongside area insiders at the barefoot chic Eco del Mare, an arched beach book-ended by huge boulders. Owned by the wife of the Italian mega-rocker Zucchero, the beach club has not only excellent food but also a clutch of romantic hotel rooms.

Best for Nimble Walkers: Of all the hikes between the Cinque Terre towns, the stretch between Vernazza and

ABOVE: Taking a break from hiking the Cinque Terre OPPOSITE: The beach club of Eco del Mar is the perfect spot to enjoy the Ligurian sunshine.

Corniglia is the most exquisite, given its sense of isolation, varied terrain, and picture-perfect views of the sea and towns. The hike takes about an hour and a half, and you must purchase a Cinque Terre card to access the trail. Then you can take the train back to where you started.

Best for Pescatarians: Take a dip at Gabbiano Beach on the island of Palmaria while looking back at the atmospheric town Portovenere. For lunch, book a table at Locanda Lorena and dig in to the *fritto misto* (mixed fried fish).

Best for Amateur Sportsmen: Schedule a sailing lesson or instruction in another water sport at Lerici's Scuola di Mare Santa Teresa with expert instruction in English or Italian. There are also summer camps for kids on-site.

Best for Spiritual Seekers: Hike to Monterosso's Santuario di Nostra Signora di Soviore, with its spectacular views on the ridges above Vernazza. The handmade bench in the middle of the hillside, on the narrow path, is reason alone to try this trail.

Best for Fishermen Souls: Make a pilgrimage to Do Spadin, a fishermen's restaurant nestled in the rocks at the edge of the sea under Camogli's Stella Maris hotel. Open only when the boats can get there with their catch of the day, the restaurant cures its own local tuna right on-site.

Best for Romantics: Hike the seaside route in Framura. Similar to the Via Dell'Amore setting in Monterosso (which closed following floods), this promenade along the water is a must.

Best for Families: Head to Santa Margherita Ligure's Bagni Fiore, which takes normal beach clubs up a notch. There is a kids' entertainer both on the beach and in the playground, a dog sitter, an aqua gym with daily classes, a spa, and a shop for picking up last-minute bikinis or cover-ups (or why not get both?). ∎

Chapter Six

EMILIA-ROMAGNA

Food central! Best in Italy? Many concur. The region cuts across central Italy, north of Tuscany and Le Marche, and south of Veneto and Lombardy. The standard of living soars in sophisticated Emilia. More often than not, extremely well-dressed, coiffed, bejeweled couples and families step out of their luxury cars and head into top restaurants. Travelers might want to stow the sneakers and T-shirts when dining well in this

food-driven destination. Chefs and home cooks revel in the abundance of Emilia-Romagna.

And why shouldn't the chefs rejoice? This place is the source of so many beloved—and delectable—foods. It contains the mother lode of sausages, as well as chestnuts, *funghi porcini* mushrooms, prosciutto, game, and the region's most famous contributions to the world's kitchens: Parmigiano Reggiano and *aceto balsamico*, that heavenly elixir. Balsamic vinegars are much maligned in supermarket versions spiked with cheap caramel flavors bearing no resemblance to authentic balsamic. Made from trebbiano grapes, the real vinegar ages at least 12 years in barrels of different woods, which lend subtle tastes. Some aficionados dine out with their private small flasks so they're assured of the real thing. Much loved *culatello,* the pig's lean back leg, is hung to age in humid, dim quarters for up to three years; a few transparent salty-savory slices grace most antipasto plates, along with crisp balls of fried bread. The prized *culatello* comes from a tiny area between Parma and the Po River, where the misty moist climate provides ideal aging conditions. Flat-dough *piadina* filled with prosciutto and cheese and flaky vegetable tortas pass for fast food: delicious with a tumbler of red wine for a quick lunch.

Traveling in Emilia-Romagna will inspire anyone who's ever lifted a wooden spoon. If you lived here, the sheer variety of pasta and sauces would entertain you every day of your life. The region's bottom-line soul food: *ragù alla Bolognese,* enjoyed throughout the world. (I make a triple recipe, simmered three hours, so I can always reach for a jar from my freezer.)

Beyond its celebrated ragù, I'm a fool for Bologna. I feel something like a magnetic force in the *centro.* Emblematic of the city's smarts, Biblioteca comunale dell'Archiginnasio, the marvelous civic library from 1563, was once part of the University of Bologna, founded in 1088. The atmosphere created by books, manuscripts, and a serene courtyard make me long for a scholarly project that would bring me here daily, as it has drawn students for centuries (witness the thousands of coats of arms they've left on the walls). One elaborately paneled room, the anatomy theater, still has the marble table for dissections, watched over by two statues of *spellati,*

WHAT YOU NEED TO KNOW...

- **BEST TIME TO VISIT:** In Emilia-Romagna, it's all about eating. Actually, there are a lot of other things going on, but avoid deep summer and winter here; the valley conditions create incredible fog and humidity.

- **TOP SPOTS:** Bologna, Modena, Parma, Ravenna

- **GETTING THERE:** Fly into Federico Fellini International Airport.

The library at Bologna's Archiginnasio Palace is only one of the city's many underrated treasures.

Traveling in Emilia-Romagna will inspire anyone who's ever lifted a wooden spoon; the sheer variety of pasta and sauces alone will entertain you.

skinned men. Looking down, an angel holds a thighbone.

Today, the city hosts 80,000 students—and what a great place to study. The young look hip in tight pants and with stylish haircuts; the professorial men wear jeans hiked up around their waists, wire-rimmed glasses, and cool white shirts; the women keep their hair long, twirl their jackets with gorgeous scarves, and favor boots. Stylish backpacks are de rigueur. Bookstores well stocked with Greek and Latin classics crop up on the porticoed streets—24 miles (38 km) of them—along with cafés that seem always to have been here.

Bologna offers many pleasures beyond academia. Here are extensive palazzi, including Palazzo Re Enzo, built in 1244, 20 medieval towers—two of which tilt—and 50 museums: from the exquisite Pinacoteca Nazionale art gallery to Museo

Emilia-Romagna's meaty Bolognese sauce is a world-famous creation.

Morandi, where you find the austere still lifes of 20th-century artist Giorgio Morandi. (And don't forget to visit the Carpigiani Museo di Gelato!)

In the Quadrilatero district, a medieval warren lined with artisan food offerings, shops include Parisian-standard flower stalls bursting with bouquets of sweet william, bunches of violets, and tin buckets of virtuous yellow tulips. They light the way toward butchers who don't shy away from the *quinto quarto* (the fifth part, aka offal), greengrocers who excel in the art of display, bakers such as the well-regarded Atti e Figli, and *pasta fresca* shops. And the bread! The senses are suffused, sending you off in search of the best trattoria you can find.

Just a half-hour trip outside the city, FICO (Fabbrica Italiana COntadina) Eataly World stuns any foodie with a phenomenal theme park showcasing Italy's cornucopia of pastas, olive oils, wines, as well as a plethora of places to eat—45 at last count. It also offers classes, exhibits, and more. The space is so large that Bianchi bicycles with carts are available. Whew!

All this in a tiny nutshell! Let this be a micro-hint of the vast pleasures of Bologna. I like to stay at I Portici Hotel (especially in the top-floor mansard room, super modern and sleek). The intimate restaurant, in a restored Liberty (art nouveau is known as Liberty in Italy) theater, serves playful innovations on the classics, with a few surprises. The gourmet cotton candy certainly surprised me.

Relatively few travelers make it to the ancient city of Ravenna on the Adriatic side. Here's early Christian Italy before it became Catholic Italy. A watery outpost of the Roman Empire, Ravenna ceded to the Ostrogoths in the fifth century; in the mid-sixth century, it became the westernmost Byzantine stronghold.

The ancient religious sites are plain on the outside, but their interior domes and walls are covered with stately mosaics. Most moving to me is the mausoleum of Galla Placidia, a Roman wife, mother of emperors, and an empress herself. Under her cupola of glittering dark blue studded with gold stars, I feel cold shivers. In the octagonal

When temperatures in Bologna and other cities soar in summer, head into the fresh air of the gentle hills nearby.

baptismal building, Battistero degli Ariani, is a mosaic of Christ—naked and young, up to his waist in water. The skillful mosaicist renders the water transparent, with the body still visible. (Not sure I've ever glimpsed Christ's penis before.) A white dove, the Holy Ghost, sprinkles water onto his head.

There are eight major Christian cultural heritage sites in the city of Ravenna. In the Chapel of Sant'Andrea, so finely are the mosaics crafted that 99 species of birds have been identified. In the monumental church of San Vitale, the artist depicts the Byzantine rulers Justinian and Theodora among white flowers—ravishing! The mosaics seem otherworldly, calling to us from the formative years of Christianity.

Ravenna, a flat city, once had canals, but now the streets are full of bicycles. Little dinging bells keep you aware of stalwart ladies, balancing their shopping bags, and kids riding with no hands. As you wend your way through these vibrant lanes, be sure to find the tomb of Dante Alighieri,

author of the immortal *Divine Comedy*. He died in exile here.

In addition to Bologna and Ravenna, Emilia-Romagna offers many other pleasures, including Parma and Ferrara, two of the most handsome and noble towns in Italy. Rich, rich Modena reigns as a world-class dining destination. Always irresistible to me, the road not taken—the turn that leads to San Leo, Brisighella, Dozza, Castell'Arquato, and other noble villages waiting all these centuries for your surprise.

Long ago, sitting in one of the arcade cafés on Bologna's Piazza Maggiore, I was trying this odd drink, cappuccino, on my first morning in Italy. And I was taking in the scene: everyone calling *buon giorno* and the ancient greeting *salve,* visiting each other among the tables, clouds of smoke from industrial-strength cigarettes, boisterous laughter everywhere. I said to my husband, "These people are having more fun than we are." I wanted what they had! That moment in the heart of Bologna was the beginning of my lifelong passion for Italy.

Whether seen from far away or close by, the Basilica of Madonna di San Luca in Bologna is a symbol of the city.

Bologna: Italy's Underrated Gem

Many whiz by this city as they speed toward Florence or up north to Milan, barely stopping to notice the beautiful dome of the Madonna di San Luca looming above Bologna's exit on the A1. It is a shame. Despite the rather flat landscape, this city, and in fact, the whole region of Emilia-Romagna, should be at the top of your itinerary for its culinary and artistic treasures.

Bologna remains one of the country's best kept secrets. With the oldest university in Europe, it hums with students. As the centerpiece of the region's food scene, the cuisine is simple but sublime (Bolognese sauce, anyone?). And the mixture of Renaissance and medieval makes it a hub of unmissable art and architecture. Today, spurred on by its robust economy (especially in comparison with other parts of Italy), new restaurants, bars, and shops are blooming in its formerly gritty periphery.

Start your tour of town with a trot up the **Torre degli Asinelli,** a 498-step medieval StairMaster. From your vista you might spy the miles of *portici,* or covered arcades, that are still intact, creating a barrier from the blistering sun in the summer and providing protection from snow and rain come winter.

The centerpiece of the city is the **Mercato di Mezzo**—literally, the market in the middle—its shops heaving with produce, wine, and *salumi,* various types of cured meats. You will have to hustle your way to the counter at **Tamburini,** the old-school deli with haunches of prosciutto hanging behind the boisterous owners and more than 200 wines by the glass on tap. Or try a panino with mortadella at **Salumeria Simoni,** a small *salumeria* that's been a local staple since 1960. Insiders take their favorite market finds to **Osteria del Sole,** where you can get a tipple of inexpensive but flavorful local vintages and watch regulars congregate to discuss sports, politics, and the weather. This joint has been around since 1465.

Caffè Terzi has a more refined atmosphere and takes its espresso *molto, molto* seriously. Stand at the bar with locals to watch owner Manuel Terzi turn beans from all over the world into some of Italy's finest coffee. Once you are appropriately caffeinated, head out for a cooking class at the **Salotto di Penelope.** It's a little tricky to find, but

so worth the effort. Best friends Barbara Zaccagni and Valeria Hensemberger weave in crucial tips—for example, that your pasta dough should be thin enough to see the Madonna di San Luca through, and that the best *brodo,* or broth, for *tortellini en brodo* should have meat in the stock as well as chicken (and, moreover, you don't need to boil it for hours on end). Finally, their recipe for ragù ("Bolognese sauce" in the rest of the world) will make you a star chef back home.

For a less traditional take on Italian food, head to **Oltre,** headed by the

young chef Daniele Bendanti, who is turning classics on their head. (He's originally from Bologna but got much of his training at the two-Michelin-star Arnolfo restaurant in Tuscany.) Located on the periphery of the city center, the restaurant uses ingredients that illuminate the region but in an unexpected way. *Sformatino di pancotto al ragù,* for example, is pasta topping reimagined as a flan. Bendanti and his partner Lorenzo Costa also just opened **Sentaku Ramen Bar.** The line snakes almost around the block most of the day—and for good reason! ▪

Bologna is one of the country's best kept secrets. As the centerpiece of the region's food scene, its cuisine is simple but sublime (Bolognese sauce, anyone?).

CLOCKWISE FROM LEFT: University students take time out to chat; residents and visitors flock to Tamburini for prosciutto and bottles of local wine; bunches of just picked asparagus are only one of the seasonal finds at Bologna's famous market, Mercato di Mezzo.

Car buffs should make tracks to the Enzo Ferrari Museum, where vintage models and new creations are on view.

Trio of Greats: Modena, Parma, and Ravenna

Much like Emilia-Romagna itself, many of its most exquisite towns stay below most travelers' radar. But once visited, they register forcefully in your memory—and in your stomach. **Modena,** of course, has its temple of food, Massimo Bottura's **Osteria Francescana,** but it deserves attention for much more. Gentle streets filled with bikers on their way to work lead past the beautiful 12th-century Romanesque duomo and the tall, Gothic-style **Ghirlandina tower,** a UNESCO-protected symbol of the city with its bells calling

out to the town the hours or warning of advancing enemy troops. The town has new cafés and bars like **Mon Café,** with mixology-perfect *aperitivi* served in a bustling space full of well-heeled locals (try the Negroni). At **Menomoka,** another trendy café, the baristas prepare their espresso with surgical precision, although draft beer and vino are also available. Wine lovers should make a stop at **Archer** for a glass of Lambrusco. For a panino that's taken up a notch, head to **Bar Schiavoni di Fantoni Sara & Chiara.** And gelato fans: Run, don't walk, to **Bloom.**

Owner Gianluca Degani is an ice cream wizard offering inventive seasonal flavors like 2788 (*fior di latte* with tonka beans, lime zest, and juniper-infused peach jam). And even those who aren't on the verge of a midlife crisis will want to make a pilgrimage to the **Enzo Ferrari Museum** (the car genius was born here) to gape at the impressive collection of super-sleek models. Cheese buffs will also want to head to **Hombre,** a short drive away, with its rounds of amazing Parmigiano. The hottest hotel in the area is Massimo Bottura's new inn, **Maria**

Luigia, named for his mother, a lovingly restored 18th-century villa that's a 12-room hideaway to showcase his contemporary art collection.

Parma's more reserved than its Modena sister, but it's a beauty. Bed down at **Hotel Palazzo Della Rosa Prati,** a noble's palace smack-dab in the middle of town that's been reinvented as an atmospheric hotel, with a chic café on the ground floor. From there, it's a stone's throw to the city's cathedral and baptistery with its medieval and Romanesque mix. When you're feeling hungry, go on a hunt for picnic fare:

Pasticceria Torino for tasty traditional pastries, **Pepèn Parma** for epic sandwiches with local Parma ingredients (beware the *cavallo* option if you're a horse lover), and **Enoteca Tabarro** for a bottle of vino. Traditionalists will want to book a table at **Leon D'Oro,** or **Cocchi;** those looking for a more updated Parma cuisine should make sure to try **Borgo 20.**

Mosaics. Mosaics. Mosaics. The elegant city of **Ravenna** delivers mosaic porn. The **Basilica di San Vitale** is literally covered in them from floor to ceiling, featuring priceless varieties

from the fifth and sixth centuries. Ravenna's **Mausoleo di Galla Placidia,** celebrated for the 900 glittering stars on its night sky mosaic, may have inspired Cole Porter to write "Night and Day." That might be just an Emilia-Romagna myth, but it makes sense. And don't miss the **Basilica of Sant'Apollinare Nuovo's** 26 mosaic scenes from the New Testament. If you can, make time for a side trip to Forli with its **Musei San Domenico,** a former monastery that hosts excellent exhibitions including a recent winner with work by Piero della Francesca. ∎

A NAME TO KNOW: MASSIMO BOTTURA

The *Chef's Table* episode with ebullient Massimo Bottura made viewers want to jump on a plane to Italy.

FOR ONE THING, the culinary star's **Osteria Francescana** has been rated top restaurant in the world by the World's 50 Best Restaurants List for two years in a row.

Bottura didn't rise to fame easily. After stints at restaurants like Alain Ducasse, his playful, rule-breaking approach made diners a little unsure of what to expect when he opened his own restaurant in Modena. Classics like *tortellini in brodo* were perfectly good just the way their mothers made them, thank you.

Until he won them over.

Today, Bottura has become an impresario whose innovative dishes have become a holy grail for international foodies and critics, turning ingredients from his region into magical reinterpretations. Plates become modern, provocative, and delicious—including Beautiful Psychedelic Veal, which looks like a contemporary art piece. Plus, he's clearly having fun doing it!

Bottura isn't just a master chef; he's a humanitarian. He has opened soup kitchens all over the world, and just launched Il Tortellante, a program that instructs teenagers with autism and other learning disabilities in Bologna how to make tortellini.

Beloved chef Massimo Bottura hails from Emilia-Romagna's Modena.

Frances's Favorites

In Your Glass

At lunch in Parma, we ordered Monte delle Vigne Colli di Parma Rosso (30 percent *bonarda,* 70 percent *barbera*). It struck such a high note with the tender saffron- and pumpkin-filled ravioli that we returned to the same restaurant that night and ordered the identical wine with roast pork. Thus, as the waiter remarked, we tasted three essences of Emilia-Romagna. A couple of other reds not to be neglected: San Patrignano (especially Romagna Sangiovese Superiore Avi) and Le Rocche Malestiane, from a vast vineyard that produces a range of varietals located in the Romagna (eastern) zone. Order Romagna Sangiovese Superiore Sigismondo.

Near Piacenza, the La Stoppa estate owner Elena Pantaleoni produces eight notable wines. Their star, organic Macchiona, blends *bonarda* and *barbera* grapes and the result is an ample-bodied red, hitting the right balance between rustic and elegant.

Gianfranco Paltrinieri's Lambrusco di Sorbara Leclisse won us over to this omnipresent regional wine. A grape cultivated as far back as the Etruscans, *lambrusco* is indigenous to Emilia-Romagna. If you've had a bad experience with a spritzy cheap export version the color of grape Popsicles, never fear: This wine can be transporting. In Parma we tried a couple of bottles of I Calanchi Monte delle Vigne, spicy and slightly dry. With the earthy cuisine of the region, just one top-quality bottle will banish the memory of the imported plonk you once knew. ■

ABOVE: Friends toast with a glass of Lambrusco, a wine that's increasingly popular. OPPOSITE: Vineyards in fertile Castelvetro outside Modena

Local Flavors: Prosciutto, Parmigiano Reggiano, and Balsamic Vinegar

Consider these numbers: 10 million slabs of prosciutto. 500 million pigs. Exports all over the world. But only 120 producers who are certified to make the world-famous prosciutto of Parma. If you have time to visit only one, make it **Fratelli Galloni,** a beloved, family-owned company that's the Maserati of pork. Housed in a state-of-the-art facility with perfectly temperature-controlled rooms for different stages of aging, it also includes—wait for it—a room where the haunches sit in ambient light, listening to classical music (relaxed muscles produce more tender meat). Only in Italy!

Mirella Galloni, the first female *capo,* boss, of the family, continues to update the business while following in her grandfather's footsteps. The prosciutto gets hand-salted (a machine can treat 1,000 haunches an hour; only 80 can be done by hand). The floors replicate those of her grandfather's cantina, and the river breezes waft through doors facing the water. Following a horrible fire on the property, Galloni added a hydroponic garden on the roof, as well as installations by contemporary artists using the steel from the former structure and a cutting-edge tasting room in glass and steel that could dou-ble as a loft in *Wallpaper* magazine. After your tour, have lunch at **Lamoretti,** a farm and vineyard in front of the fairy tale–like Torrechiara castle.

Another beloved worldwide export in addition to prosciutto di Parma is Parmigiano Reggiano. Its production also follows a strict set of ancient rules, including using milk from cows that graze in specific areas. The milk churns in huge steel vats before being aged in giant rounds for as long as four years. And in between those stages, its cloth gets changed every two hours, much like the diaper of a newborn baby. The average wheel weighs 88 pounds (40 kg) and costs more than $1,000; that's over 3.6 million wheels a year. Watch how they make it at **Nuova Martignana,** but be on time for your tour—Parmigiano makers keep strict schedules.

Balsamic vinegar is another famous export of the Emilia-Romagna region. Even if your bottle at home says Aceto Balsamo di Modena, you probably haven't had the black elixir produced at places like **Acetaia di Giorgio,** a family producer that makes the vinegar at home. Barrels lie gently in the attic as they age in oak, chestnut, and cherry wood. Giorgio Barbieri's calling came after a career in professional volleyball; when he retired, he re-created the recipe of his dear *nonna* (grandmother). Today, the family sells about 2,000 bottles a year at about $1,137 a liter: black gold that's worth the price. ■

ABOVE: Making Modena's famed balsamic vinegar, elixir for salads, is a painstaking process. **OPPOSITE:** Rounds of Parmigiano Reggiano are cared for daily by expert producers.

Hot Spot
Fellini's Hometown

Picture this: It's close to dawn. Pink and gold meet on a long stretch of horizon mirrored on a flat Adriatic Sea. In the water, grannies and mamas move in synchronized movements. Up to their midriffs against the shoreline, they walk in age-appropriate (or not) *costumi* (swimsuits). They gab; they gossip; they share secrets. It's a morning constitutional. Like flocks of seagulls, thousands of them move on the summer current, bobbing up and down.

At night, the lights of the Grand Hotel dance from the promenade; inside, waiters in starched uniforms create a sense of elegant formality. Down the beach, though, a DJ pumps techno hits to the delight of a pulsating crowd in barely-there garb.

Even for Italian insiders, Rimini is hard to grasp. Geographically it's difficult to make the connection with other parts of Emilia-Romagna. Conceptually, it's incongruous: a nightclub on the beach that is also home to grande dame hotels on the boardwalk that breathe in the ether of a more seductive time. What is it? England's Brighton? America's Atlantic City? Mexico's Acapulco?

Perhaps one can understand Rimini best as the birthplace of Federico Fellini, one of Italy's most famous directors, who was born here in 1920. Much like the trajectory of the country itself, Fellini, and Rimini too, saw the transition from a wartime, Fascist nation through a period of great artistic creativity.

Fellini watched his first films at Rimini's recently renovated Cinema Fulgor. On the flickering screen, he likely saw his first glimpse of bathing beauties in their one-piece suits emerging from the sea, swinging their hips and breasts, the precursors perhaps of Anita Ekberg in *La Dolce Vita*'s famous Trevi Fountain scene. Years later, he set up shop in the Grand Hotel (a place where diners still changed for dinner) and listened to the piano in the glamorous art deco bar, where style and the Adriatic went hand in hand. Fellini's hometown was immortalized in *Amarcord* (Romagnolo for *mi ricordo,* "I remember"), a film that mocked fascism and the church. It also won an Oscar for best foreign film in 1975. ■

A party summer town, Rimini is the birthplace of director Federico Fellini.

Chapter Seven

FRIULI VENEZIA GIULIA

In delectable Friuli Venezia Giulia, some of Italy's best wine is poured into the glasses of all the best restaurants you've never heard of. Called Friuli for short, the region's full name comes from its Venetian roots and from further back. "Friuli" derives from *foro,* forum, and *Iulii,* meaning "Julius Caesar," probably among the original founders. The small region borders the Veneto and neighboring

Slovenia, and lies just under Austria—hence, strong influences.

This wine lover's *paradiso* is still off the trodden routes of otherwise savvy travelers. Fortunately, the local cuisine is on a par with the quality of the wine. I'll walk right out on a shaky limb and say that the gastronomic experience is unsurpassed in Italy, even in justly lauded Piedmont, Sicily, and Emilia-Romagna. Of the many reasons to travel to Friuli—Trieste, clear karst lakes, the impressive Alps, Udine, the Adriatic beaches—the overwhelming motivation has to be the superb food and wine. One dinner at Agli Amici, near Udine, and one bottle of wine from Nicola Manferrari's Borgo del Tiglio prove me correct. Bookmark these for an on-point introduction.

Friuli is an easy extension from a trip to Venice. Head for the pristine landscapes of the Collio, Colli Orientali, or Isonzo wine regions, all close to Udine, that romantic remnant of the Venetian republic's glory. Check into a country inn—or a castle. Soon you can hop on a yellow Vespa and set out on empty roads to explore languid hills covered in grapevines. In early fall, the harvest over, vines blaze russet, gold, and yellow, and the cerulean sky makes you feel blessed by some pagan god. If there's a winemaker you want to visit, confirm ahead, as most do not have open tasting rooms. No mugs, no T-shirts. Make an appointment and meet the owner, just in from tending the vines, who is eager to share his treasures on a barrel top.

I prefer visiting Friuli in the fall for another reason: hunting season. With extensive forests and rugged upland terrain, game preparations lead the menus. Expect to see venison, hare, pheasant, woodcock, quail, and boar during this time and, routinely, snails, goose, frog, guinea hen, and lake fish.

What to order? Make sure to savor big bean and cabbage soups (*jota*) and delicate apple strudel. The signature dish, *frico,* crisply sautéed potatoes, Montasio cheese, and onions, appears on every menu. Even Michelin award–winning chefs avoid fussy, overarticulated preciousness that often comes with the stars. But their interpretations founded on local ingredients are not plain home cooking—no way. Inventive chefs make artistic use of the region's abundant gifts, including wild fennel, mints, greens, young hops, elderflowers, acacia flowers, and all kinds of mushrooms. Wedded to the

WHAT YOU NEED TO KNOW...

- **BEST TIME TO VISIT:** Filled with harvests, fall colors, hearty dishes, and wine tastings, September to November are among the best months to visit Friuli. The sunny, crisp days of spring are a lovely way to experience the Adriatic without the crush of summer beachgoers. Consider the area as a side trip to Venice, a quick train ride away.

- **TOP SPOTS:** Trieste, Udine, San Daniele, Collio, Colli Orientali, Aquileia, Cormòns, Cividale del Friuli

- **GETTING THERE:** The train station and airport in Trieste.

You could spend hours looking at Aquileia's Basilica of Santa Maria Assunta. It has some of the most treasured mosaics in the country.

In delectable Friuli Venezia Giulia, some of Italy's best wine is poured into the glasses of all the best restaurants you've never heard of.

diverse traditions of the area, cooks don't strain to create tortured or off-the-wall combinations of ingredients. All feels right. The word I'm reaching for: *impeccable.*

White wine, I learned in Friuli, can be just as complex as red. The lofty Venica & Venica Ronco delle Mele Sauvignon Blanc was the first step of my conversion. We were staying in Capriva at the 13th-century Castello di Spessa with our good friend, the writer Robert Draper, when I first met winemaker Giampaolo Venica. He took us to the great La Subida Trattoria al Cacciatore in nearby Cormòns. (Worth a detour!) Over many courses and wines, we hit it off, as is easy to do with *simpatico* winemakers. Friends *per sempre,* forever. We were quickly immersed—and enamored. This lucky

Udine is full of art and unmissable pastries straight from the oven.

trip began our yearly pilgrimage to taste, eat, and visit.

When we're in Friuli, we're usually based in or around Cormòns, heart of the Colli wine district. The nearby Castello di Spessa's excellent La Tavernetta al Castello has a clubby, cozy atmosphere, perfect for a first night after travel. We love staying at La Subida, which strikes me as ideal. Nothing surpasses the trattoria, mentioned above, for sampling the best of Friulano cuisine. If you can arrange to be there on New Year's Eve, you will never forget the lavish and stately dinner. The Sirk family keeps intensely close to the land. Paterfamilias Josko makes his own vinegars, and you can visit his *acetaia,* vinegar cellar.

Cormòns's enoteca, right in the *centro,* is the best wine-tasting place in Friuli. The robust and *vivace* winemakers wander in late in the day, and tastes begin to flow. You can sample local cheeses with the pinky, tissue-thin prosciutto of D'Osvaldo, the best in Italy. Only a stroll away, the friendly Trattoria al Giardinetto pleases me for the strictly local atmosphere. Just out of Cormòns, at Trattoria al Piave, you'll have a genuine welcome from the owner Patrizia, and a glorious dinner. Another place I like to stay in Cormòns: La Casa di Alice, with just four bright rooms under the care of Anna Brandolin, who keeps a lovely garden around her pool. Plus, she bakes tasty almond or lemon tarts for breakfast.

The art of the table—great food, great wine—yes. But what makes this area unique is the sense of conviviality around the everyday act of eating. Such expert service evolves from respect for the enterprise. The polished and scrumptious food comes straight out of a deep connection with the land and history of this phenomenal region.

The rest of Friuli equally attracts me. Udine: Call the moving company. This small city would be a choice place to live. Expansive Piazza della Libertà easily lands on my list of the top 10 felicitous piazzas in Italy. Sit awhile and contemplate the Venetian Gothic Loggia del Lionello, the fountain and statues, and the clock tower of Loggia San Giovanni, striped in coral and white: much to regard as you sit at Caffè Con-

After exploring Friuli Venezia Giulia's cities, take time for its natural beauty at places like this nature reserve at the mouth of the Isonzo River.

tarena and sip a tawny *ribolla gialla* or a *collio malvasia,* fragrant as crushed violets.

Venice ruled for four centuries, and Udine is one of its most winning outposts. Canals no longer exist, but various streams rush or meander along arcaded or narrow streets lined with I-could-live-here houses. The compact town offers several museums, including a modern one in Casa Cavazzini, with works by Willem de Kooning, Carlo Carrà, Frank Stella, Giorgio Morandi, Gino Severini, and Donald Judd. Isn't it sometimes a relief to see art of our own era? Another necessary pause: Caffè Caucigh, the oldest and most atmospheric in town. After my heart, the church of Madonna delle Grazie, with its cloister of votive offerings, naive paintings, usually on tin, offered in thanks for a prayer granted and depicting the lucky survivor of an averted catastrophe.

I fell for the eminently civilized town of Cividale del Friuli. You reach the center over the Devil's Bridge, originally built in the mid-15th century—but once you're there, it's closer to heaven than anything satanic. Lunch at outdoor tables at Da Feo, a leisurely look at the Museo Archeologico, a long stroll, and a stop at Tempietto Longobardo, the tiny temple where six elongated women smile at you from the eighth century.

Most astonishing: Aquileia. Please go. This Roman port, settled in 181 B.C., once reigned as a powerful trading center, one of the ancient world's largest cities, but is now a sleepy backwater. Visit to see a marvel: the fourth-century Christian mosaics on the basilica's floor. Discovered only in the early 20th century, they were uncovered from layers of straw, mud, and other flooring by Austrian archaeologists. With extraordinary skill and beauty, the mosaics reveal both the secular and the religious life of the place. Their stories are biblical—but there's also the fisherman pulling in his catch, local plants and animals, constellations, a man lounging under a pergola. Essential too is the local museum. Realistic busts and lapidary remains startle you with their vivid lived life back in the Roman era of the town.

So many enriching and beautiful places to visit as you wait for the next meal!

Built for the Austrian archduke, the white stone Miramare Castle that one can see from Trieste is an icon from the 19th century.

Trieste: Inspiration and Intrigue

Yes, there are a lot of stunning squares in Italy. But most will agree that one of the top 10 piazzas can be found in Trieste. At night, it's lit like a stage set: a wide piazza flanked by impressive neoclassical palaces. A sweeping vista runs all the way to the white-stoned Habsburg-era **Castle Miramare.**

It's a city with a complex past, hence the layers of architectural styles and influences. After a series of seemingly never ending battles with Venice, the city decided to put itself into the hands of the Austrians and became a part of the Habsburg Empire. Once it was returned to Italy, Trieste became one of Mussolini's fascist hubs. Horribly, like many other Italian cities (and despite Trieste's previous tolerance of most religions), the government not only shipped many of its Jews to Auschwitz but housed the only concentration camp in the country: the Risiera di San Sabba. Following World War II and a dalliance with Tito, Trieste was independent, rejoining Italy only in 1954. It's a painful history.

With its up close views of Slovenia and deeply rooted friendship with Vienna, Trieste in many ways is still a world apart from the rest of Italy. Behind its spectacular main square, a tangle of streets lead out of the city and up a steep hill, with views onto the town and along the coast. Make tracks to classics like **Pasticceria La Bomboniera,** a patisserie founded in 1836 that's also a design delight, with black-and-white checkered tiles, otherworldly *rigó jansci* chocolate cake, and crumbly Linzer biscuits.

The city nails neoclassical café culture—not a surprise, considering its Viennese roots. And Trieste is arguably also home to Italy's best coffee. Illy is one of the city's main producers, but there are many independent *torrefazioni,* or microroasters, too. Statistics indicate the average Italian consumes almost 13 pounds (5.8 kg) of coffee a year; in Trieste, this figure is estimated to be 22 pounds (10 kg). As one insider says, "No one dares to serve a bad espresso here, or they would close down in less than a week."

For its mixture of great caffeine and atmosphere, put **Caffè San Marco** on your itinerary. This iconic place inspired James Joyce to write his celebrated novels *A Portrait of the Artist as a Young Man* and *Dubliners* before embarking on *Ulysses.* The daytime coffee scene segues into a vibrant *aperitivo* hour,

and, in a nod to its literary roots, an in-house bookshop is in the works.

Many elegant cafés and bars line the city's picturesque canal as well as streets like Via Torino, where **Le Botti** fills with local workers at the end of the day. With dozens of excellent vintages to choose from, it's one of those rare wine bars that manages to please many generations and budgets. Nearby **Hops Beerstrò** is a must for beer lovers. Try **Miramare** for butter-thin fish carpaccio. And make sure to duck into fashionable **al Ciketo** near the Ghetto, the city's former Jewish quarter, for Friuli's answer to Venice's small plates. This chic wine bar is known for its delicious platters of salami and cheese.

When it comes to lodging in Trieste,

the grande dame **Savoia Excelsior Palace** remains the top hotel choice in the city center, for its close position to the main square, its refurbished rooms, and its panoramic views onto the Adriatic (though you might find a cruise ship blocking it from time to time). The new **Portopiccolo,** about 20 minutes from town, has become the new word for "five-star" in the region. In addition to its medical and beauty spas, two restaurants, and nautical hotel rooms, it boasts its own port: the perfect mooring for the yachts that come for the Barcolana, one of the country's most famous and historic regattas, which draws thousands of boats each year on the second Sunday in October. ∎

CLOCKWISE FROM LEFT: Trieste's expansive main piazza is lined with lively long-standing cafés; Caffè San Marco is one of the best spots for espresso and people-watching; Trieste has an atmospheric canal lined with bars.

In the Know
F-V-G: OMG the Wine

Want to impress Italian oenophiles? Get versed in this region's delightful vintages. Yes, you can inform attendees at your next dinner party, not only does Friuli Venezia Giulia lay claim to some of Italy's best white wines, but in recent years, some red masterpieces are coming into the spotlight there as well. Although there are many DOCs, keep these three on your radar: Collio, Colli Orientali del Friuli, and the less well known Carso.

Collio and Colli Orientali del Friuli separate themselves from the rest of the pack (they've been making wine here since Roman times, after all). The region, cooled by salty winds from the Adriatic Sea and protected from the harsh mountain weather of the Alps by gentle rolling hills, features varietals from both the north of Italy and Slovenia. It's a diverse and exciting time for wine here—in no small part because of passionate multigenerational-run wineries like **Marco Felluga** (Roberto took over from his father, Marco). Here, you won't find slick generic tasting rooms; instead, you'll sit around a roaring, circular fireplace and pop open a bottle while talking about terroir and the environment (and the effect of climate change on the industry) with Roberto if he's home. The main house sits in a line of vines that turn red and gold come autumn. With seven bedrooms featuring views onto the vines and over to the hills of Slovenia, it's a good place to rest after a day of tastings.

Collio may hold only 5 percent of the region's vineyards, but it's also where many of its superstars are born. Here, international varieties like sauvignon blanc and chardonnay exist alongside local varietals like *riesling italico.* You'll also find the *ribolla gialla,* a dark yellow vintage that's often sparkling and arguably has more character than prosecco. **Livio Felluga** and **Gravner** are among the deservedly famous labels you might have heard of. But make sure to also sample others like **Vignai da Duline** by cult winemaker Lorenzo Mocchiutti; his biodynamic wines are made using no herbicides and no pruning, and also happen to be both excellent and well priced.

Carso, the boho hippie cousin of Friuli wine regions, is the epicenter of the orange wine craze (actually, more of an amber hue) and the darling of the current wine world. The color comes from the skins that are left on during the fermentation process (if you want to be accurate, refer to it as a "skin contact wine" rather than "orange wine"). ∎

OPPOSITE: Nurture and nature determine the taste of the bottled products at vineyards like Vigna Petrussa. **ABOVE:** At harvesttime winemakers make predictions for their next vintages.

Frances's Favorites

Jan Morris's Trieste

Trieste lies so far east that some forget it's even in Italy. The short book *Trieste and the Meaning of Nowhere,* Jan Morris's paean to the city, chronicles a long involvement with this neglected outpost. Her personal emotional attachment and acute sense of place weave the strands of tumultuous history, ephemera, and evocative landscape.

In Morris's rendering, the Habsburg Austro-Hungarian past feels especially alive. The Jewish history is as richly compelling as it is tragic, while the high culture and intellectual backbone reveal Trieste as a complex East-West crossroads. James Joyce wrote and taught here, and the city seeped into his books. Local novelist Italo Svevo (*The Confessions of Zeno*) strongly influenced the creation of Leopold Bloom, Joyce's *Ulysses* character.

Morris doesn't shy away from the ugliness of the Fascist era or the waning of Trieste's importance as a port gateway. Read her book to understand the intricate history, but also for the sharp prose style: clipped but exacting, and well balanced between the personal and the objective.

But *Trieste* was published in 2001, and its melancholy mood and backward-glancing descriptions have faded in favor of today's more vibrant and forward city. The *bora* (fierce wind) still blows, but the vibe in Trieste is more electric than it was during Morris's times there. Maybe it's the coffee. Illy headquarters is here, and Riccardo Illy, as mayor, inaugurated fresh energy, as well as whooshes of caffeine, into the atmosphere. ▪

> **Morris's personal emotional attachment and acute sense of place weave the strands of tumultuous history, ephemera, and evocative landscape.**

ABOVE: A vintage shot of the Miramare coast on the Adriatic **OPPOSITE:** Author Jan Morris is from Wales, but she put Trieste on the map for many of her readers.

Hot Spot
Udine

On arriving in Udine, you might feel as if you've landed in a smaller-scale Venice (minus the canals, of course). The **Loggia del Lionello** mirrors the Doge's Palace; the Lion of Saint Mark, symbol of Venice, is carved into Venetian master Andrea Palladio's Arco Bollani. The duomo, with its Tiepolo-frescoed chapel, is reason enough to come here.

But what insiders know too is that this town is chockablock with very, very good food. Exemplary, in fact. At the dollhouse-size **Laboratorio del Dolce,** hidden on a quiet side street, freshly made meringues are stuffed with Chantilly or whipped cream (the Italian answer to Proust's madeleine). **La Baita** is a similarly religious experience, offering huge rounds of Montasio, a creamy unpasteurized cow's milk cheese, or soft asino, to sample on the spot or vacuum-pack for the trip home. (It also happens to have very hunky cheesemongers.) **L'Alimentare** has all the fixings for the perfect picnic, with an excellent selection of Friuli wines and freshly prepared food to go. Augment your culinary delicacies with ingredients from the outdoor market in Piazza Matteotti, where stalls are laden with seasonal produce like white asparagus in the spring and porcini mushrooms come fall. For a wonderful immersion in the city's food scene, book a tour with local resident Raffaela Graselli through Via Degli Artisti Viaggi, which will also include cultural highlights.

Don't miss a meal at **Hostaria alla Tavernetta** for its fall-off-the-bone tender lamb, trout caviar, and (for the adventurous) a signature goose dish with pears and potatoes. The intimate private rooms upstairs, with fireplaces and vintage chandeliers, make a dreamy option for groups.

Looking for something more casual? Try **Leon d'Oro** for its frittata with herbs and thick polenta grilled with cheese. Or **Vitello d'Oro,** which has become a town must for its delicate seafood tasting menus (try the one devoted solely to tuna). But the showstopper is the restaurant's tiramisu: creamy, delicate, and topped with espresso. **Astoria Hotel Italia** is close to all of Udine's highlights. ▪

Udine is the perfect-size city, full of great food and landmarks.

Frances's Favorites

In Your Glass

In a region where you hardly can go wrong, these are some of my favorite vineyards: Venica & Venica, Villa Russiz, Josko Gravner, Doro Princic, Livon, Vie di Romans, Schiopetto, Borgo del Tiglio, and Toros.

When I asked writer and almost-native son Robert Draper—we've traveled to Friuli many times together—for his top choices, he recommended our mutual favorite Venica & Venica, of course, plus Toros's Merlot and his sensational Pinot Bianco; Renato Keber's one perfect white, Friulano, which tastes like almond blossoms smell, and one perfect red: Grici Merlot Reserva. He's also a big fan of Raccaro: "the best malvasia, plus their other excellent whites, and a very nice merlot."

We both revere all of Nicola Manferrari's Borgo del Tiglio wines and have only praise for Cristian Specogna's—especially the whites: Identità, Pinot Grigio Ramato Reserva (forget the usual bar pinot grigio), Duality (100 percent sauvignon), and the full-on *rosso*, Oltre.

This short but exquisite list takes you in from the high dive. ∎

ABOVE: Pouring the tastings with a smile at Enoteca di Cormòns, a one-stop to discover some of Friuli's best wines, both white and red, plus bubbles
OPPOSITE: The Loggia del Lionello in Udine feels like a piece of Venice transported to the city.

Hot Spot
San Daniele

Name sound familiar? If you know your prosciutto, then you've probably heard of San Daniele. Many people think this iconic meat delicacy is from Emilia-Romagna. But not so.

In this small town in Friuli, a beautiful destination in its own right, nestled into the hills, the production of this heavenly ham follows a strict set of rules. The DOC-protected (since 1996) process takes more than a year and involves strict controls, from how it is salted and aged to the high-quality pork itself, which can come only from native pigs.

A visit to **Prosciuttificio Bagatto,** a three-generation establishment in town, not only offers a full education on why this variety is the couture of prosciutto but also offers the opportunity for a wafer-thin sampling alongside a delicate glass of white wine. And every June, prosciutto aficionados arrive in town to enjoy the **Aria di Festa,** an outdoor festival devoted to its cured cuts—plus stands for other food products and music.

Don't miss the frescoes at the church of **Sant'Antonio Abate** before or after your more earthly pleasures. Painted by Pellegrino da San Daniele, it's known as the Sistine Chapel of Friuli. Nearby, the city's duomo was originally built in the 14th century and refurbished in the 18th by Venetian architect Domenico Rossi.

And a private tour of **Biblioteca Guarneriana,** a library from 1466, is an absolute must, with a priceless collection of more than 12,000 volumes, including a spectacular copy of Dante's *Inferno.* Two interesting facts about the library: First, during World War II, local residents, when they heard that the German soldiers were coming, hid the library's books all over town—under beds and in stables and rural huts—to protect them from being stolen, and they returned them after the war had ended. Local lore also claims that the particular climate caused by the Tagliamento River not only cures the local prosciutto but preserves the library's books without the need for air-conditioning. ▪

San Daniele's world-renowned consortium for curing prosciutto

What a joy: the Alpine architecture, those gingerbread houses with slate roofs and balconies festooned with armfuls of flowers. Someone inside is melting cheese and fluffing down comforters and no one is ever unhappy. Or so it seems. Situated just under France's and Switzerland's Mont Blanc, Matterhorn, Monte Rosa, and Italy's own looming Gran Paradiso peaks, this smallest region of Italy wins my heart the first day.

How? Simple: The overwhelming beauty seizes all the senses at once. The intense coziness of the rustic architecture must arise from the awareness that the lofty mountains are indifferent to mere mortals. We must surround ourselves with creature comforts and domestic bliss in defiance of looming menace.

A narrow, curvy road takes us along mountain slopes thick with conifers and blazing with golden birches and chestnuts. We arrive at Prateria di Sant'Orso, a luxuriant meadow across the broad valley floor on the edge of the village of Cogne. And what luck: Our hotel faces this greensward. Mountains rise on the far side of the meadow, and through a deep V, jagged snowy peaks look like mirages in the distance. We're at the top of the Parco Nazionale Gran Paradiso, an enormous reserve. A flock of sheep munches away on lush grasses while the shepherd leans against a post talking on the phone.

We check into Hotel Miramonti, and I'm set. That's it. I want to stay at least a week. (I must make the most of three days.) The Miramonti has been in the same family since 1540. Every object has a story, especially the beguiling collection of family portraits. Not the usual dour faces here—all the ancestors look as pleasant as the current inhabitants. Honey-colored paneling, lavish use of old mirrors, antiques waxed

for centuries, crimson damask walls, and worn leather books—such refined comfort everywhere.

Our suite's three balconies overlook the valley; rich brocades and crushed velvet are fit for a Savoy princess stuck on a hunting trip to the wilds. The restaurant, Coeur de Bois, proves to be superb and civilized. For such a small hotel (42 rooms), I didn't expect an extensive spa. The hammam, with whimsically painted walls, oozes relaxation, and a number of different thermal treatments and usual spa services are hushed and soothing. I especially like the Roman *tepidarium,* a tiny mosaic steam room with a one-person cold plunge pool.

What a soporific—all night I hear the tinkling of sheep bells.

Within walking distance, about an hour, from Cogne is Lillaz, a tiny settlement at the end of the road. We followed along a mighty stream until we reached a pair of high *cascate,* waterfalls plunging into clear pools. The village of Gimillan is close too, but quite vertiginous for a hike. Drive up for the

WHAT YOU NEED TO KNOW...

- **BEST TIME TO VISIT:** Year-round (but in the season between summer and winter sports, many businesses are closed)

- **TOP SPOTS:** Courmayeur, Aosta, Cervinia, Gran Paradiso, Cogne

- **GETTING THERE:** Fly into Turin then head north by car or train to Valle d'Aosta.

There are almost as many cows as people in the gentle rolling hills of the Aosta valley, framed by the Italian Alps.

Located on the other side of the French Alps in Italy, this small region has many of its neighbor's assets, from winter skiing to summer hiking.

stupendous views and for a peek into life in such a remote spot. Outside the typical rustic log and slate-roofed houses, compulsively neat woodpiles are ready for what winter surely brings. Already, in October, the smell of wood smoke puffs into the air. From here, the ski slopes down mountainsides look challenging, to say the least. Cogne's environs inspire you to lace up those hiking boots and take off. When I return, I'll try the village's rustically elegant Hotel Bellevue, closed right now for a season break. Looks divine!

In the off-season, all is quiet, and many shops and restaurants are closed for a preseason break. Fine with me. All the walking trails are empty, and I could be John Muir tromping in these woods! Valle d'Aosta is well organized for outdoor activities; local tourist offices are staffed with knowledgeable people and equipped with trail guides. Ask for the one called simply *Hikes*. It has a good map and is in English. Every day, we choose one of these well-marked paths that show at the outset the degree of difficulty.

In winter, the Sant'Orso meadow becomes one of the best cross-country skiing places in Italy. Fifty miles (80 km) of trails begin right outside the Miramonti's door. This seems like the least hassle skiing possible. Other slopes are close for downhill, and a *funivia* runs you up to Montzeuc for panoramas and downhill pistes. Rent skis in the village, and set off from there. There are ice skating and snow walks as well.

When we return in late mornings, invigorated and exalted, it's time to settle in to the Miramonti's cozy library of leatherbound books. This spells *vacation* to me. For lunch at rustic Brasserie du Bon Bec in the village, there'll be fontina fondue with crisp polenta bread to dip and a copper pan of baked chopped veal, potatoes, and onions under a blanket of crusty cheese: the lusty food *valdostani* have eaten for centuries. Back to the hotel for a soak in the warm hammam, then a twilight walk along the meadow. Dinner as it should be, leisurely paced and delicious. A Jerusalem artichoke flan; gnocchi of potatoes and chestnuts filled with Blu d'Aosta cheese, butter, and salvia; goose confit with vegetable *mostarda* (mustard, vinegar, aromatics) and pumpkin. Like that. Easy to love.

Next day: repeat. Repeat as often as needed to restore a lightness to your step, to clear your head of unimportant minutiae, and to feast your eyes on rare beauty.

All of Valle d'Aosta works this way. What a mellow town, Aosta, the region's capital and the shopping magnet for all the villages around. The ancient grids, the *decumanus* (east-west) and *cardo* (north-south), still function as main streets, long and straight in the Roman way. And extensive ruins—a theater, a bridge, the Porta Pretoria, and a monumental arch from 25 B.C.—are as much a part of the cityscape as the busy

Cold cuts and salami accompanied by homemade bread with figs and nuts

Like its French counterpart Chamonix, Italy's Courmayeur turns into an idyllic winter sports destination with plenty of other distractions off piste.

shops and cafés branching off from the grand neoclassical Hôtel de Ville (town hall) on Piazza Chanoux. I always love how at home with time the Italians are, and Aosta proves that once again. The ruins set you dreaming of ancient eras but meld naturally into daily life.

Up, up out of the *centro*. If you're a brave heart, you can experience the ultimate mountain high: a balloon ride over the Alps. I wish I had the courage! It must be divine to float above the coruscating silvery colors of snow, sipping a glass of prosecco and catching views of the slate-roofed houses, the Matterhorn, Monte Rosa, and Mont Blanc. Bundle up! It's cold up there.

See and be seen in Courmayeur. The shop names reflect the clientele at this super-glam ski resort: Rolex, Maserati, Balenciaga, Moncler. Obviously, this is the place to find cool boots or a feather-light winter jacket the color of fog. Or one for your dog! Cashmere boutiques (did I count three?), a

tempting toy shop, and the friendly bookstore Libreria Buona Stampa all invite lingering.

Aside from retail therapy, this village is so superbly situated that images imprint forever on your brain. The surrounding area is rich in castles, mysterious and aloof. Mont Blanc juts up to a lofty 4,810 meters, which sounds higher in feet—15,781—the highest mountain in Europe. Naturally, this is ski and après-ski paradise. But it's also a great destination in other seasons.

Courmayeur: yes, fashionable, but also a place of wild nature and extravagant beauty. Friends own a house here and have come every winter since childhood. Now the tradition passes to their son. I can imagine all their layered memories: challenging days on the slopes in glittering sun; hot chocolate with mounds of whipped cream; family times around a table laden with cheeses, sausages, wild boar pasta, and local strong wines. A sense of place deeply embedded in their spirits. Lucky they are.

At nighttime, cozy Courmayeur is lit up with pretty streetlights so one can still have a stroll after dinner.

Alpine Villages: Valle d'Aosta's Hidden Charms

Many Italians head to this region come fall for a specific reason: to celebrate apples, one of its main products. You might be interested to know that the farms here produce a ton of them—literally, 5,000 tons (4,500 t). And happily, there are plenty of festivals celebrating Valle d'Aosta's famed exports. The apple festival in Gressan and the **Mele Vallée festival** in Antey-Saint-André both happen in October, when the extraordinary fall foliage further enhances Valle d'Aosta's cozy charms.

Located on the other side of the French Alps in Italy, this small region possesses many of its neighbor's assets: excellent skiing in winter and hiking in summer, small family-run restaurants, and charming small towns. In Aosta, for example, if you aren't a sporty type, you will find lots of distractions in the form of small one-of-a-kind shops. A must stop is **Nicoletta's** for cheese like aged fontina as well as *tomme,* a buttery soft cheese that can be made from cow, ewe, or goat milk, and goat cheeses (the competition from the French on the other side of

the mountains has only improved Aosta's goat cheese). For dried mushrooms, an easy-to-pack delicacy to take home, head to **Il Boschetto. San Pasquale Ferramenta** nearby showcases the handsome ironwork the region is also known for: hinges, locks, door knockers, keyholes, and door handles. **À la Page** is the well-curated bookstore you wish every town had, filled with a great selection of titles, including some English guidebooks, and inviting tables for reading and research. Wood carving, an ancient craft of the region, also continues to thrive; the winsome **Wood Sweet Wood** sells intricate models to challenge little geniuses, along with nostalgic musical toys that feature rotating figures around a scene.

Come winter, the town of **Courmayeur** becomes the region's primary ski destination—but it's a great launch point regardless of the season. Make **Villa Novecento,** an art nouveau–style restaurant and inn, your base, and plan on eating and drinking your way through town. **Pierre Alexis 1877** provides a quick study in a higher end Valle d'Aosta cuisine; be sure to sample dishes like a crème brûlée "al parmigiana" with black truffles and gnocchi with leeks and snails. And save room for desserts like a *ganache al cioccolato bianco* (white chocolate cake). For coffee and cocktails, try **Caffè della Posta;** since 1911 residents have gathered to enjoy this fireplace-warmed space. And if you're in the mood to shop, stop in at **Andrè Maurice,** with its rainbow of soft cashmere sweaters, scarves, and throws.

In nearby **Saint-Vincent,** the gambling casino may draw the Italian crowds, but the real winner is the village itself. The water that runs through the city's pipes from the nearby lake is

Chestnuts with cinnamon and whipped cream are the perfect post-slope snack.

heralded for curing any liver problems, and strolls along the flowery (or snowy) pedestrian street give you a sense of the town's gentle rhythms. Have lunch at **Olympic** for local specialties—perhaps after viewing the evocative 15th-century frescoes in the parish church (which depict, among other subjects, a sleeping woman, the Crucifixion, and St. Lorenzo, who became the patron saint of cooks after being martyred on a grill—yikes!). For dinner, the most atmospheric restaurant in the area is **Le Grenier,** located in an old granary. Sit by the huge copper fireplace for a romantic meal among the grain racks and sculptural tools.

As for where to stay in Saint-Vincent, the **Grand Hotel Billia** is a belle epoque delight that unfortunately has been marred by an intrusive, corporate-looking entrance and deck. But it still retains some of its historic charm, glimpsed in the lobby's painted, coffered ceiling and the formal dining rooms with mountain vistas. ∎

DINING WITH A VIEW
Adventurous visitors to Valle d'Aosta are rewarded with fine dining among breathtaking mountains.

FULVIO DI ROSA, top restorer of old houses in Tuscany, has a family place at Courmayeur and knows the region's secrets. Here are the restaurants where he takes his family, when not stirring his famous risotto al Barolo at home: **La Chaumière,** with stunning views; **Rifugio Maison Vieille (Giacomo's),** reached by night cable car; **Ristorante Chiecco,** also by cable car; **Château Branlant;** and **Auberge de la Maison,** both inn and restaurant.

Di Rosa also is enthusiastic about a small restaurant in Val Ferret that you can get to in winter only by cross-country skiing or walking on the snow by the river, but it's easy to find by car in summer. The place is called **Lavachey.** "A bit adventurous," he says, "but it pays back with a lot of soul and wonderful authentic food."

For an idyllic hotel, he recommends going to Cogne, as I did. But near Courmayeur, there's a simpatico inn with mountain atmosphere: **Hotel Hermitage.**

To glimpse Di Rosa's work, check out **Podere Paníco,** the rental at Montroni d'Arbia, near Siena, and the restored medieval village near Cortona, **Borgo di Vagli.**

In the Know
Frenchie Cultural Influence

Although its Dolomite counterparts tend toward German influences, the Valle d'Aosta region instead leans French. Quite French, in fact. If you're staying here, fluency in both French and Italian is always useful. This mix of cultures—a type of French Provençal meets northern Italian—is known as Valdostana. From architecture to food and even wine, this region of Italy is often hard to distinguish from its neighbors across the Alps.

One of its most prized secrets is its distinct wine scene. Although Valle d'Aosta may be the smallest of the viticultural areas, insiders know it boasts very good, little-known labels, with eminently reasonable price tags to boot. The network of vineyards—some at fairly steep elevations—produce more common grapes like *nebbiolo* and *pinot noir;* they also grow varieties you may not have heard of before, like *prié* and *cornalin.* These are not sophisticated, Bordeaux-style wines, but energetic, changeable, young beverages, much like the weather here. A Noussan Cuvée de la Côte (even the names of the cantinas are Frenchified) is a good example of the drinkable nature of the vintages.

As it happens, mulled wine is as popular here as it is across the border in France. A difference, though, is in the *grolla* (etymology: grail), or Italian-style cup. Here, traditional "cups of friendship" filled with mulled wine and spiked with potent coffee and citrus are set aflame, then passed around the table,

everyone sipping from a different opening. It's bad luck if the cup is set down before it's empty.

Perhaps not surprising, given its history and proximity, when it comes to cuisine, the Valle d'Aosta region relies on many of the same staples as France. Cheese here looms large, with goat cheese as a standout. But don't dismiss niche markets like fontina, which can be made only from full-cream unpasteurized milk of Valdostan cows above a certain altitude.

One of the region's most prized entrees is the *carbonada,* a meat dish stewed with wine and spices. *Crespelle,* the Valle d'Aosta's answer to the crepe, is generally filled with ham and cheese. Try it at Aosta's **Trattoria Praetoria,** a restaurant that beautifully showcases the French influence alongside more Italian mountain staples like polenta and fresh pasta. **Il Vecchio Ristoro** also elegantly melds the two cultures, fea-

turing homemade breads like an unforgettable chestnut loaf and rabbit stuffed with *lardo,* fat.

Located in a lovely mountain lodge, Courmayeur's **La Maison de Filippo** serves up a cheese fondue, an excellent *carbonada,* and wines from both sides of Mont Blanc. And up the mountain from Courmayeur in the small hamlet of La Palud, **Dandelion** showcases "cuisine de montagne" including a beef fillet with green pepper and foie gras. (Make sure that **La Chaumière** by the cable car is also on your list for the outstanding polenta and wine list.)

The architecture of the Valle d'Aosta, spawned during the Middle Ages between Italy and France, reflects the region's hybrid routes. Despite being called *castelli,* the names of this region's castles belie the French roots. There are 150 fortified structures dotting the small region including **Château Sarriod de la Tour,** one of the most picturesque. ◼

OPPOSITE: Fontina is one of the delicious cheeses on hand in this mountainous area. **ABOVE:** Sharing the *grolla,* a wooden bowl with spouts for communal sipping of mulled wine, is an enduring tradition.

Frances's Favorites

In Your Glass

Believe it or not, vineyards thrive among the crags of this dramatic region. For such a small production area—only 1,144 acres (463 ha)—the variety of grapes is staggering. Many little-known varieties, such as *fumin, vuillermin, cornalin, prié,* and *mayolet,* create a sense of exploration when facing the wine list. These are high-altitude wines, and something is working beautifully. I was entranced every night with the superb quality of the Valle d'Aosta producers' bottles.

Look for the Les Crêtes label. Among this maker's consistently standout wines, I recommend Valle d'Aosta Syrah, compatible with the many dishes featuring local cheeses. Light but not lightweight, this wine is meant for food. A shade more meditative, its *nebbiolo* Sommet, *molto corposo,* with a very generous body, puts forth some spice with softened tannins. The lauded Chardonnay Cuvée Bois is heady and fresh as a mountain stream. It's possible to visit the vineyard's "mountain hut," the inspired Rifugio del Vino designed by Domenico Mazza.

I also frequently ordered the Anselmet wines: Henri, Torrette Superieur, Pinot Noir, and La Touche.

Finishing several dinners, Liquore di Pino Mugo came to us in little glasses—an Alpine-scented sip that reminded us, at the end of the evening, of our walks in the forests. ▪

Believe it or not, vineyards thrive among the crags of this dramatic region. These are high-altitude wines, and something is working beautifully.

ABOVE: Les Crêtes winery is a strikingly modern structure, but the estate started making wine back in the 1880s. OPPOSITE: Cut through by rivers and lakes, the fertile Valle d'Aosta is perfect for vines.

Best Of

Outdoor Diversions in All Seasons

Despite being the smallest of the regions in Italy, the Valle d'Aosta boasts one of the best and most spectacular settings for summer and winter sports.

Best to See the Views: Located at the base of Mont Blanc, the resort town Courmayeur, on the other side from Chamonix, has the same excellent ski trails and hikes up one of the world's most beautiful mountains. You can also view the incredible panorama from the cable car.

Best for Winter Sports: Breuil-Cervinia, at the base of the Matterhorn (Monte Cervino in Italian) is the region's other unmissable ski area. As one of the highest resorts in the Alps, the pistes get good snow from early November to early May. And since it shares a border with Switzerland, it's even possible to ski into the resort town of Zermatt for more challenging runs: There are over 100 miles (160 km) of intermediate options in Cervinia. Ice skating and ice climbing, as well as paragliding, are on offer for sporty types. The après-ski scene goes full cylinder here in high seasons, with bars offering mulled wine and hot chocolate. For the perfect stay, try Hotel Hermitage; its slope-side location is one of the best in the region, with a pampering Le Prairie spa and a destination restaurant.

Best for Wildlife: Valle d'Aosta is also home to the Gran Paradiso, the country's oldest national park. Populated with ibex, eagles, and chamois among other protected animals, it offers beautiful summer hikes through meadows of butterflies (the Giardino Alpino Paradisia is one of the most spectacular Alpine botanical gardens in the world).

Best for Adventure: Plan to make the Cogne Valley your general base for excursions in the park. When winter falls, try the cross-country trails deep into the forest. In the summer, hike or take an electric bike through the valley to the 492-foot (150 m) Lillaz waterfall. The Cogne is also a big draw for climbers; rock faces offer different levels of expertise, and ice climbers can hit the more than 150 icefalls in the area. Along with the storied Hotel Miramonti, Cogne's other choice hotel is the Bellevue; its four-table Le Petit Restaurant is one of the best places to eat in the region. The property also sits right on the edge of the Sant'Orso meadow, a stunning location.

Best for Wildflowers: Another protected area worth the hike is the Pavillon du Mont Fréty Nature Oasis and its famous botanical garden. Tucked in between glaciers are miles upon miles of excellent trails, including the Sentiero Francesco e Giuditta Gatti options, some of the most beautiful walking routes in the area.

Best for Bathers: After all the rigorous activity, your body might be ready for some pampering. In the town of Valdigne, the Pré-Saint-Didier has been famous for its thermal waters since Roman times. With its pool, spa, and hotel cradled beneath the mountains, it's a great spot for total relaxation. ■

ABOVE: A child is towed by sled near Cervinia's ski resort. OPPOSITE: The thermal pool at Pré-Saint-Didier in the Aosta Valley

Part Two

Central Italy

Emerging from the mist is Podere Belvedere, one of the picturesque farmhouses that dot Val d'Orcia's rolling countryside.

From wine to sculpture, hikes to bucolic hot springs, the middle of the country quite literally offers the best of Italy.

Filled with gently undulating hills, golden stone buildings, pristine vineyards, and glorious art, central Italy epitomizes the joys of this country. Do you love exquisite Renaissance architecture, painting, and sculpture, along with artisanal shopping? Florence will give you Stendhal's syndrome (that phenomenon where art makes one woozy). Or do you seek medieval winding alleys and formidable fortresses along with adrenaline-filled festivals? Head to Siena, where a central grand piazza hosts the Palio, the bareback horse race that has been a town fixture for centuries. Perhaps you love pasta along with architecture? Head to Rome, where layers upon layers of history unveil themselves as you walk past treasures like the Forum or the Circus Maximus, all within sight of vibrant new cafés and bars and beloved trattorias.

There's Etruscan culture to discover too, with fascinating ruins that speak to its roots throughout the Lazio and Tuscan regions, not far from contemporary art installations. All across central Italy, art and hill towns coexist alongside rolling green fields dotted with cypresses—and in the spring, bloodred poppies. The acres and acres of vines that crisscross the region are a backbone of the country's wine history, each grand estate or humble *agriturismo* with a story and stretch of soil different from the next.

With all the pleasures of the countryside, you might be tempted to skip a trip to either the Mediterranean or Adriatic coast. Don't. The experience of a briny spaghetti with clams and crisp white wine at a beachside club is sublime, as is a siesta accompanied by the soundtrack of the sea.

In the center of the region are the Apennines, a majestic mountain range that houses protected national parks and remote villages that have scarcely changed in centuries. Truffles, earthy sausages, and other local delicacies await, as well as pastas unique to each hamlet. East to west, south to north, here is a region for every sort: those in search of the country's greatest hits or those who prefer to just meander without a plan.

CLOCKWISE FROM TOP LEFT: Brunelleschi's famous dome of the Florence cathedral with the city beyond; a painted door in the village of Lucca; the pedestrian-friendly streets of Rome; artichokes, featured in Roman dishes at traditional restaurants

Chapter Nine
TUSCANY

From my house outside Cortona, I see in the distance a villa built for a pope's visit in the 1700s. Legend says that he stayed only one night. Thanks, anyway, for the inheritance of this mellow golden facade the sun catches late in the afternoon. The sweeping view he must have seen on his one morning hasn't changed since, and certainly not during the 30 years I've been looking. Instead of development: a medi-

eval tower, a few *case coloniche* (old farmhouses), terraced hills, olive groves, and towering cypress trees punctuating the landscape. No rash of condos mars the valley; strict zoning forbids. Thanks, again. That's why much of Tuscany remains idyllic: Those forbidding rules in rural zones keep someone from adding an ugly garage or even nonconforming windows.

Timeless, the plotted and pieced landscape remains, timeless—as are the villages, where if someone came back from the dead after 300, 500 years, often she could find the place where she was married, hear the same bell from her parish church, or knock on the door where she was born. Tuscany—land of ancient architecture, endless art, olive groves—is mysterious because this invisible but palpable flow of time comforts. *This is for always,* we sense. And Tuscans are not retro people. They simply have the sense to bring the past forward with them rather than destroying it.

And isn't this fundamental truth at the heart of why so many love Tuscany? At taproot, the feeling of being at one with time gives a metabolic connection to a place. *I'm home.* When I felt that on arrival, I assumed I was unique. Since then, I have met so many first-time and return visitors who have had the identical experience.

Beyond these visceral feelings (*I surrender*), I can list hundreds of reasons to find Tuscany spellbinding. Everyday beauty becomes a profound revelation. In my adopted hilltop town of Cortona, you may feel nourished just by sipping a cool drink in the lively piazza and following the chromatic shifts falling across the rosy, ocher, and saffron palazzi. In June, brides from many countries descend the steep steps of the town hall, down into the piazza filled with well-wishers. Artists flock here, propping their easels on roadsides and sketching in the park. Writers! Cortona has given me 11 books. Unparalleled, I think, the always surging inspiration and romance that arise in this ancient and *incantevole,* enchanting, town.

Cortona was one of the original 12 Etruscan strongholds. My house takes its name from a remnant of the original town walls that looms above us—Cortona was larger so many

WHAT YOU NEED TO KNOW...

- **BEST TIME TO VISIT:** April to late June, September to mid-November. Many hotels in the Tuscan countryside tend to close from November 1 until March, but city properties remain open and have many fewer tourists than in the summer. They are particularly atmospheric over Christmas and New Year's.

- **TOP SPOTS:** Florence, coastal gem Capalbio, Lucca, Cortona, Siena, Pienza, Greve, Montalcino and the hill towns of the Val d'Orcia

- **GETTING THERE:** There are airports in Pisa and Florence, as well as Perugia.

A quintessential Italian invention, a vintage Vespa scooter is a striking way to navigate the rolling Tuscan countryside or zip through the towns.

Tuscany—land of ancient architecture, endless art, olive groves—is mysterious because the palpable flow of time comforts. *This is for always,* we sense.

centuries ago. The inheritance remains in the exceptional MAEC museum, an excellent introduction to the culture that underlies Tuscany.

Renaissance artist Luca Signorelli was born in Cortona, and we're lucky to have a trove of his work at Museo Diocesano, along with the great "Annunciation" by Fra Angelico, who worked in Cortona for several years. We all love his angel with orange curls. The futurist painter Gino Severini left many works in his hometown. My favorite is the stations of the cross walk below Chiesa di Santa Margherita. Each station is a stone shrine with mosaics illustrating the saga.

Of all the hill towns, Cortona may be the liveliest and the friendliest. The two harmonious piazzas in the *centro* zing with life far into the night in summer. Families stroll with gelato, the young gather at Piazza Signorelli's outdoor cafés, and kids

Diners gather in Cortona's vibrant main piazza.

kick a soccer ball against the museum walls. All this summer fervor reverts to ancient stony silence in deep winter.

Beautifully placed on a long spur of Monte Sant'Egidio, the town is protected by gigantic Etruscan walls topped with smaller stones in medieval times. Within the walls, *vicoli*, tiny streets, with poetic names like "path of the dawn," "of the night," radiate off the Rugapiana, the flat street, which is lined with boutiques. From Piazza Garibaldi, you look out at the serene Val di Chiana, where all the great produce and fruits are grown, and the curve of Lake Trasimeno, where Hannibal defeated the Romans in 217 B.C. In this timeless city, you could be convinced that he's coming any minute, riding his last elephant into the idyllic landscape.

Consider what follows a memo, brief and incomplete, a *gita,* little trip, around the region pinpointing a few favorites.

Bisected by the Arno, Florence, we all know, is a wonder of the world, dominated by Giotto's bell tower and the great Brunelleschi dome of Santa Maria del Fiore, so gaily adorned with green and pink marble. And the ancient city of Siena's duomo is striking in somber black and white stripes. The city's sweeping shell-shaped Piazza del Campo is one of the great sites. The surrounding medieval buildings in broad sunlight look like a stage set for a rollicking opera. But at midnight under the moon, the mood turns as stately as a Bach fugue: What a showstopper. How proud and amazing a place can be. How humanity can soar.

I love so many of the smaller towns in Tuscany. Who could forget Lucca, with Barga and the Garfagnana mountains and woods above that jewel box town? Bagno Vignoni's thermal pools and streams are where the Medici soaked their tired dogs and aching backs. Severe Massa Marittima, gateway to the western coastal area of the Maremma, is an old favorite, with its off-kilter piazza and friendly natives. The medieval towns of Sansepolcro, Anghiari, and nearby Monterchi make a lovely threesome for a day. The great Piero della Francesca paintings in their home territory, the plethora of

The view of the rolling hills surrounding Cortona from Bramasole, Frances Mayes's home

truffles and mushrooms, and the Busatti headquarters of traditional Tuscan fabrics are strong attractions that draw me frequently. And unforgettable: lunch on the beach at Ristorante La Pineta, near Marina di Bibbona, where the waves practically fall in your lap and the salt-crusted fish reinvents the concept.

In the village of Pienza, planned as an ideal Renaissance city, you sit on sun-warmed marble ledges around the noble piazza, then stroll along town walls for the Val d'Orcia view: cypress-studded serpentine white roads meandering into the tawny hills. This infuses you with happiness.

Tuscany is truly endless!

Other ways to rejuvenate your spirits include a visit to Lucignano, a quiet village with a gorgeous elliptical piazza, where on the walls of the church of San Francesco black-robed Death on horseback drags a scythe and aims a bow and arrow. Or proud Castiglion Fiorentino, an intact medieval center and the home of incredible olive oil. I love Pietrasanta, a contemporary art town full of Boteros, and Etruscan Vol-

terra, with a superb small archaeological museum and alabaster crafts.

Easy—jump onto a frequently running ferry from Piombino over to Isola d'Elba, where Napoleon was exiled. What a laid-back spot to decompress and play in small coves you reach only by boat, drive around the hilly island, and test your ability to unplug and chill out. Check into the waterfront Hotel Hermitage or the smaller Villa Ottone (sea view room only), and you may want to become an exile yourself.

Enough! But only a hint of the possibilities.

When it comes to Tuscany, I have the rapt, perhaps capricious, preferences of a native. After all, I've lived here longer than anywhere else in my life, even my primordial Fitzgerald, Georgia. Tuscany is my heart's needle, although I'll always be a *straniera,* a foreigner. Departing for my other American life is always hard. I leave the book I'm reading open on the bedside table as a promise: *I'll be back.* Returning, I feel the surge of pure joy: the sensation of riding a big wave onto shore. What a soft landing.

Wine 101: Brunello to Super Tuscans

Starting your Italian wine education? Look no further than Tuscany, a top destination for oenophiles. One of Italy's most celebrated regions pairs diversity and elegant settings with excellent vintages, as well as small productions with regional cuisine. Even after multiple trips here, you'll still enjoy the discovery of new labels at every turn.

Among the musts for your wine pilgrimage through this territory will be a stop in the vineyards around **Montalcino** for a wine named Brunello. The superstar DOC, made only with *san-giovese* grapes, came onto the global stage later than its counterparts in Chianti—but once the large estate of Banfi vaulted it into the spotlight in the 1990s, the international market took notice.

Smaller estates and producers started proliferating here, and part of their beauty is how the different terroirs around Montalcino demonstrate the various environments, types of soil, and how the wine is stored while using just one type of grape. While there are a plethora of labels to love, a few favorites include producers like **Il Cupano,** for its almost French-style vintage; **Podere Le Ripi,** owned by one of the Illy scions; and **Poggio di Sotto,** for its exemplary *vino rosso.* And of course, make sure to try the one of the region's top Brunellos (with their specific aging process)—**Casanova di Neri,** which always attracts accolades in wine publications and from critics.

You may have heard of the "Super Tuscans," the term for imaginative wines that use unique grape blends devised by their producer. But nothing beats the experience of seeing where huge wine stars like **Ornellaia, Sassi-**

Antinori's strikingly modernist winery, opened in 2012, was designed by architect Marco Casamonti and Archea design studio. Circular metal staircases have views over the extensive vineyards.

caia, and **Antinori** make their famous vintages. These celebrated vineyards create their own blends but are also influenced in some ways by their Bordeaux counterparts—for example, with their use of oak barrels. Don't miss the smaller players too; they offer a considerably more reasonable price tag. Try **Aia Vecchia** or family-owned **Caccia al Piano.**

Montalcino may receive bigger billing than the Sangiovese counterparts near **Montepulciano** because of their international reputation. But the Vino Nobile, also an only-*sangiovese* wine, deserves its own look—especially at vineyards like **Poliziano,** or the sustainability-focused **Salcheto.** And the well-reputed producer **Avignonesi** winery has become a stalwart in the area, as well as abroad.

In **Chianti**—perhaps Tuscany's best known wine destination—the offerings are fit for every occasion. Here, you'll find inexpensive bottles to bring on a picnic that are still more than drinkable (try **Castello di Gabbiano**) or occasion-worthy prize vintages from celebrated

Enoteca Italiana in Siena features signature blends called "Super Tuscans."

labels like **Mazzei.** You must also make time for a stop in at **Antinori**'s new winery, an architectural showstopper to showcase the vintages of the famed Tuscan wine family.

Other wine areas should be on your radar too—the village of **Scansano** in the Maremma coastal region of Tuscany, for example. One of the joys here is the ability to travel all over the region and find a wonderful glass of something local wherever you go. ■

TUSCANY'S WOMEN IN WINE

In a region and country mostly known for male producers, the new generation of female stars is one of Tuscany's most exciting trends. Among the ones to follow:

THE BRUNELLOS of Stella Di Campalto's **Di Campalto** have achieved an almost cultlike status. Her love for the region extends to the care she took in restoring an estate, left abandoned for almost half a century, which she transformed into this peaceful and fertile property. Along with her husband, Marco Pallanti, Lorenza Sebasti made **Castello di Ama** into one of Chianti's star vineyards—and they also happen to have a museum-worthy contemporary art collection, featuring international superstars Louise Bourgeois and Anish Kapoor.

Roots run deep for Elisa Sesti. Her father, Giuseppe, planted the vines at **Castello di Argiano** before she was born. Under her watch, it's become one of the region's Brunello producers of choice, with a love of the terroir that justifies its place in the constellation of top vintages.

Gemma Marcucci has dedicated her career at **San Carlo** estate in Montalcino to keeping the quality of her father and grandfather's wines at top billing while making them accessible—with a dedication that especially shines in her wine tours. And since Miriam Caporali's father, Giulio, gave her the reins at Montepulciano's **Tenuta Valdipiatta,** she has been preserving his legacy for over a decade while advancing its reputation on the international stage. Her innovations include an on-site winemaking class.

Sign up for a cooking class with wine pairings at the Desinare school in Florence, named for the midday meal that Florentine families share.

Florence: Navigating the Renaissance Masterpiece

When you plan a trip to Tuscany, Florence has to be on your itinerary. How could it not be? Packed with Renaissance treasures, it's a destination that's deservedly high up in the travel hall of fame. The **Duomo,** the **Uffizi Gallery** with its priceless Botticellis, Michelangelo's "David," the views of Florence stretching along the banks of the Arno. What's not to love?

With fame, though, the less palatable aspects of a destination beloved for centuries have grown worse. Common sights: massive tourist groups,

vendors selling counterfeits of the main Italian brands, an overwhelming sense of congestion at the city's heart.

Luckily there are still ways to get away from the crowds. Companies like Context Travel and Personalized Italy bring you to the "best ofs"—but off-hours or privately. Try a tour of the city's celebrated kilometer-long (0.6-mi) **Vasari corridor,** connecting the Uffizi Gallery to the **Palazzo Pitti,** after the museum officially closes; cooking classes in noble palazzi normally closed to the public; or a private pottery or leathermaking lesson with a local artisan.

Exploring museums and churches that are smaller, or less written about, gives major artistic pleasure without having to compete for space with a selfie stick—spots like the exquisite Chapel of the Magi in the **Palazzo Medici,** which is open only by appointment. Renaissance painter Benozzo Gozzoli's "Procession of the Magi," commissioned by Cosimo de' Medici, is full of vivid imagery. Kids and adults alike will enjoy the armor collection at the **Stibbert Museum. Palazzo Strozzi** hosts some of the most important retrospectives in the country, hanging contemporary art on its stately palace walls.

Walks in less frequented neighborhoods like **Fiesole,** a stroll down the tree-lined avenues of **Villa Bardini's** baroque gardens, and a visit to **Piazza di Bellosguardo** (where Florence Nightingale and Henry James lived) give peeks into Florence at a quieter pace.

Oltrarno, on the south side of the river, is Florence's equivalent of Paris's Left Bank, centered around the Palazzo Pitti. Here is where local residents escape the tourists, as well as enjoy less crowded cultural treasures and up-and-coming restaurants. Among the highlights is Brunelleschi's stunning **Basilica di Santo Spirito,** near the artery of San Jacopo. The **Brancacci Chapel** not only has priceless frescoes depicting the life of St. Peter but also has quiet cloisters and interlocking courtyards that transport visitors to centuries past.

Florence's modern opera house

A number of the city's best bars and restaurants have grown up in Oltrarno, enjoyed after a stroll in the **Boboli Gardens.** Try **Il Santino,** where over 150 Tuscan handpicked vintages come with local cheeses and cured meats from farms not far from town. At **Gurdulù,** named for the Italo Calvino character, regulars congregate for artisanal cocktails, while **Burro e Acciughe** showcases a beloved Italian snack—bread topped with butter and anchovies—

alongside a stylish local crowd. And at **Le Volpi e L'Uva,** Tuscany's best wines are served up with plates of salami and cheese to its loyal clientele. **Essenziale,** located in a 19th-century warehouse, is helmed by one of the city's rising chefs, Simone Cipriani (try the *baccalà carbonara,* pasta prepared with peanut and mint!).

Looking for a stylish place to stay in the neighborhood? Book a room at **SoprArno Suites,** an 11-room guesthouse in a 14th-century palazzo run by young designers who have added custom beds and stand-alone tubs to the original high-ceiling rooms, some with original frescoes.

In the last few years, Florentine insiders have also created locations that tourists can enjoy but are mostly designed for residents. The **Mercato Centrale,** for example, showcases artisanal products and vendors of everything from gelato to olive oil, with food

CHECKING IN

From reinvented palazzi dating back to the era of the Grand Tour to sexy modern hideaways, Florence's hostelries know how to charm.

PORTRAIT FIRENZE: The latest venture of the Ferragamo family, founders of the design label, is right on the Arno with unbeatable views of the Ponte Vecchio.

J.K. PLACE FIRENZE: Fashion editors and insiders book early for a room at this intimate boutique hotel right on Piazza Santa Maria Novella, one of the loveliest squares in all of Florence.

ADASTRA SUITES: Overlooking Europe's largest private garden, the nine-room hotel has great original details, like frescoes and antique chandeliers, mixed with vintage pieces.

FOUR SEASONS HOTEL FIRENZE: The ubiquitous luxury group took two palazzi from the 15th and 16th centuries and transformed them into a quiet oasis right in town, with a pool and spa.

RIVA LOFTS: A former tannery from the turn of the 20th century, this chic lodging was reinvented as nine airy apartments by Florentine architect Claudio Nardi.

HOTEL SAVOY: Recently renovated, this property from Italian hotelier Rocco Forte has a wonderful address, on the Piazza della Repubblica, and large, stylish rooms.

IL SALVIATINO: Located in a green enclave in Florence's Fiesole, this restored villa has become a preferred stomping ground for paparazzi-averse VIPs.

GRAND HOTEL MINERVA: Smack dab on Florence's Santa Maria Novella square, this newly renovated hotel has much to recommend it, including a rooftop pool with a panoramic view of the city, architectural bones from mid-century master Carlo Scapa, and amenities including a hot tub.

ABOVE: A panoramic view of Florence on the banks of the Arno OPPOSITE: Shops like Marie Antoinette in Florence are known for both their vintage picks and new designs in cozy ateliers.

stalls so that you can sit down and sample the wares right there. At **Barthel,** a vintage furniture and kitchen store, the owners have opened a cooking school, **Desinare,** that attracts chefs from town, as well as visitors. The **Gucci Museum,** which debuted in 2011, showcases the archives of Italy's most important brands for the city's fashion students, as well as label mavens from all over the world, and a restaurant outpost from Massimo Bottura.

Eating well and relatively inexpensively is a Florentine art. Easygoing and unpretentious, **Il Santo Bevitore** doubles as the fashionable lunch spot for nearby executives. The owners recently also opened **Il Santino,** a good spot for wine and small plates like the Tuscan tomato soup *pappa al pomodoro.* Fabio Picchi is one of the city's most famous chefs. Part restaurant, part cultural enclave, **Teatro del Sale,** a former

theater, has become a Florentine insider favorite for both its performances (music, dance, and theater) and simple staples. If you need a break from the classics, **Cablèo,** Picchi's latest venture, is where Asian meets Tuscan.

Choosing one spot to try the Florentine staple *bistecca alla Fiorentina* (Florentine steak) will elicit an argument between city residents. But most agree that **Regina Bistecca's** authentic version of the T-bone offers a version so good that local residents and visitors alike are clamoring for a table. One of the most romantic dining rooms in the city, **La Bottega del Buon Caffè** is also home to some excellent cuisine thanks to the owners' ingredients sourced from their own farm; try the tasting menu from up-and-coming chef Antonello Sardi.

Despite megabrands and plastic menus proliferating in the city, Florence's side streets are still known for

their small shops and cafés. **Amblé,** for example, draws well-heeled locals for an Aperol spritz (it also happens to sell vintage furniture and accessories). **Marie Antoinette** and **Boutique Nadine** are treasure troves for designer labels, and consignment, while the new **OBO la bottega** is where Florentines go for tableware and gifts. **La Ménagère** showcases the city's new penchant for multipurpose spaces—here you'll find an exquisite kitchen flower shop, cocktail bar, restaurant, and a basement spot for live music.

One of the city's greatest pleasures is finding destinations that Florentines love but are actually tucked away near the most touristy spots in town. **'Ino,** just off the old stone Ponte Vecchio, sells panini with freshly baked bread, filled with cheese and ingredients selected by its local owner from small producers. ∎

Best of

Biking and Hiking: Sightseeing as You Go

The curse of local drivers, bikers nonetheless swarm to Tuscany for its combination of stunning scenery, variable terrain, and cycle trails lined with country inns. You can also go off asphalt on foot and hike the true back roads Italians call *strade bianche* (unpaved roads).

Best for Bucket List Seekers: One of Italy's best biking routes was born only a few decades ago in Tuscany. The L'Eroica, inaugurated in the late 1990s by a passionate Italian cyclist, Giancarlo Brocci, is the pinnacle of specialty races, featuring some of Tuscany's most beautiful roads. It leaves the village of Gaiole in Chianti and travels south past Siena to Montalcino and back north in a loop. Cyclists can

ABOVE: A gritty participant in Tuscany's L'Eroica bike race OPPOSITE: A hiker takes in the view of the Mediterranean from Monte Capanne on Tuscany's Elba island.

pick different distances, from a relatively short 29 miles (46 km) to a 130-mile (209 km) version. The mix of vintage bikes and nonasphalt roads has garnered a loyal annual following. If you don't want to participate in the official version in October, just download the maps and follow the route solo. Cruise past Brolio Castle, classic vineyards, and the medieval village of Buonconvento, and don't forget the numerous enticing food stops.

Best for Secret Itineraries: Cicloposse tour company specializes in Tuscany biking itineraries and knows the region intimately (the owners showcase the southern area near the Val d'Orcia particularly well and have a good selection of high-end bike models). Urban Bikery rents electric bikes out of Montepulciano, one of the preferred modes of transport after toiling up one too many hills. International companies like DuVine and Backroads have excellent guides and plan everything in advance, from bike pickups to where to stay.

Best for Walking Meditation: Walking in Tuscany is a delight. Landscapes change at every turn. On one excursion, the route winds through the *crete,* distinctive clay hills, of the Val d'Orcia, while another passes through farmland and lush hills around Greve. Other trails traverse bluffs overlooking craggy coves in nature reserves on the coast. Meditative and hidden away, these paths offer elegant sights: a line of cypresses on a dirt road, a small church inaccessible to cars, or, in spring, fields of poppies and other wildflowers.

Best Guides for Insider Tips: A beloved resource for walking the region is James Lasdun and Pia Davis's *Walking and Eating in Tuscany and Umbria.* Some favorite hikes include the trek from Montalcino to the Abbey of Sant'Antimo, and the ring walk of Laimole. For customized itineraries, Trufflepig is a small artisanal company that focuses on important details that make your experience unique, while guides at the stalwart Butterfield & Robinson have years of expertise unlocking the Tuscan hills by bike or foot. ∎

A beach near the spectacular village of Populonia. It's one of Tuscany's prettiest options, backed by shady trees and frequented by surfers.

Coastal Escapes: Tuscany's Lesser Known Stars

Swaths of beaches with secret coves. Storybook towns perched above the sparkling Mediterranean. Plates of fresh seafood on white-washed terraces. Many visitors head inland when they book their trips to this beloved region, but Tuscany insiders know that the coastline here deserves its own spotlight.

In the southern part of the region lies **Capalbio,** a weekend and summer playground for holidaying Romans, many with second homes here. One of the best beach clubs in Italy is **Rosso e Vino alla Dogana** near the town's marina. Here, plates of *spaghetti alle vongole* (clams), served at tables with views of the sea, and a nap on one of the beach beds after lunch become welcome summer rituals. At nightfall, drive out of town to **Locanda Rossa.** Recently restored, the resort has two pools, a playground, a small spa, and an excellent restaurant in the former lemon greenhouse, **La Limonaia.** Near Locanda Rossa is the **Tarot Garden,** the surreal art installation in a space inspired by Antoni Gaudí's Park Güell in Barcelona. It comes with oversize mosaic sculptures by original owner and artist Niki de Saint Phalle depicting different tarot cards throughout the impressive gardens.

Farther north, the Argentario peninsula gained fame as a yachters' paradise. It is also home to **Hotel Il Pellicano,** a family-owned and much photographed resort that's been the hideaway for the fashionably fabulous since the 1960s. For a less pricey option, try the lovingly restored **Casa Iris** in the port town of Orbetello.

Little known outside Tuscany, the tangle of streets of the beautiful village of **Talamone** is close to the nature park

Parco Regionale della Maremma. Formerly part of the Duke of Tuscany's private estate, it's now home to wild boar, deer, and beachgoers who sit next to magnificent sculptural pines. Those who live nearby also head to the beach club of Talamone's **Bagno delle Donne** with its enviable position under the nearby castle.

Set in the hillside of the delightfully uncrowded Vetulonia, **Il Baciarino** is a truly unusual hotel: five cottages with solar-powered wooden hot tubs that jut out from the mountain. Another highlight? The exquisite fish dinners cooked up by the chef-owner. Day trips should include a hike to **Cala Violina,** a perfect cove of powdery white sand and a turquoise stretch of sea.

Populonia, home to Etruscan ruins and a wall-encircled village perched above Baratti Bay, takes photo ops to the next level with 360-degree views of the sea and national park from its 15th-century fortress. Make a stop for *fritto misto* (mixed fried seafood) at **Ristorante Canessa.** Or visit **Poggio Ai Santi** near San Vincenzo for epic views (and food to match).

Up an avenue of majestic cypress trees is **Bolgheri,** the anchor of the Super Tuscan wine region and a town easily walked in half an hour. Here try an artisanal ice cream at **Ti Amo** or a wine tasting at **Bar Enoteca Tognoni.** Outside town, the boutique hotel **Relais Sant'Elena** is a quiet oasis of gardens, pretty rooms, and unbeatable sunset views.

Nearby, **La Pineta** in Marina di Bibbona draws Italians and foodie travelers alike to its small dining room for *crudo* (raw fish) and just-caught seafood. The gruff but charming *capo,* Luciano Zazzeri, who was once a fisherman before becoming a stellar chef, sadly passed away, but his son Daniele has taken over the helm.

If you are in search of a villa to rent seaside, Trust and Travel and Cedric Reversade's portfolios have a good inventory. ∎

Many visitors head inland when they book trips to this beloved region, but Tuscany insiders know that the coastline here deserves its own spotlight.

CLOCKWISE FROM LEFT: The picturesque harbor of Porto Ercole on the Argentario peninsula; one of the striking sculptures by Niki de Saint Phalle in Capalbio's Tarot Garden; a delectable fish soup from Michelin-starred La Pineta restaurant in Marina di Bibbona

Frances's Favorites
Sunday in Arezzo

The nearest "big city" to my home in Cortona is Arezzo (around 100,000). I've furnished two houses from its **Fiera Antiquaria,** a sprawling antiques market held the first weekend of every month.

What's for sale? Some flotsam, some garage sale stuff—but otherwise, you'll find treasures, especially paintings. I'm amazed that I can buy chestnut tables, iron wine racks, gilded candlesticks (to turn into lamps), heavy monogrammed napkins, even 1930s aluminum cookware, which has acquired a worn patina by now.

Arezzo also has antiques shops along **Corso Italia,** the main street, and on radiating *vicoli*. (How easy it is to ship a large 18th-century *armadio* [armoire] with painted doors.) I've found everything under the sun and then some.

After a morning browsing the market or people-watching at **Caffè Dei Costanti** (where part of *Life Is Beautiful* was filmed), try lunch at **La Lancia d'Oro** right in the midst of the market and overlooking the **Piazza Grande,** one of the greats of Italy, lined with narrow medieval buildings.

Afternoon allows time for Arezzo's other abundant charms: the duomo's small Piero della Francesca painting of Mary Magdalene with wet hair after she washed and dried the feet of Jesus; the house of Petrarch, who profoundly influenced Western poetry; the memorial statue of Guido Monaco, a native boy who invented the musical scale; and the **Museo Archeologico,** located in a park that was once a Roman amphitheater.

But the magnetic draw to Arezzo is a major fresco cycle of the Renaissance: "The Legend of the True Cross" by Piero della Francesca in Chiesa di San Francesco, painted in 1452–1466. He depicts the history of the wood that became the Cross on which Christ was crucified, back to its beginnings as a seed placed in the mouth of Adam when he died. The cycle reads like a book, and was indeed inspired by the 13th-century *Golden Legend,* which chronicled the journey of the wood toward the Crucifixion.

Arezzo is the perfect place to participate in the Sunday evening *passeggiata* (promenade). Droves of Italian youth out to see and be seen stroll along the Corso. Laughing, arm in arm, advertising their flush of shining energy, sporting their fitted clothes and good haircuts, they embody the fervor for enjoying this place, these friends, this moment. Families with strollers meet friends, ladies with tiny dogs gossip, and men, hands behind their backs, look into shop windows. Everyone stops to gaze at the displays at the super-fashion house **Sugar,** in a transformed palazzo, now the most aesthetic retail space in Tuscany.

Late afternoon: Waiters with trays of spritzes aloft, the clanging of bells, exuberant life, Italian life, as enduring as ever. A Sunday in Arezzo raises my hopes for the world. A sweetly curated dinner at **Le Chiavi d'Oro** ends a memorable day. Stay, if you can, at **Sugar Rooms,** also dazzlingly restored. ∎

ABOVE: One of the restaurants tucked under Arezzo's arches OPPOSITE: Piero della Francesca's sublime fresco of Mary Magdalene at Arezzo's Cathedral of San Donato

Pienza: A Renaissance Haven

In Pienza, a long-dormant volcano crowns a wide valley that turns fluorescent in spring and gold-brown by late summer; sometimes snow falls on the cypresses in winter. Inside the city walls, a white, unadorned cathedral is the centerpiece. Residents here compete in cheese-rolling contests and run through the undulating countryside to honor the pope who put this town on the map. With the formidable help of architect Bernardo Rossellino, Pope Pius II, who was from the tiny village and wanted to transform his birthplace into a sort of summer Vatican, constructed the perfect Renaissance town. It's not coined "the ideal city" lightly. Pienza and the Val d'Orcia below it are now both UNESCO protected.

In the past decade, as travelers realized its immense beauty and resource, Pienza's popularity has soared. **La Bandita Townhouse,** the town's former nunnery, was lovingly converted into a 12-room hotel with a restaurant designed to showcase the flavors, rhythms, and strong local community of this jewel-like town. Elisabetta Giannetti offers an intimate bed-and-breakfast at **La Bellavita B&B.**

Restaurants here draw a loyal clientele for *pici,* the area's fatter answer to spaghetti. At **Latte di Luna,** a suckling pig (*maialino*) and roast potatoes are legendary for good reason, so it's essential to make a reservation. At **Sette di Vino,** grilled pecorino comes with a layer of pancetta melted on top (think of it as Pienza's answer to the croque monsieur but without the bread), as well as bruschetta with ricotta and spring onions and a bean soup that will become your new standard-bearer. At sunset, congregate

Known as Tuscany's ideal city, Pienza has sweeping views of the Val d'Orcia and a spectacular Renaissance main square, among other attractions.

at **Il Casello** bar to watch the deepening pink-gold light over an Aperol spritz.

One of the exciting aspects of Pienza is to see the new generation of businesses that have taken their place alongside the city's classics, including many delectable pecorino shops, the long-standing wine store **Enoteca di Ghino,** and classic artisan shops like **Bottega Artigiana del Cuoio** (known for its beautifully simple leather bracelets). The butcher, **Macelleria Scroccaro,** has been in the same family for generations, as has the vegetable and fruit shop, **L'Orto di Silvia.** The piazza in front of the bar that's been there since the pope's time is where kids run freely and grown-ups sip on *aperitivi* at **Bar La Posta.**

Within this ancient village, new creativity abounds among craftsmen and -women. At **Officine 904,** leather bags come in modern shapes and vibrant colors, while **La Porticina** owner Diletta Biagiotti curates a collection of local jewelry, clothes, and accessories that showcases young Italian designers.

Artisan Anna Porcu designing her antique cameo jewelry

Anna Porcu at **Antichità Caratelli Beatrice** reinvents antique cameos on leather cuffs, and Raffaella Zurlo uses recycled materials for furniture, glassware, and jewelry at **RiCreaRe.**

At **Prosit,** in addition to offering samples of local wine, cheese, and specialty items on-site, the owners have set up shipments of seasonal goodies they will send to you at home. There is even a juice bar; at **Buongusto,** try a green smoothie or unusual but delicious homemade gelato like *pesca lavanda,* peach with lavender. But perhaps no place better exemplifies the city's new energy than **Idyllium,** where artisanal cocktails with local herbs are served in a space almost reminiscent of Williamsburg in Brooklyn, New York. It's open late and serves up the perfect club sandwich to a crowd that spans many generations of Pientini. ∎

THE TALE OF THE TRAVELING SHEEP
Pecorino di Pienza has become its own brand. The milk is local, but the flocks had a long journey.

AS YOU DRIVE THROUGH the Val d'Orcia, you might start to notice them: flocks of sheep moving through the spring grass. The little bells around their necks tinkle in the distance. Snowy white sheepdogs keep watch over them, sometimes with a shepherd lying nearby looking up at the sky. The tableau seems conceived as an aesthetic pleasure for those traveling through the valley, but they offer something even more valuable—pecorino cheese.

Even if the milk comes from these nearby flocks, their story is one of migration. After World War II, many farm residents left the countryside with the dream of a better life in the cities. Many of their properties and surrounding land were left abandoned and fallow.

In the 1960s, though, the government came up with an idea to revitalize the lush settlements, offering Sardinian farmers the opportunity to come north with their sheep.

They sweetened the deal through incentives and low-percentage loans on stupendous parcels of land.

And so it was that the sheep came to their new home and became irrevocably connected to one of the area's best products. The cheese reflects what these ewes graze on. Marzolino, for example, the fresh version of pecorino, comes when the spring grass, full of herbs, is at its sweetest. Semi-aged rounds wrapped in grape leaves create a strong smell from streets away.

For a tasting, head to Pienza's **Marusco e Maria** with its full menu of different types—try the one wrapped and aged in walnut leaves—or to **Cugusi di Cugusi Silvana,** one of the most respected producers in the valley. **Agriturismo Bagnolo** remains a working farm; a tour there will give you a 101 in pecorino and other cheesemaking and you can bed down in one of their cozy apartments.

Frances's Favorites

In Your Glass

The quintessential grape of Tuscany is *sangiovese.* That the word means "blood of Jove" indicates how far down into the roots of the region these vines reach. We know *sangiovese,* at apogee, as Brunello di Montalcino, welcome at the best celebrations. At its friendliest, Vino Nobile di Montepulciano, and at its most accessible, Vino Rosso di Montepulciano. Many of the best Chiantis are 100 percent *sangiovese.*

When I first came to Tuscany, the question of what wine to drink was "Red or white?" The answer was always red, and the pitcher was poured from a green glass demijohn. Now the wine culture has exploded all over Italy— nowhere so brilliantly as in the coastal Maremma region, where Sassicaia, all cabernet sauvignon, holds court along with Ornellaia, a cabernet sauvignon with merlot and cabernet franc. The new blends acquired the name Super Tuscans, and the village of Bolgheri became a destination.

Less familiar, Carmignano—also a blend but from traditions harking all

the way back to the Etruscan—has a devoted following. High on spice and body, it's lawfully wedded to down-home, *genuino* Tuscan cooking.

Starting from practically zero, the Cortona area has become a serious contender for top syrahs. First came Luigi d'Alessandro's Il Bosco, a staple at my house, as is Baracchi Cortona Syrah Smeriglio. I'm partial to these; they resonate with the *terra* I call home. Stefano Amerighi sets a high mark with his biodynamic syrah, and upstart young vintners such as Mirko Zappini, who makes Calice, are right on his coattails.

Out of hundreds, I'm enamored with these spectacular Tuscan wines:
- Baracchi Brut Trebbiano (Metodo Classico), also Ardito
- Sette Ponti Crognolo
- Mastrojanni Brunello di Montalcino Vigna Schiena d'Asino
- Poliziano Nobile di Montepulciano Asinone
- Tenuta Le Farnete/Cantagallo Carmignano Riserva
- Grattamacco Bolgheri Superiore

Don't miss the traditional Tuscan after-dinner *vin santo* (sacred wine), a nutty elixir. Avignonesi's Occhio di Pernice (partridge eye) is one of the best.

Two special vineyard inns: Relais Mastrojanni in Montalcino and Il Falconiere in Cortona, which has the bonus of a Michelin-starred restaurant and an excellent cooking school. ∎

ABOVE: Huge metal barrels are a relatively recent addition to the wine cellar of legendary Tuscan producer Mastrojanni. OPPOSITE: The redbrick winery of Barone Ricasoli, an antique structure in Gaiole in Chianti

Best of
Tuscan Hill Towns

The scattering of hilltop fortifications and villages that dot Tuscany's countryside provide some of its greatest attractions. Here are some must-see spots.

Best to Rub Elbows With Nobility: Grab a coffee in Cetona's main piazza. The city's grand public square and beautiful houses have inspired expats and Romans alike to buy second homes here.

Best to Get Garden Envy: La Foce, an incredible villa with landscaped gardens designed by Cecil Pinsent, put the Val d'Orcia on the travelers' map. Free tours are held on the hour, but check their website.

Best for Oenophiles: Try a tasting at Montalcino's La Fortezza, where it's possible to sample many of the great Brunello wines all in one stop. Across the street, the new Locanda Drogheria Franci also has an excellent wine list.

Best to Go Off the Beaten Path: Visit Pitigliano, a town literally carved into the area's *tufo,* a type of creamy yellow stone. As well as being one of Tuscany's most picturesque villages, it has one of the most important former Jewish ghettos in the country.

Best to Take the Waters: Luxuriate in the natural thermal baths of Bagno Vignoni (Adler Thermae Resort is fab) or in the pools at San Giovanni d'Asso, Saturnia, and Rapolano Terme, among others.

Best to Get Transported: Dream of living in the village of Massa Marittima. Its uncrowded atmosphere and perfect architecture make it one of Tuscany's hidden gems.

Best to Join the Party: Take part in a local festival like Montepulciano's Bravio delle Botti, where muscly men in tights (well, you know what we mean) roll huge wine barrels up the precariously steep streets.

Best to Go Spiritual: Visit Benedictine abbeys like Sant'Antimo, outside Montalcino, for the evening vespers service, or San Galgano, near Siena, for its haunting missing roof and summer opera programs.

Best to Feel the Cinema: Follow in the footsteps of great movies filmed in this area—for example, walk along the *Gladiator* road, where Russell Crowe galloped home to try to save his family from the Roman legions; visit Juliet's family home as seen in Franco Zeffirelli's *Romeo and Juliet;* experience the town of Cortona, immortalized in the best-selling memoir *Under the Tuscan Sun;* tour Sant'Anna di Camprena's exquisite chapel, commemorated in *The English Patient;* or get to know Arezzo through the Oscar-winning lens of the magnificent film *Life Is Beautiful.*

Best to Make a Memory: Take a jaunt into tiny Monticchiello. Not only is it home to Ristorante Daria (don't miss a plate of the *tagliatelle* pasta with black truffles), it's also the birthplace of Teatro Povero, plays written and performed by village residents.

Best to Join the Pilgrimage: Follow the monks along the Via Francigena, the 1,100-mile (1,700 km) pilgrim route that runs from Rome to France.

Best to Go Gourmet: Book a table at Arnolfo, the town of Colle di Val d'Elsa's Michelin-starred restaurant, which very much deserves the hype. But work up an appetite in the hilly old town first.

Best to Go Back to the Earth: At Podere Il Casale, a sustainable farm with all kinds of animals from goats to donkeys, the Swiss-Italian owners make cheese and honey and serve up delicious homemade lunches overlooking the Val d'Orcia. ▪

During Montepulciano's Bravio delle Botti festival residents dress in medieval garb and race wine barrels down the streets.

In the Know

Where to Stay in the Hill Towns

Tuscany has always had a particular draw for those, whether local or expat, who want to open a small hotel, often with a restaurant attached. Food and hospitality come at different prices and with a particular audience to coddle.

Monteverdi Tuscany: This tiny, picturesque hamlet, perched in the hills above Sarteano, has been reinvented as a boutique resort with guest rooms spread through the stone buildings, a fantastic spa with an indoor Roman-style pool, a gallery, a restaurant, two bars, and cultural events.

Villa Bordoni: One of the fore-runners of the new generation of countryside boutique hotels that have become the Tuscan ideal, this 16th-century, 10-bedroom property outside Greve in Chianti was transformed by a Scottish couple with an eye for Italian authenticity but with new flair. Spend chillier evenings alongside the fire roaring in the excellent restaurant.

Villa Fontelunga: This red-painted villa close to Cortona, surrounded by olive groves and pretty gardens, makes for a great launchpad into the surrounding area. Rooms are romantic, and the twice-weekly dinner parties are one of the most fun events in "the Valley." The owners will be opening Borgo 69, a new resort and restaurant.

Borgo Santo Pietro: Once a pilgrimage stop for monks on their way to or from Rome, this painstakingly restored property was the brainchild of a Danish couple looking for a new Tuscan life. Elegant details include verdant gardens, antique chandeliers, and claw-foot bathtubs.

Tenuta Santo Pietro: This lovely family-owned estate sits just outside Pienza and is a well-priced option surrounded by vineyards, olive trees, and beautiful views of the Val d'Orcia.

Follonico B&B: More like staying at the home of a good friend, Follonico's four suites immerse guests into country life with dogs and geese wandering through the grounds, the smell of fresh bread wafting through the property, and co-hosts offering insider tips on the nearby area.

Locanda al Colle: This beautifully appointed boutique hotel close to Pisa mixes five-star amenities—a pool, private beach club access, perfectly appointed guest rooms—with warm hospitality.

Rosewood Castiglion del Bosco: This 5,000-acre (2,023 ha) resort, originally opened by the Ferragamo family and now run by Rosewood, is one of the most luxurious in the region, with a golf course and its own spa. Be sure to visit the small chapel with its exquisite fresco by Pietro Lorenzetti as well as the vast kitchen garden full of seasonal produce. The spacious guest rooms feel like their own fiefdom outside of Montalcino.

La Bandita Countryhouse: An eight-room farmhouse lovingly transformed into a boutique hotel offers 360-degree views of the Val d'Orcia, an infinity pool overlooking Pienza, and an orange-tiled hammam.

Borgo Pignano: A 750-acre (303 ha) estate with an 18th-century villa as its centerpiece, this is an impressive organic farm that's well worth the visit (they make exquisite honey). Featuring an unusual infinity pool built into a former quarry, this hotel offers a lovely sense of seclusion, even though it's a close drive to cities like Volterra.

Fonte Bertusi: This charming family-owned spot (helmed by a father and son who also happen to be artists) has a wonderful annual music festival and is perfectly priced.

Rent Your Own Pad: Lots of visitors to Tuscany rent their own villa, and it's a particularly good option for special celebrations, destination weddings, and family get-togethers. Among the agencies to check out are Unique Properties and Events, Merrion Charles, and Via Villas. ▪

A good night's sleep awaits at La Bandita Countryhouse, a boutique hotel in Pienza.

Hot Spot
Siena and Lucca

Bareback horses gallop at full pace around a wide piazza. Jockeys in silk costumes emblazoned with symbols shout insults to each other as they flick their whips at one another. The crowd roars as they jostle for position on the starting line. The race begins, riders are thrown—and no matter, the competition continues, the steeds career in and out of the colorful group. This is the Palio. This is Siena.

Much as Florence is the model for Tuscany's Renaissance period, so is **Siena** the epitome of the medieval era, carved up into different *contrade,* or neighborhoods. At the Palio, an age-old horse-racing competition, the city once again turns insular, its families divided back into the areas where they were born.

But the race is not the only ritual here. Climb the **Torre del Mangia,** Siena's iconic tower, to get a sense of the city's layout. At **Nannini,** a beloved pastry institution, sample *panforte* and *ricciarelli,* the crunchy almond cookies best enjoyed alongside an espresso. Insiders grab a table on the ground floor of **Le Logge** for a plate of *taglierini al tartufo,* fresh pasta with truffles. Or stock up on picnic supplies at **Antica Pizzicheria** with its wild boar sausages and bottles of local vintages. In the evening, join locals at **Da Trombicche** for an *aperitivo* and plate of salami. And after hours on the weekend, live music sets the tone at **Un Tubo.**

If Siena veers medieval, **Lucca** is all about Romanesque architecture. There are more than 100 churches. At Lucca's duomo, **San Martino,** art history buffs are besotted by Jacopo della Quercia's exquisite tomb for Illaria del Carretto. And the town's **Piazza del Anfiteatro** still exemplifies the perfect shape of Roman construction.

The centerpiece at the fifth-generation **Pasticceria Taddeucci,** among the other appealing sweets, is *buccellato Lucchese,* a cross between bread and a sweeter coffee cake. *Tortelli Lucchese* is another specialty, this one stuffed with meat and topped with ragù. Try it at **Ristorante Giglio** on the idyllic piazza of the same name, or **Da Francesco,** which arguably has the best version in town. ▪

One of Lucca's many photo options, San Francesco church and monastery

Chapter Ten
UMBRIA

Green heart of Italy: that's what the tourist brochures say about Umbria. And they're right. Velvety hills everywhere, villages decorating all the dips and surges. To travel well in Umbria means giving in to the urge to take that alluring turn, follow that spire, veer into the narrow gate of a village on market day to buy grapes and slices of *porchetta,* that super-savory roasted whole pig. • The joy of Umbria, just over the border from Tuscany,

is the close-to-the-earth way of life preserved here. Take your time; no rush. The lofty white village of Spello has spread across the hillside forever. Assisi, Spoleto, Montefalco, Bevagna: Something unique marks each of these towns. Assisi may have a parking lot with escalators conveying thousands of pilgrims up to the center—but once there, you'll find this place possesses something profound that throngs can't alter. The calm spirituality of San Francesco emanates from the pale stones, and seeing Giotto's paintings is on any art lover's wish list. Roman remains at Spoleto, frescoes of Benozzo Gozzoli in Montefalco, the haphazard architecture of Bevagna's piazza—all are far from madding crowds. To those contemplating a move to Italy, I always say, "Look into Umbria."

On a tufa stone lookout, the Orvieto duomo's glittering facade could welcome us to heaven. Inside, the fresco cycle of heaven and hell by Luca Signorelli is one of the glories of the Renaissance. His vivid depiction of hell must have scared the populace into virtue. Look for the blond woman riding the back of a demon; her expression of fear is unforgettable. The paradise sections seem quite bland in contrast.

From our land outside Cortona, we look into Umbria: hills with shadows in the folds, an ancient tower, and the blue crescent of Lake Trasimeno. Often on day trips, we head that way.

We especially love livable Città di Castello, with its bookstores and café-lined piazza guarded by twin clocks: one for minutes, one for hours. Rich with palazzi and churches, Città is also home to two museums spotlighting the work of Alberto Burri. A doctor in World War II, he was captured and sent as a prisoner of war to Texas, where he began making art out of found materials such as cardboard and cellophane. After the war, he never went back to medicine; instead, he continued his experiments, eventually influencing Robert Rauschenberg and many others. He left his work to his hometown. Città is a proud market town, surrounded by impressive double walls.

WHAT YOU NEED TO KNOW...

- **BEST TIME TO VISIT:** As in neighboring Tuscany, Umbria's countryside tends to close down after Epiphany (January 6) until mid-March (although bigger towns like Perugia remain vibrant due to the thriving university student population). Since Umbria is a real foodie region, you may want to align your dates according to the seasonal produce you like best.

- **TOP SPOTS:** Perugia, Assisi, Lake Trasimeno, Orvieto, Città della Pieve, Sibillini National Park, Bevagna, Montefalco, Gubbio, Spoleto, Todi

- **GETTING THERE:** Outside Perugia, the small airport of San Francesco d'Assisi serves private planes and low-budget airlines. Alternatively, fly into Rome or Florence and rent a car; it's about a two-hour drive from either city.

Novella Nicolini's ceramic workshop, a third-generation family-owned business in Deruta

The joy of Umbria, just over the border from Tuscany, is the close-to-the-earth way of life preserved here. Take your time; no rush.

With the nearby Tiber, chestnut woods, and lush countryside, this is one of Umbria's sweet spots.

Umbria may be landlocked, but Trasimeno, the largest lake on the peninsula and fourth largest in Italy, provides nine beaches, as well as a lovely loop of medieval villages along the shores. Bike and walking trails are numerous, and late afternoons are glorious, with luminous marigold and rose sunsets smearing the sky and tinting the water.

The castle town Castiglione del Lago juts into the water. Children can scramble among the ramparts and parapets. Several shops sell the *fagiolini del Trasimeno,* a small prized bean. Restaurants feature yellow eel, perch, carp roasted like

The hand-weaving atelier of Giuditta Brozzetti in Perugia's church of San Francesco delle Donne

porchetta, and other lake fish. We go there for *serpentone,* a snaky-shaped pastry filled with fruit and ground almonds.

From there and from Passignano, just around the bend, catch a boat for a tour of the lake's three islands. Isola Maggiore, where St. Francis spent a Lenten season, was once known for fishing and lacemaking, Now, only about 20 inhabitants remain. The simple Hotel da Sauro offers a respite for lunch after walking around the island.

In Passignano, stroll along the lake and stop by the two shops selling the famous Umbrian Deruta pottery. Some are well-priced seconds. It's a sweet overnight too, especially if you choose the intimate Il Fischio del Merlo (The Blackbird's Whistle) for dinner.

Umbria maintains a strong craft tradition, especially wrought iron, textiles, and ceramics. If you live here (or in Tuscany), it's likely that you have a preferred *fabbro,* blacksmith, for your iron gate, lanterns, fireplace tools, pergola, drain covers, and holders for roof gutters. Textiles in Umbria go back to medieval guilds; contemporary fabric designers still take inspiration for their weaving patterns from Renaissance fabrics, often those seen in paintings.

Linens are my weakness, second only to the colorful majolica pottery historically associated with the region. In the main street shops of the hilltop town of Montefalco, I find tablecloths and placemats (made for Americans, as they are not traditional in Italy) in the soft rose, wheat, plum, and chalky blues of the frescoes. Aprons and hand and kitchen towels make exquisite gifts, especially paired with a few bars of the marvelous Italian soaps sold everywhere.

Gualdo Tadino, Orvieto, and Gubbio are major ceramic towns. Often a pattern is associated with a location. Who can resist one of the cheery red, blue, and white rooster pitchers from Orvieto? Gubbio artists seem to favor pomegranate bor-

A road twisting through Passignano sul Trasimeno, one of the charming villages scattered on the shores of Umbria's Lake Trasimeno

ders. The large platters are dramatic and useful for lavish selections of antipasti. After touring this proud town, try the Umbrian specialties at Porta Tessenaca.

Especially tempting for ceramic lovers is the hill town of Deruta, about 12 miles (20 km) from Perugia. It's command central for majolica and has been since 1200. First, visit the Museo Regionale della Ceramica di Deruta for historical context. The town burgeons with shops, and often an artist is demonstrating her Raphael-stylized dragon or grapevine border. On the edge of town, the venerable workshop Ubaldo Grazia offers a large showroom of wares. Some are seconds, and you see on the bottom which U.S. store the piece was destined for before it got a dust mote embedded in the glaze. Small flaws, big savings. Also, it's possible to order a set of tableware tailored to your designs or monogrammed. I ordered and shipped a set of 12 place settings—plates, pasta bowls, salad plates, and espresso cups. The colorful fruits and vines on a white background please me every time I take them from the cupboard.

Of the many attractions of Perugia, paramount is the Galleria Nazionale dell'Umbria in the Palazzo dei Priori. On display are many works by the majors—Piero della Francesca, Perugino, Fra Angelico, Duccio, and others from the 13th century onward. Afterward a visit to the atelier of Alvaro Breccolotti, called DUCA, offers a complementary experience. DUCA's work, primarily still lifes, is more real than real. He infuses a pot of garlic, a single cabbage, a ripe persimmon with presence and luminosity. (For an appointment, info@ducanet.com.)

Many small moments make up the pleasures of Umbria. Lunch under a grape arbor outside the hilltop town of Todi, with the scent of figs warmed by the sun. Buying tiny lentils and sausages in the village of Norcia, where heads of wild boar look down from the walls of the shop. In Città della Pieve, standing transfixed by the Perugino painting "L'Adorazione dei Magi," and then realizing the landscape behind the figures is the beautiful and familiar Lake Trasimeno. Hills at evening spreading like a blue pleated skirt, sunset over autumn vineyards lit copper and gold. Umbria moves quietly into your heart.

Insider's Guide

Perugia and Assisi: A Crossroads of Art and Spirituality

Poor **Perugia** has suffered its share of bad publicity in recent years. In October 2016, newspapers published slightly misleading maps of its proximity to the epicenter of a series of nearby earthquakes. The multiple murder trials of American college student Amanda Knox brought a deluge of negative attention to the city (although even as a backdrop, its undeniable beauty shines through). And despite the lures of its annual summer jazz festival, Perugia tends to lose out to Florence when it comes to travel coverage in glossy magazines.

But travelers who do make the trip here will discover lovely surprises around every corner: one of the oldest universities in Italy, set within a series of exquisite palazzi; new bars and restaurants, set alongside city institutions. Art history and architecture buffs will find 18th-century buildings mixed in with Etruscan structures, Gothic style among medieval, all lining long thoroughfares that spill down the hill into smaller neighborhoods.

Start your rambles at the church of **Sant'Angelo,** one of the most unusual in Italy with its circular structure atop a pagan temple (16 columns from different ages surround the altar). Next, stroll along Corso Vannucci, Perugia's main drag, with a stop in at **Pasticceria Sandri,** a beaux arts—or *bella arte*—fixture from 1860, for espresso and a slice of Sacher cake, a chocolate delicacy transported from Austria. Once you're sufficiently refueled, head to the **Galle-**

Magical light at the Basilica di San Francesco in Assisi, a UNESCO World Heritage site and the city's spiritual heart, named for its patron saint

ria **Nazionale dell'Umbria,** housed in a 13th-century palazzo, to see some of the region's finest artworks.

Umbria is celebrated for its artisanal ingredients, and Perugia showcases them exquisitely at restaurants like **Osteria a Priori,** specializing in food from the region (olive oil and truffles, please!). **Trattoria del Borgo** offers dishes like handmade *strangozzi,* a typical Umbrian wheat pasta, with pesto made of Umbrian wild herbs. Before or after, have a cocktail at **Mercato Vianova,** a stylish cocktail bar that serves up all the classics.

After Perugia, make the pilgrimage to **Assisi.** It's hard to overstate this city's religious importance for Catholics, but even atheists will feel its deep spirituality. The heart of town lies near the **Basilica di San Francesco d'Assisi,** where frescoes by Giotto and other masters bring the story of St. Francis to life in glorious detail (and might just bring you to tears). Busloads of devotees come to town for the pleasure of experiencing one of the most powerful spiritual and artistic masterpieces in Europe, but it's

Delicate desserts at Pasticceria Sandri in Perugia

easy enough to lose them if you head to the main sanctuaries early in the morning or late in the day. The **Bosco di San Francesco,** the little park alongside the basilica, provides a green canvas in which to absorb all this beauty. And a visit to the **Basilica di Santa Chiara,** the monument for Francis's first "sister," or first nun of the order, should also be on the itinerary.

Walking up the **Corso** to the **Temple of Minerva** puts the history of Assisi into high relief: The Middle Ages reside above you in the medieval buildings, with the Roman ruins below. Foodies flock to **Osteria Piazzetta dell'Erbe** for good reason: The fresh, seasonal menu keeps local residents coming back, and in the summer, you can snag an outdoor table in the tiny square. ∎

CHECKING IN

Whether drawn to the region for a spiritual retreat or for more gluttonous pastimes, visitors will discover that this region tends to run the gamut when it comes to lodging options. Here are some spots from which to launch your expeditions.

SINA BRUFANI: Despite a slightly threadbare initial impression, this inn's perfect position at the start of Corso Vannucci, along with an affordable price tag, makes it one of the best choices in Perugia.

LOCANDA DELLA POSTA: Talk about a storied past: Goethe and Hans Christian Andersen are among the famous guests who have bedded down here during a stay in Perugia. Following a complete renovation in 2017, the luxury town house now offers original frescoes alongside modern bathrooms and sleek wood floors. Snag a fourth-floor room to enjoy the fireplace and balcony.

BORGO DEI CONTI: For a more rural experience—think acres of olive trees, terraced gardens, and a peaceful swimming pool—book a room at this estate that's about a half-hour drive from Perugia. (You might just end up staying in the spa instead of sightseeing.)

NUN ASSISI: This boutique hotel is pretty flawless, especially when it comes to the spa housed in the Roman ruins beneath the former nunnery. The restaurant—despite the rather unfortunate name, Eat Out Osteria Gourmet—is also excellent. (Poached egg with pecorino cream and truffles? Yes, please.)

Hot Spot
Lake Trasimeno

T hose who love a good sunset (and who doesn't?) understand that driving past this heavenly lake on the Perugia SS 71 at the end of the day is, well, transcendental. The clouds are reflected in the water's surface; the outline of the islets sits against the orange horizon; the lake's curves become shaded and illuminated as if the Ascension really is about to take place.

Yes, **Trasimeno** is indeed very special, both historically and in its present-day incarnation. This was where Hannibal defeated the Romans and where Puccini found inspiration for many of his operas. Celebrated Star Wars director George Lucas has an estate on these shores, and British heartthrob Colin Firth (*Pride and Prejudice* and *Bridget Jones's Diary*) makes this place his second home with his Italian wife and kids. (Take that, Como!)

Once you explore the lake for yourself, you'll understand why the area's an overlooked gem with tiny villages. For example, **Monte del Lago** is populated with little houses and perfectly tended gardens, like the one that surrounds the grand villa that Puccini once loved. Its main thoroughfare leads down to a pier that seems constructed for a quiet meditation overlooking the water.

Seafood lovers head to Castiglione del Lago's **L'Acquario** for *regina carpa* (queen carp), smoked eel, or *tegamaccio,* a type of fish soup that's particularly good with a glass of Vino Colli di Trasimeno. Passignano's **Trattoria del Pescatore** dates back to 1947 and is housed in a former olive press. Once you've had your fill, you can take a boat ride from the main dock to islands like the uninhabited **Polvese,** where you'll find a public park with a monastery, the church of San Giuliano, and a 14th-century castle.

History buffs will want to take a tour of **Tuoro sul Trasimeno,** an ancient Etruscan city that saw Hannibal's epic victory over the Roman army. And in the tiny village of **Castel Rigone,** make sure to visit the **Sanctuary of Maria Santissima dei Miracoli,** one of the most beautiful examples of Umbria's Renaissance architecture. ∎

A sweeping view onto Lake Trasimeno's Polvese Island

Frances's Favorites

In Your Glass

Sagrantino, the pinnacle of Umbrian wines, is not for sissies. The wine's tannins can be tongue-twisters. Although some appreciate that jolt, I rely on my good wine guide and app to lead me to tamed but still forceful bottles. Sagrantino stands up to a pork roast and acts its part with a roast guinea hen, but pour a glass late at night by a fire and you'll see just what "meditation wine" means. Maybe I'm a big fan of Arnaldo Caprai's versions because his were the first ones I loved. But around the town of Montefalco, there are several other awesome producers of this native grape known as little holy wine: Lungarotti, F.lli Pardi, Tudernum, and Tenuta Bellafonte.

The area of Orvieto produces casual whites that go so well with summer lunches and picnics. Decugnano dei Barbi's Orvieto Classico Superiore Il Bianco represents the area well. Tenuta Le Velette produces another good Orvieto Classico called Berganorio.

From the shores of Lake Trasimeno, look for Castello di Magione's Colli del Trasimeno Grechetto, and Pucciarella's numerous offerings of both red and white. ∎

> Sagrantino acts its part with a roast guinea hen, but pour a glass late at night by a fire and you'll see just what "meditation wine" means.

ABOVE: A street leading to Orvieto's spectacular and unmissable 13th-century duomo filled with priceless frescoes by Fra Angelico and Luca Signorelli
OPPOSITE: A bunch of grapes to make the famous Orvieto Classico, a drinkable and well-priced white vintage

Built into multiple elevations on a formidable hill, Gubbio is one of Umbria's prettiest and best preserved towns.

Insider's Guide

Hill Towns of Umbria:
One for Every Season, One for Every Reason

The rivalry between Tuscany and Umbria is legendary. For every Tuscany lover, an irate Umbrian will assert that its counterparts are better: My castle is older. My *borgo* is less touristy but MORE beautiful. My fresco was more painstakingly restored. My food is more sustainable. The best way to determine who's right? Explore Umbria's hill towns yourself.

Just over the border from Tuscany, **Città del Pieve** is an exquisite medieval village formerly inhabited by Etruscans and Romans. The birthplace of the great Renaissance artist Pietro Vannucci (more often known as Pietro Perugino), the town is home to several of his works, including the fresco of the "Adoration of the Magi" and "Madonna and Child." Robert Wirth, the owner of Rome's celebrated Hotel Hassler, has recently bought the **Hotel Vannucci,** which significantly upped the luxury quotient in the area.

Sure, Italy's chockablock with insanely beautiful cathedrals, but the city of **Orvieto** should be high on the list for any visitor to Umbria. Inside the striped duomo dating from the 13th century, you'll find exquisite frescoes from Fra Angelico and Luca Signorelli. Afterward hit **Trattoria dell'Orso** for seasonal standouts like fresh tagliatelle with truffles.

The walled medieval town of **Bevagna** oozes charm—especially if you're sitting at an outdoor table at **La Bottega di Assù,** the restaurant that inspired the owner of New York's beloved il Buco. Here the focus is on only Umbrian producers, with the olive oil, honey, and cheese used in the restaurant's sumptuous dishes also available from the shelves to take home. A visit to the 12th-century church of **San Michele** in the beautiful Piazza Silvestri is a must too.

Perched high above the Umbrian Plain, **Montefalco** not only boasts some of the best views in the region but is also known as its finest eating town. Among the many excellent restaurants there, **L'Alchimista** in the main piazza is a standout: the kind of homestyle cooking that could have been created by your Umbrian *nonna. Gnocchi al Sagratino,* for example, comes cooked in the town's celebrated wine. Afterward, stop in to the **Museo di San Francesco,** located in a former church dedicated to the saint featuring beautiful works by Perugino (the teacher of Raphael) and Benozzo Gozzoli.

Do you like wildflowers? If so, plan to visit the remote Piano Grande in the **Mount Sibillini National Park** in June, when the entire plain is blanketed with blooms. In the tiny nearby village of

Flowerboxes hung from the town of Città della Pieve's distinctive redbrick facades

Castelluccio, have an espresso before taking in the views; the feeling of solitude is deeply restorative.

Like their neighbors in Tuscany, Umbrians take their olive oil very seriously. Surrounded by acres of olive groves, **Trevi'**s liquid gold has its own DOP. Try it in local dishes at **Taverna del Sette,** also known for its truffles.

Antique lovers should make tracks to the monthly market in the main piazza of **Pissignano** (yes, you read that right). On the first Sunday of every month, the FairTrade event is filled with

CHECKING IN

Many of Umbria's fans tend to make repeat visits and set up shop for a good amount of time. Thanks to the sense of refuge in the hotels here, one can understand the loyalty to the region.

EREMITO: This former hermitage qualifies as one of the most unusual hotels in Italy, with single bedrooms in the former monks' cells and a steam room built into the old rock foundations. The views are epic, overlooking the bluff and forest below, and the style epitomizes monastic-chic with throw pillows and candles for meditation—perfect for the spiritually minded or just those who need a break from civilization.

TORRE DI MORAVOLA: The love child of Christopher Chong, a former Norman Foster architect, and his wife, designer

Seonaid Mackenzie, these seven suites are flawlessly encased within a former 12th-century tower. And the rooftop pool is truly unparalleled. This boutique retreat is a must-stay for design lovers.

PALAZZO SENECA: The main draws of this 16th-century structure are its stunning position in Norcia (famous for its truffles) and its perfect access point into the Mount Sibillini National Park. A candlelit spa, intuitive service, and a recent Michelin star provide just a few of the others.

vintage furniture and clothing. Afterward, head to the remarkable Roman *tempietto,* a tiny temple, at the **Fonti del Clitunno.** Lord Byron and Virgil were only two of the poets won over by the beauty of this little park.

Perched on Monte Ingino, the town of **Gubbio** is one of Umbria's true treasures. Start in the medieval Piazza Grande, framed by the 14th-century Palazzo dei Consoli and the Palazzo del Podestà, before walking through the impeccably preserved town. Despite its rather rickety look, the *funivia,* cable car, that whisks you up to the top of the hill, offering views of the town and countryside stretching below, is worth the fright. Insiders bring a picnic to match the epic panorama.

Arched street in Città della Pieve

Even compared with Umbria's steepest hill towns, **Todi's** vertical streets are off the charts. But it's more than worth exploring this old town, ringed by three walls like something out of a fairy tale. (The interior wall dates back to the Etruscans, the middle the Romans, and the outer to the Middle Ages.) Although it has become a little more touristy than its counterparts since it was deemed one of the world's most sustainable towns, you can still participate in the quiet routine of the residents or visit during the **Todi Festival,** the town's annual music and art festival.

Umbria's full of festivals during the year, and **Spoleto** gets its turn with the Festival dei Due Mondi, offering more than two weeks of music, theater, and dance. But whatever the season, this town is a stunner, sitting with the grand Apennines at its shoulders. ■

ABOVE: The grand palaces of Piazza dei Priori in Perugia look like a film set when lit up at night. **OPPOSITE:** An aerial shot of Perugia shows the Umbrian city's impeccable layout overlooking the plains below.

In the Know

Local Flavors: Truffles, Cheese, and Lentils

Umbria's food roots run deep. These are not necessarily Michelin-starred places, but rather simple, traditional restaurants with an emphasis on seasonal and local ingredients. Truffles loom large; although the white ones are available only in the fall, you can get your hands on the black ones year-round. **Norcia** offers up some of the very best in the region, often served on *strangozzi,* a long, thick pasta. And the town produces a salty but delicious prosciutto.

One of the most inspiring aspects of Umbria is the food shops that sell only products made in the region. **La Vostra Cantina** in Castelluccio di Norcia is a marvelous emporium featuring pecorino, lentils, honey, and olive oil; go for the *norcerie*—rustic salamis and other cured meats. Another shop that prizes the region's DNA is Perugia's **Umbrò,** a spot that sells organic ingredients from local farmers. Try the olive oil from the groves between Spello and Spoleto.

In Umbria, mushrooms, wild asparagus, and herbs come foraged from the woods and plains that characterize its craggy terrain. Legumes like lentils and beans grown organically figure prominently as the base for hearty winter soups when temperatures drop. Game comes roasted in large, wood-burning pizza ovens or in pasta sauces. Cheese from the region includes a goat variety from **Diego Calcabrina,** whose fame might seem a little exaggerated until you try it and become a convert too.

His production sells out quickly and you can visit his farm, but only with a reservation.

Above Spoleto, visit **Agriturismo Bartoli,** a huge truffle reserve, with truffle hunting available with the owners' pair of well-nosed canines. Afterward, you can eat your spoils with homemade pasta.

And what about the vino? In Umbria, you'll find less well known and less pricey wines than in neighboring Tuscany. One of the main offerings comes from **Montefalco** with a 100 percent *sagrantino,* the world's most tannic wine. Perfect for heavier dishes, it is reputed by fans to have antiaging antioxidants. Paolo Bea's "Pagliaro Secco" Sagrantino di Montefalco 2006 has cult status. The regular Montefalco Rosso is a lighter blend: a ruby red vintage that goes down easy right after harvesting. Torgiano, close to Perugia, got a DOCG upgrade back in 1990; its wines are a mix of *sangiovese* and *canaiolo* that need to be aged at least three years. Try the Lungarotti Rubesco Riserva "Vigna Monticchio." For white wine lovers, go for the Orvieto DOC, a mix of *grechetto,* trebbiano, and other white aromatic grapes; many good bottles cost less than $20. ∎

OPPOSITE: Caciotta is only one of the delectable cheeses available in Umbria's town of Norcia.
ABOVE: Dried lentils ready for hearty stews and soups are another of Norcia's staples.

Frances's Favorites

La Fioritura (The Flowering)

My Italian neighbors love their motorcycles even if they rarely use them. When on early summer weekends I see them roar off, I know they're headed to Piano Grande to see the poppies.

The slopes of the Sibillini Mountains surround a high plain, a former glacial lake of about six square miles (16 sq km). Depending on fluctuations of weather, the plateau puts forth a breathtaking display of wildflowers in May, June, even into July. The blood-red poppies are only the most brazen of the unfurling, which also includes wild tulips, muscari, gentian, narcissi, oxalis, violets, cornflowers, chicory, asphodels, cyclamens, and crocuses.

Looking down from a distance, it seems that fallen rainbows are melting onto the fields. The flowery expanse lies at 4,166 feet (1,270 m) within the **Parco Nazionale dei Monti Sibillini.** Its many walking paths are marked, and a trail map is widely available. The shores of blue, blue Lake Fiastra and the trails up Mount Vettore (8,100 feet/2,476 m) are lovely for walks.

Where is the cave of the namesake prophet Sibilla? Lost in myth. What does remain (though severely damaged by the 6.6 earthquake of 2016) is the village of **Castelluccio,** famous for tiny organic lentils always paired with the pork charcuterie of the area. Most Italians cook lentils at New Year's, as the coin shape symbolizes prosperity to come. Known as *lenticchie di Castellucio,* they are done in 20 minutes and require no presoaking.

Food-focused **Norcia** is a splendid little town within the park. Also badly shaken by the quake, the *centro* has remarkably recovered (but for the Basilica of San Benedetto). Food shops decorated with mounted boars' heads soon reopened, displaying their wares out front: baskets of dried porcini, sacks of local polenta, strings of sausages, and hanks of prosciutto. In fall and winter, black truffles are on show. Truffle biscotti? Not sure about that. The *tartufo* even flavors a grappa and an *amaro,* an after-dinner bitter.

So known are the local pig butchers that all over Italy a pork butcher shop is known as a *norcineria.* Every bit is used in the sausages, *salume,* and cured meats. Try the popular salami *coglioni di mulo,* mule's balls. Don't worry; the name is based on the shape, not the ingredient. Minced and seasoned pork is formed around a center of *lardo,* dorsal fat. How pleasant, lunch while sitting outside at **Locanda del Teatro** and tasting the array of boar and pork *salume,* along with some local pecorino and a bowl of that famous lentil soup with rustic bread. Stay overnight at **Palazzo Seneca,** with its candlelit restaurant, Vespasia. Or try the same family's atmospheric restaurant, **Granaro del Monte 1850.** For a country stay (and this area is wonderful for that), check out **Agriturismo Il Casale degli Amici,** also with a restaurant serving authentic Umbrian dishes.

The vast park spreads into adjacent Le Marche. Since they're so close to *la fioritura,* why not cross the border and visit two more enchanting towns, Visso and Ascoli Piceno? ■

ABOVE: Horses run free in the idyllic landscapes of Umbria's Mount Sibillini National Park. **OPPOSITE:** *La fioritura,* "the flowering," brings the incredible fields of blooming poppies and other wildflowers.

The work of Alberto Burri, one of Umbria's most famous artists, is housed at Fondazione Palazzo Albizzini in Città di Castello.

Insider's Guide

Umbrian Art: From Craftsmen to Contemporary

Umbria has a long history of craftmanship, and many of Umbria's products, from textiles to clothing, come from small, often family-owned workshops. One of the best of these is Perugia's **Giuditta Brozzetti,** housed in the 12th-century church of San Francisco delle Donne. Four generations of the same family have created textiles on 18th- and 19th-century wood looms, an intricate and time-consuming labor. The details are exquisite.

Even larger companies focus on keeping Umbria's productions ethical and local. Cashmere king **Brunello Cucinelli** has reinvigorated the town of Solomeo, outside Perugia, by establishing his factory in an old castle and founding a school for the art of creating handcrafted clothing. It is replete with acres of olive trees and vineyards, and there are plans for a hotel in the future. Cucinelli wanted the business to become an example of how local economy, artistic collaboration, and teaching could inspire future generations to continue old methods of craftsmanship. His cashmere is heavenly soft.

From food to architecture, Umbria tends toward the traditional—which is why the new movement to highlight contemporary art feels so fresh and exciting. Massimo Lauro, one of the forerunners in contemporary collecting, is originally from Naples (his wife and fellow art lover, Angela, is an American), but in the 1960s, his family bought a house outside Città della Pieve and fell in love with the area. The couple opened a contemporary art museum there in 2009.

Today, the **Giardino dei Lauri** has become more than a collection; it's more of a collaborative lab that specializes in promoting artists under 40 years old. Admission is free, to encourage people to visit the former warehouse that is now a light-filled space that includes site-specific pieces. More than 70 pieces of art—paintings, sculptures, installations, and multimedia—are in rotation, with works by a variety of renowned artists, including Martin Creed, Ugo Rondinone, Takashi Murakami, Maurizio Cattelan, Urs Fischer, and Rudolf Stingel. Out in the garden, an enormous rainbow sculpture reads "Where do we go from here?"

Umbrian artist Alberto Burri landed pieces in New York's Guggenheim and London's Tate among other museums. He died in 1995, but his abstract collages and cracked paintings live on in his hometown of Città di Castello, showcased at **Palazzo Albizzini.** Later installations are exhibited in evocative, former tobacco-drying warehouses on the outskirts of town. The foundation also boasts a research library that's a treasure trove for contemporary art students.

One of the most interesting collections of outdoor pieces has to be **Sculptori a Brufa,** which since 1987 has been installing art in the town of Brufa and in the surrounding rolling hills (it's not uncommon to be hiking through the deep country and suddenly come across an evocative steel sculpture). Its program BrufArte Giovani highlights younger artists.

Flash Art, a well-regarded Italian magazine, also put contemporary art on the map here. The publication's editor is from Umbria's Trevi, and he launched an art festival in partnership with the **Palazzo Lucarini Contemporary** that is now an annual event. ∎

Umbria tends toward the traditional—which is why the new movement to highlight contemporary art feels so fresh and exciting.

CLOCKWISE FROM LEFT: "Untitled (The Thing)" at Giardino dei Lauri; another piece at Giardino dei Lauri; an installation at Palazzo Lucarini Contemporary

Mezzogiorno: midday. This word applies to sun-blessed Lazio. Maybe it's the *laz . . .* in Lazio. Just saying the name induces a slowdown, a definite lazy lean toward la dolce vita. Securely, this south-central region possesses one of the best climates on planet Earth. (I've had dinner outside on New Year's Eve in Rome.) In other cities— New York, London, Istanbul—a frenetic momentum prevails. But Rome lures you to

a long lunch, to frequent café stops, window shopping, gelato strolls, and late dinners on terraces where balmy breezes barely stir the palm branches.

Rome invites. Invites walks under the sycamores along the Tiber, through the Borghese gardens, along the Via Veneto, from fountain to fountain, up the city's seven hills, and down the Corso. Of all the major cities, it's the greatest for walking, especially in the morning as the city awakens.

A man in a beret is playing the xylophone in the rain. Two lovers seem to be drinking a case of each other on the bridge. Three African nuns sail along in white habits, each eating a *cornetto.* A Moto Guzzi blasts off at the light, weaving among Fiats and leaving them in his dust. Domes and sudden columns from antiquity appear, even a gigantic marble foot, all that's left of someone colossal. A metal shade roars up: shop opening. Cats sleeping in the ruins. A roof garden to envy. More gelato. Shops with killer shoes. Roma, not built even in a millennium, but yours in a day or three or ten.

Everyone enters Rome with a to-do list: Colosseum. Sistine Chapel. Spanish Steps. Trastevere. Campidoglio's Capitoline Museums. The thrilling walk through the ruins in the ancient heart. And the Pantheon. (Try to stand under the oculus when it's raining or—rare and magical—snowing.) That's a start.

To that list, add: Galleria Doria Pamphilj, in the palace still occupied by the noble family, whose superb art collection includes Caravaggio, Bernini, Titian, Correggio, and many others. Here's a chance to glimpse old-world villa splendor. Palazzo Barberini, where in usually uncrowded ease, you can discover three Caravaggios and major works by Bronzino, Filippo Lippi, Reni, Raphael, and more. Count on the Scuderie del Quirinale, housed in the former stables of government palaces built in the 18th century, to have a compelling exhibit. MAXXI and Macro, two contemporary museums worth the out-of-the-way locations, represent our own time.

In Basilicata Santa Maria del Popolo, find two more Caravaggios depicting the crucifixion of Saint Peter and the conversion of Saint Paul, and his celebrated triptych, "The Calling of St. Matthew," in the church of San Luigi dei Francesi. Make your way to the Galleria d'Arte Moderna for a visit to 20th-century Italian modernist painting. And back to the

---

WHAT YOU NEED TO KNOW...

- **BEST TIME TO VISIT:** Rome goes on all cylinders all year round, except for August, when anyone with any sense goes to the beach. The Christmas season is atmospheric, and the crisp days of spring and fall bring the city's luminous light into exquisite focus.

- **TOP SPOTS:** Rome, Ponza, Viterbo, Civita di Bagnoregio

- **GETTING THERE:** Fly into Fiumicino or Ciampino airport.

Piazza Navona in Rome used to be flooded by the ancient Romans for amusing boat races.

Lazio: Just saying the name induces a slowdown, a lazy lean toward la dolce vita. This south-central region possesses one of the best climates on Earth.

beginnings, Ara Pacis, built from 13 to 9 B.C. The monument was Emperor Augustus's altar to peace, now encased in a glass museum designed by American architect Richard Meier. What a privilege for him. The marble altar is intricately carved with vegetal motifs and highly individualistic Romans in procession. Outside, Meier's fountain plays, the plainest in Rome.

These treasure troves are major stakes in the culture of the West. Then there's gelato. At the paradigm Gelateria del Teatro, Via dei Coronari, 65/66, the melon, lemon, and other fruit flavors reveal their true essences. Can chocolate bring tears to your eyes? See for yourself at Moriondo & Gariglio, Via del Piè di Marmo, 21/22.

In Rome, my favorite things to do tend to skew off the trodden paths. I like to stroll the Monti neighborhood, the oldest in the city. Here, you'll find tiny shops, pop-up fashion sales, hip restaurants, and good oldies, such as Le Tavernelle, where a gifted waiter can hold 30 empty wineglasses in his two hands. Or score a last-minute ticket to an opera or concert at the magnificent Renzo Piano concert hall, Parco

Gelato breaks are a savior on any sightseeing tour of Rome.

della Musica: great acoustics and enveloping warm wooden walls, like musical instruments. Slightly north of the *centro,* how spellbinding the Gino Coppedè quarter, constructed from 1913 to 1927. A cluster of about 30 Liberty houses are built around a frog-themed fountain. Step under the entrance arch decorated with a large spider and into a neighborhood that resembles a children's book of fairy tales. Once considered a weird aberration, Coppedè's fantasy land became exclusive over time. Whimsy rules, and the underlying Gaudí-influenced architecture pleases with its arches and symbols and human scale.

I like the pilgrimage up the Janiculum hill to the miniature but perfect Tempietto (little temple) in the courtyard of the church San Pietro in Montorio. Round and ringed with severe Doric columns, Il Tempietto is one of the great buildings of the Renaissance, as well one of Christianity's bedrock holy sites. Inside marks the spot where St. Peter was martyred— crucified upside down, since he didn't feel worthy to be positioned as Christ had been. Donato Bramante designed with strict classical references and proportions. Walking through the ruins in Rome, you can imagine him studying the fragment of the house of the Vestal Virgins, and even the Temple of Hercules, for inspiration.

Such marvels are found everywhere. There's hardly a lane I don't want to turn down, or a produce stand where I don't want to pick up a tangerine, or a street market where I don't buy spices or a beach wrap. My ludic list is just for example; you'll easily discover your own Rome.

Maybe someone else has, but I've never encountered a rude clerk, driver, or waiter in Rome. The only crass employees I've experienced were at the Sistine Chapel, where they shout and herd and make that experience less than pleasant (*"Silencio!"*). But here's a codicil to this ode to my favorite city. There are tides of tours traveling as one big tsunami, and you had better step aside as they crash along. Traffic? Oh yes. But happily, much of the historic center is closed to cars. The city center is walkable and compact. Maneuver the

A view onto Lazio's town Sperlonga overlooking the curving beaches and sea below

metro easily; avoid crowded buses. Go to a bar twice, and the third time, the barista is likely to remember you. Become a regular at a trattoria, and you're welcomed like family. Frequent a *salumeria,* and you'll be given tastes of cheeses and prosciutto. Rome's humanism remains intact.

Heading out of Rome into the pleasures of Lazio, I recommend several stupendous destinations. Just east of the city, Hadrian's villa was constructed for the emperor during 118–134. That long ago, Hadrian did not lack for comforts. We see the enduring remains of his sauna, heated floors, swimming pool, and *frigidarium* (cold pool), as well as his love of beauty in the layout of the gardens and water features. Read Marguerite Yourcenar's *Memoirs of Hadrian* before you go; she will bring this complex emperor to life. Another four miles (7 km) to Tivoli and you're at one of the most studied and admired of Italian gardens: Villa d'Este, a 16th-century palace known for monumental scale, elaborate cascades, and water jokes. (Apparently it was fun to get sprayed unexpectedly.) The Sabine Hills always have been an escape for popes, wannabe popes, rulers, and ordinary Romans who enjoyed country pleasures.

My favorite part of Lazio lies about two hours southeast of Rome: the two beach destinations of Sperlonga and Sabaudia. They could not be more unalike. Sperlonga, perched above the sea, looks exactly like an ancient Greek village: whitewashed, cubical, cobalt blue doors, and doorways strung with bougainvillea. Beaches flank the town on either side.

Sperlonga's opposite, Sabaudia is a strange architectural gem. When Mussolini drained the malaria-ridden Pontine Marshes, a feat that had been attempted even in antiquity, he enabled the construction of several settlements for workers and for those then able to move into the area. Sabaudia is entirely composed of rationalist/fascist architecture. Begun in 1933 and completed in an astonishing 250 days, the town must have looked bleak as it rose from the swamps, but now has mellowed into a holiday destination. The soldiers' stiff boots have morphed into flip-flops, for today the attraction of the area is a 14-mile (23 km) beach with polenta-colored sand and dunes backed by four lakes.

Either Sperlonga or Sabaudia makes a good base for discovering the old port town of Gaeta; Sermoneta, a medieval hill town slightly inland; and the sublime Ninfa gardens.

Lazy days in Lazio—you can't go wrong.

An ornate corridor in Rome's Villa Doria Pamphilj gallery, one of the city's most spectacular buildings, lined with ancient statues and gilded ceilings

Insider's Guide

Rome: A Jumble of Sensory Treats

There's no place like Rome. The Colosseum, the Trevi Fountain, Saint Peter's, the Spanish Steps, and Piazza Navona: Oh yes, you must hit them all. But for a sense of real Roman life, go off camera. Give yourself time to wander into the quieter corners and neighborhoods, to the churches with priceless and little-visited works of art, to cafés and people-watching (and wonder how Roman women successfully navigate the cobblestones in sky-high stilettos).

Although the Romans themselves can be gruff and abrupt, try drawing them out with talk about football (soccer), the weather, the best carbonara, and politics. Talk about opinionated!

Make sure to carve out time for the smaller museums in town, a digestible alternative to those with lines around the block. The **Galleria Doria Pamphilj,** for example, holds one of the world's most important collections—Caravaggios, Brueghels, and Diego Velázquez's famous portrait of a scowling Inno-

cent X (which became the basis for Francis Bacon's Screaming Pope series). The still family-owned palace is a masterpiece in its own right. At the **Borghese Gallery** too, built as the family's 17th-century villa, the museum houses plenty of impressive baroque art. And it's the sculptures you won't forget, such as Bernini's "Rape of Proserpina," where you can actually see Pluto's fingers indent the flesh-like marble of Proserpina's thigh (it's still hard to fathom how the sculptor pulled it off).

In Rome it's all about walking. Walk, walk, walk, and then walk some more. Rather than getting on the metro or in a taxi, explore the city by foot. It's an easy way to get a structural sense of the chaotic metropolis and duck into quiet residential neighborhoods. Don't miss **Via Giulia,** a peaceful cobble-stoned street that's home to antique shops, ivy-draped town houses, and churches like Santa Maria dell'Orazione e Morte. **Via Margutta,** right off Via del Babuino, is lined with galleries and has a quiet residential feel, even if it's steps from the hordes on the Spanish Steps.

Via dei Coronari has to be one of Rome's most beautiful roads, leading past antique shops and cafés before arriving just a block from the Tiber and a spectacular view of Emperor Hadrian's mausoleum, **Castel Sant'Angelo.**

There are a number of excellent outfitters that allow you to see Rome through your belly, and all come with a different emphasis. Katie Parla tends to highlight satellite neighborhoods and up-and-coming chefs, even if she also covers restaurants of the city center. Veteran Elizabeth Minchilli homes in on the classics and includes institu-tions in the Jewish ghetto, now a celebrated foodie destination, near her home in the neighborhood of Monti.

Rome's café culture looms large. You may have heard of **Sant'Eustacio**'s legendary coffee, but try broadening your horizons after sampling its espresso and head to something less guidebook favored. You *must* hit **Roscioli** for lunch, but its café also offers impeccable espresso and a cozy back room that's the perfect respite from sightseeing. At **Panella,** Valentino-clad matrons and tattooed hipsters rock up to the counter for *squaglio con panna* (a

A NAME TO KNOW: SCOOTEROMA
Forget getting stuck in traffic or with other tourists: Get on a Vespa and drive the streets like a local.

WHAT BETTER WAY to experience Rome than by Vespa? (Audrey Hepburn would approve!) The best outfitter by far is Scooteroma, a well-oiled operation helmed by its dynamic owners, American Annie Ojile and Italian Giovanni Nerone. Don't be intimidated by the thought of navigating the Eternal City's legendary traffic; each bike comes with its own driver/guide, all passionate experts on the city. Here are some of Ojile's insider discoveries: "I like to compare the hip neighborhood of Monti to NYC's Nolita, since it has the same fantastic combination of old and new. You can find a 50-year-old butcher joint next to the local wine bar next to the vintage clothing shop," she says. "Between tours, I love the tiny yet chic Zia Rosetta. They have salads and juices—hard to come by in the land of pasta, pizza, and *pane!*" In the evening, she says, "Head to the lively main square of Piazza della Madonna dei Monti to hang with locals drinking cocktails." Another must? "La Fontana dell'Acqua Paolo, in Trastevere atop Gianicolo hill. It was designed by Bernini using recycled marble from the Roman Forum. Since it's so high up, you don't see the same crowds as at the Trevi Fountain."

Scooteroma offers personalized Vespa tours all over the Eternal City.

ABOVE: A sweeping view down the iconic River Tiber and Sant'Angelo bridge OPPOSITE: Roscioli Caffè, one of Rome's best spots for city classics like *cacio e pepe* or an *aperitivo* at cocktail hour

chocolate treat stuffed with whipped cream) and reenergize with the special *cappuccino dei carbonari* (just a splash of alcohol in the zabaglione foam). You will remember it for the rest of your life—seriously. Normentano's **La Portineria** is local residents' pick for the best *cornetto alla crema* to go along with your cappuccino (and the pastrymaker Gian Luca is quite easy on the eyes). Brunch is the new *aperitivo* in Rome. Make tracks to **Marigold,** founded by alums of Alice Waters's American Academy restaurant, where freshly baked pastries like sourdough cinnamon rolls tempt alongside classics like eggs Benedict, buttermilk pancakes, and perfectly ripened avocado on toast. It's also worth a detour for dinner.

Yes, yes, yes, you must go to the Vatican, see the Sistine Chapel, and maybe even hear a homily in St. Peter's Square. But there are other churches in Rome where there will be less jostling

and shorter lines. In Piazza del Popolo, for example, the tucked-away basilica **Santa Maria del Popolo,** once said to be haunted by Nero's ghost, comes with exquisite side chapels painted by Caravaggio. The **Basilica di Santa Maria** in Trastevere is said to be one of the earliest churches dedicated to the Virgin Mary, dating back to the second century—but it's the 12th-century mosaics inside that really dazzle. And **San Clemente** offers an extraordinary example of 2,000-year-old layers of Roman history in just one site: a 12th-century basilica atop a fourth-century church sitting on a second-century temple on a first-century Roman house. Talk about repurposing! For the perfect guide to the monuments (who also preorders tickets and helps get you to the right spot at the perfect time), look to Imago Artis Travel. The outfitter also customizes itineraries for children or specific interests.

One of the sad results of globalization has been the emergence of big international brands replacing the mom-and-pop shops or independent boutiques. But despite the H&Ms and Sephoras, Rome still has small stores that offer something less mass market. At **Chez Dede,** for example, everything from perfume to bags to jewelry is curated by Andrea Ferolla and Daria Reina, a couple who use both their hometown sources and farther-flung travels to create a one-stop that you want to put in your suitcase. In the neighborhood of **Monserrato,** two female designers are reinvigorating prêt-à-porter at **G.A.N. Gaia & Anne** with locally sourced fabrics and intricate detailing. And while the new designer at **Maison Halaby** may be Lebanese, his brightly colored leather bags have full Roman DNA, sparking the attention of Italian *Vogue* editors and travelers in search of one-of-a-kind creations. ■

Rome's Neighborhoods off the Main Drag

Many of Rome's masterworks lie in the part of town known as the *centro storico,* the historic center. But many of the city's neighborhoods, still nearby, have a lot to offer and many fewer tourists. Pick a few, or just one, and see where Romans live and play.

Prati: One of the residential neighborhoods right by the Vatican, this leafy enclave is an insider favorite for its mix of pretty town houses alongside bustling local bars and restaurants. With 273 stands, Mercato Trionfale is one of Italy's biggest food markets, with stalls of fish, produce, and even housewares, and dates to the 1800s. Il Sorpasso, a bar and restaurant, is a buzzy meeting point for Romans. As you enter, a long bar fills up with locals looking for a cocktail (or, earlier in the day, a healthy smoothie). Grab an *aperitivo* and a plate of prosciutto and cheese, or wait for a table in the main room for *trapizzini,* a Roman take on pizza, or thinly sliced *baccala,* cod, carpaccio (reservations are highly recommended).

Testaccio: One of Rome's trendiest neighborhoods is home to restaurants, nightclubs, bars in former warehouses, and food markets that draw hipsters in search of an after-hours scene. Before digging in to your food and nightlife, check out MACRO, located inside the area's former slaughterhouse and now home to one of the city's new contemporary art museums. Afterward, fuel up with a plate of *cacio e pepe,* a pasta dish featuring cheese and cracked black pepper sauce, at Felice a Testaccio before heading to Angelina a Testaccio with its terraced bar and artisanal cocktails.

Piccola Londra: Most visitors haven't even heard of this tiny neighborhood on the city's north side, but "Little London" remains one of a kind, replete with multicolored, art nouveau-style town houses. Designed by architect Quadrio Pirani in the early 20th century, it's a secret worth experiencing.

Centocelle: If you like your atmosphere gritty, this up-and-coming neighborhood about five miles (8 km) from the city center should be on your list. Restaurant Mazzo, a 12-seat restaurant that's become one of the hottest reservations to snag, is largely to thank for the spotlight. In 2015, the area became more connected to central Rome with three new metro stops; now, locals head to Via delle Palme's Menabo for organic wine.

Monti: Tucked into the hills above the Forum and Colosseum, this quaint neighborhood is close to the city center but gives off the authentic vibe of real-life Rome. Stroll its enclave of cobblestoned streets and try restaurants like Urbana 47, a spot that concentrates on local organic ingredients (the industrial chic design also feels fresh). Afterward, wander along Via Urbana with its stylish boutiques. For a glass of good local wine, try either hidden gem La Barrique or Al Vino Al Vino with its large selection of Italian vintages. ■

OPPOSITE: Monti's Piazza della Madonna **ABOVE:** *Cacio e pepe* at Felice a Testaccio, located in one of Rome's trendiest neighborhoods

Local Flavors: Keeping It Classic

Fried artichokes. *Cacio e pepe. Carbonara. Bucatini all'Amatriciana. Supplì.* If you know these dishes, your mouth is probably already watering. Rome is known for its humble cuisine—but it's also one of Italy's best, based on relatively simple recipes and ingredients that are easily accessible and seasonal.

Let's start with the artichokes. Between December and April, they make their way happily onto city menus. It's Rome's favorite vegetable, a staple since ancient times and further popularized when Jews came to the city after being expelled from Spain and southern Italy. The *alla romana* style means the vegetable is simmered in mint, garlic, and olive oil; *alla giudia,* or Jewish style, is fried. One of the foodies' favorite versions is served up at **Giggetto** (named for the Jewish ghetto that used to be here).

Now for the pasta. Some carb fans save their calories just for Eternal City dishes like *cacio e pepe,* creamy sheep's cheese with cracked black pepper. As always, weighing in on the best might cause anarchy, but Testaccio's **Flavio al Velavevodetto** learned his version from the *cacio e pepe* king, Felice (of Felice a Testaccio) himself, before the great chef passed away. But you can't argue with the version at **Armando al Pantheon** either. And **Cesare al Casaletto** is worth a tram or cab ride for its version of *cacio* (as well as other exemplary takes on Roman trattoria staples).

Looking for the hottest reservation in town that takes on the classics with aplomb? **Santo Palato** quickly became the restaurant that insiders put on their must-try list, with young chef Sarah Cicolini at the stove of the kitchen they are calling "trattoria moderna" (watch out for gruff service, though). And **Retrobottega** has given true ingenuity and passion to every dish at the restaurant with its slate countertops and open kitchen—it's hard to find better vegetarian plates in Rome.

Yes, yes, maybe Naples does have the country's best pizza. But, damn, it's not bad in Rome either. Roman pizza ranges between pieces of flatbread that you can eat as you go or pie that's big enough for a full meal. For the first version, you must, yes, *must,* go to **Bonci Pizzarium** for pizza by the slice (though it seems blasphemous to call such a delicious thing just a slice); the *supplì,* or tomato croquettes, aren't half bad either (GASP!). At **Antico Forno Roscioli,** the so-called slice is also exemplary; try the *bianca* with just olive oil and salt, or the *rossa* with its idyllic tomato sauce. The owners have also opened **Emma** nearby as a temple for thin-crusted pie; the results are a new standard in town. ■

ABOVE: Divine fried artichokes at the Giggetto **OPPOSITE:** Bonci Pizzarium is a Roman institution, famous for its freshly baked bread, pizza by the slice, and *supplì,* croquettes.

Cocktail or Bust: Rome's New Bar Scene

Being ahead of the curve is not how most aficionados would describe Rome; the city's signature trattorias, classic architecture, San Pietrino cobblestones are fine as they are, thank you very much. But for those interested in a cocktail that's more than a Negroni or Aperol spritz, the emergence of a new generation of speakeasies, or lounge bars, has been a boon.

In 2010, **Jerry Thomas,** a bar named after the New York saloon owner from the 1800s, kicked off the trend and became the forerunner for treating the art of the cocktail with a reverence that borders on the religious. To gain admittance, you will need a password (go to the website to get it; it's often the answer to an alcohol-related question). When you arrive, you will think for a minute that you've landed in a 1920s Prohibition-era bar, complete with live jazz, plenty of cigarette smoke, and concoctions including "Ten Collins" with gin and bitters.

At **Derrière,** behind a restaurant and through the kitchen door is a small, smoke-filled room with a long backlit bar and sexy bartenders. Get the whisky sour. And even cocktail snobs are impressed by **Suburra 1930,** with (naturally) a 1930s vibe. Try the Bronx with gin, vermouth rosso, dry vermouth, and bitter Campari.

Most cocktail lovers give Monti's recent arrival, **Drink Kong,** a high rating for good reason. It's the latest offering from master mixologist Patrick Pistolesi. And **Il Marchese** is the first Amaro bar in town—it has at least 500 bitters.

Hotel bars in Rome are more than an afterthought: The new cocktail bar at the **Hotel de la Ville** has a great view and artful drinks. **Charade,** in the new de Ricci hotel, is ideal for a tête-à-tête, or an after-party like the ones held there during the Rome Film Festival. Oh, and if you have an interest in body art, **Wisdomless** offers up cocktails while you get inked. It's best to consider what tattoo you'd like before you get too drunk. ■

Artisanal cocktails at spots like Suburra 1930 are Rome's hottest trend.

Checking in Rome

From tucked-away hideaways to restored grande dames to new boutique arrivals, the capital's hostelry choices rank among the best, and most diverse, in all of Italy.

St. Regis: Fresh off a complete multimillion-dollar overhaul, this iconic palace hotel comes with a quiet location near the ancient Caracalla Baths and a spa that even the Romans would have enjoyed.

Portrait Suites: This 14-room pied-à-terre, has wonderful details like a rooftop terrace with an outdoor fireplace and luxurious rooms.

Palazzo Dama: An outdoor pool right by the Tiber, surrounded by a pretty garden in central Rome? Yes, please.

Hotel Eden: This secluded and storied property recently had a complete renovation and style makeover. The bar with its views over the city is one of the best spots in the city for cocktails at sunset.

Hotel Vilòn: A new insider favorite in Campo Marzio, this 16th-century palazzo was once a Borghese family home that was recently converted into an 18-room hotel. One of the best properties in town.

Papal Palaces: A number of historic properties that hosted popes past have been turned into luxury apartments that give a sense of pomp without being pompous. The Costaguti Experience, on the periphery of the former Jewish ghetto, comes with its own billiard room, a fabulous living room with large windows overlooking the Piazza Mattei, and five guest rooms. The owners of the Holy See have taken the former apartment of Pope Innocent X's mistress Olimpia (yes, popes had powerful consorts) and transformed it into a two-bedroom luxury hideaway with a terrace overlooking the Piazza Navona. It's a religious experience that comes with the high price tag to match.

Hotel de la Ville: The latest from luxury hotelier Rocco Forte (also behind the stylish Hotel de Russie) just opened in 2019 and has instantly drawn buzz for its rooftop bar overlooking the Spanish Steps and spa for tired sightseers.

J.K. Place Roma: With outposts in Florence and Capri, this third arrival adds 30 boutique rooms close to the sights but perfectly outside the tourist fray. Vintage furniture, antique fireplaces, and a cozy living room–like lobby keeps it chic but unpretentious.

Corso 281: A number of small properties with hotel-worthy services have sprung up in recent years, a kind of hybrid between a service apartment and a boutique option. This one, right by Piazza Venezia, is a successful example of the model with its central location, helpful staff, and large rooms.

First Roma Dolce: This new arrival right on the Via del Corso, the Eternal City's main artery, is housed in a 19th-century building designed by Giuseppe Valadier, who also masterminded the layout of the Piazza del Popolo. Along with the First Roma Arte, its sister hotel just a short walk away, the two properties combine boutique chic with kind service. ■

ABOVE: Hotel Palazzo Dama has an enviable address and an outdoor pool. **OPPOSITE:** New arrival Hotel Vilòn is one of Rome's chicest options, where fashion types meet in the lobby.

Frances's Favorites

Righteous Roman Restaurants

Where shall we eat? Plan ahead. Research the possibilities—there are thousands in *bella Roma.* Bookmark, keep a list, or tear out articles. Reserve trendy hot spots such as **Salumeria Roscioli** or perpetually popular **Pierluigi** in advance. Then you won't have to take time finding a table when you'd rather be sipping a spritz.

It's easy to plan dinner in advance, but at midday *pranzo,* you often find yourself at some out-of-the-way site—or you're in a crowded tourist area and you end up taking the "looks OK" approach. I found **Da Fortunato** near the Pantheon that way, so sometimes following your nose leads to a discovery—but you can also face a tired tourist menu or cardboard pizza. Go for savvy apps that list by neighborhood. Or preempt hassle by scouting out what's near your general location come one o'clock—for instance, Roman specialties at **Armando al Pantheon, Tempio di Iside** for seafood near the Colosseum, and **Al Moro** for true Roman classics near the Trevi Fountain.

Of the many contemporary, experimental newer places, I like **Il Convivio-Troiani,** exclusive (ring the doorbell on arrival), quiet, and playful. Who could resist photographing the artfully presented and delicious food? **Glass Hostaria** in Trastevere also serves forth the unexpected. Try the fantastic vegetarian tasting menu. For seafood, book **Il Sanlorenzo,** grown-up and elegant with impeccable choices. I love the old-school trattoria atmospheres of **Colline Emiliane** (recipes from Emilia-Romagna), **Trattoria Monti** (recipes from Le Marche), and **Osteria La Gensola,** serving all the great Roman pastas. Their spicy *amatriciana* sauce is just what it should be. **Ristorante Matricianella** features old-fashioned red-checked tablecloths. I like to sit at one of the sidewalk tables and order both the fried artichokes *and* the Roman artichokes. Matricianella is situated off the elegant Piazza San Lorenzo in Lucina, with cafés serving light lunches outside. For tasty small plates after a gargantuan *pranzo,* tiny enoteca **Il Goccetto** features 850 varieties of wine. ∎

ABOVE: Seafood lovers adore Pierluigi restaurant in Piazza de Ricci, where outdoor tables book up fast. **OPPOSITE:** After exploring the nearby monument of the same name, Armando al Pantheon is the go-to for classic pasta dishes and an old-school atmosphere.

Outlying neighborhoods have become hubs for street art like this installation by renowned artist Blu, on Rome's Via del Porto Fluviale.

Insider's Guide

New Art Stops in the Eternal City

You need, must, *have* to hit the major museums, ancient Roman sites, and exquisite churches in Rome—but also make sure to give yourself some time to explore the new modern art galleries, the major contemporary museums, and the city's street art, which has given it more relevance within a modern context. Rome has always featured layers of art and architecture, one on top of the other—so it makes sense that it would continue to evolve century after century.

One of the first modern buildings to be constructed in the historical center

in about 100 years, Richard Meier's **Ara Pacis,** was also one of its most controversial: a glass box that encloses an ancient Roman altar dating to 9 B.C. Despite many naysayers, the light and views onto the Tiber create an installation-like effect, especially from the interior of the structure.

In 2010, the Zaha Hadid–designed **MAXXI Museum** opened its doors to contemporary art exhibits. A masterwork of suspended staircases and grand spaces provides the modern backdrop to installations and performance areas. The permanent collection

includes international work by Kiki Smith, Ed Ruscha, and Gerhard Richter, as well as pieces by young and established Italian artists. Visiting exhibitions have ranged from retrospectives of photographers like Paolo Pellegrin to performance art.

Galleries too took notice of the audience that wanted some Cy Twombly after their Caravaggio. **Larry Gagosian** opened the Italian outpost of his namesake gallery not far from the Spanish Steps (in addition to Twombly, exhibitions have included Rachel Feinstein and Richard Serra). And Lorcan O'Neill was one of the forerunners of visionary gallerists here; his exhibition space became the heart of the new scene for artists and their champions. He continues to introduce the city to up-and-coming artists, as well as respected names including Francesco Clemente and Rachel Whiteread.

One of Rome's exciting new arrivals, **Rhinoceros,** is the brainchild of Alda Fendi. With the help of the celebrated architect Jean Nouvel, she has transformed a palazzo into a home for her arts foundation. The museum showcases experimental installations, performance art, and plays within the modern-meets-17th-century space, as well as exhibits of more classic fare like intricate Michelangelo drawings (there are apartments also designed by Nouvel upstairs and a restaurant with caviar and champagne among the offerings).

Rome's emerging art isn't always displayed in conventional spaces,

Rome's Gagosian gallery, the Italian outpost for world-famous art dealer Larry Gagosian

however; some of the city's neighborhoods feature it right on the buildings' facades. Rome's **Ostiense,** for example, features portraits of history greats from Dante to Elvis, with a very pop art effect. One of Rome's exciting young street artists, Alice Pasquini, is now world renowned but found her calling in her hometown and in creating outdoor installations there. ■

MUSE, STAR, BACKDROP, INSPIRATION: ROME AND FILM
Even if you haven't been to Rome in person, you have most likely seen it in cinematic glory.

ROMAN HOLIDAY, from 1953 and starring Audrey Hepburn and Gregory Peck, immortalized the city for legions of fans as they zipped through town on a Vespa and ate gelato as they walked down the Spanish Steps. The film also has made every visitor since wish they, too, had an Eternal City pad to live out their Italian escape from reality.

In the 1960s *La Dolce Vita* brought viewers to the Trevi Fountain and made women everywhere wish they could frolic in the water as sensually as Anita Ekberg did in her stunning strapless evening gown. And *The Talented Mister Ripley,* directed by Anthony Minghella and released in 1999, gave the city a seductive if sinister veneer as Matt Damon and Gwyneth Paltrow lingered in gold-lit cafés and palazzi that could double as museums.

More recently, in 2013 Paolo Sorrentino's *La Grande Bellezza* (*The Great Beauty*) caught the Eternal City at its best angles. Despite a plot showcasing a Rome full of decadence and slow decline, the sublime locations stun. The opening scene at Fontana dell'Acqua Paola, the visiting nun on her knees climbing the Scala Sancta, the long pans of glowing patinas and lamp-lit streets, as well as visits to secret gardens and noble hideaways, linger for months after a viewing.

Of course, Rome—Italy's equivalent of Hollywood—has always been associated with film. It began here in the 1930s at the city's Cinecittà, spawning great classics like Vittorio De Sica's 1948 *Bicycle Thieves,* which showed the dark side of the city in a neorealist film that's still considered one of the screen's most important works. Whatever their angle, both Italian and foreign directors have been inspired to bring Rome into the spotlight, a tradition of the silver screen that continues to memorialize the city for the next generation of cinephiles.

Hot Spot
Escape the Urban Jungle

Although most visitors concentrate on the capital, there are plenty of reasons to make a side trip from the metropolis. **Civita di Bagnoregio,** the medieval masterpiece atop a cliff, is one of the prettiest towns in Italy—and that's quite a claim in a country that's got pretty towns galore. Nicknamed "the dying city," both because it is slowly losing residents and its soft limestone base is eroding, it elicits only wonder for now. The village of tiny streets seems to sit on the clouds, accessible only by a crooked little bridge; visit the lost-in-time alleyways and Chiesa di San Donato just for the day. Or book into **Corte della Maestà,** a lovingly restored villa with five suites. Opened by one of Rome's most famous psychiatrists, the spot mixes impeccable original details with a sense of warm hospitality. It's best to go to the hamlet midweek, though, to avoid the weekend day-trippers.

Insiders highly rate **Castel di Tora,** about an hour outside Rome, with its emerald green lake and child-size carp. The sense of getting away from it all is at full effect. Rent a boat for a couple of hours, and then head for lunch at **L'Angoletto** for a seafood feast. For thermal spring lovers, **Viterbo** has always been a popular spot for Romans to relax, and continues to draw spa lovers and history buffs from all over Italy. The village has intact 11th-century walls and an atmospheric historic center.

Book a trip with Personalized Italy to discover **Ciociaria's** exquisite Benedictine monasteries, about two hours southeast of Rome, with a delicious meal along the way. Or plan a hideaway at **La Posta Vecchia Hotel,** the former villa of J. Paul Getty, which is still full of the antiques he collected. Located right on the sea, it's the perfect place to hole up for a couple of romantic nights, taking time to lounge at the exquisite indoor pool, experience the new spa, or browse the archaeological findings discovered under the structure that are now housed in a small museum. ■

Civita di Bagnoregio sits atop a limestone cliff that is quickly eroding.

Frances's Favorites

Leaving Roma

If leave you must, flights are often early. But no need to stop your pleasures at a dreary airport chain hotel in order to be at the terminal early in the morning. I'm a regular at the **Seccy** in the working port town of Fiumicino. An inexpensive hotel on a nondescript street, the friendly Seccy is lovely inside, with well-appointed, spacious rooms. The bonus is dinner. **Fiumicino** has ter-rific restaurants within easy walking distance, from the casual pizza place next to the hotel to two-Michelin-starred seafood temples **Pascucci al Porticciolo** and **Il Tino**. For years, my family has dined at the softly lit **Zi' Pina** in winter and under their grape pergola in warm seasons. **Cielo** is a recent and winning discovery: supersophisticated and chic.

Several times I've chosen **Hotel QC Terme Roma** for five-star luxury in a park setting. The hotel's old-world patina and new-world comfort, extensive spa treatments, beautiful pool, and memorable restaurant may make you want your flight to be canceled. Hard to believe you're only a stone's throw from the runways.

Both hotels, less than 10 minutes from the airport, arrange transport. ▪

> If leave you must, flights are often early. But no need to stop your pleasures at a dreary airport chain hotel to be at the terminal.

ABOVE: Although known for its airport, the town of Fiumicino also has a port and spots to hide in before a flight. **OPPOSITE:** QC Terme Roma features natural thermal baths, a chic restaurant, and a luxe hotel, all close to the airport.

Ponza: Romans' Island Escape

Fishing boats moored along the port; small bars, cafés, and restaurants snuggled along tight alleyways; vintage scooters zipping up the hill with sea views in all directions. No over-the-top hotels or camera-toting tourists here; **Ponza** is Lazio's magical island getaway: simple, low-key, and lost in time.

Start your exploration at Ponza's port, where you duck through an arch and find hidden-away seafood joints like **Restaurant Eea,** a place that has some of the best fish on the island. **Aqua Pazza** is the Michelin option with evocative views over the port.

As for hotels, the **Chiaia di Luna** has an unbeatable position, perched on the hill facing a white limestone cliffside that looks almost like the surface of the moon. With a long pool and whitewashed rooms that would cost triple on an island like Capri, this retreat is the perfect getaway. The Fendi family has long been a champion of the island, and opened a small hotel hideaway here. **Villa Laetitia** might be a tad faded in parts but still draws loyal fans to its six rooms with views over the port.

The island makes the perfect long weekend destination or a few days midweek for an even more low-key escape. On your first day, stay on the island. Swim off the rocks at **Spiaggia di Frontone** and make the hike up to **Associazione Culturale Cala Frontone,** known by locals simply as Da Gerardo, where Gerardo Mazzella and his family opened a small museum and restaurant. Plates of anchovies, mozzarella from his own buffalo, and salads from the garden are served under a vine-covered pergola.

A boat trip to **Palmarola** should also be on the itinerary. Rent a boat through Diva Luna: Options include a private boat with skipper or group excursions. Stop for a dip in the green-blue sea by the cathedral-like blue grottoes. Lunch at **O'Francese** is a rite of passage; here, sailors and visitors sit at long wood tables on a simple terrace facing the sea (there are a couple of rooms upstairs too). ■

The island of Ponza is one of Italy's best kept secrets.

Frances's Favorites

In Your Glass

The majority of Lazio's wines are white. Frascati is ubiquitous. There's that word: *drinkable*. And they are. Light and summery, they're able to heft a bit of gravitas too. Make sure to check out Frascati Superiore Eremo Tuscolano, made by Valle Vermiglia. Volcanic soil and an herbal terroir distinguish this wine in your glass. From the island of Ponza, Casale del Giglio sends forth the chalky, fruity Biancolella Faro della Guardia. *Biancolella* is a grape variety grown only on the island. Our trusty Gambero Rosso *Italian Wines* guide led us to these.

Three vineyards stand out for consistent high quality. Falesco, in northern Lazio, makes Est! Est!! Est!!! di Montefiascone, which (despite the dubious name) is a pleasing trebbiano and malvasia blend. Montiano, a merlot, is one of the region's best wines. Next is the Sergio Mottura winery, known for its *grechetto,* Poggio della Costa. This pale beauty, with a whiff of citrus blossoms and stone, garners top ratings and the bonus of being well priced. Poggio Le Volpi's Bacca Rossa, from the *nero buono* (good black) grape, makes an earthy and spicy partner to pasta with sausage and four cheeses.

In Rome, wine nuts must feel a magnetic pull to Ristorante Casa Bleve. Not only is it set in a romantic glass-roofed courtyard, but the wine list rivals the Bible in thickness. When I was last there with friends, we drank a thrilling couple of bottles of Antonello Coletti Conti's Cesanese del Piglio Superiore Hernicus, from just southeast of Rome. Ask the waiter for a tour of the subterranean wine cellar, which has a Roman wall to sustain the vast collection. ▪

> Frascati is ubiquitous. There's that word: *drinkable*. And they are.
> Light and summery, they're able to heft a bit of gravitas too.

ABOVE: Castel Gandolfo, one of Lazio's village treasures and a summer papal home, peeks out over the calm oasis of Lake Albano. OPPOSITE: *Risotto alla pescatora*, a typical regional dish, comes with mussels, clams, and other seafood bounty from fishermen's nets.

Chapter Twelve

LE MARCHE

This surf and turf region invites you to go off course. Take the little road where a sign points to a 13th-century abbey. Or come upon a truffle festival. Or (mea culpa) spend a stack of euros at the Prada or Tod's outlets. Just a skip from Umbria and Tuscany, the green, green hills—and mountains—of Le Marche border the Adriatic for 107 miles (173 km). Travel feels intimate, as most of the attractive towns are small or midsize.

Everywhere, you'll be assured of a warm welcome. Local food is consistently *delizioso*—the big *brodetto* soup that contains 13 types of seafood; crispy *fritto misto,* grilled meats, the well-loved *vincigrassi,* a signature lasagna amped up with a mixture of meats in the ragù, including giblets and sometimes cockscomb. Often a little marsala is worked into the pasta dough. *Passatelli* is a specialty. It looks like pasta but is formed from eggs, bread crumbs, and Parmigiano, then poached and served in broth. Simple, delicate, and typical.

The name *Le Marche* comes from *marches.* Not at all swampy marshes, the word means "borders," the territory so named by the Romans for the edges of their domain. I'll travel here without reservations, since so many appealing overnights are possible on the *agriturismo* farm-stay program. Le Marche is right for country sojourns. Not an *agriturismo,* La Casa Azzurra near Loro Piceno nevertheless feels like someone's home. A rather plain, yes, blue, farmhouse, it has a common room full of art and design books, two adorable truffle dogs—the breed is Lagotto Romagnolo—a spa, yoga, and Seta Cruda, a restaurant locals rightfully seek out for a special dinner. Best pizza in Le Marche? *Sì, signora.* In July, the fields all around blaze with sunflowers. Find the right spot, like this, and check in. Nearby you'll come upon a handful of beguiling villages to explore.

Fermo! What an astonishing remain from Roman times—30 underground cisterns—soaring, vaulted, cavernous brick chambers, built from the first century B.C. to the first century A.D., complete with vents, pipes, and sophisticated channels for the egress and cleaning of springwaters for the town's use. Not only builders of roads for the ages, those Romans were hydraulic engineering geniuses. Aboveground, Fermo is an elegant and lively town. Il Teatro dell'Aquila, the opulent five-tiered and frescoed opera house, has regaled locals with performances since 1790.

About 30 miles (50 km) up the coast, Recanati is the birthplace of the 19th-century poet Giacomo Leopardi. He's certainly remembered in his hometown: His poems are posted on flower boxes, his home still lived in by relatives, and a statue of the poet himself lords over the handsome piazza. He's frowning. I wonder if he's remembering his

---

WHAT YOU NEED TO KNOW...

- **BEST TIME TO VISIT:** Outside peak summer season on the coast and during the truffle season in the fall, many tourist amenities will be closed, but you can still fall into fun adventures. Spring and fall colors, not to mention incredible local produce, keep fans coming back in the shoulder months too.

- **TOP SPOTS:** Urbino, Senigalia

- **GETTING THERE:** There are airports in Ancona and Falconara.

Cònero is a national park and one of Le Marche's unexpected treasures.

Pretty Sirolo has old houses and a shady piazza situated for views of the coast. Church bells hush the singing birds and reverberate far out to sea.

unhappy childhood in a dysfunctional family long before the term existed.

If you're near Macerata, just 20 minutes down the road, the under-the-stars summer opera attracts both famous and promising young singers. Music is all over Le Marche. The city of Pesaro, perched on the Adriatic, honors its native son in August with the Rossini Opera Festival. I think no other region has as many seemingly out-of-the-way but fascinating small towns to discover.

Then there's the odd find. I happened upon the magnificent Roman Catholic complex at Loreto. The basilica of the Santuario della Santa Casa complex contains the house of the Virgin Mary. As the legend goes, the structure was flown by angels from Nazareth to Illyria and then deposited on the shore near Loreto. Miracle of the muscular angels! Passionate scholarly studies definitively connect the house to cave structures in the Holy Land; others cry fantasy and twaddle. Regardless, anything with such a swarm of legend and history has to be interesting.

So there's the house, placed inside the basilica, its marble surrounds worn to a shine by generations of kneeling pilgrims. More compelling to me are the art treasures, including a rich group of works by Luca Signorelli: "The Doubt of Saint Thomas," "The Conversion of Saint Paul," and musical angels and medallions in the vaulted ceilings. I'd thought we'd spend an hour, but we kept finding works by Guido Reni, Cristoforo Roncalli (Pomarancio), Lorenzo Lotti, Bellini, on and on. We stayed all morning.

Every December 9, a statue of the Black Madonna is taken out of her house for a grand procession. Fires are lit on the coast and in the fields, to light the way for angels. I'm not kidding: She is carried aloft on the broad shoulders of earthly fliers, the pilots of the Aeronautica Militare—the Italian Air Force!

Intrigued by its unique towns, I frequently feel the call of this region's myriad pleasures. "Let's go over to Le Marche for a couple of days," I'll say. Then to choose where: Grottomare, for its medieval upper town and fanciful villas along the sea walk. Ascoli Piceno, for the grand Piazza del Popolo, one of the most admired in Italy—and the local specialty, *olive ascolana* (stuffed and fried olives) to enjoy while sitting out with an *aperitivo* in that exquisite space. Or, as often happens, to a beach escape: the Roman market town of Senigallia, which has two famous and outstanding restaurants—Uliassi and La Madonnina del Pescatore—plus casual fish shacks along the wide, seven-mile (12 km) *velutato,* velvet, beach. We check into Hotel Terrazza Marconi for its hammam, sea view rooms, and bicycles to use on the shady pedestrian street along the water. These towns are only a few of many perfect ones for a weekend getaway.

Fermo's picturesque Piazza del Popolo has architectural treasures at all angles.

Ascoli Piceno's festival of La Quintana brings pomp and circumstance to Le Marche in July, but the city is full of gems throughout the year.

Not at all a secret discovery, the walled town of Urbino attracts art lovers from all over the world. The Montefeltro clan had ruled here since 1234, but Federico da Montefeltro put the town on the map in the 15th century as a major center of humanism. His image is well known from the Piero della Francesca portrait in the Uffizi Gallery in Florence. He lost an eye in a sword fight and is seen in profile—his good side—looking stern and hook-nosed. Wearing a flat-topped red hat, he faces the portrait of his wife, Battista Sforza.

When Montefeltro gave up fighting (he made his fortune as a skilled and successful mercenary) he turned to art, attracting the great painters, sculptors, marquetry artists, poets, and scholars to his court. His Palazzo Ducale reveals his passion for the good life, from the light-filled courtyard to the aesthetically pleasing rooms throughout, especially Lo Studiolo. His personal small study is a marquetry marvel: a room within a room, made by some master of inlay. On the walls and trompe l'oeil cabinets, the inlay artist has depicted books, lutes, other musical instruments—even a squirrel. The palace also houses the major Piero della Francesca paintings, the strange "Flagellation of Christ" and the "Madonna of Senigallia," and others by Alberti, Titian, Uccello, and Raphael, who was born in Urbino.

The other major hot spot of Le Marche is the Cònero Regional Park, the coastal area below the capital city of Ancona. Pretty Sirolo has appealing old houses and a shady piazza situated for prime views of the coast. Church bells hush the singing birds and reverberate far out to sea. The area is home to the sand beaches Mezzavalle, La Vela, stunning Due Sorelle, and Portonovo, where the rocks look like small fallen moons. Translucent water deeply regenerates what needs regenerating.

You can even stay on the beach at a strategically located Napoleonic fort, built in 1808, now the Hotel Fortino Napoleonico. At the small town of Numana, hire a boat for swimming in clear coves. Fish and mussels are abundant all year, but locals wait for early summer, when the particular wild mussel, *mosciolo,* can be harvested from the rocks.

I'll take a Le Marche week anytime.

A view of Urbino's duomo, one of the UNESCO-protected city's many highlights, which include the artist Raphael's birthplace and a vibrant university

Insider's Guide

Urbino: Renaissance in Miniature

Framed by the Apennines on one side and the Adriatic Sea on the other, Le Marche has never had the traffic of better known neighbors like Tuscany and Emilia-Romagna. And although magazine editors and trend predictors like to say it's the country's next up-and-comer—a tagline for about a decade now—you get the sense that residents want it to stay just as it is: a place for quiet hikes and authentic meals, filled with secluded abbeys, undervisited artistic masterworks, and pretty beaches. Once you see it, you're likely to feel the same way.

Exclusion from Italy's official list of must-sees has proved especially kind to the city of **Urbino,** arguably Le Marche's star attraction. This compact gem manages to exist in a way that feels civilized but alive. Despite its UNESCO designation and bevy of art treasures, you'll find no throngs of day-trippers with flag-wielding tour leaders or kiosks of kitsch memorabilia here.

The university town instantly draws you in, filled with easy, pleasant streets that wind past grand, stately buildings and student-filled cafés. Urbino's compact Renaissance heart is due to the efforts of Federico da Montefeltro, a fierce one-eyed warrior who used his battle winnings to invest in the art and architecture that would make his hometown an ideal city. Montefeltro designed his palace, the Palazzo Ducale (now the **Galleria Nazionale delle Marche**), to showcase a series of noble bedrooms as well as a library, a chapel, and dining halls. The palace was stripped after Montefeltro's death, but it still houses masterpieces from artists and architects including Piero della Francesca, Leon Battista Alberti, and Raphael.

Montefeltro's small private study—made completely of trompe l'oeil intarsia (inlaid wood)—is particularly exquisite—the perfect setting from which to plot his next war escapade or art commission.

While you may not have heard of Montefeltro before visiting Urbino, the same is probably not true of the painter Raphael, the city's more famous resident. The artist was born here in 1483, spending his childhood with his family in an atmosphere that called to mind a miniature Florence. Today, Renaissance fans continue to make the pilgrimage to Via Raffaello to see where little Raffaello laid his head at night and gained his significant talent. Near his childhood bed is a small fresco of the Madonna and Child that Raphael painted as a boy.

When it comes to cuisine, Urbino's dishes are reminiscent of those found in Emilia-Romagna and Tuscany, featuring such staples as mushrooms, truffles, and preserved meats like the famed prosciutto di Carpegna. Try a *crescia sfogliata,* flaky flatbread, at **Osteria Km 0** opposite the duomo. Le Marche's take

Le Marche's truffle dish comes with *passatelli,* the region's traditional pasta shape.

on a *piadina,* this tasty treat is stuffed with locally produced cheese and salami, melted between freshly baked, flaky bread. And warning: The cheeses are extraordinary. Legend has it that Michelangelo so enjoyed the *casciotta d'Urbino,* a sheep-cow variety, that he actually bought farms nearby to guarantee a lifetime supply of the stuff.

At the tiny **La Trattoria del Leone,** the emphasis is on local dishes. Make sure to try their memorable vegetarian take on *passatelli,* the Marchigianian pasta made out of bread crumbs, eggs, lemon, a dash of nutmeg, and grated Parmesan in a touch of broth. The country inn **Cà Andreana,** a short 10-minute drive outside town, comes with cozy rooms and simple, meaty dishes; try the Urbino *agnello al forno* (oven-crisped lamb). ◾

CHECKING IN
Countryside villas are symbolic of the region's larger appeal.

WHILE THERE ARE A NUMBER of small hotels and inns from which to set up shop in Le Marche, renting a villa or farmhouse is a great option (and will set you back considerably less than counterparts in Puglia or Tuscany, especially in high season). One to consider: **Malatesta Maison,** a kind of surprise behind closed doors that most people have not had the time to discover. This lovingly restored farmhouse was the brainchild of an Italian Chilean couple, Carlo Ruzza and Claudia Orellana, who have transformed it into a modernist but cocooning space. Formerly a hotel, the property now offers weekly or nightly rentals—perfect for a family reunion (though it's probably not advisable for

smaller kids) or groups of friends discovering the region.

Be sure to spend time at the pool, in the small spa area, eating meals under the pergola, or contemplating a view that changes with the clouds. Inside, open-plan living areas with cozy white sofas and an industrial-size kitchen make this the perfect fall and early spring hideaway—just the place to drink wine and cook before taking day trips to nearby towns.

Villa Olivo is a new addition to the rental market that should be on your radar. It offers a beautiful infinity pool, private gym, enough space for 12 guests, and a location close to the area's beaches.

Frances's Favorites
In Your Glass

How can such good wines be so inexpensive? That's the question I've asked here and in only two other parts of Italy: Puglia and Sardinia. And given the quality and value, why aren't the Le Marche vineyards much better known? The favored white grape, *verdicchio,* "needs some love," according to wine writer Tom Hyland, who also wondered why the wine isn't being snapped up all over the world. Too cheap, producers told him. No one trusts what isn't pricey. Others mentioned that the traditional amphora shape of the bottle was off-putting to some buyers. Such a mistake—Le Marche is one of Italy's prime wine regions.

Verdicchio has *verde,* green, in its name and in the glass: a faint spring tinge. This lovely summer-sipping wine pairs naturally with seafood. Across Le Marche, the tastes are nuanced with almond, grass, or the scent of grass after rain. Some vineyards age their *verdicchio* in wood for a year, adding a faint hint of smoke. A few taste unremarkable.

Grown in two areas, Castelli di Jesi and Matelica, the *verdicchio* has other variations. Experts find more refined floral, citrus tastes from Jesi, and more herbal notes, sunny yellow color, and fuller body from Matelica. I'll take either. Some of the best we've poured: La Monacesca Verdicchio di Matelica, and Villa Bucci Verdicchio Classico Superiore dei Castelli di Jesi. A *verdicchio* wine that truly catches that sparkle on the waves: Tenuta di Tavignano Misco Superiore. Gambero Rosso

recently selected it for the white wine of the year for all of Italy.

Given that Le Marche food leans heavily toward prosciutto, pork, and grilled meats, what about reds? The Cònero area south of Ancona is known for Rosso Cònero, a *montepulciano* grape sometimes blended with up to 15 percent *sangiovese.* The result: clean, velvety, and happy to stand up to any wild boar or woodcock. Look on wine lists for Umani Ronchi's Cùmaro and Campo San Giorgio (both 100 percent *montepulciano*). You can book a vineyard stay at Umani Ronchi's appealing Villa Bianchi Country House in the Jesi production zone.

Another able-bodied red: Velenosi Rosso Piceno from the desirable area of Ascoli Piceno. ∎

ABOVE: Matelica's panorama includes acres of local wineries. **OPPOSITE:** Ascoli Piceno wine bar Siamo Fritti comes with plenty of local vintages for sale and a restaurant for oenophiles after the tastings.

In the Know

Seni-What? Italy's Seafood Pearl

Senigallia. It looks just like an ordinary seaside village on the Adriatic (though to be fair, the old town is quite charming and Italians love the summer rockabilly festival there). But this tiny place is home to some of the most creative seafood in Italy, with not just one but *two* Michelin-starred restaurants: Madonnina del Pescatore and Uliassi.

Getting a consensus on which is better could take a lifetime of meals and interviews (although Uliassi just scored its third star, making it one of only 10 restaurants in the country to snag this particular honor). Ratings aside, suffice it to say that both restaurants are quite revelatory and happen to be very important launchpads for young Italian chefs looking to make their mark.

In a light-filled dining room with views of the sea (as well as of the shrine to the Madonna who protects sailors, after which the spot is named), the two-starred **Madonnina del Pescatore** was inspired by chef Moreno Cedroni's trip to the Cape of Good Hope almost 30 years ago. Using the culinary concept of the Indian and Atlantic Oceans meeting at the cape, his tasting menus and à la carte combinations are divided between dishes closer to home and those farther afield. Dishes like a perfectly rendered risotto with oysters, Moreno's "Suchi" (the misspelling intentional), and a take on *tortellini in brodo* (where the *brodo*, broth, comes in savory cubes), reference the original recipes, then tweak them with delicious results.

At **Uliassi** the competition with neighboring Madonnina served to raise its culinary evolution to new heights. Chef Mauro Uliassi has deep roots in Senigallia. His spot between the beach and the port's canal began in 1990 as a simple beach bar, growing a reputation over the years that rightly puts him in the top tier of Italy's finest chefs. His dishes always keep ingredients of Italy's east coast in mind while adding new elements. His tagliatelle with cuttlefish, for example, comes with nori pesto and fried quinoa, while just caught red prawns are enlivened with lemon water and pineapple sage flowers. Like many of Italy's other best restaurants, the establishment is very much a family affair—Mauro's sister Catia runs the front of the house, and his son Fillipo is the sommelier.

If you have time to experience both places, you'll have hit the seafood jackpot in a town that—despite, and because of, its humble roots—allows chefs to shine within their own terroir.

P.S. For a launchpad into the town's old port and promenades along the sea, book a room at **Terrazza Marconi,** which provides free bikes to work off some of those tasting menu calories. ▪

OPPOSITE: One of the delicate seafood treats at Michelin-starred Madonnina del Pescatore **ABOVE:** Senigallia goes rockabilly during its summer festival, with 1950s style from dress to music.

Best Of

Le Marche's Travel Experiences

One of Le Marche's joys is that you can enjoy them practically in your own company. This allows visitors to experience how this region felt even centuries ago.

Best for the Meditational: Le Marche is home to some of Italy's most important and impressive abbeys. Start the pilgrimage at the 10th-century Benedictine monastery of Fonte Avellana, mentioned in Dante's *Divine Comedy*.

Best for the Nature Lover: The hills around Monte Catria draw hang gliders and nature fans for its otherworldly setting. Its pristine roads wind through the mountains, surrounded by an undisturbed countryside.

Best for the Aesthete: The country has designated certain towns in Italy as their most beautiful. In some regions, the certification can bring too many curious visitors, but in Le Marche, they are still unspoiled and solitary. Frontino, for example, has fewer than 400 residents and an unusually high clock tower tangled in ivy that turns russet red come fall. Entering through the arch of Corinaldo feels like an abandoned film set with sets of steps leading to small churches and perfectly preserved medieval walls.

Best for the Bargain-Minded Gastronome: Hit the White Truffle Fair in the town of Sant'Angelo in Vado in October, with fewer people than at some of the other country equivalents and a plethora of options from Tuscany, Umbria, and Le Marche.

Best for the Slow Food Devotee: Take your time at Bargni di Serrungarina's Da Gustin. This authentic trattoria, managed by three successive generations, comes with steak roasted over a wood fire and truffles from the surrounding forest. At Antico Furlo, you'll find earthy and delicious dishes like white truffles in tagliatelle that epitomize the region's unpretentious and well-priced approach.

Best for the Wanderer: For those interested in natural treasures, don't miss the Frasassi caves near Genga. This underground karstic complex located near Genga is a fantastical place full of stalagmites and stalactites that look like upside-down melted candles. ∎

ABOVE: Le Marche's unmissable Apennines **OPPOSITE:** Bikers explore the countryside around Fonte Avellana, a working monastery and quiet enclave for Romanesque architecture lovers.

Chapter Thirteen
ABRUZZO

Something happens when you cross from the Le Marche into Abruzzo. Undefinable. Just a sense that you're passing into the wild heart of Italy, a place of indomitable mountains studded with isolated villages cut off not only from the outside world but from each other. The wildness must be a scent on the air; you sense it. • Abruzzo and its twin region, Molise, located just above the spur of the boot, used to be known

seamlessly as Abruzzi. In 1963, they untethered into separate regions, but a symbiosis remains. Both possess extensive forests and wildlife, the Apennines' rugged terrain, and sun-washed Adriatic beaches without the influx of visitors that Puglia, their neighbor to the south, experiences.

The Costa dei Trabocchi, as this section of the Adriatic is called, is named for the rickety fishing structures that dot the coastline. Built out into the water, these *trabocchi* look like wooden spiders suspended in the waves, flimsy and ready to collapse. Nets and pulleys could bring in big hauls. Most now have become the ultimate fish shacks. Don't miss a chance to eat just caught seafood at one!

Come here for the beaches, yes, but stay for unspoiled nature. More than twice the size of Molise, Abruzzo boasts higher summits. The Maiella massif reaches 9,753 feet (2,973 m), while dramatic Gran Sasso climbs to 9,553 feet (2,912 m). Both ranges are in superb national parks that offer winter sports and summer hiking—but surprisingly, the area feels undiscovered.

A bonus: Hotels and restaurants in Abruzzo are inexpensive. The food is best described by that expressive Italian word, *genuino,* genuine: parallel to *terroir* but with an additional kick of passion. Traditional recipes from one's *nonna* figure prominently on most menus. Not that there's a lack

of innovation; along the coast, the fish couldn't be fresher, and if the chef bakes his *spigola,* sea bass, in a potato and almond crust, I'm sure *nonna* wouldn't mind.

Vasto, a wide beach resort, is a choice spot on the Abruzzo coast. At secluded Villa Vignola, just outside town, our white room overlooks the sea. The lawn invites reading and napping on a chaise longue under an umbrella. I make a dent in the 500-page novel my book club has chosen. A lone man walks down the slim, pebbly curve of beach, wades in, and quickly drops into deep water. The hotel's restaurant downstairs confirms that this is the place to be; nothing compares with grilled prawns, a sprightly white wine, the whoosh of waves, and a slender crescent moon over the water.

Set on a hill with broad sea views, Vasto won my heart when I saw the main piazza, named for Gabriele Rossetti,

---

WHAT YOU NEED TO KNOW...

- **BEST TIME TO VISIT:** Winter for snow buffs, spring to see parks like Gran Sasso in all their glory, and the coast during the shoulder months. Each *paese,* or town, has its own local *festa,* so try to time your visit accordingly to really get into the spirit.

- **TOP SPOTS:** Gran Sasso, Castel del Monte, Santo Stefano di Sessanio, Sulmona, Vasto

- **GETTING THERE:** You can fly into Pescara, but renting a car is essential to really see the region.

Produced in Majella National Park, these well-cured salami and hearty sausages are among the staples of an Abruzzo table.

Here is the wild heart of Italy, a place of indomitable mountains studded with villages cut off not only from the outside world but from each other.

whose statue centers the town. He left here as a political exile, later fathering two pre-Raphaelite poets, Christina and Dante Gabriel Rossetti in London. Cast in bronze, he's back again, benignly overlooking his hometown.

Busy Vasto has a medieval heart, a castle, and endless little alleys. Groups share meter-long pizzas at outdoor tables. Kids on bikes zoom around fountains, women hoist grocery bags and think of the dinner they'll cook, and the church at the end of the street keeps its doors wide open so we pagans outside with gelato can see the service we are missing.

Only an hour north, Chieti, rich in archaeological ruins, is an ancient city said to have been founded by Achilles: that old. (*Chieti* evolved from "Teate," the name of his wet nurse.) We find a yellow brick, ivory stone, and butterscotch stucco city with a wide pedestrian street, gracious arcaded sidewalks, an evocative Liberty-style café, and attractive shops. Walking along Corso Marrucino, we forget history for a few minutes of indulgent clothes shopping at Gio and DD Boutique, then pick up fig jam and chocolates at the Antica Bottega del Caffè. At a bar, I ask the barista, "How's life in Chieti?" "*Tranquillo,*" he answers.

I stop in to the historic Marrucino theater, built in 1817.

Chieti's picturesque cathedral bell tower is visible from miles away.

Though closed for renovation and entry forbidden, the workers let me in anyway (it's Italy, after all). Filled with four tiers of red velvet box seats, the interior space looks like gilt-frosted spun sugar. Among the curlicues on the ceiling, allegorical female figures decorate a rose window surrounded by medallions of famous playwrights and composers. Evidently performance has always been important in Chieti; both a theater and an amphitheater were discovered in the acropolis of the first century B.C.

All this seems enough for one town, but there's another reason not to miss Chieti: the superb Museo Archeologico d'Abruzzo. The museum cases display everyday objects gathered from ancient graves: belts, daggers, headbands, perfume bottles, a collection of votive hands from a shrine, and some startlingly large statues (especially the one of seated Hercules, who was widely worshipped in this area). I've never seen funeral biers made of finely carved and decorated animal bones. All fascinating to contemplate—especially a pair of gold circular earrings with semiprecious green stones. They must have been the rage in 200 B.C.

In a small room you find the star attraction. One of the premier archaeological finds from all of ancient Italic culture is the mysterious sixth-century B.C. statue known as the Warrior of Capestrano. At 6.8 feet (2.09 m), he's a strong man carved from limestone, white as a ghost. To stand face-to-face with the earliest art of the area is a profound experience. He's dressed enigmatically, with what appears to be a partial facial mask and a broad-brimmed hat. The mask connects him to Mycenaean Greek funerary customs, while the hat adds to his mysterious purpose. Was he upright or buried? With muscular thighs, tight, round butt, and weapons, he exudes force. But the crazy hat gives him a Don Quixote air. Carving on the stone along his side reads: "Me, beautiful image, made by Aninis for King Nevio Pompuledio."

In 1934, he was found in a vineyard, cracked into two separate pieces, with his hat some distance away. Near the hat, a torso of a woman, much smaller scale, came to light too.

Dancing female figures adorn the curved ornate ceiling of Marrucino's theater cupola in Chieti, an artistic hub for the city from opera to jazz.

She's displayed here, her hand almost touching the throat that's not there. Where is the rest of her? Who were they?

One of my favorite towns in Abruzzo is Sulmona, located in Valle Peligna, a green bowl surrounded by mountains. Ovid was born here. A medieval aqueduct runs by the main Piazza Garibaldi. Endearingly, Sulmona's claim to fame is *confetti,* the sugar-coated almonds given as favors at every Italian wedding. They're for sale everywhere, often fastened together and arranged like bright flowers. Wander the calm streets and dip into art at the Museo Civico, located in the most beautiful building in town, the Santissima Annunziata complex. Best to enjoy a simple and perfectly prepared lunch at Ristorante Clemente. I liked retreating to the hotel and dipping into Ovid's *Metamorphosis* with a few *confetti* to munch on. In the evening, a stroll again through the civilized town and a really fun dinner at Buonvento, an intimate osteria stacked with books and frequented by locals. Stefano, at the end, poured a glass of *genziana,* gentian root *digestivo,* straight.

Close by, the village of Pacentro is a sleeping beauty.

Strangely quiet on a misty September morning, the lower piazza is enlivened by a lone farmer selling vegetables and the area's red garlic from his truck. In the upper piazza, three men sit in front of the café looking at their phones while a woman plays solitaire. The barista tells me that the town is full of life, just not today. She's proud that Pacentro is listed as one of the *Borghi piu belli d'Italia,* most beautiful villages in Italy. We wander the pretty stone lanes with houses displaying coats of arms of their *contrada,* neighborhood district. These are important medieval designations; festivals, sports, and racing competitions among *contrade* emphasize close ties.

On the way home, we come upon a roadside restaurant with a smoking grill outside. They're serving sausages, *scamorza,* the local cheese for melting, and *arrosticini,* sizzling lamb skewered on thin sticks. I'm imagining this is what those shepherds ate on the 621-mile (1,000 km) transhumance, the epic migrations of sheep to greener pastures. The man next to me smells like wet wool. We huddle in the light rain under umbrellas. The tastes are savory and rich. Tradition runs strongly in Abruzzo.

Cows calmly graze on the vast pastures of Abruzzo's Gran Sasso National Park, underneath the cloud-covered peaks of the stately Apennines.

Gran Sasso: Abruzzo's Natural Gem

Swaths of green meadow with 360-degree views as far as the eye can see. A vertical massif rises from the low pastures, turning dramatically pink at sunset. Down below on the plain, flocks of sheep look like slow white clouds on a sunny day. Wildflowers peek up from below the rocky soil.

Even for seasoned Italian travelers, **Gran Sasso and Monti della Laga National Park** thrills. There is something otherworldly about it. The breadth of the plateau and height of the great massifs recall other spectacular natural beauties: Norway, perhaps. Patagonia, maybe.

Part of the park's appeal is the sheer size. It's one of the largest in Europe. Plains and valleys alternate between the peaks; little fortified towns provide picturesque rest stops. The Gran Sasso massif itself is second to the Corno Grande, the highest peak of the Apennines.

Today the territory is filled with gentle grazing land perfect for sheep, dotted with small rock dwellings that once provided shelter for shepherds. Flocks have been tended here since Neolithic times, and the area has always relied on their wool, a main engine of the Abruzzo economy well into the 19th century. There are also more than 100 miles (160 km) of trails for horseback riding and hiking.

The park is full of surprises. The **Calderone,** Europe's southernmost glacier, feeds a lake that is dreamy blue and perfect for canoeing. And in addition to the Sasso range, the park includes the other massive rock formations of **Monti della Laga,** which also spill into Le Marche and Lazio. Large snowfall in winter draws skiers.

In this beautiful expanse, wildlife abounds. Wolves prowl (watch out, sheep!), thousands of migratory birds flow south, peregrine falcons soar overhead, and butterflies (like the magical Apollo with its exquisite pattern of black, white, and red wings) flutter through the wildflowers. Marsican brown bear, roe deer, and the Apennine chamois, a species of deer indigenous

to the region, frolic in the meadows.

The tiny towns that dot the park sit high in the mountains and stun in their simplicity. Spots like **Castel del Monte** offer an arresting mix of medieval and Renaissance architecture (beginning in the mid-1500s, the Medici ruled the town for a century). Encircled by defensive walls and five gates to keep the bandits at bay, the town, with its pristine layout, is one of the most beautiful in the park. The ancient fortress of **Rocca Calascio,** the highest castle in all of Italy, is also a must-see. Its function was to protect the mountain roads that

allowed wool to travel from Tuscany all the way down to Puglia. When the Medici took over the castle and surrounding area in the 1500s, the wool would go back to Florence to supply the court's finery. Finally, movie buffs may be interested to learn that Jean-Jacques Annaud's 1986 film *The Name of the Rose* was shot here.

Book a night at Niko Romito's **Casadonna** and its Michelin-starred restaurant, **Reale,** housed in a 16th-century former monastery in Castel di Sangro, or at the simple but intimate **Le Case della Posta** in Santo Stefano di Sessanio. ∎

A NAME TO KNOW: MARGHERITA CARDELLI

Since their wedding in Gran Sasso National Park made it into the pages of *Vogue,* Margherita Cardelli and her husband, Gerardo Cavaliere, have become the unofficial ambassadors for Abruzzo.

THE COUPLE MET at Gerardo's Neapolitan atelier, and after joining forces, they resuscitated the idea of exemplary tailoring for women: think fitted jackets, made-to-measure suits, and belted overcoats in luxurious fabrics. Many of these come from the flocks of sheep near Cardelli's family home, Le Siepi Country Farm, a stunning equestrian center and *agriturismo* (roughly, "agriculture tourism," a style of vacation featuring farmhouse resorts). Their timeless fashion line, the Giuliva Heritage Collection, was picked up by Net-a-Porter and Matches.com, to reach an even broader audience.

Cardelli's favorite place in Abruzzo is the lowland of Campo Imperatore, an immense labyrinth of lights, hills, and mountains at the base of the Gran Sasso mountain. "I love driving there from Santo Stefano di Sessanio, where a small road, that starts above the lake, brings you into the middle of the wildest Italian nature, in the center of Italy, but only an hour and a half from Rome. The surprise that grows meter by meter really explodes when you arrive on top of the hill overlooking the lowlands. There's no stronger emotion for me. That is also the place where I got married two years ago. It is called the Little Tibet, and it literally seems to be in Tibet, or Mongolia, or Montana."

Margherita Cardelli, designer of Giuliva Heritage Collection, is from Abruzzo.

Emidio Pepe and the Superstar Wine of Abruzzo

Even for those who know their wines well, it's easy to confuse Montepulciano Vino Nobile with Montepulciano d'Abruzzo. The former is from Tuscany, and the latter from Abruzzo. Vino Nobile is made from *sangiovese;* Abruzzo's Montepulciano is its own varietal using the grape of the same name. Okay, now that's sorted.

But what's the name you need to know if you only try one wine from Abruzzo? Emidio Pepe. Legend. Superstar. Cellar keeper. Inspiration to many other winemakers around the world.

Emidio's pedigree goes back a long way—to 1889, to be exact, when his *nonno* (grandfather) started growing grapes on their land. Emidio worked alongside his grandfather and father

until he felt ready to produce his own vintages in 1964. He's now a cult figure for wine nerds, as well as any wise soul who likes individuality and complexity in a bottle. If there were ever a model for Italian wine, Emidio in his signature elegant, but jaunty, cap has to be it.

Long before the "Made in Italy" philosophy was born—the idea that excellent, local products would be the country's economic savior and preserve the ancient knowledge and workmanship at risk of being lost—Emidio was living it. His wines showcase the literal roots of his home region; he was one of the first to feature the *Montepulciano d'Abruzzo* and trebbiano grapes that are indigenous here. No chemicals are used in any stage of production, and long aging helps draw out the full potential of these vintages.

Emidio views wine agriculturally and environmentally rather than scientifically and was a pioneer in Italy's biodynamic movement long before it was cool. Grapes are still crushed here without machinery: red grapes by hand, white by foot. Pruning and picking are also all done by hand. Each step of the process uses as little human or artificial interference as possible.

Today, Emidio's daughters and granddaughter are taking over the reins of the family empire. You can stay with them on their estate's charming *agriturismo* and see the process up close. Three generations committed to the land. Made in Abruzzo DOC indeed. ∎

ABOVE: Emidio Pepe, one of Italy's most respected and innovative winemakers **OPPOSITE:** Pepe's estate has been in the family for generations and includes an inn for guests.

Hot Spot
Sextantio

It's happening all over Italy: Depopulation. Low birth rate. Movement from countryside to city. Leaving home to look for more economic opportunity.

You need to see only a few villages around the country to get visual confirmation of these troubling facts: beautiful crumbling towns where you might come across only a handful of residents. *Vendita,* for sale, signs everywhere.

But entrepreneurs and Italy lovers are coming up with creative ways to counter these trends. In January 2019, the mayor of Sicily's Sambuca offered up homes for a dollar to entice buyers to refurbish them using local craftsmen and materials and thus reinvest in town. The story went viral and put this very beautiful village on the tourism map too.

Few other people have been as interested in bringing the local hamlets back to life as Daniele Kihlgren, the owner of the **Sextantio Albergo Diffuso.** Inside the fortified medieval village of **Santo Stefano di Sessanio,** the hotel gives new meaning to remote; its 4,000-foot (1,219 m) setting is like being in an eagle's nest. The isolated town was slowly becoming abandoned when Kihlgren found the dwellings he wanted to convert. He resolved to restore it while keeping the original details as intact as possible.

The result is a living museum for traditional Abruzzo architecture. Fires roar in the enormous fireplaces. Rooms restored with terra-cotta and oak are scattered through the hamlet, with hotel guests living alongside the village's remaining residents. Uneven walls, heavy wood doors, and small windows to watch for bandits recall the place's ancient past.

The food here features the humble but delicious ingredients of a 16th-century dining room: hearty stews of legumes and sausage, hunks of bread with local cheese, pork liver sausage, and pastas like *chitarrina,* "little guitar," with ricotta.

Part of the hotel's greatest appeal is the romance that goes hand in hand with the overall authenticity. Stand-alone bathtubs sit next to rough-hewn original walls; at night, candles and heated floorboards line the way to bed. Wool blankets made from nearby flocks of sheep keep things cozy. ■

A unique hotel has helped revive the hill town Santo Stefano di Sessanio.

Frances's Favorites

Confetti

onfetti: sugar-coated almonds, ubiquitous at every Italian wedding reception, first communion, and baptism. (*Confetto* means "sweetmeat," from the Roman *confectum,* something prepared.) These authentic treats are usually presented in a little white net sack, tied with ribbon, and laid beside your plate. The best ones have a layer of chocolate and no additives in the sugar.

Most *confetti* comes from Sulmona, home to the Museo Confetti Pelino, confectioners since 1783, and dedicated to preserving their history. Prior to that time, nuns made the sweets. Along the streets, many vendors display the candies arrayed as multicolored flowers in bright finger-paint colors. At a glance, they're so stylized that you wouldn't imagine them as edible. A whole town, crazy for *confetti!*

What's fascinating is the background. Since recorded history, objects have been tossed at processions—flowers, rocks, eggs full of perfume, candied coriander seeds, and rotten eggs. In medieval Sulmona, candied almond *confetti* were thrown at the bride and groom; the egg shape indicates a fertility wish. Only later did cheaper cut-up paper begin to be tossed and called, in Italy, *coriandoli,* coriander seeds (though in English, the candy's name transferred to our paper confetti).

Recently on church steps, I saw that plastic rose petals had been strewn. Not nearly as good a start to marriage as the tasty almonds! ■

Vendors display the candies as multicolored flowers in bright finger-paint colors. At a glance, they're so stylized you wouldn't imagine them as edible.

ABOVE: *Confetti,* the traditional sugar-covered almonds made in all colors and designs to celebrate big events around Italy, originated in Abruzzo's town of Sulmona. **OPPOSITE:** Organizing the wares at Pelino Confetti, one of the town's oldest manufacturers of the sweets

Best Of
Hideaway Towns of Abruzzo

Scattered throughout the region, Abruzzo's towns feel frozen in time and offer the strong possibility of escaping other tourists. Here's how to seek out your particular craving:

Best for Beaching: Vasto, a low-key, unpretentious Roman fishing village perched over the Adriatic, makes the perfect launchpad for the surrounding beaches. Have lunch at Castello Aragona, overlooking the bay; grab a seat on the shaded terrace for the town's famous fish soup or tortellini with shrimp and truffles. The Pineta of Teramo beach is worth the drive. Part of the "blue flag" network, which designates the beaches with the cleanest water in Italy, it remains pristine in high season despite the many beach clubs and lidos along the way.

Best for Nature Lovers: At the heart of the National Park of Abruzzo, the town of Pescasseroli sits in the middle of the mountains, drawing hikers and wildlife seekers in the spring and ski buffs in the winter. It also marks the beginning of the famous Pescasseroli-Candela *tratturo,* first a military route for Roman legions, then a road for moving sheep from Abruzzo into Puglia, and now a beautiful trail for intrepid walkers.

Best for Photography Buffs: Sitting on the banks of the large lake of Scanno, this town of the same name is one of Abruzzo's most beautiful (Henri Cartier-Bresson and Mario Giacomelli were only two of the photographers seduced by it). Getting there is half the fun; the road snakes precariously through the Sagittario Valley while providing lots of photo ops before the main event of the town itself. Don't miss the venerable church of Santa Maria della Valle on the main piazza.

Best for Chefs in Training: In the seaside town of Pescara, a mother-and-daughter team, Rosaria Mastrodicasa and Annabella Cermignani, have taken their considerable combined culinary talent and created Cooking With Rosy. They invite guests into their home for cooking lessons or take them on a tour of their favorite winery or *trabocchi,* former fishing platforms that sit on the sea like art installations. As Abruzzo's main coastal town, Pescara can be somewhat overwhelming, and this is a wonderful way to get the inside take through local eyes. It's also fun to learn how to make traditional pastas like the *chitarra* through a board with stainless steel guitar–like strings (hence the name). Another dish to make when you get home? The *ravioli dolce alla Teramana,* pasta stuffed with ricotta with just a dash of cinnamon and sugar. If you want a more gourmet experience, book a table at Café Les Paillotes. Heinz Beck, the star chef behind La Pergola in Rome, received a Michelin star here as well. Don't miss the *scampi crudo* with mint, celery, yogurt, and raspberry; the delicate combination is a memory maker. ∎

ABOVE: Dressing for Ju Catenacce, a festival in the village of Scanno
OPPOSITE: *Trabocchi* fishing rigs converted into restaurants

Frances's Favorites
In Your Glass

Pecorino is not only a cheese; it's a grape much appreciated in Abruzzo and in Le Marche, just to the north. The Pecorino Pasetti's version, with pear aroma and a hint of stoniness, complements the area's marvelous seafood. Equally good: Cataldi Madonna Giulia Pecorino Biologico. This easy wine is also well balanced, with a light citrus touch. From the fine winery Luigi Cataldi Madonna comes Pecorino Giulia (the label shows the ancient statue of the Warrior of Capestrano). A slight tang of grapefruit does not overwhelm the other light fruit notes.

The famous red wine of the region is Montepulciano d'Abruzzo (not to be confused with Vino Nobile di Montepulciano, which is made of, at minimum, 70 percent the famous *sangiovese,* known in Tuscany as *prugnolo gentile*). Abruzzo *montepulciano* is its own grape variety. Castorani Amorino Montepulciano d'Abruzzo is a beauty that complements a savory beefsteak brushed with rosemary or the popular grilled lamb.

Also appealing: big-mouthed and juicy Montepulciano d'Abruzzo Ursonia, Il Feuduccio di Santa Maria D'Orni.

After dinner, try the popular *digestivi centerba* and *genziana* to end your hearty meal with a bang. *Centerba* means "100 herbs." The taste bears that out, dense and grassy, with a piquant edge. *Genziana,* the color of candlelight, is yellow and bitter. Though gentian flowers are often shown on the labels, the ingredient actually comes from the macerated dried root. ∎

> After dinner, try the popular *digestivi centerba* and *genziana* to end your meal with a bang. *Genziana,* the color of candlelight, is yellow and bitter.

ABOVE: Semivicoli's atmospheric tasting room is housed in the castle's ancient cellar; hotel rooms sit on its upper floors. OPPOSITE: Barrea, a town known for its wine as well as being a launchpad for hikes, spills down the hill to the lake.

Chapter Fourteen
MOLISE

Welcome to Termoli, a sparkling gem on the Adriatic. The ideal place to stay is the old quarter of town, where a castle soars above a stretch of golden beach. The café-strewn piazza, grounded by a graceful Romanesque church, opens to the bluest sky, and the white travertine streets gleam like slabs of wax. • Our upstairs room in the Residenza Sveva, an *albergo diffuso* (rooms scattered around town managed by a

central office), is dominated by a big window filled with the view: turquoise waters lashed with dark blue. The floor, laid with big aqua tiles, looks wet. On an early September weekend, the sea remains warm enough for swimming. Our first act: lunch at the brilliant Ristorante Svevia. "Just a glass," we demur. But when the waiter refills, we don't object.

Corso Nazionale bisects the newer section of town, a few steps away. As in every Italian town, a *passeggiata*, promenade, takes place in early evening. Every couple with a stroller to push comes out; so do a cluster of men in wheelchairs and teens in laughing gaggles. Smart shops open their doors wide, and waiters bear trays of sunset-colored *aperitivi*. All of us delight in the balmy air with nothing on our minds, for an hour, but the palm trees, the coming dinner, and this *now* with others, all caught in the spell of a communal rite.

When dark falls, we settle at Osteria Dentro Le Mura, an outdoor table on the sea walk in old Termoli. Lapis lazuli night sky with flecks of stars, fireworks shooting off in the distance, some accordion players and screechy singers. A feast of everything just caught, brought to us fresh and grilled.

Molise, a microcosm of Italy, has beaches, mountains, olive groves, lost-to-time villages, authentic food, and wine. I find everything I love about traveling right here. Molise—no one knows what the word means—is the second-to-smallest

Italian region, with only 2,758 square miles (4,438 sq km). Seeing the sights is easy, right? But when I make a list of inland villages I want to visit, I find that they are so far apart I can visit only two or three in a day of driving around mountains, often on secondary roads through untainted wilderness. What a pleasure to come upon towns refreshingly themselves, not catering to tourism but existing for those who live there.

We strike out from Termoli. In the village of Larino, close by, we sit in a sunny piazza overlooking the impressive 1319 duomo, where local people are filing in. By the second coffee,

WHAT YOU NEED TO KNOW...

- **BEST TIME TO VISIT:** Unless you are specifically in the region for skiing, it's best to avoid visiting here in January and February, when the already difficult-to-navigate roads become even harder to manage. Christmas will give you the chance to witness a variety of atmospheric festivals, and in the spring, you'll enjoy the crisp, sunny days without other tourists.

- **TOP SPOTS:** Agnone, Termoli, Rochetta a Vulturno, Saepinum, Venafro

- **GETTING THERE:** Molise doesn't have its own designated airport, so fly into Pescara or Naples, then drive (renting a car here is a must). If you're feeling adventurous, try Italy's "Transiberian train," which winds through Abruzzo, Molise, and some of the wildest landscapes in Italy.

Tuscan and Piedmontese truffles may get more press, but Molise's variety is also excellent, especially served up in a plate of risotto.

Molise, a microcosm of Italy, has beaches, mountains, olive groves, and lost-to-time villages. I find everything I love about traveling right here.

mournful music swells out the doors, and a full-ritual liturgical procession passes. Unlike many Masses I've witnessed with a congregation of 10 ancients, this one is packed. I photograph the arched entrance of receding columns and the intricate stone rose window. I take my time, lingering on carved lambs, mythic griffins (they lifted bodies into heaven and therefore symbolize ascent), and representations of the winged evangelists: ox, lion, man, and eagle. Lapidary remnants of graves, ornaments, and markers fill the church cloister, including a massive grinding wheel that pressed many an olive in ancient times.

Besides its ravishing church, Larino has Roman mosaics, an amphitheater, and beckoning lanes to wander. Row-house doors open directly onto the street. No room for trees, but

The bell tower of Santa Cristina in Sepino provides an evocative view.

residents garden with pots. One doorway with four sleeping cats on the mat is draped with pink and white mandevilla vine, which is trained around the windows as well. Next door, the neighbor methodically lined her plot with plastic water bottles laid end to end. Thereby hangs a long-brewing feud: Plastic bottles around doors deter cats from peeing against the walls. I wonder if the neighbors speak. I hope so, as they live so close to the lane named Paradiso.

After an hour of hardly passing another car, we come to Agnone, a vibrant town of 5,200 souls settled by the pre-Roman Samnite warriors. I want to say we're out in the middle of nowhere, but it's such a somewhere! Significant churches, a wide, tree-lined main street with many bakeries and butcher shops alongside bars and stores selling old copper and antiques. The local industry is the Marinelli family's production of bells. For more than a thousand years they've been casting by the lost wax method. Bells, bells of all sizes, from gigantic duomo bells to tinkly dinner bells. I would like to hear each one's particular *ting* or *gong*. The Campane Marinelli foundry's museum preserves the entire history.

Agnone's old quarter is alluring, with Venetian-influenced palazzi, stone stairs leading up to the next level of streets, a barny church where four brindled cats take the sun, and historic Caffè Letterario's inviting terrace overlooking a fountain and small piazza.

Wandering in the villages all over Italy, I'm always struck by what intact worlds they are. People living their intense and private lives: nothing at all to do with the soon-gone voyeur. I'm the ghost figure, moving invisibly through the dramatic or ordinary scenes lived out in this place. That sensation is vivid in Molise, where you see pale villages from afar, cascading down a mountainside or capping a peak. They're storybook inventions, appearing almost real.

Pull into irregularly shaped Piazza Nerazio Prisco, *centro* of Sepino, ready to be surprised. The buildings are apricot, marigold, blood orange, turquoise, rosy dark plum, apple

Larino's wagons come painted with local images and vegetation like art installations.

green. The Chiesa di Santa Cristina is ethereal blue with a unique swirling iron cupola. But nothing prepares you for the white-trimmed buttercream interior. I can sometimes get churched out, but this one intrigues me mightily. The *pietra dura* (inlaid colored stones) altar is merrily bedecked with sunflowers and watched over by an Annunciation, the most mysterious of religious subjects. But the ceiling is what astonishes me. Painted by the Molesano artist Amedeo Trivisonno, whose life (1904–1995) spanned the century, the arresting frescoes make me want to lie on the floor and look up. Usually, 20th-century interventions in duomos are cringe-worthy, but these biblical scenes are illuminating, with a mellow and exacting color sense. Trivisonno—why have I never known of him?—painted in 37 churches and also worked in Egypt. I'm inspired to make a quest of his frescoes. This is when travel flies outside expectations.

The town of Oratino, just 30 minutes away, seems asleep when we arrive. That's because at this hour, almost everyone sits around a table for Sunday lunch. From the open windows in the lanes, I hear clinking forks against plates and competing voices. Argument. Laughter. Aromas of roast pork. Plaques on many palazzi record painters, architects, writers; this must have been a center of culture. We follow our noses to Ristorante Olmicello, joining dozens of local families for the ritual weekly *pranzo*. They order copious platters of antipasti and pitchers of house wine, and then proceed to visit from table to table, their returns to their seats admirably timed for the next course. So much of Sunday remains in rural Italy.

We too order too much. Little ravioli with walnuts, *medaglioni* (pillows of potato-filled pasta) with speck, zucchini, and pistachios. Other pastas are treated to pumpkin and sausage, or served with *spigarello,* a local green close to broccoli rabe. So tasty: roasted *scamorza* cheese with radicchio and crisp pancetta; *bocconcini,* bites of chicken with arugula. Everywhere the local *pecorino* wine pours freely. Beware—it's so friendly and drinkable that you might not notice how quickly the pitcher empties.

We have only three days to find these secret realms, and there are dozens we miss. We return to Tremoli for a final night in this enchanting town: pizza in an intimate piazza where everyone knows everyone on this late summer night.

In the Know

An Introduction to Italy's Youngest Region

Ma sai qualcosa del Molise? Do you know anything about Molise? *No mi dispiace, non sono mai stato*. I am sorry, I have never been.

In Italy, that exchange is typical. Even seasoned travelers, native and foreign, are hard-pressed to locate this tiny region next to Abruzzo. Poor Molise gets made fun of in other parts of the country for its remoteness. (There was even a Facebook page called "Molisn't," or "I don't believe in the existence of Molise," which garnered over 60,000 followers before a kind soul took it down.) Still, this far-flung expanse may end up getting the last laugh as a new wave of visitors eager to escape other tourists unearths a multitude of treasures.

Here are some facts to know. The region was first settled by the Samnites, a warrior tribe of fierce native Italians who ruled the area before being conquered by the Romans. The Goths became the next set of invaders, followed by the Lombards.

In the 19th century, many of Molise's residents fled the area for other parts of the country or emigrated abroad because of poverty and more than the occasional earthquake. During World War II, the region was a front for intense battles between the Allies and Germans and was heavily bombed. As a result, many "ghost towns," or villages that are partially or completely depopulated, are common here.

Considered the gateway to the south of Italy, Molise is the very youngest of Italy's regions, established only in 1965 after being separated from its neighbor, Abruzzo. Earthquakes in 1980 and 2002 resulted in another wave of emigration. No wonder the people here have gained a reputation for being incredibly resilient.

Dubbed Italy's "wild west" because of its bandit past, Molise feels the most remote of its many regions. There's no airport, and traversing mountainous territory involves crazy, curvy roads. But that's part of its charm—and why, once intrepid travelers do make it there, they are deeming it Italy's "new" must.

Villages in Molise seemingly defy gravity, especially those around the **Parco delle Morge,** a string of little towns that seem to be about to precariously tumble down the side of the mountain. Refreshingly, traces of a simple, traditional life that has disappeared in many parts of the country linger on here.

The region is chockablock with antique treasures, once you know where to look. Roman Empire buffs will want to put it on the itinerary. The mausoleum outside Atilia, for example, also has an impressive theater located by the tiny town of **Pietrabbondante** (literally, "the town abundant with stone"), and the viaduct over Lake Guardialfiera that curves gently around **Monte Pelosi** sits over the ruins of a Roman bridge.

Castles from the Norman period also abound here, including formidable structures like the **Angevin Castle** of Civitacampomarano and the **Monforte Castle** of Campobasso. These imposing buildings show how often this area was under attack by marauding troops and itinerant bandits. ◾

OPPOSITE: Artisans in Molise handcraft *zampogne* (bagpipes). **ABOVE:** Monumental ruins excavated near the town of Pietrabbondante date back to the Roman era, and even the Samnites before them.

Best Of

Molise's Towns: From Romans to Ghosts

With its layers of history and natural beauty, Molise makes the perfect destination to slowly wind your way from town to town, stopping for ruins in one spot and a feast in another.

Best of the Ghost Towns: After the 19th century, many residents took off for America or bigger Italian cities. As a result, many towns in Molise became a living museum and monument to what was left behind. Such was the case in Rocchetta a Volturno, which suffered extensive damage during World War II (and a landslide to boot). But this older settlement on the hill was once one of Molise's most central areas; the important abbey of San Vincenzo, ancient tombs, and an aqueduct are only some of the remnants of its former history. In the municipality of Civitacampomarano as well, there may now remain even fewer residents (about 400 to be exact), but it was once an important town. The number of inhabitants swells significantly every June for the CVTà Street Fest when international and local street artists reinvigorate the neighborhood with bright murals and site-specific art installations. Whatever the season, the haunting *borgo,* hamlet, is worth a side trip.

Best for Roman History Buffs: The town of Saepinum might be one of Italy's best kept secrets. Formerly a Samnite settlement, it fell into Roman hands in 293 B.C. Its well-preserved forum and Roman baths let you quietly explore the settlement without the jostling crowds of Pompeii and Rome. Particularly sweet is the remaining inscription telling the citizens there to allow the shepherds and their sheep to pass unhindered, a custom that is still respected. In Venafro, head to the Roman theater, located in the center of the more modern part of the city, before going up to the old town, with its traces of Roman ruins under every structure. After working up an appetite, try *la signora di Conca Casale,* a local sausage originally prepared for nobles with various cuts of pork and seasoned with black peppercorns, peperoncino, cumin, and fennel pollen (it's one of the region's true specialties). And in Larino, the Roman amphitheater built in the first century A.D. remains a grand visual reminder of Molise's deep Roman roots.

Best for Ski Bunnies: Only an hour-and-a-half drive from the Adriatic beaches, Campitello Matese lays claim to the greatest snowfall in central southern Italy. With a wide network of runs, the fun goes on over a number of different mountains, like the Monte Croce and Miletto, drawing downhill skiers and snowboarders galore. Come spring, nature buffs take their place.

Best for Truffle Hunters: Truffle connoisseurs should put Molise on their radar, as the region is the second biggest producer in all Italy. And Carovilli is at the heart of it all. While the black varieties are more ubiquitous and less prized (though certainly delicious), the white varieties come with a creamier, more distinctive taste. For a real farm-to-table experience and to sample local products from truffles to mushrooms, book a table at Masseria Monte Pizzi (before falling asleep in one of its delightful rooms). ■

ABOVE: The town of Venafro OPPOSITE: Rocchetta al Volturno was full of residents until landslides forced them to relocate to the valley.

In the Know

Festivals: The Heartbeat of Molise

While local festivals remain popular all over Italy, some feel less authentic because of how many tourists join the fun. In Molise, however, they remain a traditional backbone of the region and a way to come together in a territory where the population tends to be spread out and relatively isolated for months at a time.

Every May in the region of **Ururi,** oxcarts career dangerously close together during the Carrese, a deeply entrenched event that pays homage to the importance of the bovines here. The event starts with the blessing of the animals before the races begin; then adult farmers steer older animals, while adolescents and preteens follow with the calves, which also pull small carts. The lucky winner, who arrives first in front of the main church of the **Santa Maria delle Grazie,** celebrates the victory by carrying the relic (said to be part of the holy Cross) in a townwide procession that precedes an epic feast. The rest of the year, the town continues its rural rhythms, tucked into the lush countryside where the cattle graze.

In the village of **Agnone,** the Christmas festival of Ndocciata is one of the most authentic in Italy. Hundreds of residents come together to light torches, creating a beautiful light show through the streets of town before gathering for a huge bonfire. The *ndocce,* torches, were originally used by the Samnites to move secretly through the countryside at night to avoid their enemy in broad daylight, then by farmers to light their way to Mass on Christmas Eve. And the lights are used by local Romeos who try to woo their Juliets with the most impressive torch creation they can muster (a look of appreciation from her window is a *sì,* while a bucket of water to snuff out the fire is a definite "no thanks"). While in Agnone, don't miss the **Museo Storico della Campana.** The town is also known for its church bell, *campana,* production.

Termoli, a small port town with whitewashed and pastel-colored houses, truly comes to life every August 15 for the Ferragosto festival, when townsfolk reenact defeating the Turkish invaders in a David and Goliath–like battle that happened in 1566. Fireworks, belly dancers, and youths dressed as marauding Turks create a spectacular show. The walled village deserves a visit even if you can't make it on that date; it was the site of a monumental battle between British and German forces during World War II, and now has become a preferred escape to the beach (ferries also leave from here to Puglia's Tremiti Islands). Don't miss the town's 13th-century Norman castle, the striking Romanesque cathedral, and a raucous fish market on Tuesdays and Thursdays.

At the village of **Pescolanciano's** Festa di Sant'Anna, held in late July, the town's inhabitants celebrate the harvesting of grain and honor their patron saint Sant'Anna, with an outdoor Mass and procession through town. Intricate wheat creations top the heads of local women in traditional dress. ▪

OPPOSITE: The Ndocciata festival in Agnone sees the lighting of thousands of torches to celebrate an ancient Christmas rite. **ABOVE:** Bovines take to the streets to celebrate Carrese.

Frances's Favorites

In Your Glass

Although small in size, Molisano wines walk tall. For all the super-fresh fish on your plate along the coast, try a Molise Falanghina DOC, Borgo di Colloredo, or the Molise Falanghina, Di Majo Norante. The *falanghina* wines are pale straw in color, with a faint scent of orange blossoms and a bit of stony-beach minerality.

Inland, with grilled or roasted meats and robust pastas, check the wine list for Molise Aglianico Contado Riserva, Di Majo Norante. This is a big, balanced red that you'll want to hold up to the light to enjoy the rich crimson color, then sip slowly. It hits the top on wine charts, and the price is so low I thought there must have been a misprint. Molise Rosso Passo alle Tremiti, earthy and fruity, comes from a vineyard that overlooks the five tiny Tremiti Islands, an hour by ferry from Termoli.

Nocino, a favorite *digestivo,* must be made from still green walnuts gathered on the feast day of St. John the Baptist, June 24. (That's when they're just right.) The cut-up walnuts macerate in alcohol, lemon peel, clove, nutmeg, and vanilla bean for around 38 days; then a sugar syrup is added. Bottled, it's then aged for a few months. Dark and spicy, *nocino* seems perfect to sip in winter by the fire. ■

Check the wine list for Molise Aglianico Contado Riserva, Di Majo Norante.
Hold it up to the light to enjoy the rich crimson color, then sip slowly.

ABOVE: Lines and lines of *falanghina* grapes **OPPOSITE:** Have a glass, or a bottle, of Tintilia wine at San Martino in Pensilis's Catabbo cellar.

In the Know

Hiking Ancient Pathways of Soldiers and Sheep

Suddenly you find yourself thinking that you hear the sound of bells—faint at first, they grow steadily stronger. Then the sound of little hooves, clicking along like hundreds of high heels. Around the corner, you spy them: a current of sheep making their way down the street, moving in their own particular rhythm, and nudged along by the dogs that escort the slower ewes. At the back of the line or in the middle of the crowd, a shepherd walks with purpose. Steady, watchful, moving in a way that can only be described as meditational.

The phenomenon of the *transumanza,* or transhumance migration, has to be one of Italy's most fascinating and enduring. This network of ancient trails has been used by flocks of sheep and cattle for centuries, as shepherds take their flocks from the highlands down to warmer countryside during winter and then back up again when the temperature starts to rise. In places like Lombardy's Po Valley, much of the network has been interrupted by the construction of suburbia or highways (although many intrepid herders still follow the same route, wending their way through the new development).

Here in Molise, however, the *tratturi,* or trails, are much easier to see as they were intended. The tracks follow in the footsteps of the Roman soldiers who first used these routes as they moved south, conquering as they went. The vein through Molise is considered one of the major arteries of the *transumanza,* taking the valuable animals from the steep mountainsides of Abruzzo, through Molise, and then down into the gentle flatlands of Puglia (wool was the main industry for much of the region's history). Recently, UNESCO recognized the historical and cultural importance of such a migration. More than 150 miles (250 km) of pathways through these neighboring regions are also a hiker's dream.

The best way to start your exploration is the route between Pescasseroli and Candela. Ask at Pescasseroli's tourist office for a map of the hike. ∎

OPPOSITE: Cattle make the journey from north to south on the *transumanza,* or transhumance, migration, one of Molise's most evocative sights.
ABOVE: Sheep have traveled the same trails for centuries.

In the Know

Local Flavors: Natural and Earthy

Despite its small size, Molise has a wide-ranging cuisine and specializes in dishes and products that you might not see in other parts of the country.

Caciocavallo di agnone, for example, is an ancient local cheese made from cow's milk and dates back to Roman times. You'll know you've found the right one when you see the telltale white cord around its slender top. It resembles a teardrop, and hence its nickname: *lachrymose,* dialect for "tear." Another top *formaggio* is the *caprino di Montefalcone nel Sannio.* This goat's cheese comes from a province of Campobasso and boasts the subtle taste of the herbs and flowers the animals enjoy in the nearby meadows. If you get lucky enough to be invited to a special event like a wedding, the antipasto will be sure to include *stracciata,* a delicate rindless cow's cheese typically served with prosciutto.

Meat lovers will be in heaven in Molise—particularly those who adore cured meats, and most especially those who enjoy sausages. Among the specialties is the *Ventricina di Montenero di Bisaccia,* a succulent salami aged anywhere from seven to 18 months. The distinctive smoky taste comes from being dried by a fireplace before being hung from the rafters. Other sausage staples include the *salsiccia di fegato,* stuffed with pork liver and seasoned with orange peel and bay leaves, and *torcinelli,* with sheep liver rather than pork.

As in most other areas of the country, Molise creates its own pasta shapes, as well as sauces, that are distinctive to the region. And as with everywhere else, there is often disagreement as to who can lay claim to each celebrated invention. Here, chefs own the *cavatelli.* This delicately imprinted pasta usually comes with ragù, a meat sauce, topped with sausage, or, for vegetarians, with broccoli (known as *spigarello*). Another popular pasta shape, *fusilli,* was also first used here, but with variations where spinach or beets are added to the dough to lend its distinctive, vibrant color.

The rugged and fertile land here provides the perfect soil for vegetables. A local endive, the *scarola venafrana,* comes in delicate salads or is cooked in hearty dishes with beans. The Isernia onion, also known as the *cipolla di San Pietro,* is a particularly sweet varietal often featured in a frittata (the onion has its own festival every June). And even in the colder months, tomato lovers will find the *pomodori gialli invernali:* literally, yellow winter tomatoes. These firm, juicy *pomodori* provide a steady, delicious staple to be served on grilled, thick bread or with homemade pasta. And the way they hang suggestively from the farmhouse beams gives them the look of a food magazine cover shot! ■

ABOVE: *Caciocavallo* cheese is prepared every morning at Agnone's Caseificio Di Nucci. **OPPOSITE:** Owner Antonio Di Nucci shows off the excellent results of his caciocavallo.

Part Three

Southern Italy
and the
Islands

Capri's iconic view of the Faraglioni rocks provides a stunning focal point for boats and island visitors.

From maurading pirates to sea lovers, the south of the country has aways seduced visitors. Expect beaches, castles, and plenty of good food.

Filled with azure seas, hearty food, and historical treasures, the south of Italy beckons: a mystical land that feels like another country. Every church and tower here has a story. The south was repeatedly invaded, and the architectural treasures left by waves of conquerors are a road map for the area's history. In Naples, you'll find glorious chaos and mouthwatering pizza. In Sardinia's Cagliari and Alghero, you'll encounter historic universities bustling with students; in Lecce, fanciful carvings on ornate churches; and in Matera, a vision of a city that seems plucked from the Middle East.

The food in this part of the country is nothing less than mouthwatering: fat eggplants and sun-ripened tomatoes; buttery mozzarella and ricotta cream–filled cannoli; and freshly caught fish from the sea. The wine flows all over the south, and Mount Etna has become one of the most exciting regions in the country.

Visiting here, you can't go wrong with an expedition to the beaches: the blindingly white and turquoise of Sardinia and Puglia, the stretches of natural park in Sicily, the treasured islands off Campania like Ischia and Capri. Sailboats nod nonchalantly off the coast. The summer lingers longer here than in the rest of the country, and you'll enjoy balmy sunny days even in April or late October.

If you're in search of a cone of pistachio DOC gelato in Sicily or an ice-cold Ichnusa beer in Sardinia, head to the small towns dotted throughout the south. Time stops. And perhaps you'll remember the people here most of all. Kind strangers become friends over the course of an espresso or an *aperitivo* in a sun-drenched café. The south was (and still is) the poorest part of Italy; many of its former residents immigrated to the United States. Their relatives who remain are warm and receptive to visitors from other places. Meeting them, you'll immediately understand the deep connection with family, with friendship, and hospitality. This alone will keep you coming south for a long, long time.

CLOCKWISE FROM UPPER LEFT: The circular whitewashed *trulli* houses of Puglia are seen in Alberobello and scattered in the countryside; traditional bread cooked in a wood-burning oven is served with olive oil in Matera; the catch of the day being offloaded in Puglia's Trani; the world-famous lemons of the Amalfi Coast.

Chapter Fifteen

CAMPANIA

For sheer beauty, few other places on Earth compare with the Amalfi Coast's flower-tumbled villages and vertigo views over the Tyrrhenian Sea. The gods live here, all the good ones; we just can't see them. Unbelieving of such beauty, we mortals think we're dreaming, even as the benison of light falls over us. • The person you become here seems like the person you always meant to be. Or so I feel, among the

jasmine vines on a terrace in Ravello, the jewel box of Amalfi. My neighbors are ancient Roman emperors with their stone faces overlooking the sea, overcurried dogs on jeweled leashes, and a few other wonder-struck tourists snapping a hundred photos a minute and possibly forgetting to look, just look.

The Amalfi Coast starts at Sorrento, just over an hour south of Naples. The narrow, vertiginous former donkey track road hugs cliffsides overlooking plunging sea views. Once you've driven that coast, you never forget it. How could you? Your heart was in your mouth, and your brain hardly could absorb the beauty. The fabled coast ends at the town of Vietri sul Mare, famous for ceramics.

From many departure points along the sea, take a private boat or a ferry to Capri, which has attracted emperors and movie stars, pederasts and writers, aesthetes and oligarchs, as well as cascades of day-trippers spilling off those ferries for six dazed hours. No wonder why. Sheer glamour smacks you like a sneaker wave. Capri embodies all the fantasies of a paradisiacal Mediterranean island. The whitewashed houses bear sweet names, the water is bluer than your true love's eyes, and the craggy coast seems operatic, as if some forlorn hero will climb ashore singing an aria learned from the Sirens. Former goat paths climb up and down and wind around precipitous edges, luring you to discover every inch of the island.

By 4 p.m., boatloads of tourists depart, and the island returns to itself. Don glamorous sunglasses and head straight up to the tiny village of Anacapri in a white open-top taxi. Wander the lanes, explore shops, and visit Villa San Michele, the garden and estate of Axel Munthe, a Swedish doctor and writer who loved Capri. There's Café Casa Oliv within the lush grounds.

Even better, come in spring or fall. I was there late one October when the winter shutdown was beginning. Bliss. I discovered that the island offers the best walking imaginable. I could read—Munthe's *The Story of San Michele* and Shirley Hazzard's *Greene on Capri*—on the beach without getting fried, and local people suddenly had time to talk.

A short hydrofoil ride away (also leaves from Naples) lies

WHAT YOU NEED TO KNOW...

• **BEST TIME TO VISIT:** Like many of Italy's other regions, Campania is best to visit in the shoulder season; Naples and Amalfi are less crowded, better priced, and cooler. Come August, many of the pizza masters will be on their own beach vacation, and temperatures become sweltering. Like to party? Few other places in Italy are as jovial as Naples come Christmas and New Year's Eve.

• **TOP SPOTS:** Naples, Ischia, Cilento, Capri, Amalfi

• **GETTING THERE:** Naples International Airport—or hop on the hour-long Frecciarossa train from Rome.

Vines embrace the inviting entrance to Villa Cimbrone, a private home reimagined as a hotel in Ravello, a quieter outpost on the Amalfi Coast.

Campania has been desirable from the eighth century B.C.
The Greeks were all over it, colonizing as fast as ships could get there.

the island of Ischia, whose main attractions are the many thermal pools, spas, good seafood, a laid-back atmosphere.

Besides these legendary coasts, the region of Campania, just south of Rome, has been desirable from the eighth century B.C. The Greeks were all over it, building massive structures and colonizing as fast as ships could get there. For a fascinating look at what remains of the ancient world, I propose an unforgettable tour, beginning with the Greek port city of Paestum. A cluster of three monumental ruins dominates: the Basilica, the Temple of Athena, and the Temple of Neptune. Surely these colossal colonnades are unreal, looming so suddenly out of the backwash of time. An oracle might step from behind a column in the dusk. Have a picnic, or step up, channel an orator, and declaim. From Paestum, a magnetic strength seems to emanate.

Each ancient site is singular. Rich and powerful Capua, just north of Naples, became a major city, second to Rome in size. Now known as Santa Maria Capua Vetere, what remains from the classical era is a phenomenal amphitheater that

seated 60,000, second only to the Colosseum in Rome. The city changed hands, from Etruscan to Samnite to Roman and then over to Hannibal. What convoluted waves of conquerors: Visigoths, Vandals, Ostrogoths, Longobards, Saracens. Rolling with the times, Capua remained a top city during those successive eras. Check out the colosseum and Museo Campano in modern Capua. The ticket also admits you to a *mithraeum,* a vaulted underground frescoed space dedicated to the mysterious pagan cult of Mithras, which originated during the third-century Roman Empire and filtered to Italy via Greece. Here, Mithras strides a bull as he kills it. A startling image.

Next up, Pompeii and Herculaneum, the two cities destroyed in A.D. 79 by the eruption of Mount Vesuvius. How quickly they alter your perception of how life was lived. At Pompeii, reach out and touch the deep past, from lava-charred loaves of bread to delicate frescoes of baskets of figs. The remnants of quotidian life put you in immediate contact with those citizens who had no time to flee the onrush of Vesuvius's fiery lava. Unforgettable: a charred man and woman caught forever in a spooning embrace. Don't go on a sweltering day; it's still fiery hot in the ruins.

Only five miles (8 km) from Naples, Herculaneum's mosaics, frescoes, and architectural ruins present an even closer look at sophisticated daily life. There's more to find (the work continues today); after all, Herculaneum was buried under 60 feet (18 m) of mud and lava.

Ending this tour in Naples makes sense. The Museo Archeologico possesses troves of objects from Campanian excavations, allowing you to put history into context. Belt buckles, sieves, pans, jewelry, everything scraped up from the homes reminds you of the hands that made them, the work in the kitchens, the adornment of the dress. Truly flabbergasting, the quantity of what remains. The erotic frescoes used to be closed to the general public. Now you can see them, dominated by brothel humor. One man's phallus is so large that it's carried before him on a tray!

Serving up espresso at Gran Caffè Gambrinus, a historic café in Naples

Campania is full of archaeological treasures like the UNESCO-protected Roman ruins of Villa Poppaea, located in the town of Torre Annunziata.

Now you're free to explore one of the most vibrant cities on Earth. They used to say, "See Naples and die." For the beauty, of course: beauty beyond measure with its bay and looming Vesuvius. But Naples also is a swarm of southern craziness and energy. Four on a Vespa, *no problema.* Drivers of minute cars put NASCAR champions in the dust. Friends born here say if you are native, no other city ever can compare. You always will long to be back in your fabled Napoli! Stand in line for one of the primo pizza places (Sorbillo, Da Concettina, Da Michele). Explore the ancient Roman east-west thoroughfare, the *decumanus maximus,* now called Spaccanapoli: the "split-Naples" street with tiny dark shops, gelato sellers, and *friggiatorie,* quick fried-food stands serving *arancini,* crispy fried rice balls filled with cheese or ragù. Offshoot lanes are crowded with artisan makers, since the 17th century, of the revered *presepi,* Nativity scenes, complete with pig roasting, weavers, candlemakers, bakers, donkeys, and sheep to complete your manger scene. Baby Jesus lies on electrified hay, and there's even the witch Befana, who refused to follow the Wise Men but atones by bringing gifts to good children on Epiphany, January 6. How *bellissima:* The church of Santa Chiara provides an oasis of calm in a majolica-adorned courtyard among the cloisters.

What a treat to attend a performance at Teatro San Carlo, the grand opera house built in 1737. Wander in the *centro,* including Via Calabritto for the best shops, and the Via Chiaia, a palazzo-lined street where the trees meet overhead. I always stop at the historic Gran Caffè Gambrinus for a pastry. Coffee in Naples is the best, brief and intense, and always served with a small glass of water. Nearby, you find the glass-domed Galleria Umberto I: traditionally the place for fine shops, now dingy but still impressive. For views, and a more refined Naples, take the funicular up to upscale Vomero's pleasant neighborhoods, shops, and restaurants.

I like the pedestrian Lungomare walk along the water, and the Quartieri Spagnoli, a decadent and bawdy neighborhood. No one does decadent like Naples: dreamy, decrepit palaces with broken shutters and stucco peeling off in layers of burnt umber, putty, and apricot; iron balconies swagged with bougainvillea; massive doorways with giant lion's head knockers; laundry strung haphazardly. And, see through the window, magnificent ceiling frescoes inside? That's Naples: city of contrasts. Staggering natural beauty, squalor, exuberance, and hidden moments of grandeur.

Many visitors use Naples as a launch point for the islands of Ischia and Capri, but the city itself is more than worth exploring.

Naples: Finding Beauty in Chaos

Vespas career down tight streets. A family of three sit on top of one, wearing no helmets; they buzz up the narrow alley the wrong way. Laundry hangs between buildings as grandmas shout gossip to one another. Markets heave as the greengrocers call out their specials in an unidentifiable dialect. Pretty women get their fruit and vegetables from a greengrocer's *ape,* the country's ubiquitous three-wheeled vehicle.

This is Naples. But there's another Naples too: Grand, exquisite palaces. New galleries and sweet cafés. Some of the kindest-hearted people in all of Italy. Pizza: lots and lots of pizza. Gobsmacking views of Mount Vesuvius.

To Naples lovers (and they are legion), this city takes many shapes—and that's what makes it glorious. In a single day you can see a performance of an opera like *La Bohème* at the **San Carlo,** experience the trippily opulent interior of the church of **Gesù Nuovo,** join strolling couples along the **Lungomare** (mercifully free of the traffic that keeps you on your toes in the rest of the city), and cheer along with the Napoli fans at their beloved *stadio* of **San Paolo.** Football (soccer in the U.S.) is a religion all over Italy. But if you can make it to only one game, try to experience it here.

Food figures large in this city, and Neapolitans have ample appetites. They love their pizza, incredibly so. Everyone will tell you which is best (more on that later). But they also have a penchant for street food like *sfogliatella* (a pastry filled with ricotta cream) and *babà* (cake doused in rum) served along the heaving historic alley of **Spaccanapoli,** a bustling, chaotic artery of the city for Neapolitans and visitors alike with one-of-a-kind shops and food stalls.

The Christmas market along Via San Gregorio Armeno is one of the country's most unusual and a city must: It runs year round (although it reaches its apex at the holiday). Here you'll find Nativity scenes that are surreal with life-size Wise Men and all assortments of Baby Jesus, joined by celebrities and royalty like Prince William and Kate Middleton as guest stars in the scene. One wonders who buys the outlandish figures, but they get plenty of window traffic for sure.

Make sure to explore the trendy neighborhood of **Chiaia,** Naples's answer to New York's SoHo or London's Notting Hill, where, come nightfall, **L'Ebbrezza di Noè,** "Noah's drunkenness," transforms from wine shop to intimate bar lined with a plethora of various glasses and bottles to sample and a restaurant. Also make sure to visit **L'Antiquario,** a sexy speakeasy bar with painfully earnest but impressive mixologists.

Part of the beauty of Naples is the mix of restaurants, which creates one of the best culinary scenes in the country. Insiders gather at the tiny **Pescheria Mattiucci** for *crudo* and crustaceans in a spot that doubles as a fish shop. For Neapolitan classics, head to **Osteria Donna Teresa,** a place that feels like a *mamma*'s kitchen with insanely good meatballs. Another traditional spot, **Trattoria Da Ettore,** has a briny al dente *spaghetti alle vongole* (pasta with clams) and a loyal fan base. (Book in advance; there are only eight tables.)

Naples doesn't offer nearly as much choice in hotels as Rome or Florence, but **Palazzo Caracciolo** has a good location close to the highlights. **Costantinopoli 104,** an ornate villa has a quiet garden, and the **Romeo,** facing Mount Vesuvius, provides a more updated boutique option (along with a pool overlooking the Bay of Naples). For a great price and location, make a reservation at **Hotel Piazza Bellini** in the heart of the historic center. ∎

Food figures large in this city, and Neapolitans have ample appetites.
They love their pizza, incredibly so. Everyone will tell you which is best.

CLOCKWISE FROM LEFT: Look both ways to avoid the fast-moving Vespas often driving against traffic; *sfogliatella,* a flaky traditional pastry, is only one of Naples's culinary musts; the city's archaeological museum is stuffed with treasures like this statue of Atlas.

In the Know

Elena Ferrante Novels

If you love literature and keep an eye on the best-seller lists, you've definitely heard of *My Brilliant Friend,* the first in a four-part collection of novels known as the Neapolitan diaries. Elena Ferrante, the pseudonym for the author who was anonymous until outed by the Italian press, became an international literary sensation. The books—as much a depiction of Naples and its surroundings as of the female friendship at its heart—capture a seductive, mysterious place that's full of contradiction. Their popularity (as well as the success of an elegant HBO tie-in miniseries) has spawned a spate of walking tours of the city.

Elena (Lenú) and Lila, the novels' co-heroines, do not inhabit a grand Naples. In fact, their neighborhood, depicted during the 1950s, is one of the city's poorest, located just east of the chaotic central station. Poverty, crime, domestic violence, and depravation are all around them. And yet there is something deeply seductive in the way Ferrante renders their environment: a peek into an underbelly of the south that somehow seems real without being sensationalized. When the main characters make it into grander parts of the city, you can sense its beauty through their eyes.

The working-class neighborhood of **Rione Luzzatti,** where the girls grow up, is a concrete representation of the city's contradictions: a run-down neighborhood that hasn't really changed, but also a place where the heart of the city beats loudly. In the raucous market of **O'Buvero,** for example, the street vendors, selling everything from tomatoes to contraband, recall the distinctive business owners of Ferrante's books—for example, the Solara brothers, who control the neighborhood's crime arm.

Food is much at the heart of both the novels and their settings. The **Pasticciello** is known for its iconic *pagnottiello,* a Neapolitan street bite made of cheese and ham within freshly baked bread.

You might feel a little voyeuristic, or apprehensive, about visiting the novel's celebrated "tunnel with three entrances" on **Via Gianturco.** A pivotal setting in *My Brilliant Friend,* it's the place where Lenú and Lila first leave their neighborhood for a glimpse of the sea. Seeing the city through their eyes brings another level of understanding to its many and complex layers. Take a tour with Sophia Seymour's Looking for Lila, which curates specific itineraries based around the novels. ■

OPPOSITE: Modernity encroaches on the old-school working-class neighborhood Rione Luzzatti, which features large in *My Brilliant Friend.* ABOVE: The series, set mostly in Naples, has become a worldwide success and a miniseries on HBO.

Frances's Favorites

In Your Glass

What did the ancients drink? Horace, Pliny, and Virgil mention *vinum falernum.* In the 1960s lawyer Francesco Avallone, intrigued with the legendary grape, began to scour Campania for lost vines. After long research, scientists identified a few scragglers as *falanghina,* and Avallone planted them in Monte Massico, where they originated. Probably Greek imports originally, the vines flourished in Roman times. Avallone later brought in *aglianico* and *piedirosso,* other historic stock, developing wines steeped in deep identity with Campania.

I met Maria Ida, Avallone's daughter, at their Villa Matilde vineyard. We shared a lunch with liberal tastings, and I have been enthusiastic ever since with both the story and the wines. Look for their friendly whites: Greco di Tufo, the Falanghina Rocca dei Leoni, and Falerno del Massico. You can now stay at their Locanda del Falerno. Enjoy the vineyards, pool, and simple rooms, and, best of all, dine in their restaurant featuring local recipes and all their wines.

Two other favorite Campania wines: the complex white I Favati, a local *fiano* grape from Avellino, and Feudi di San Gregorio's Taurasi red, which attained *tre bicchieri,* the highest three glasses status, in Gambero Rosso's *Italian Wines.* High praise indeed.

Limoncello after dinner on a high terrace over the sea tastes much better in Campania than anywhere else. The lemons along the Amalfi Coast drench in sun and breezes from the sea. Nightingales sing in the lustrous dark green leaves. Scrape the skin with your fingernail, and the pith sends out a mist. Taste in place: There's the small crystal glass, the blossom scent, then the sharp/sweet hit that makes you purse your lips. A fire goes down. Slowly. Sip slowly. One sip for each glance at the moon. ∎

> Limoncello after dinner on a high terrace over the sea tastes much better in Campania than anywhere else. One sip for each glance at the moon.

ABOVE: In addition to its archaeological finds, Pompeii is home to vineyards framed by Roman walls and beautiful ruins. **OPPOSITE:** Limoncello, made with fragrant lemons from Campania, is a popular after-dinner drink and a recommended bottle to bring home for friends.

In the Know

Naples's Underground Contemporary Art Scene

Y ou would be forgiven for not thinking of Naples as a hot spot for contemporary art. But beneath your feet—literally—is a network of innovative installations. Housed in the metro stops below the city, it's the brainchild of Achille Bonito Oliva, a former director of the Venice Biennale. The epic project called on 100 artists and architects—including Gae Aulenti, Sol LeWitt, Robert Wilson, and Karim Rashid—to contribute individual creations that artfully connect classic with contemporary. At the Gae Aulenti–designed Museum station, incredible black-and-white photos by artist Mimmo Jodice feature Greco-Roman statues found at the Villa dei Papiri in Herculaneum; at the Toledo stop, a Robert Wilson "Crater de Luz" installation with classical music playing evokes the feeling of floating beneath the sea; and at the Dante station, a Nicola De Maria mosaic fresco entitled "Universo senza bombe" ("A Universe Without Bombs") captures a moment of hope in a city where bombings continue to be a reality.

The action isn't limited to just below ground. The **MADRE Napoli** is the city's contemporary art complex. Housed in a 19th-century palazzo, it includes two rooms dedicated to hometown heavyweight artist Francesco Clemente, plus spaces for international stars like Richard Serra, Daniel Buren, and Anish Kapoor. Here, as in the subway system, the curators did an excellent job making connections between ancient and modern. Site-specific work includes French-Italian artist Paul Thorel's "Passaggio della Vittoria," a mosaic wall that is an homage to the city's iconic Galleria della Vittoria, a tunnel that connects the city's east and west sections. Female artists loom large too, with work by Cindy Sherman, Marina Abramović, and Tomaso Binga (the male pseudonym adopted by Italian artist Bianca Menna). Binga's mural "Alfabetiere Murale" uses the artist's own nude body to imitate each letter of the alphabet.

Each December, Naples's **Piazza del Plebiscito,** the city's most famous square, gives the contemporary art world a shout-out too. Richard Serra and Anish Kapoor have been among the artists given the public space as a place to feature their art and to bring Naples's connection to modern works into high relief.

Smaller galleries have proliferated too. **Galleria Fonti** and the unmissable **Lia Rumma** feature masterpiece contemporary stars like Vanessa Beecroft and Anselm Kiefer on the roster.

Bear in mind that Naples has been drawing artists since the 1960s, yielding the mix of grit and beauty that continues to intrigue intrepid visitors. In 1974, after years of collecting work by Cy Twombly, Dan Flavin, and Sol LeWitt, Pasquale Trisorio opened the **Studio Trisorio** gallery.

Even Banksy has made an appearance in town. "Madonna With a Pistol," the artist's only known preserved work in Italy, was recently put under a cover to prevent vandalism. His other Naples offering depicted a female saint in a state of ecstasy, accompanied by a McDonald's meal and Coke. It was covered in graffiti in 2010. ▪

OPPOSITE: Naples's metro stops feature installations like this one by American Robert Wilson. ABOVE: MADRE exhibited *"Axer/Désaxer"* by French conceptual artist Daniel Buren from 2015 to 2017.

Best Of
Neapolitan Pizza

In the much beloved song "That's Amore!" Dean Martin croons about the moon, love, and a big pizza pie. Now who in the world connects love with pizza? The Neapolitans, for one. And who can blame them? After all, they own the pizza game. But where to get the best pie? That question always ignites a pizza oven debate that pits residents and food writers against one another. With more than 500 pizzerias in town, only a fifth are certified by the True Neapolitan Pizza Association, the regulatory organization that ensures that both ingredients and preparation style are in line with tradition. They even hold a pizza-making championship every summer. (Neapolitan pizza masters create their dough in advance in order to prevent any ensuing bellyaches from the fermentation.)

Now it's time to decide for yourself. Try to eat your way through as many restaurants as you can before making your final choice. It's not the most onerous of homework assignments!

Pizzeria Sorbillo will make anyone's list. The family-owned restaurant now has two outposts: the latest in Chiaia and the original back in the *centro storico,* the historic city. For owner Gino Sorbillo, pizza is in his DNA. He is a third-generation *pizzaiolo* and inherited the place from his *nonno* (grandfather), who opened it back in 1935. While you wait in line, pick up a cold beer from the *acquafrescaio* (a Neapolitan drink stand) alongside.

Pizzeria Di Matteo remains an old-school contender. It's been around since 1936 and specializes in pies often eaten standing up: a folded-up, heavenly experience that costs only a few euros. If you would like to top up your cholesterol count, order the *pizza fritta,* a ricotta and provolone cheese pizza that's deep-fried deliciousness.

L'Antica Pizzeria Da Michele dates back to 1909. This place is no frills, and proud of that too. Only two styles of pizza are served: the Margherita and the Marinara. There are no reservations, and the atmosphere is less than *romantico.* But who cares? The pizza is divine.

Attilio commands great respect for its pies, and for good reason. Don't miss the Carnevale; the outside dough is shaped into eight little crowns *(cornicione)* filled with ricotta, the pizzeria's trademark.

50 Kalò is the current pizza darling in Naples, as is its pizza maker, Ciro Salvo, a god in dough circles. In dialect, *50* means "dough" and *kalò* means "good." But after trying even a simple Margherita, just tomatoes and cheese, one might want to say, it's orgasmic.

Pepe in Grani was named numero uno in Italy in 2017 by the prestigious 50 Top Pizza organization, and is most certainly worth the pilgrimage. International fans line up for hours for Franco Pepe's signature Margherita *sbagliata,* baked first with mozzarella and cooked afterward, brushed with tomato puree and basil. (This trick stops the pizza from getting soggy: genius indeed!) But it's not Pepe's only innovation; he prefers his own local tomatoes over the traditional San Marzano variety and uses his own blend of flour, which he says is easier to digest. ∎

ABOVE: A pizza fresh out of the oven at Pizzeria Sorbillo. Sorbillo and other *pizzaioli* were designated as a cultural heritage by UNESCO. OPPOSITE: A stop for a slice at legendary Di Matteo

BUON APPETITO CON
Coca-Cola
94
PIZZERIA
DI MATTEO
SALA SUPERIORE
E
SALA IN ERNA
CLIMATIZZATE
UNICA SEDE
DA' 1936
PEUGEOT

Hot Spot
Capri

Even if you've never been to Italy, there's no way you haven't heard of Capri. Glamorous Capri, where Jackie Onassis stylishly showed the world how to wear the island's signature pants (she bought a dozen at a time) and chic sandals. Before Jackie O, the island was the place where Odysseus reluctantly resisted the Sirens' call.

But there are two Capris. The first is the island that brings day-trippers from cruises moored in Naples to clog the main square and the designer shops that line the main arteries of town. The second is the island that many don't walk far enough away to see, where sun-dappled pathways are perfumed with the scent of myrtle and juniper and the lazy sound of cicadas. Up and up you climb to **Villa Jovis,** where Capri's most famous and truly horrible residents once lived. Emperor Tiberius got up to all sorts of trouble here, engaging in debauchery that was the talk of Rome; he also reportedly threw wayward subjects off the dramatic cliff.

Make sure to reserve a table nearby at **La Fontelina,** the chic beach club and restaurant with views of the iconic Faraglioni rock outcroppings. A lunch of fresh grilled *orata,* sea bream, and crisp white wine before taking a siesta on a daybed by the sea is one of the island's true pleasures. Reserve in advance and note that they have two seatings—1 p.m. and 3 p.m.—in case you're looking for a later meal. For shoppers, those carefully crafted Capri sandals await at **Canfora.**

If you stay on the island in the heat of the day, head to the more low-key village of **Anacapri** and cool down under the lemon trees of **Da Paolino.** Try some bruschetta served with sun-warmed tomatoes and tangy capers, and a plate of *paccheri,* Campania's signature tube-shaped pasta, with fresh lobster. By sunset, the day-trippers disappear, and you can enjoy the main *piazzetta* as it should be seen.

Looking for stylish digs? Stay at **J.K. Place Capri** with its languid blue pool and nautical chic rooms, or the newly renovated **Capri Tiberio Palace** featuring a cocktail bar and a mosaic hot tub that even the emperor Tiberius would have liked. ▪

Capri has drawn honeymooners and a crazy emperor over the centuries.

Frances's Favorites

The Gallery by John Horne Burns

John Horne Burns was an American officer stationed in Naples at the close of World War II. He centers his odd novel *The Gallery* in the glass-enclosed shopping center in the *centro* of Naples, the partially bombed Galleria Umberto I. Published in 1947, the book became a best seller and an object of envy from the most famous writers of the time. Now, few have heard of him.

What is worth the horrors of war? The episodic book flips between nine portraits—Neapolitans, madam of a gay bar, military personnel—and eight "promenades," chapters in the writer's own voice. Because of his imagistic and raw language, Burns is good at pulling readers close to the city. He was well placed to gauge the exploitation of Italians at the hands of American captors, and more—the disillusion of victory. Read it after seeing Naples.

Burns describes Neapolitan dialect, which he calls "Italian chewed to shreds in the mouth of a hungry man." Even within the city, it varies:

The fishermen in the bay talk differently from the rich in the Vomero. Every six blocks in the squashed together city there's a new dialect. But the dialect is Naples and Naples is the dialect . . . And O God, their gestures! The hand before the groin, the finger under the chin, the cluckings, the headshakings. In each sentence they seem to recapitulate all the emotions that human beings know. They die and live and faint and desire and despair. I remember the dialect of Naples. It was the most moving language I ever listened to. ■

ABOVE: American troops in Naples during World War II OPPOSITE: Galleria Umberto I was built in the late 1800s as a way to move the city toward a new era. The building became a centerpiece of Naples and of a 1947 novel by American soldier John Horne Burns.

Amalfi Coast: From Steinbeck to the Seaside

Hairpin turns on cliffside roads. The smell of lemons ripened in the sunlight. Rocky coves nestled beneath blue sky. Towns that hang above the sea with church domes that double as reflectors for the long sunsets.

In many ways, the real start of the Amalfi Coast's fame can be traced to the celebrated author John Steinbeck. In 1953, friends in Rome suggested he visit the village of Positano as a place to hide away from the busy capital with a respite on the coast (the author was on a European trip with his wife). He dutifully arrived there after hilariously and accurately recounting the trip up the coast for an article in *Harper's Bazaar* (words to the wise: Unless you are a particularly skilled or fearless driver, consider hiring someone to take you).

"Flaming like a meteor we hit the coast, a road, high, high above the blue sea, that hooked and corkscrewed on the edge of nothing, a road carefully designed to be a little narrower than two cars side by side," he writes. "And on this road, the buses, the trucks, the motor scooters and the assorted livestock. We didn't see much of the road. In the back seat my wife and I lay clutched in each other's arms, weeping hysterically." Luckily Steinbeck arrived in Positano safely. And like many others who make the journey, he became hooked.

Positano on the Amalfi Coast is arguably one of Italy's prettiest villages, especially at sunset, and has become extremely popular as a romantic getaway.

Despite the countless honeymoon couples and tour buses in high season, **Positano** is still one of the prettiest seaside villages in Europe; pink, yellow, and red buildings cascade down to the beach below. Splurge for a room at **Le Sirenuse.** This family-owned property is legendary for good reason, filled with antiques and prints. The terrace pool overlooks town, and its iconic gold-and-green mosaic dome glitters in the sunlight. The current owners, Antonio and Carla Sersale, are always adding new amenities like **Franco,** a bar named after Antonio's father, a store with elegant cover-ups and frocks perfect for dressing in the "dolce vita" style, and fitness retreats.

Ravello's a quieter town than Positano—or at least, it's easy to find peace in the cool gardens of **Villa Rufolo.** The villa also hosts the town's annual music festival from April to November. If you make Ravello your

Villa Cimbrone's beautiful gardens in Ravello

base, both the **Belmond Hotel Caruso** and the **Cimbrone** mix luxury with old-school glamour. Meander the streets past lemon groves to **Villa Cimbrone,** a formerly private home now turned hotel, or take in views of the Gulf of

Sorrento. Gore Vidal made his home here at a beautiful villa called La Rondinaia ("the swallow's nest"), where he happily lived until the death of his partner.

Praiano provides another less crowded option to Positano. Even if you don't stay at the stylish **Casa Angelina,** you will want to visit its **La Gavitella Beach Club,** reached by an elevator carved into the dramatic cliffside. Or take a boat to **Da Adolfo,** a simple but wonderful seaside restaurant featuring just caught tuna carpaccio.

An American woman, Bianca Sharma, fell in love with a 17th-century monastery outside Conca dei Marini as she boated up the coast. Now her retreat, **Monastero Santa Rosa,** has been transformed into a hotel and destination spa. The pool here is one of the most beautiful in Italy, but leave the kids at home—this photo op is for adults only. ■

SORRENTO

En route to Positano or Amalfi, most drivers don't even notice the hidden gem Sorrento as they pass by.

THE TOWN ON THE SEA possesses many of the assets of its better known neighbors—but without the prices and attitude. Start your exploration on the newly pedestrianized main *corso* and the network of little streets that make up its *centro storico* (historic center). Sorrento's a hub for shops, restaurants, and bars, and the signage from the 1950s will appeal to those who appreciate old-school typography. Tuesday is market day, and the town heaves with vendors, including those with huge, fragrant lemons (with leaves attached) that are famous throughout the country.

In a destination full of beautiful churches, the 15th-century Sorrento Cathedral on Via Pieta remains a showstopper, complete with triple-tiered bell tower and intricate examples of intarsia (a unique type of wood mosaic). Come summer, the **Chiostro di San Francesco** becomes the setting for concerts and exhibits, but this cloister is a lovely place to linger all year—especially in the spring,

when its trees and bushes flower into a lush green space for meditation. **Gelateria Davide** is a different kind of religious experience, pulling in ice cream connoisseurs for such seasonal flavors as wisteria and wild strawberries.

Marina Grande, the fishing village and seaside promenade down below the historic center, offers views of Mount Vesuvius and Naples, along with seafood lunches at spots like **Trattoria Emilia.** Here, the tables almost touch the fishing boats that deliver the catch of the day early in the morning.

Book a room at **Bellevue Syrene**—preferably one with a view of Vesuvius, of course—for Amalfi-like accommodations at a much more affordable rate than properties in Positano. An elevator brings you right to a seaside lido, and the port is only a short stroll away. Even if you don't end up staying, make sure to turn up for a sunset *aperitivo*.

In the Know

Local Flavors of Campania

As it happens, many of the most classic and popular Italian dishes in the United States originated in Campania and its environs. When immigrants left Naples or the countryside, their most beloved recipes came too—pizza, for example, and eggplant parmigiana.

It's no wonder that the food of Campania is the foundation of how Americans view Italian cuisine; its natural resources are remarkable. Lemon trees here are bigger, bolder, more astounding than their stateside counterparts; they produce large fruit with a thick peel that makes limoncello, the typical liqueur of the Amalfi Coast, as well as tangy granita and gelato. (These lemons are so exemplary that they have been given protected status by the European Union.) Capers bloom on bushes and become a tasty addition to pastas. Tomatoes are so delicious that they have their own DOC (San Marzano, to be exact). *Mozzarella di bufala* is a wonderful complement to those sun-ripened tomatoes, along with a drizzle of extra virgin olive oil and fresh basil. The buffalo that produce this cheese are the VIPs of bovines; dairy farmers employ everything from massages to music to help them produce their tasty milk. Visit these doe-eyed creatures at farms like **Tenuta Vannulo** (which also happens to be close to the less visited but unmissable ruins of **Paestum**).

Thanks to its Mediterranean location, Campania's seafood is also remarkable. Platters of *gamberi* (shrimp) and *spaghetti alle vongole* (spaghetti with clams) are plentiful. *Totani e patate,* a delectable dish of potatoes and squid, is a popular menu item. *Fritto misto* with crispy but delicate octopus is a must. And don't miss *colatura,* an Italian version of fish sauce dating back to the Roman period.

Oh, and let's not forget the *polpette*. These meatballs that have become an Italian-American staple hail from Naples. In many traditional meals, pasta is served with the *polpettes' sugo,* or sauce, while the meatballs themselves become the second course. ▪

Mussels and clams figure large in Campania's hearty seafood dishes.

Hot Spot

Ischia

With the tourist spotlight on glamorous Capri, many travelers forget about its bigger sister, Ischia. That suits the devotees of this island just fine; in fact, they'd prefer to have its natural hot springs, hidden beach clubs and pristine seas all to themselves.

Anyone who has seen the Oscar-nominated film *The Talented Mr. Ripley* has witnessed the breathtaking beauty of Ischia (and if you haven't, now's the time!). In an iconic scene, American grifter Tom Ripley, portrayed by Matt Damon, "happens" upon the tanned, gorgeous Marge Sherwood (Gwyneth Paltrow) and her lover, Dickie Greenleaf (Jude Law), lounging on a golden beach with an exquisite castle in the background. That castle is actually across from Ischia's Forio; the castle behind is the island's Castel Aragonese. The beach? The **Spiaggia dei Pescatori.**

Lounging on the beach beneath that castle is enough to keep any vacationer content for days. But Ischia's got many gems to uncover, including the island's multitude of hot springs. Try any of a dozen natural pools of varying temperatures at the hotel and spa of **Aphrodite Apollon.**

To enjoy the full complement of Ischia's pleasures, rent a boat for the day. Circling the island languidly, you can enjoy the coastal highlights and stop in for a dip at a plethora of coves. The beach club of **La Scanella,** is straight out of a Slim Aarons photograph with a swimming pool at the edge of the sea and melt-in-your-mouth mozzarella fresh from the owner's buffalo up the hill. Docking in the port of **Forio** feels like crossing a portal to a perfect Italian fishing village, circa 1950—except it's real.

But word of the island's charms is spreading, which is heating up the hotel scene. The **Regina Isabella** used to be the only game on the island; the medicinal spa is authentic, to say the least. But the **Mezzatorre Hotel and Thermal Spa** owned by the family behind the esteemed Il Pellicano on the Tuscan coast has given the grande dame new competition. With a position on the sea and a perfect location for exploring the island, the 46 rooms have a crisp updated feel. ▪

Sailboats bob in Ischia's Sant'Angelo harbor.

Frances's Favorites

The Caravaggio Quest

The rowdy baroque artist Michelangelo Merisi da Caravaggio spent the year 1606 in Naples, fleeing from a murder charge in Rome. He moved on to Malta, where he found more trouble to get into. In 1609, he returned to Naples for another stint. He left behind great late work, all of it permeated with the violence and drama of the life he lived.

Full of furious energy, his paintings have immense narrative power because they occur at a moment of change: Something has just happened or is just about to. He chose to work directly on canvas rather than from drawings, and he used live models who didn't look like the Renaissance ideals but instead had realistic, warts-and-all faces. In this, Caravaggio was a harbinger of modern art. He is the artist of darkness. Faces and actions emerge from shadows and gloom, with piercing light hitting his subjects and glancing off objects. The viewer is left to scrutinize the darkness for other faces, animals, objects that tantalize with their obscurity.

While much of his late work has disappeared, three magnificent canvases remain in Naples. At **Pio Monte della Misericordia,** Via Tribunali 253, you'll find Caravaggio's "Le Sette Opere di Misericordia," "The Seven Works of Mercy." Based on the New Testament verses of Matthew 25:35-36, the painting depicts the acts of mercy: I was hungry and you gave me bread, I was thirsty and you gave me drink, etc.

Caravaggio has crowded all seven acts onto a large vertical canvas, with two angels and the Madonna and Child looking down on all the activity. Study each episode closely, then back up to take in the whole.

"The Martyrdom of Saint Ursula," thought to be Caravaggio's last work, lives at **Palazzo Zevallos Stigliano,** in a busy shopping district at Via Toledo, 185. Ursula was martyred in Germany, after sailing with 11,000 virgins from England. She'd refused her father's demand for her to marry the warlord Conan. Caravaggio's composition shows her in scarlet, brilliant as blood, just as the arrow enters her breast. Her face and skin have the white-gray pallor of death. The grizzly and gnarled old man who shot her looms close, bow in hand. The crux: just where

Caravaggio chose to seize his subject.

Taxi up to **Museo di Capodimonte,** allowing a few hours because there's much to see. This is the largest museum in Italy. Built as a palatial residence for the Bourbon rulers, the sprawling museum oddly lacks visitors. Hanging in the vast rooms are Correggio, Masaccio, Titian, Parmigianino, and so many more, plus the grand royal apartments. Caravaggio's "Flagellation of Christ" hangs in lone splendor. The buffed and luminous Christ commands all the light, while his shadowy torturers obviously relish their work. What a mighty painting: the suffering palpable, the contrasting light increasing the tension, the rigorous composition intensifying the emotion. Caravaggio: all drama and momentum. ∎

ABOVE: "The Seven Works of Mercy" by Caravaggio is the highlight of the Pio Monte della Misericordia church in Naples. OPPOSITE: Caravaggio's masterpiece "Flagellation of Christ"

Hot Spot

Cilento National Park

When exploring Campania (and Italy in general), it's important to take a moment to appreciate the country's extraordinary natural beauty (and the entities who had the wherewithal to protect large swaths of the land from development). Italy has a long history of preservation, begun after World War II, that spared many places and monuments from being ruined.

Cilento National Park, which stretches from the sea to the foot of the region's Apennines, is one of Italy's great examples of conservation. It achieved protected status in 1991—relatively late in the game—and later as a UNESCO World Heritage site in 1998. Encompassing the remains of the Greek town of **Paestum** (one of the country's best preserved and undervisited ruins), pristine seafront, and acres upon acres of mountainous region, it's one of those places that makes you wonder why a park this marvelous is not better known.

Palinuro makes a good spot to start your tour. With simple fishing boats and gentle coves, the vibe feels very far from high-wattage spots like Positano. From there, you can take some easy excursions along the coast or visit the **Spiaggia di Marinella** (its extensive cerulean sea caves are seemingly lit by floodlights from below). Nearby, Ernest Hemingway lived in **Acciaroli** around when he was writing *The Old Man and the Sea* in the 1950s; the atmosphere hasn't changed much since then.

Rock climbers adore the park, as well as the high-altitude walks through the craggy mountainside (don't miss **Monte Cervati** and **Monte Gelbison** with their soaring views of the region). But sybarites can just put down a picnic blanket and snack on Cilento white figs (brought here by the Greeks) and *muzzarella co' a murtedda,* mozzarella preserved in myrtle branches, a regional method that infuses a unique and delicious flavor. It's still unclear how these buffalo who made this cheese arrived here, but they resemble the water buffalo from Asia. The mix of simple ingredients and cinematic surroundings is sublime. ▪

Cilento National Park is also home to the Greek ruins of Paestum.

Chapter Sixteen

PUGLIA

From space, the many white villages of Puglia must look like someone spilled a basket of pearls. They run the length of the region, making up the spur and heel of the boot, and dot the inland, gleaming from afar like apparitions. Is this Italy? Looks like Greece. Or Tunisia? Or cubist paintings? • Inside the villages, the mystery deepens: Stone lanes twist, dead-end, and climb to ramparts where often the sea view is a thin

aquamarine ribbon. Some invader was always threatening, and small windows and strong doors are remnants of protection. Whitewash was thought to prevent plague. The Greeks were here first, and it shows: Traces of their language linger in dialects and in the bone-white houses. Towns feel as secretive as medinas, even with balconies of spilling surfinia and geraniums. Ostuni may be the prime example, but rivals include Trani, Monopoli, Marina Franca, Peschici, Vieste, and Locorotondo.

The gleaming villages characterize settled Puglia, but the landscape is defined by older structures: the mysterious stone dolmens, menhirs, and *trulli*, scattered in the fields. Despite centuries of looting, development, and weather, a surprising number endure. Sometimes you catch a glimpse of one as you speed down a highway lined with ugly industry; often, one just appears, old as time, in an olive grove. Clusters survive around the coastal cities of Taranto and Otranto, in the Bari province, and far south into the Salento at the tip of Puglia.

No one knows the function of these ancient stone structures. Dolmens—simply a flat stone on top of two vertical ones, like a table—might have been tombs or places of sacrifice, while the monolithic stone menhirs from 4000 to 1200 B.C. are thought to have been places of worship connected to fertility or sun cults, with possible astrological purposes. If both seem primitive, even foreboding, the *trulli*

are fanciful conical dwellings skillfully made from stacked, upwardly spiraling stones, ending in a pointy top often adorned with an ornament. Though they have older roots as shelter in agricultural fields, *trulli* became easy housing in the 16th century, when overlords allowed their peasants to build such structures. Or, as some believe, the canny peasants built them for a specific purpose: When the owners came every few years to visit, they could pull out the keystone and the whole thing collapsed, saving them from paying tax. Owner leaves; house rebuilt.

Today these strangely endearing *trulli* are coveted and cared for, and often they are still inhabited. They're thrilling to spot in a field of wheat or wildflowers, but when

WHAT YOU NEED TO KNOW...

- **BEST TIME TO VISIT:** Many of the hotels and restaurants in the larger towns remain open most of the year. But if you want to explore the unique countryside hotels, you will probably want to wait until spring or fall. The coastal areas are teeming with tourists in summer, but the local festivals are lots of fun and if you time your comings and goings with when everyone is taking a nap or at the beach, you can still explore the highlights without a crowd.

- **TOP SPOTS:** Lecce, Otranto, Ostuni, Polignano a Mare, Gargano

- **GETTING THERE:** Bari and Brindisi have airports.

Polignano a Mare in Puglia hangs over the Adriatic.

Inside the villages, the mystery deepens: Stone lanes twist, dead-end, and climb
to ramparts where often the sea view is a thin aquamarine ribbon.

concentrated—the town of Alberobello has more than 1,500—there's a unique atmosphere, as though you've crossed over into the land of elves and gnomes.

More than that of any other region, the cuisine emphasizes vegetable and fish recipes that hark back to the roots of ancient life, when the rural folk were abjectly poor. Resourceful by necessity, they even gathered wheat grains that remained when the fields were burned after harvest; the charred grains were called *arso*. Make do with what you have! As it turned out, incorporating *arso* into the dough gave the bread a toasty aroma. The practice continues, but now by roasting, not by stoop-labor gathering.

Massive loaves are one of the joys of Puglia: the best bread

A sweet piazzetta hidden in the seaside village of Polignano a Mare

in Italy. Foraging for *cicoria* (chicory), dandelion, hyacinth bulbs, as well as growing turnips, chickpeas, *fave*, and every legume possible led to the vegetable-based cuisine that now seems so contemporary. Chefs have a high awareness of *biologico*, organic products—more than I've seen in any other part of Italy. What a joy to graze through Puglia.

There's not a more stimulating region to visit in Italy. Everyone comes here for the secret beaches and limpid water, but there's much to do in Puglia other than bask in the sun. In addition to the characteristic white towns, some favorite stops along the way, zigzagging north to south:

The "spur" at the top of the heel—the forested and hilly Gargano promontory—rivals the Amalfi Coast for scenery, especially around Vieste and Mattinata. Dine at a rickety *trabocco*, an old fishing structure built in the water. At the ancient town of Manfredonia, the facade of 12th-century Basilica di Siponto has been treated to an imaginative intervention by the innovative young architect Edoardo Tresoldi. The ruined church in the rear has been completely reconstructed—but in wire. The ghost of the former inhabitant!

Romanesque churches in the particular Puglian style are balm to the eyes of architecture buffs. Especially moving are the ones located in Trani, Ostuni, Ruvo, Otranto, and Bitonto. Trani's has the most dramatic setting, on a windswept piazza facing the sea. Across looms what looks like a sand castle but was built in 1233 by Frederick II. Slightly inland in Troia, I found my favorite church, Santa Maria Assunta. I'm mesmerized by its magnificent stone rose window. Begun in 1093 but not finished until 1127, it anchors the town in an intimate way and reveals successive influences of Byzantine, Saracen, Norman, and Pisan Romanesque architecture. Staring up at the window while having a coffee is a double pleasure, since the bread and pastry aromas of two bakeries waft into the piazza.

A short look at other pleasures: The village of Polignano a Mare stands right on the sea. Flowery and seductive, it's a lively place to wander, buy a few ceramics, have a drink, and hear music (often "Volare," since the composer, Domenico

Bordered by centuries-old sculptural olive trees, a field of blooming red poppies makes the Valle d'Itria even more spectacular.

Modugno, was born here). For dinner, there's serious magic on tap. You can dine in a grotto above the sea, sipping prosecco as the big sunset melts the sky pink and violet. Reserve a ringside table in advance at Grotta Palazzese, which is also a hotel.

Puglia is serious about castles. Frederick II was known as Stupor Mundi, wonder of the world, and as the king of Sicily, Germany, Italy, Jerusalem, and Holy Roman Emperor, he earned the title. Castles were his hobby. He built many. The 1240 Castel del Monte, near Andria, is the most arresting: octagonal and formidable. The number eight must have been significant: eight sides, eight towers, and eight rooms on each floor.

Called the "Florence of the South," Lecce is the gateway to the Salento, the far south, with seemingly endless beaches. Renowned for frothy baroque architecture, *cartapesta* (papiermâché) as an art form, and a Roman amphitheater, it's also a good place to sample the area's cuisine. Try *salsiccia leccese,* sausage of veal and pork seasoned with cloves, cinnamon, and lemon. *Orecchiette,* ear-shaped pasta, is most often served with *cime di rapa,* broccoli rabe. At the exuberant and youthful restaurant Bros', the food is locally sourced and wildly presented; they're clearly having fun in the kitchen. Lecce

makes an excellent base for exploring *borghi* and beaches all the way to southernmost Capo Santa Maria di Leuca.

Wandering: the best. Go onto back roads to see *oliveti,* groves of massive olive trees that must have been twisting in the wind for a thousand years to shape themselves so forcefully. Indulge your inner tree hugger. In spring, yellow and white flowers dazzle the grasses, and fields of almond and fruit trees emanate a haze of white and pink. Prickly pear, orange and lemon blossoms, pomegranate, mimosa, broom, as well as wildflowers, grace each season. *Parietoni,* low stone walls that crisscross enormous areas, may have been boundaries or definitions for fields. They look like extensive archaeological remnants of lost cities.

Puglia's glory lies along the coasts. It's easy to hire a boat or climb aboard a scheduled tour at most marinas. The cliffs and coves, Robinson Crusoe beaches, and startling rock formations all are seen from a different perspective from the water. A private hire allows you to stop and rinse your soul in one of the hidden bays.

Is there a more exhilarating place to travel? Puglia runs deep. What I've mentioned is only the tip of the *trullo.*

Where to Stay in Puglia

With all due respect to other regions, Puglia arguably has the best hotel scene in all of Italy. Long, low buildings encircled by blinding white stone walls. Gnarled olive trees outside. The sound of cicadas that call to each other by long cobalt swimming pools. Plump green olives in deep ceramic bowls. Simple pleasures abound at the *masserie* farmhouses that once protected residents from Turkish and Greek invaders. But even after the unification of Italy, the fortunes of the region did not improve; it became one of the poorest in the country. Many residents left to find a new life in the United States, abandoning their homes. As it happens, these compounds possess the perfect configuration for a boutique hotel: a principal stately building surrounded by annexes, olive mills, and acres of land. The new owners, many of them from outside Italy, noticed that a new generation of travelers is flocking to the region for its beautiful beaches and towns, creating a need for luxurious lodgings. Try some of these enticing options:

Masseria Trapanà: Located just a half hour from Puglia's anchor city of Lecce, Trapanà is owned by a charming Aussie, Rob Potter-Sanders. Its design ethos is stunning. Antique rugs cover the restored stone floors of the 16th-century structure; coffee-table books sit atop mid-century tables, while Moroccan pillowed nooks and wrought-iron lanterns dot the property, offering endless opportunities to hide away. A fire pit invites commingling at *aperitivo*, or solitary stargazing after dinner.

Masseria Torre Coccaro: A style forerunner that first brought guests to Puglia, this property was recently bought by famed hotelier Rocco Forte. It oozes rustic charm, with original stone troughs in the bedrooms and an Aveda spa housed in the caves of the former olive mill. Another asset? Two chic beach clubs about a 15-minute bike ride from the hotel.

Borgo Egnazia: If you've already heard of one *masseria,* it's likely to be this one, where Justin Timberlake and Jessica Biel got married and where Madonna spent a few of her birthdays. The scale here is much larger than most other Pugliese properties, with multiple pools, an excellent spa, and private villas surrounded by acres of land.

Masseria Potenti: Located near Manduria in the center of the region, this spot has more of a family feel. Each season, it draws regulars to both the nearby beaches and its homegrown charm. Each of the Pugliese antiques has a story to tell, and the food comes from the property's sustainable farm.

Convento di Santa Maria di Costantinopoli: Return visitors regard this as their own lair and jealously guard the secret. Owner Athena McAlpine and her husband (who passed away a few years ago) lovingly restored the former convent, filling it with antiques and art from Africa, thousands of books, and gardens of cacti and rare flowers. The bed sheets are heaven, and the breakfasts look like an art installation with a long table laden with fruit, freshly baked pastries, and juice just squeezed from the harvest of the nearby trees.

Palazzo Daniele: The owners of Rome's stylish G Rough recently opened this spot in Salento. It has tucked-away spaces in the orangery, by the black-bottom pool, and in the shaded courtyard. Simple but luxurious rooms are lit up by exquisite tilework and frescoed ceilings.

Masseria Moroseta: Foodies must make tracks to Moroseta, where chef Giorgia Goggi has put its wonderful restaurant on the international culinary map.

Private rentals: If travel includes family or a group of friends, rent an entire *masseria* through agents like Charming Puglia or the Thinking Traveller. ▪

A distinctive bedroom at Masseria Potenti, one of Puglia's fortified farmhouse hotels

In the city of Lecce, the historic center is full of distinctive churches like the Basilica di Santa Croce with carvings covering nearly the entire facade.

Insider's Guide

Lecce: Puglia's Crowning Jewel

Long dubbed the "Florence of the South," this nearly 2,000-year-old city is considered one of the most important in southern Italy. But the truth is that the moniker doesn't really fit. For one thing, it's smaller than its northern counterpart. It has many fewer tourists, and its architecture is much more baroque than Renaissance.

But it is indisputably a beauty on its own terms. Pretty baroque churches with carvings that can hold your attention for an hour line small pedestrian streets. Food from tiny bars and homestyle cooking are washed down with

glasses of robust local red wine. Little shops with Pinterest-worthy ceramics and handmade textiles are everywhere. On a summer day when everyone is at the beach (or taking an epic siesta; here they can last from after lunch until 6 p.m.), this gem of a city is yours for the wandering. Tanned locals trickle in for a late meal. By midnight, Lecce heaves with life.

At **Caffè Alvino,** try the Lecce signature of *caffe latte di mandorla in ghiaccio* (espresso on ice with almond milk) and a *pasticciotto* (custard pie) before getting lost in the sculptured exterior of

the nearby **Basilica di Santa Croce.** Mermaids in saucy poses, dragons, turbaned warriors, sheep, and cherubs prowl across the facade of this amazing structure. Next up is the city's duomo and its adjacent bell tower; the former was originally built in 1144 but received a face-lift, and its new neighbor, in the 17th century. It's a truly spectacular monument. Afterward, saunter into **Doppiozero** for a plate of local cheese and salami (the deli has now expanded into a proper restaurant, if you feel like a bigger meal), or grab a gelato at **Natale Pasticceria;** its chocolate with *pepperoncino* is not for the faint of heart. (But if you like spicy, you must try it!)

Lecce, and Puglia in general, is famous for its *cucina povera*—literally "poor kitchen"—which means that the best of its chefs use simple ingredients in incredibly delicious ways. **Le Zie,** for example, feels like your grandma's house. There are no menus, and dishes change almost every day, but staples include a traditional *pure di fave con cicoria* (fava bean puree with bitter greens). The chef and waiters seem straight out of central casting, which only adds to the appeal.

Wine lovers in Lecce flock to **Mamma Elvira Enoteca** for more than 250 vintages by the glass, thanks to the state-of-the-art enomatic machines. And **Mastro Enomaltoteca** also has hundreds of samples—not to mention 150 craft beers, served in a beautiful white-stone space. (Try the 12 e Mezzo line from the Varvaglione Winery; the organic white is a winner.) **Quanto Basta** turns out a mean cocktail and has all the musts of a hipster bar, from bearded bartenders to foraged ingredients.

For shoppers, **IJO'** tempts with sustainable textiles made on antique looms, while **Vico dei Bolognese** is a new concept store with pretty chunky jew-

Lecce's boutiques are one-of-a-kind stops for artisanal wares.

elry, as well as clothes and accessories. And you never know what you might score at **Vergini Suicide**—but Gucci bags, 1960s jumpsuits, and other vintage treasures are often on sale.

There are a number of *masserie* hotels outside of Lecce—but if you prefer to be in the heart of the action, set up base at **La Fiermontina** in the historic center. A tribute by Giacomo Fiermonte to his grandmother, this self-proclaimed "urban resort" features crisp guest rooms, inviting public halls with modern art, and design pieces from the likes of Le Corbusier mixed in with family mementos. (The outdoor pool is also a draw.) **Palazzo de Noha** is another boutique option close to the city amphitheater with well-priced rooms, considering the enviable address. ◾

A TABLE TO BOOK

Restaurants in this region are a vegetarian's dream but include plenty of fish and meat too if you're in the mood.

Masseria Il Frantoio: Just northwest of Ostuni, this *agriturismo* estate with thousands of olive trees is a veritable education in *cucina povera,* with most of the organic ingredients grown right on site. Nightly feasts of four to six courses include local wines paired with each.

Da Tuccino: Polignano a Mare on the sea is one of Puglia's loveliest towns. This restaurant, offering the region's answer to sushi, *crudo,* gives you another reason to visit.

L'Altro Baffo: Close to Otranto's 12th-century cathedral, this restaurant draws Puglia regulars who enjoy excellent seafood with a twist. Think fresh-caught sea bream in a broth with a touch of lemongrass.

Osteria del Tempo Perso: Ostuni's old-school osteria is lost in time indeed—in the best of ways. Try the eggplant parmigiana (it will offer you the new standard for the dish) and *scampi crudo* with burrata.

Frances's Favorites
In Your Glass

Even in the most casual trattoria, waiters know their wines. The Pugliese live close to the earth; I never went wrong taking a suggestion. The grapes of choice, *negroamaro* (black bitter) and *primitivo,* are a genetic match to zinfandel. Usually the house wine made by someone's dad is full of body and juice and light on tannins (hats off to papa Mario or Piero!). Puglia grows more grapes than any other region in Italy, so there's much to choose from. I always peruse the wine list for Tenute Rubino and Cantine Due Palme wines.

After a visit to the Chiaramonte vineyard, I came home with a case of Gioia del Colle Primitivo. Such an elegant but earthy wine. Gambero Rosso's *Italian Wines* agreed; the guide recently selected it as red wine of the year in all of Italy. My husband also loved the Torrevento Castel del Monte Nero di Troia. We drank quite a bit of that around the cities of Troia and Lucera. They're mighty partners with the super-robust food of the area. We saw a couple enjoying it with their long-simmered horse stew!

With so much fish on the menus, it's surprising that more white wine isn't produced—only 20 percent. Red is fine with octopus, anchovies, and hearty fish preparations, but for a delicate white fish gently treated with lemon and olive oil, I prefer white, so I was happy to meet the Masseria Li Veli Askos—both *verdeca* and their *fiano.* The big bonus: Wine is shockingly inexpensive. ∎

ABOVE: Primitivo, one of Puglia's classic vintages, is a deep, dark tannic wine that goes well with hearty dishes or walnuts from a nearby tree. OPPOSITE: Acres of vineyards are often part of a cooperative run by villages or groups of farmers.

Greek and Norman Architectural Influence

Driving through Italy's boot offers a powerful visual reminder of the many conquerors who left a significant mark on the land and cities here. After the fall of the Roman Empire, waves of invaders battered the territory: Byzantines, Normans, and Ottoman Turks, among others.

Frederick II is a name you should know before your trip. Who was he? The king of Sicily from 1197, the king of Germany from 1212, the king of Italy and Holy Roman Emperor from 1220, and the king of Jerusalem from 1229.

This same Frederick (called Stupor Mundi to commemorate him as a wonder of the world) built a lot of imposing castles up and down Europe, especially in southern Italy. But if you get to only one, make sure it's Andria's medieval masterpiece, **Castel del Monte.** It might seem a trek. But just do it.

The octagonal building has a tower protecting each angle. It has eight rooms on each floor; even the courtyard is octagonal. Not only is this an incredible feat of architecture (it's a UNESCO-designated building), but it speaks to Frederick's love of astronomy and geometry. In other words, it will delight the kids in tow who like castles and anyone young or old who thinks that great buildings demonstrate a kind of white magic.

For the Greek side of things, look to **Ostuni.** Nicknamed the "White City," it looms above the valley. And the close-up is even better. White-washed buildings punctuated with colorful doors line cobblestoned lanes. Greek gets mashed up against a Gothic cathedral.

Stay at Ostuni's **La Sommità,** a restored 16th-century palace, and plan to make day trips to other architectural musts nearby. Make sure to see the distinctive *trulli* (circular structures) that characterize local architecture in **Alberobello, Martina Franca** for its baroque and Gothic masterpieces, and beautiful **Locorotondo** with its labyrinth of lovely winding streets and Romanesque churches.

While many visitors head to **Otranto** for its picturesque position on the sea and beautiful nearby beaches (many sunbathe on the rocks in front of town), art history lovers make a pilgrimage to one of the world's most beautiful mosaics, located in the city's cathedral. Covering the entire floor at 700 square feet (65 sq m), the masterpiece depicts the tree of life in an exquisite and unusual way: Two elephants support the trunk, with subjects including mythology, biblical scenes—even King Arthur. The zodiac signs make an appearance, as does the story of Adam and Eve. Deucalion and Pyrrha are depicted being rescued on the back of a giant fish while griffins cavort near goddesses like Diana. Incredibly intricate, and with so many references from different cultures and countries, this magical floor exemplifies just how many strands tie Puglia itself together. ◾

OPPOSITE: Martina Franca's Basilica di San Martino has an exterior that draws architecture buffs.
ABOVE: The tree of life depicted on the floor of Otranto's cathedral is a true masterpiece.

In the Know

Local Flavors: Scarcity as the Mother of Innovation

Despite being one of the poorest regions in Italy, Puglia possesses many of its natural resources, including more than 60 million olive trees and much of the country's olive oil production. You'll also find vegetables: some of the fattest eggplants and tomatoes you've ever seen, along with succulent figs and pomegranates. Fields of wheat help make the region's pastas and exports. Seafood, sourced from fishermen on both sides of the coast, is plentiful. And best of all, gloriously diverse food markets put their northern counterparts to shame.

Some of the basics you should know:

Friselle, the distinctive crunchy bread cooked in a stone oven. *Taralli,* Puglia's circular addictive answer to a pretzel (it's divine with some fat olives and a crisp glass of white wine). *Orecchiette,* the little ear-shaped pasta made to cup a sauce of broccoli rabe with garlic and bread crumbs or tomato sauce with creamy ricotta. Most of the pastas here, which you won't see much in the rest of the country—*roccoli, cavatelli, stacchiodde, curti, gruessi,* and s*agne ncannulate* (a long, twisted shape)—are made with just flour and water. (For a long time, eggs were a luxury hard to come by daily.)

And, oh, the cheeses. The *burrata di Andria,* with a creamy heart that seeps out as your knife cuts into the harder exterior. *Caciocavallo,* that cow cheese where you swear you can taste the spring grass and wildflowers.

Meat appears for special occasions, like lamb that was butchered and grilled only for important festivals or Christmas. *Turcinieddhri* is only for the true meat eater (roasted heart, lungs, liver, and cooked fat from goats or lamb), while pescatarians enjoy *purpu alla pignata* (simmered octopus), and baccala, Salento style, cooked in the oven. ∎

ABOVE: Farm-fresh figs in Apulia OPPOSITE: *Taralli,* **similar to pretzels or breadsticks, come in many flavors.**

Best Of
Puglia's Beaches

From secluded white-sand spots for picnics à deux, to chic beach clubs that stay open well into the night, to miles-long nature reserves, Puglia's seafront is one of its best assets. The best time to enjoy it without hordes of other sunseekers? May and June, September and October.

Best for Flower Power: Named after the white blooms that flower here in Eden-like abundance come springtime, the Baia delle Zagare also has a stretch of powder sand beach bookended by limestone cliffs and cornflower blue water.

Best for Nature Buffs: With its distinctive watchtower, Torre Guaceto includes a protected reserve for birds and marine life, cave dwellings, and beaches that go on for as far as the eye can see. Nude, gay, family, solitary: There is a stretch for everyone.

Best for Adrenaline Seekers: Love to dive off a rocky outcropping with lithe adventurous types? Polignano

a Mare has become a mecca for cliff divers and has even hosted a number of Red Bull championships in the sport. Or head to Fiordo del Ciolo, where the Adriatic and Ionian meet, and take photos of the fearless jumpers plunging from the cliff into the bay below. (Those with a fear of heights and deep water should definitely look away.)

Best for Club Types: You aren't going to find the same kind of Champagne-guzzling celebrity types and prices as beach club options in the south of France (thankfully). But Puglia has some seriously fun beach clubs like Mora Mora. An excellent seafood restaurant, a stylish but low-key bar, linen-draped daybeds, the occasional DJ, and the turquoise sea are among the draws.

Best for Gay Men: Puglia has a number of gay beaches on both coasts, but residents and visitors favor Gallipoli's Punta della Suina, with its pine forest–backed dunes and pretty coves. Book a daybed at the G Club and discover why Gallipoli has been nicknamed the capital of "Gay Salento."

Best for Photo Ops: San Pietro in Bevagna is a protected beach in the Maruggio region with sweeping white-sand dunes, transparent water, and a chill vibe outside the high season.

Best for Island Adventures: The Tremiti Islands lie off the Gargano coast. Only two of the five islands are inhabited—and that term comes with a wink, as these fishermen have lived here since ancient times and still speak in a Partenopean dialect (so, yes, they are from here and you are not). Joking aside, these isles are a revelation: part of a marine reserve, with mythological-like rock formations that give Aquaman a run for his money. Come here to see subterranean caves and deep-sea floors. ■

OPPOSITE: The Baia delle Zagare is home to a collection of spectacular white-sand beaches and turquoise sea, one of the series of beaches that make Puglia famous for its coastline. ABOVE: San Pietro in Bevagna near Taranto

Frances's Favorites

Companions for Puglia

Oddly little is written about Puglia, but what first drew me there was a book, *Honey From a Weed,* by Patience Gray. She moved here in 1970 to live a basic life close to the land. And I do mean basic—no plumbing, heat, hot water, or electricity for 30 years, and way far south in Puglia near the town of Spigolizzi. Formerly the editor of the women's section of London's *Observer,* she abandoned her English life for wild Puglia. Her memoir is quirky, personal, full of exciting recipes to try (and some not to try—for example, fox).

Gray got to know the wild herbs and weeds of the region, much of which ended up in her pots. A locavore before we knew that word, she was a forager who became a scholar of both flora and fauna. She also became adept at skinning and dressing game, outdoor roasting, and sausage making from the nether parts of the pig. I would love to have tasted one of her weed salads.

She is truly one of the great food writers. Adam Federman has written an excellent biography, *Fasting and Feasting: The Life of Visionary Food Writer Patience Gray.* She died in 2005.

When I come to these parts, I also pack *Old Puglia: A Cultural Companion to South Eastern Italy* by Desmond Seward and Susan Mountgarret. Reading it led me to see Byzantine cave paintings, to know the background of the landscape's archaic stone dolmens and menhirs, the history of *trulli,* and the shaping power of Frederick II, who said, "It is clear that the God of the Jews did not know Puglia, or He would not have given His people Palestine as the promised Land."

Old Puglia sharpened my appreciation of how the transhumance, the seasonal movement of sheep between summer and winter pastures, influenced the region's history. And how could it not? By the 17th century, there were four and a half million sheep in Puglia to manage and transport, an imbroglio involving customs stations, absentee owners, and nomadic months on the hoof. Small flocks of 300 were joined to a *punta,* a vast flock of 10,000, with a caravan of shepherds.

The authors explore the mysterious tradition: the tarantella. The dance is said to have originated with a poison tarantula bite that set the victim in wild motion, inciting others to gyrate and fling their bodies until the sufferer was cured. The authors provide gentle correction. Tarantism, they write, is exorcism, a way to cure mental problems. But a copious background of spider lore points to something deep in the psyche that kept people dressing in spiders' colors and to begin to dance by imitating the movements of their furry-legged enemy. ▪

ABOVE: Sunset makes the lone Torre Squillace even more evocative. OPPOSITE: Puglia still operates according to its age-old timetables; here, sheep move between their farm and verdant pastureland.

Hot Spot
Gargano

Mention Gargano to a Puglia lover who knows it well and you might notice a particular light come into that person's eyes. Puglia is beautiful, yes. But the Gargano is a supermodel.

Green. Mountainous. Punctuated by miles of olive groves and forest. Formidable white limestone cliffs that spill down to long, sandy beaches. Happily, much of this breathtaking area has been declared a national park. Its protected status secludes it from mass tourism, except for the coastal properties that become packed in the height of summer.

Start your exploration at **Vieste,** a city on the sea with a path along the water and a Norman castle as its anchor. Traditional fishing boats bob in the port and supply just caught fish to waiting restaurants and residents. As they're being cooked, a delectable smell wafts down the alleys from the white-washed houses. Nearby, a rock tower called **Pizzo-munno** is said to house the soul of a lovelorn fisherman who turned to stone after Sirens tempted his lover to her death.

While the beaches at the front of town might be more crowded, it's easy to get away from them by bike, or boat north to **Peschici** or south to **Mattinata.** In each direction, there are dozens of beaches in hidden coves.

The sea isn't the only attraction here. In fact, it's the small hill towns up in the mountains that preserve a quiet and gentle pace of life. Stop by **Monte Sant'Angelo,** filled with steep alleys and gently flapping laundry lines between the buildings. Here, you will find the **Santuario di San Michele Arcangelo** with its bell tower from the 13th century and the wonderful restaurant of **Li Jalantuùmene.** Chef and owner Gege Mangano creates reinterpreted Pugliese classics like *orecchiette* pasta, with bread crumbs and broccoli rabe—but his pasta is made from buckwheat rather than white flour.

The **Foresta Umbra** ("Forest of Shadows") showcases Puglia's ancient woodlands of Aleppo pines and oaks, with wildlife like roe deer and foxes. This large nature reserve, about a 30-minute drive from Vieste, makes one especially grateful for Italy's large network of protected parks. ▪

The town of Vieste is the perfect base to explore the area of Gargano.

Chapter Seventeen

BASILICATA

My introduction to this mountainous, mysterious region in the instep of the boot was Ann Cornelisen's memoir, *Torregreca*. • Ann was my neighbor in Cortona. As a young woman, she'd spent several post–World War II years in the remote town of Tricarico, working for Save the Children Fund. Single and intrepid, she lived in a cold barracks-like building with erratic water supply; piglets and chickens ran in the stairways.

She oversaw the building of nursery schools and soon found herself involved in the life of the village, becoming the confidant of neighbors.

From that experience, Ann also wrote *Women of the Shadows*, a searing look at the passionate, hard lives of southern women during that era of extreme poverty. The intensely moving book reveals their survival qualities: perseverance, fatalism, humor, suspicion, and an unrelenting work ethic. I also admired her austere prose style. One hot summer— must have been 1997—in her non-air-conditioned Alfa Romeo, she took my husband, Ed, and me on a trip.

Entering Basilicata—which she called by its old name, Lucania—from the north, she took on her role as tour guide and began to show us castles. (Frederick II built them with abandon all over neighboring Puglia, as well as here.) At the blocky fortress Castello di Melfi, located at the foot of Monte Vulture, Frederick drafted the Constitutions of Melfi in 1231, bolstering control over his burgeoning empire. Nearby, Castello di Lagopesola, with thick, square towers, looked suited to legends of knights and fair ladies. Though she felt bound to show them, castles didn't interest Ann much. She soon insisted that we push on to Matera, one of the world's oldest, and possibly strangest, towns.

Twenty-odd years ago, I was horrified at this jumble of caves where people lived for 9,000 years. Haunted and dark, the almost abandoned Sassi (stones) area was a catacomb, a labyrinth, a beehive. From a distance, the view seemed to be a scene from prehistory: stacks of openings in the earth, several stories high, scratched out of the hillside—some with fancy facades belying humid, primitive abodes within. Interspersed among the domestic dwellings were 150 rupestrian churches, some with faded Byzantine frescoes.

Ann, of course, knew Matera from the 1950s and recalled its teeming squalor. Even then, the 16,000 residents were gradually being relocated into modern quarters via government programs. The change was spurred by the publication in 1945 of Carlo Levi's *Christ Stopped at Eboli*. The meaning of the title? Christ stopped short in Basilicata, leaving the lands beyond the town of Eboli to their pagan, unlucky, unredeemed ways.

WHAT YOU NEED TO KNOW...

- **BEST TIME TO VISIT:** Spring brings meadows of wildflowers; summer, festivals and concerts; and fall, autumn temperatures and great food. You will find hotels open throughout the winter in the main city of Matera, but they may be closed elsewhere.

- **TOP SPOTS:** Matera, Maratea, Pollino

- **GETTING THERE:** The closest airport is Puglia's Bari International. Basilicata's roads are famously remote, so you will want your own car to explore properly.

Every road trip through Basilicata should include a stop in Maratea.

Despite modern innovations, you can still taste what earlier life must have been as you plunge below Matera's upper town into renovated cave dwellings.

Fast-forward to the present. I'm shocked to find Matera lively with tourists. They can sleep in comfort, thanks to the *albergo diffuso*, hotel rooms located in the caves around town. Sleek bathrooms, candles, and duvets. Wouldn't the old signoras be shocked? Not to mention thankful for the banishment of infant mortality, tuberculosis, and malaria. The current revival is undoubtedly best, even though I can imagine what Ann would say about how "tarted up" the place is. She would not be staying in a luxury cave where people used to live side by side with their animals—but I would!

Despite modern innovations, you can still taste what earlier life must have been as you plunge below Matera's upper town into the twisted, stacked passageways and renovated cave dwellings. Many are now inns, restaurants, galleries, and jewelry boutiques. Old-timers speak of the

Exploring the old town of Matera, carved into the local rock

intense community bonds among those who lived here—but indeed, who would now want a cozy straw bed with a few chickens as bunkmates? Unredeemed parts of the original town endure. Wander to the edges of the settlement, where caves are still abandoned, and into the Crypt of Original Sin for its ninth-century fresco of Adam and Eve. "Tarted up" Matera is still disturbing. It transports you so forcefully that you emerge into the upper town dizzy and startled from the intimate slip behind our time.

In the sunny and open upper town, suddenly you're among cafés, vibrant young people promenading around the leafy streets, baroque heritage churches, buzzing Vespas and Fiats.

Back then, in Ann's small car, we pressed on to Tricarico, which in her book she renamed Torregreca in homage to the Greek heritage of the area. Medieval in aspect, Tricarico is older. The name derives from *tricargos*, Greek for "three mountains." The village seemed almost unrecognizable to Ann—more prosperous, but not improved in beauty. The sites she'd poured her life into looked derelict. We did meet several of her friends who remembered her as if she were a saint. She was glad to return one last time and glad to leave. A book slammed shut.

This affecting journey with Ann allowed Ed and me to get a sense of the isolated lives in the rough mountains, where until recently, brigands ruled, people lost their youth in their 20s, and dentistry was an unattainable dream. We felt too a renewed admiration for our friend, who had tried to help. I remember vividly the villages scattered along the hillsides, the women in black with wizened faces (and there are still a few now), and Ann looking stony herself as we zipped through her past in those wild and beautiful mountains. How odd travel can be. Such a memorable journey, and mostly I remember being drastically hot and cramped in the back seat of her car.

I especially love the charismatic town of Maratea on the Tyrrhenian coast. Taking the train is the best way to arrive,

A suite at Matera's Le Grotte della Civita, a boutique hotel in one of the city's caves (*sassi*)

because the line after Sapri, where you change from Naples, is the oldest train in Italy. Wooden seats, rickety tracks, windows open, whistle blaring—off on an adventure!

Because the original settlers wanted to hide from passing pirates, the pretty village, 2,000 feet (610 m) up, has no sea view. In the harbor below, you can charter a boat to explore coves, hidden beaches, and caves along the coast. We stay at the Liberty hotel Villa Cheta just outside town. Big windows overlook the sea, and the rooms are airy and light.

The view lures you down to Porticello beach. Although it's only April, I brave the chilly water and take one of the most deeply refreshing swims of my life. The utterly clear Tyrrhenian Sea makes me feel oddly buoyant. (Take beach shoes; the strand is pebbly.) I play dolphin, as in childhood.

Walks from the hotel follow old mule tracks crisscrossing hills blowsy with wildflowers. We encounter no one. Maybe best of all was dinner on Villa Cheta's sea view terrace. The fish are well prepared and fresh as can be. I loved the *paccheri*, big tubular pasta, with lusty eggplant and tomato sauce. (Tomato sauces all over Basilicata are made with gusto.) Scents of lemon and myrtle from the garden waft in on breezes, and palms rustle softly. "Cue the full moon!" Ed calls out. The moon is a gold Greek coin tossed in the air.

There's deep red wine filling our glasses. We clink *cin-cin!* The night quickly engraves on my memory.

Basilicata's coasts are short but front both seas, the Ionian and the Tyrrhenian. Near Maratea, where the sands are gray and sometimes rocky, the beaches to find are Cala Ficarra, Acquafredda, Castrocucco, Maccaro, Anginarra, Fiumicello, Cala Jannita, Spiaggia Nera (black sand), and d'Illicini. On the Ionian side, where some beaches are golden sand, good choices include Scanzano Jonico, Nova Siri, and Policoro. Another hotel to consider near Maratea: Il Santavenere, serene luxury overlooking the sea, extensive spa, and Ristorante Le Lanterne.

Happily, dramatically beautiful Basilicata is no longer abjectly poor. Skiing and trekking vacations, hotel and restaurant development along the fabulous beaches, good roads, the slow rise of the whole south: All of these are bringing Calabria, Abruzzo, Molise, and Basilicata into the charmed circle of Italian tourism. The region's unblemished nature—especially in Parco del Pollino, the largest national park in Italy, and frontage on two coasts—offers splendid outdoor possibilities for renewing and active vacations.

Matera: Basilicata's Unique Monument

Even within a country where each region seems like its own fiefdom, Matera is a city unlike any other in Italy: Its arid, gold-white imprint feels as though it were conjured from the Middle East. (The city's nickname is, in fact, "Little Jerusalem," which is why so many religious films have been shot here. More on that later.) The tumbledown effect of caves and houses, cut into yellow and white *tufo* stone, creates a craggy, moonscape effect as it follows the curves of the surrounding gorges.

Matera's rising status as a tourist destination comes in part from proximity to its neighbor Puglia (many low-cost airlines arrive at the Bari International Airport). As that region emerged as the new "it" destination in Italy and tourists came south, Basilicata—and particularly Matera—began to emerge from the shadows too.

There is nothing hip about the city (although one could argue that it has serious wabi-sabi credibility). It's a serious, somber, mysterious, and deeply atmospheric place. And as such, its quiet paths make a wonderful place for writers, artists, musicians, and filmmakers to find their muses. It wasn't much of a surprise in the artistic community when Matera was designated a 2019 European City of Culture.

Matera is one of the oldest inhabited

Residents of the Sassi district of Matera once lived in underground grottoes without running water or electricity, but thanks to relief programs in the 1950s, their homes are now aboveground. The old cave dwellings have been renovated so visitors can experience the city's unique culture and history.

cities in all of Italy; it predates Rome by centuries and is on par with Istanbul and Jerusalem in terms of its rich history. Start your exploration in the *sassi*, the unique caves that have become its symbol. These dwellings once housed the city's residents but have been reimagined as hotels, bars, and restaurants in the wake of the old town's UNESCO World Heritage site designation in 1993. Prior to the 20th century, the homes of the nobility would have sat atop the town; the caves below contained the quarters of servants and poor peasants.

To get the lay of the land, start with a visit to **Casa Noha,** an interactive museum in the former home of a noble; it's a great introduction to a town that has seen huge strides since World War II, particularly in the past decade. (The evocative multimedia presentation is courtesy of FAI, Italy's admirable historic foundation.) **Casa Grotta nei Sassi di Vico Solitario** depicts a humbler rock dwelling, in which families and livestock cohabitated. Also make sure to take a peek into one of the remarkable rock-cut churches here and in the surrounding countryside. There are more than 150 of them, a

Come nightfall, residents and lucky visitors head to Matera's Piazza Vittorio Veneto.

sign, perhaps, of how much faith was needed amid such destitute conditions for most city inhabitants.

It's not just sightseeing here, though. Stop at **Osteria al Casale** helmed by chef Fabio Paolicelli for such dishes as cavatelli with local caciocavallo cheese and mushrooms. Or join locals at **Area 8** after work hours—the space doubles as the office of a video production company—when this vintage furniture-filled property transforms into a buz-

zing bar featuring small plates and cocktails like the current Italian favorite, the Moscow mule. Or book a table at **Soul Kitchen.** This relative newcomer has reinvented the typical fare with dishes including "burnt" wheat *troccoli* noodles with a sauce of buffalo with pumpkin. And for gelato, make tracks to **I Vizi degli Angeli,** which features unusual flavors like milk and lavender, seasonal sorbets, and stunning staples including chocolate and hazelnut. ∎

CHECKING IN
Ever wanted to stay in a cave? It may sound a bit macabre, but these days, the converted *sassi* are quite romantic.

SEXTANTIO LE GROTTE DELLA CIVITA: This 18-room hotel—the product of more than a decade of restoration—features original experiences like breakfast served in a 13th-century church. With huge white candles in every wall crevice, stand-alone bathtubs, and views of the Murgia National Park, the spot is atmosphere incarnate.

PALAZZO GATTINI: Formerly the palace of one of Matera's most important noble families, this 20-room property features a Turkish bath in the spa and suites that include private swimming pools on the terrace.

IL PALAZZOTTO RESIDENCE & WINERY: This 10-room hotel in a 16th-century palace places natural wood and stone alongside modern lamps and luxurious bathrooms to create an organic connection between modernity and the 1700s. The balconies with vistas over the old town are also a boon.

L'HOTEL IN PIETRA: Located in the middle of the *sassi* behind the cathedral, this cozy hotel features rooms in former caves; the lobby used to be a church. Regulars love to hear the bells resonate throughout the gorge. Wake up early and wander into town on your own.

The Writer Who Brought Basilicata Onto the World Stage

As Matera turns its cave dwellings into boutique hotels, restaurants, shops, and the like, it's hard to imagine that this city and region were once called the "shame of Italy." Before and after World War II, Basilicata encapsulated the poverty and unsanitary conditions that particularly haunted the south of the country. Families were crowded into unlit caves with numerous children, living alongside their livestock without plumbing, electricity, sewers, and running water. The infant mortality rate was nearly 50 percent.

Carlo Levi, a Roman Jewish writer and artist, was instrumental in documenting the region's extreme poverty. A loud and persistent critic of the fascist movement, he was sent into exile by the government in 1935 to the tiny town of Aliano as punishment for his political activism. His memoir of his time in the region, *Cristo si é fermato a Eboli* (*Christ Stopped at Eboli*), was published in 1945, just as World War II was ending. (Eboli is a town in Campania near Salerno where, according to Levi, civilization ended.)

In many ways, Levi's masterpiece was a *denuncia,* or formal complaint, on fascism as he experienced it. This concept of the *denuncia* is an important idea in Italy: a fundamental and popular way to register displeasure, usually anonymously. The book was essentially saying, publicly and vocally: Italy, shame on you. Shame on you for let-ting Basilicata become so poor and unhygienic. Shame on you for not taking better care of your citizens. Shame on the gentry who treat peasants like animals. Shame on the church, which succumbs to the status quo to keep their adherents in poor living conditions. Shame on both the secular and religious leaders for doing nothing and looking the other way.

With his memoir, Levi was continuing an important dialogue about the south and north of Italy as the country emerged from World War II, beset by a large swath of economic, political, and social problems. By illuminating the enormous poverty and despair in Basilicata, Levi was forcibly bringing "the problem of the South" onto the national stage.

And despite the inhumane conditions, Levi also documented Basilicata's deep beauty and community. His great affection for his new neighbors is immediately apparent, which infuses his book with great emotional resonance. "Anyone who sees Matera can't not be impressed," he wrote. "It's so expressive, and it touches you with its painful beauty." ▪

ABOVE: Carlo Levi was exiled by the government to the Basilicata town of Aliano. OPPOSITE: Levi, one of Italy's most important writers, was responsible for bringing Basilicata's deep poverty to the country's attention.

Hot Spot

Palazzo Margherita: An Ode to the *Nonni*

You might not expect to find one of Italy's loveliest hotels in Basilicata. Hidden away in the working-class town of **Bernalda,** it also happens to be owned by one of the world's most famous film directors, Francis Ford Coppola.

But let's start from the beginning.

In the early 20th century, many Italians left their birth country to escape poverty, lured away by the American dream. Many hailed from southern Italy—including Coppola's grandparents, who in 1904 bundled up their possessions and took off across the ocean to embark on a new life. Coppola would grow up hearing their stories of Bernalda—"*la bella Bernalda*" as his grandfather (*nonno*) Agostino called it—while eating dishes that transported them back to the old country. Coppola started to discover his roots. On one of his most memorable trips, he recounts watching the local *festa* of San Bernardino from the windows of a dilapidated 19th-century villa: the spot that would become both a family home and a luxury hotel.

Part of what makes **Palazzo Margherita** so special is that it pays homage to the Coppolas' tastes and interests; the rooms are named after family members (including his children, Roman, Sofia, and Gia, who helped envision the details). But the property also ticks the boxes for guests. Additions like one-of-a-kind bathtubs and huge custom beds come alongside original details like ceiling frescoes and large neoclassical windows.

It's hard not to enjoy a screening in the ballroom, which features a collection of films based on the suggestions made in Martin Scorsese's *My Voyage to Italy,* the documentary he made about the country's greatest hits (film nerds, swoon now!). Also make sure to take advantage of the vintage jukebox at the **Cinecitta** bar, which plays Italian classics to the mix of local residents and hotel guests spilling out into the street. ∎

The Palazzo Margherita hotel is owned by Francis Ford Coppola.

Frances's Favorites
In Your Glass

Calabria and Basilicata have the soil and climate to soar in the wine world. As of now, the two regions are just beginning to realize their potential, whereas nearby Puglia already has solidly placed itself on the viniculture map.

In Basilicata, *aglianico del Vulture*, named for an extinct volcano near the city of Potenza, is the grape of note—and no one performs its alchemy better than Elena Fucci. Her highly acclaimed Titolo, a DOCG, speaks for the power of the landscape, and the elegant heights *aglianico* can reach. I immediately grabbed a case; only 25,000 bottles are produced yearly. Another claimant for champion of Basilicata terroir is Basilisco's Aglianico del Vulture Superiore CR. Monte Vulture is a zone in northern Basilicata where most of the region's wines originate.

Another rising-star red grape, the *primitivo,* comes from Matera. Three to introduce you: Tenuta Parco dei Monaci, Cantine Cifarelli, and Taverna. ■

> In Basilicata, *aglianico del Vulture*, named for an extinct volcano, is the grape of note—and no one performs its alchemy better than Elena Fucci.

ABOVE: The rooftops of the village of Ripacandida with the imposing peak of Monte Vulture in the background OPPOSITE: A wine tasting at the cellar of Elena Fucci in Potenza

A Triumph Spitfire from 1962 rides a curved road above the Gulf of Policastro, part of a vintage car tour.

Maratea and the Coast: Amalfi Without the Crowds

Roads curve above the blue-green sea. Colored fishing boats bob on the waves like children's toys. Beaches alternate between black-ink smooth pebbles and buttery caramel-colored sand. Villages breathe freely as residents move through the day with dogs and strollers and gentle breezes. Roses of all colors cascade down the sides of walled gardens, lining alleyways where the only sound is cutlery against china, urging you toward a speedy lunch.

Maratea? Mara-what? It doesn't help that the spelling of this city's name is similar to "Matera," its UNESCO-protected counterpart to the east. But for those who love it, the confusion is just fine; the dearth of tourists and tour buses suits its gentle, pleasant nature. Amalfi, its neighbor to the north, can keep the honeymooner mill—and the high prices too.

Part of Maratea's great appeal is that it is really two towns. The first, located in the hills, was a highly fortified watchpoint from the time of the Greeks. The second is the port, separated by mere kilometers from the historic center, its coastal gem. That proximity means you can have two vacations in one: some days spent in the upper hill town, ducking into one of the 42 churches or relaxing in the quiet local cafés, and others spent on the sea, exploring the beaches and craggy coastline by car or by boat. Or follow the residents, who spend the morning at the sea and evenings in town, which offers up a rich cultural life in the summer with festivals, concerts, and exhibitions.

Make the **La Locanda delle Donne Monache,** a former monastery transformed into a 27-room hideaway, your base. The design in the rooms might need a reboot on the style front, but the pool below the property's former chapel more than makes up for it. Spend a few hours there before spilling out into the backstreets past a scattering of shuttered buildings for sale (so tempting), small bakeries, and family-owned restaurants like **La Merenderia,** run by a father and son. With its tables scattered in a back alley under black-and-white photographs from Maratea in the 1950s, Merenderia is a dream *enoteca,* featuring plates of cheese and meat and carafes of local wine (for the adventurous, the pistachio liqueur keeps things interesting). For a taste of rugged, mountainside cuisine, opt for **Il Giardino di Epicuro,** where foraged herbs accompany organic meat and produce from the restaurant's farm. Pasta lovers should order the ravioli stuffed with ricotta, sausage, and herbs, or the homemade *pappardelle* with porcini when in season.

On the port, **Zà Mariuccia** is the insider's pick for *spaghetti alle vongole* (with clams) before a nap at **Acquafredda** beach or a swim at **Spiaggia Nera,** the pebbled cove with emerald sea. For a more serviced setup, opt for **La Secca di Castrocucco** with its sun loungers and beach umbrellas.

There are natural caves all along the coast, heaven for divers. Don't miss **Macarro Beach** for epic laps in clear blue water. At the port, rent a little boat for a solo trip, or wink at a fisherman to get a skippered ride. ∎

Villages breathe freely with gentle breezes. Roses of all colors cascade through walled gardens, lining alleyways where the only sound is cutlery against china, urging you toward a speedy lunch.

CLOCKWISE FROM LEFT: Dried peppers and other wares at a deli in the coastal town of Maratea; the port below Maratea has boats to rent to explore the nearby coves and beaches; local residents chat at Caffè e Dolcezze bar.

In the Know

Cinema's Favorite Southern Italian Location

With its evocative stark towns, arid landscapes mixed with green lush countryside, and diverse coastline, Basilicata has become a preferred backdrop for films, both international blockbusters and Italian art house favorites.

Little Jerusalem: There's that comparison again. Matera is so similar to that all-important religious landmark, in fact, that it was used as the backdrop for Mel Gibson's controversial *The Passion of the Christ*. Look for the rock church of San Nicola dei Greci; Gibson filmed the Last Supper scene here, and ghostly Craco was where Judas was hanged in the film.

Bible-focused films have proliferated here before and since Gibson. In 2018, a star-studded cast arrived to film *Mary Magdalene*, where Joaquin Phoenix played Jesus to Rooney Mara's Mary. The movie itself is a bit of a plodder, but the city and beach scenes are utterly transporting. And it's not the only Mary tale that was filmed here. A winner of four awards at the Venice Film Festival back in 2005, Abel Ferrara's *Mary* featured Juliette Binoche, Heather Graham, and Marion Cotillard.

But let's not talk just Hollywood-marketed films. Pier Paolo Pasolini's *Gospel According to St. Matthew* depicts Jesus' birth until his resurrection and is considered one of the most important films in the director's canon. The screen adaptation of Carlo Levi's celebrated Basilicata memoir, *Cristo si è Fermato a Eboli*, powerfully brings the masterpiece to life by filming in the village of Aliano, the real-life inspiration for his fictional Gagliano. Another powerful screen adaptation, mainly filmed near Basilicata's Melfi, is *Io non ho Paura (I'm Not Scared)*, released in 2003 and based on the book of the same title by Niccolò Ammaniti. The film shows images of the main character, a young boy, running through fields of grain under a huge sky. Then the plot turns dark and wrenching.

And to understand Basilicata's history of *brigantaggio,* a movement that rose up in the 19th century against the unification of the country, turn to the classic film *Il Brigante di Tacca del Lupo.* The rebel force—Robin Hoods or just plain bandits, depending on your interpretation—was composed mostly of farmers who were strongly opposed to being under the control of the more powerful north. The movement was doomed, and many of the insurgents ended up in concentration camp–like prisons. The film helps explain the freedom fighter legend that grew up around it. ■

OPPOSITE: Pier Paolo Pasolini shot *The Gospel According to St. Matthew* in Basilicata, a popular region for movie settings. **ABOVE:** Rooney Mara as Mary Magdalene, on set in Matera

Best Of
Basilicata's Hill Towns

I n addition to its stately cities and secluded countryside, Basilicata offers lots of small villages to lose oneself in—whether for epic views or little-known art and architecture.

Best for History Buffs: Go Greek at Metaponto. It is one of the most important ancient colonies in the region—especially the ancient temple to Hera set above wheat fields and the Ionian Sea.

Best for Ghostbusters: Seeing is believing at Craco, only one of Basilicata's ghost towns. This eerie hamlet was deserted back in 1963 following a huge landslide.

Best for Thrill Seekers: Adrenaline junkies will enjoy Il Volo dell'Angelo, a zip line that runs between Pietra-pertosa and neighboring Castelmezzano in the Lucanian Dolomites (Dolomiti Lucane).

Best for Oenophiles: Set on top of an extinct volcano, the lovely lake area of Vulture is home to the *aglianico* grape, which produces Basilicata's strong red wine.

Best for Photography Lovers: Get inspired by the Calanchi, where the natural clay formations create a moon-scape effect. Henri Cartier-Bresson and other photographers have taken spectacular shots here.

Best for Taking in the Sun: Rest up at Torre Fiore Hotel Masseria. The bright white compound outside Pisticci features red-paneled walls and a poolside restaurant.

Best for Ramblers: Trek through the Pollino, Italy's largest national park. The park offers something for every level of fitness, from a gentle stroll to cross-country skiing or canyoning. It's also a wonderful place for bird-watching. ■

The archaeological site of Metaponto comes alive in spring when the wildflowers bloom.

Frances's Favorites

Tasting Basilicata

No other region in Italy has a more robust, traditional cuisine than Basilicata. *Cucina povera,* the poor kitchen, spurred women into invention. What's in the cupboard? Invent around what's at hand! Local products—the pig, peppers, the range of pastas, wild herbs—combine to create flavor-bursting, close-to-the-earth dishes. Peperoncini play a leading role, especially in sausages, but also in stews of pork and tomato. *Pupazzella* is a hot pepper filled with anchovies and herbs, marinated in vinegar. There's also *cotechinate,* rind of pork stuffed with the fiery peppers, herbs, and garlic, all braised in tomato sauce. (Yes, spicy!) Traditional great grills of lamb and pork spiked with rosemary and peppers—yes, again. Even the rustic bread gets its hit of peperoncini. Grilled, thick slices with provolone, bacon, peppers, and tomatoes: a meal.

> **What's in the cupboard? Invent around what's at hand! Local products—the pig, peppers, pastas, wild herbs—combine to create flavor-bursting dishes.**

ABOVE: The production of *caciocavallo podolico* is a laborious process by hand with delicious results.
OPPOSITE: Dried sweet peppers are examined for quality and taste.

I always gravitate to a region's cheeses. In Basilicata, seek out these unique treats: *caciocavallo podolico.* (*Caciocavallo* is popular all over the south.) Translation: horse cheese, maybe from how its gourd shape dries over a structure that resembles a saddle? Or not. Whatever the etymology, the Basilicata version notches up the taste because of the rich milk of the native free-range cow, *podolico,* whose milk is redolent of herbs and wild shrubs, lending richness and flavor. An aged cheese, it's firm but with give, and especially delicious for breakfast with warm rolls and honey.

What choices! Ubiquitous provolone, dense ricotta, *cacioricotto,* a slightly salty ricotta, and excellent mozzarella. I'm a fan of *scamorza,* a cow's milk cheese that we often melt in the fireplace and spread on bruschetta. *Scamorza* looks like a fat golden purse, tied off at the top.

Others to look for: The pecorino of Filiano, made from native *razza gentile* sheep's milk and aged almost a year: particular and nutty. *Burrino,* a goopy *caciocavallo* formed around a heart of butter. (Burrata has become trendy. I wish this had as well.) *Casieddo di Moliterno,* a sheep's milk summer cheese. The curds are flavored during the process with *nepeta,* wild mint, which gives a faint aromatic hit to the semisoft texture. The white balls are wrapped in fern leaves and tied with a sprig of *ginestra,* the wild yellow bloom that sparks the hillsides in summer. ▪

Chapter Eighteen

CALABRIA

"Un altro mondo," a Tuscan friend said. Calabria, another world. What's otherworldly is the beauty. Long flour-white beaches bordering a sea shifting across the blue spectrum. Roadsides dizzy with wildflowers. Purple asters, Queen Anne's lace, pink morning glories, blooming cacti, and tumbles of vulgar magenta bougainvillea. If you drive north from the Reggio di Calabria airport, you want to pull over often, for below

lies the turquoise and cobalt and indigo Tyrrhenian Sea.

Calabria's location—the misshapen toe of the boot poking into the sea—determined that this land would be an object of desire. Of the many invaders, the major influence is obvious from its Roman name: Magna Grecia. Archaeological sites dotting the map show the extent of their colonization; as in Puglia, some areas retain Greek words in dialects.

The landscape underscores Calabria's tumultuous history. The last upheavals of the Apennines striate the region, dropping straight into the sea and creating a sensation of geography in motion. What stunning land—the west coast bordering the Tyrrhenian, the east bordering the Ionian Sea, and the tip of the toe poking into the Strait of Messina.

On the Tyrrhenian side, Capo Vaticano, six miles (10 km) from the dreamy destination Tropea, is a primo first stop—especially if you arrive as the sun sets. Streaks of rose gold exactly match the Aperol spritz delivered on a tray, and sunset tessellates a path all the way to shore. Are the puffy clouds skywriting the word *relax*? The super-contemporary Capovaticano Resort Thalasso and Spa stands on grassy bluffs bordering the beach. Palms reflecting in the long pool curving along the beach look like mirages. (Maybe it's all a mirage, and I'm only imagining arriving at such a place.) Another excellent hotel choice: the Altafiumara Resort and Spa, set above the sea with extensive gardens.

Tropea rises dramatically out of the rocks, 200 feet (61m) above a beach lapped by clear-to-the-bottom waters. In mid-May, only five people are swimming. Flowery piazzas lined with umbrellas, a crumbling three-story palazzo, shops hung with braids of hot peppers, and the prized red Tropea onions, tart and sweet. The vanilla-tinged-with-coral buildings are just decadent enough to make me think this is one of the most romantic towns in Italy.

At lunch, Ed orders the famous local sausage *'nduja*—almost silent *n*—which derives from "andouille," spreadable and rusty red from spicy peppers, tripe, and pork. Also on the antipasti platter: soppressata laced with fennel and hot peperoncini, and tasty capocollo, made from pork loin and cured for a hundred days or more. Oh, pickled Tropea onions—and *ricotta affumicata,* ricotta smoked over chestnut wood and herbs. Red Tropea onions dominate the menu at Ristorante Alice. We order crisp *frittelle,* onion fritters, then

WHAT YOU NEED TO KNOW...

- **BEST TIME TO VISIT:** April to June, September and October

- **TOP SPOTS:** Tropea, Reggio Calabria, Le Castella, Capo Vaticano, La Sila

- **GETTING THERE:** There are three airports (Lamezia Terme, Crotone, and Reggio di Calabria) plus a ferry service to Sicily.

Painted changing rooms on the Calabrian waterfront

Streaks of rose gold match the Aperol spritz on a tray, and sunset tessellates a path all the way to shore. Are the puffy clouds skywriting the word *relax*?

Ed moves on to the *frittelle di neonati,* newborn fish. (Minnows!) I'm on firmer ground with sturdy pasta, tomatoes, and pesto.

In the afternoon lull, I notice the angle of the Benedictine monastery Santa Maria dell'Isola against the sea; twisted streets only two donkeys wide; small carved masks hung on palazzi to scare off the evil eye; shadows of palms printed on the streets. The strong sun of the south beats down a tranquil somnolence over the whole town. "Sunscreen," I say. "Number 70."

Just up the coast from Tropea, I discover the seaside town of Scilla. The namesake, Scylla, was the nymph turned monster who devoured several of Ulysses' men. We leave the car at the broad crescent beach and walk around the bend to Chinalèa, a district of narrow lanes and fishermen's cottages along the water. It's easy to find a terrace for dinner overlooking the sea. At Il Casato, it's swordfish, of course, here in swordfish central. After dinner, the streets are dark. Everyone sleeping—possibly dreaming watery dreams.

Pass through Gerace's Piazza Tribuna to find the Vescovi archway.

The Ionian side of Calabria beckons. The narrowest crossing to the opposite, eastern coast spans only 20 miles (32 km) through groves of citrus trees. First quest: Capo Colonna, a lone Doric column surviving from a lost temple to the Greek goddess Hera on the easternmost promontory of Calabria. This lonely marker from the fifth century B.C. rises from the poppy-strewn rubble of antiquity, outlined against the same sky that was there when this largest temple in Magna Grecia loomed over the sea. Spooky, one column standing. A stray cat wraps around my ankle. I feel a quick chill. The cat's sinuous tail, or the single column's mighty symbolism of Calabria's history?

What draws the traveler to eastern Calabria? Beaches. Hundreds of them. Hill towns and food. The seafood here is oh so fresh. I happened into Gambero Rosso Ristorante e Enoteca in Marina di Gioiosa Ionico: a lucky stop. Memorable, those gigantic grilled scampi. Two other of Calabria's most lauded and starred restaurants are on the Ionian side. Pietramare is housed at the small and exclusive Praia Art Resort in Isola di Capo Rizzuto. Ever seen hammocks swaying in the shallows? Can you find a more sybaritic spot than this? The young chef Ciro Sicignano's kitchen is a Calabrian wonderland. Little ravioli filled with smoked mozzarella and tomato followed by the most pristine fish, the tenderest pork, and a fine finish: seductive cherry soufflés served in individual copper pans beside a scoop of cherry gelato. Probably because we're enthusiastic about every bite, the waiter brings Ciro over for toasts all around. We leave with pastas and local honey. These generous gifts! All over Calabria, we've been given sauces, jams, and biscotti.

The next night we dine at another temple to Calabrese cuisine, Ristorante Abbruzzino. Chef Luca Abbruzzino shows us the kitchen, which provides insight into how calm and organized he is. Every morsel is carefully crafted—ravioli with truffles, *tortelli* filled with ricotta, almonds, and mackerel; then pigeon with plums. The chef reappears. He wants to know what we didn't like. We loved everything.

La Cattolica church in Stilo is the earliest Byzantine structure in Calabria.

The inland hill towns, which protected residents from sea raids, commanded panoramic views of whomever might be headed for them. I chose Monasterace as a good location for explorations. We checked into the Agriturismo 'A Lanterna: new, furnished serenely in white, and situated above a lighthouse.

Off we go. Santa Severina sits upon a tufa promontory like a ghostly ship. The prize is the exquisite, tiny Byzantine church of Santa Filomena. Topped by a cupcake-shaped cupola ringed with 16 slender columns, this beauty from the 10th to 11th century endures.

Stilo's jewel is La Cattolica, the earliest Byzantine structure in Calabria. The brick roofs ripple like crimped pie crusts.

My favorite hill town is Gerace. The Bar Cattedrale's outside tables overlook the largest church in Calabria. In their flavors of granita, those refreshing icy slushes, you can catch a whiff of Arab heritage: bergamot, almond, pistachio, peach, fig, prickly pear, and black mulberry. Yes, the Norman church, dating from 1045, is grand. Each of the majestic columns along the aisle is different, suggesting that they were taken from ruins, especially from the nearby Greek town of Locri.

At the end of the trip, I circle back around to Reggio di Calabria. Destroyed in an earthquake in 1908, then bombed in World War II, it retains its tropical atmosphere, with twisted banyan and blooming jacaranda trees along the fabulous sea promenade, Lungomare Falcomatà. The prime attraction is the Museo Nazionale Archeologico, one of the best in Italy. The treasures include a *dolium,* a six-foot-high (1.8 m) olive oil storage jar from 1150; the grave of a Hellenistic woman, which yielded delicate earrings set with gems and, inside her mouth, a gold coin, to pay for her passage to another world but unspent.

Then we arrive at the bronze Riace Warriors. Two glorious nude men, six feet six inches (1.98 m) and six feet five inches (1.95 m). Found in the sea just off the town of Riace, they might have been jettisoned from a fifth-century Greek ship in distress. Warrior A and Warrior B are their pedestrian names. No one knows their origins. But here they are. They show their teeth. Silver, along with silver eyelashes and ivory irises, copper mouths and nipples. Their buttocks are taut, their beards groomed, their poses powerful.

Calabria: *un altro mondo,* another world, I was told. These mysterious visitors from the beginning symbolize Calabria. Sensuous and aloof. Ancient. Fierce and proud.

Tropea: Calabria's Seaside Treasure

White-sand beach beneath a cliff. Twisted cobblestoned lanes that converge onto a dazzling panorama of Caribbean-blue sea. Shops selling reddish purple onions that seem to gleam in the sparkling sunshine.

Of all the seaside towns in Calabria, Tropea is arguably the most ravishing. It's also one of a kind, offering a bird's-eye view over its much photographed powder beach, located under a sharp cliff 200 feet (61 m) below the main village, a vista that stretches all the way to the volcanic island of Stromboli. This is not a spot for ticking off on a tourist checklist; instead, savor a walk past the town's faded 18th-century palazzi and along the **Corso Vittorio Emanuele** to the *punti di visto,* public balconies, which provide the irresistible viewpoints at the end of the town's walls.

Despite a turbulent and very multicultural past featuring invasions by Arabs, Swabians, Byzantines, and Normans, among others, Calabria today is really on the radar for Italians and a few lucky insiders who know about its series of gentle beaches and sweeping coastline. In truth, the area does not have the same infrastucture as some of its neighbors, very few locals speak English, and there is not the range of accommodation as in spots like Puglia or Basilicata. But that's its charm too, watching other Italians on holiday.

The region becomes a party during the summer, as families flock to wade

Tropea is full of treats like this white-sand beach sitting underneath Santa Maria dell'Isola, a church with one of the most spectacular positions in Italy.

in the balmy clear water and beach-goers set up umbrellas in a kaleido-scope of yellows, reds, and greens. There are also the visitors from the United States, here to discover their family lineage. Although many Cala-brese left this poverty-stricken region for a better life in the new country, Ital-ian Americans strive to keep their con-nection to the food, the broad dialect, and the beautiful land, even in its most difficult moments of history.

Tropea's duomo, a Norman cathe-dral, provides a formidable centerpiece to town, with an icon of the Madonna of Romania on its altar. She is the city's protector in times of war and duress (during her eponymous festival every September, she is paraded through town to remind citizens of her impor-tant role in the life of the town). Next door, the Bishop's Palace in the **Palazzo Vescovile** houses relics and religious iconography that hint at the region's deep Catholicism.

But most of Tropea's focus centers on the beach, rated by various publica-tions including *Condé Nast Traveler,* as one of the 10 most beautiful in the country. It's at the foot of the spectac-ular **Santa Maria dell'Isola,** located on a

Restaurants with outdoor tables are among the distractions in Tropea.

rugged promontory; there isn't much inside, but travelers can climb to the roof to admire the view of the beach and the sea stretching toward Sicily's Aeolian Islands. Swimming and volley-ball are the main pursuits, with tanned bodies of every description enjoying their sunbaths.

At dusk, the attention turns back into town for a sunset *aperitivo* at

Al Migliarese or a plate of *pesce spada,* swordfish, at **Osteria del Pescatore** tucked into a backstreet. At **Vecchio Granaio,** part of Italy's slow food net-work, locals congregate for pizza, while **Incipit** is the town's more gourmet choice, with offerings like *moscardini,* baby octopus, cooked with Tropea onions, and tuna with a currant sauce. ▪

CHECKING IN
Although Calabria's hotel offerings are quite small, they are memorable.

The choice of hotels in Calabria remains quite small com-pared with the diverse lodgings in Puglia or Sicily. Book well in advance to get a room in the summer.

VILLA PAOLA: This 16th-century former convent in a quiet spot outside Tropea is (so to speak) divine. The 11-room boutique hotel offers flowering gardens and an infinity pool: the perfect respite after day trips to town and along the coastline.

PRAIA ART RESORT: In many ways, this resort put Calabria on the boutique map. Located on the edge of the Marine

Resort of Capo Rizzato, it features tiled floors, hammocks hung above the sea, and a large pool: the perfect home base for day trips to other destinations.

TROPEA BOUTIQUE HOTEL: A quick walk to the Marina dell'Isola beach, and with views over the sea from the breakfast and *aperitivo* terrace, this cheap but sweet hotel is a fraction of what rooms cost in better-known Italian resort destinations. Ask them to rent you a boat or go for an excursion in a group vessel for a truly raucous and memorable experience. Italian summer incarnate!

Local Flavors: Think Simple but Spicy

Calabria often seems like its own country within Italy, and that singularity is reflected in its cuisine. With only a sliver of sea separating them, the region shares ingredients with Sicily. But Calabria has even more of a penchant for the spicy.

There are over 150 different types of peperoncino, chili, here. The fairy dust of Calabrian dishes, these peppers are often worked in to pasta for an extra kick. Some varieties, including the celebrated Diamante, are potent enough to be used sparingly. The town of the same name hosts a festival in its honor every September; be sure to try the 'nduja, the Calabrese sausage flavored with chili pepper. A few miles away, in Maierà, there's even a museum devoted to peperoncini, tracing the little red pepper's 6,000 years of history.

Another mainstay of Calabrian cuisine comes in the form of an onion: the Tropea onion, to be exact. A sweet incarnation of the vegetable, it's one of Italy's most famous species, grown by hand on the clay cliffs. Its color, a purple pink, looks almost like a Pantone shade, giving dishes a special glow as well as a light sweetness. Tropea onions can be made into a marmalade to top crostini or shaved into a salad. Gently grilled, the bulb also serves as a great accompaniment to grilled fish or roast meat. Its fans claim that it has health benefits too, from lowering blood pressure to anti-inflammatory properties. Plus it's said to ward off the evil eye.

Considering the economic hardships of the region, it's easy to see how the Calabrese became creative at fixing simple dishes that were still tasty—for example, the *caviale del poveri,* or poor people's caviar: herring roe in oil flavored with sardines and onion. Or *stoccofisso,* stockfish with potatoes, tomatoes, and capers. *Pasta e patate ara tijeddra* comes from Cosenza, where pasta, potatoes, tomato sauce, cheese, and bread crumbs are served with a crispy crust thanks to a quick stint in the oven.

The region also boasts a wide range of natural resources. The most celebrated among them include swordfish; the largest wild mushroom cultivation in Italy; *arancia calabrese* (also known as bergamot), an orange grown only in Calabria; and *caciocavallo,* the area's signature cow's cheese. The best one to sample has to be the Ciminà *caciocavallo,* a Slow Food–protected product.

Finally, when eating Calabrese style, don't forget the wine accompaniment! Cirò, considered the world's oldest vintage still in production, is also the region's best known; the designation starts in the eastern foothills of La Sila and runs down to the Ionian coast. Try a bottle of Librandi, a fourth-generation producer, or 'A Vita, a delicious organic interpretation of the *gaglioppo* grape. ■

OPPOSITE: The beautiful purple onions of Tropea, used in local dishes and touted as an anti-inflammatory **ABOVE:** Yet another type of *caciocavallo* cheese; this is known as the Silano.

In the Know

The Bronze Statues of Riace

It seems unlikely that a snorkeling enthusiast would stumble on one of Italy's most important archaeological finds. Yet that is exactly what happened one August morning in 1972 when the bronze statues of Riace (named after the nearby town of Riace Marina) were discovered on the floor of the Ionian Sea.

At first, the vacationing Roman thought he had found a dead body that had been thrown into the watery depths. But on further inspection, he realized that it was a bronze arm that had caught his attention and that there were, in fact, two statues side by side. He alerted the authorities, who soon pulled them up from their sandy seabed.

Why are these statues so famous and beloved? For one thing, the Greek men represented are life size and incredibly well preserved (especially given that they date back to between 460 and 450 B.C.). They were most likely not sculpted by the same artist, but both were masters of their time. Some experts believe that the subjects were warriors; others think they were renowned athletes, while still others deem them characters from a Euripides play. The general consensus is that during a storm, they were tossed out of a boat on their voyage between Greece and Rome.

It's the sense of extreme vitality that makes these statues truly compelling: their mass of hair and beards, their ripped muscles revealed in their full naked glory, and the exquisite attention to detail (glass and calcite were used for their eyes, for example, and their teeth are made of silver).

This idealized human beauty is crafted with such detail and precision that it's hard to believe they were produced by sculptors who lived 2,000 years before the Renaissance masters lauded for creating perfect beauty in hard-to-ply materials. The fact that these bronze statues were some of the only ones remaining from the period (since many were melted down for their metal) made them an even more celebrated find.

In today's age of fast-moving headlines, it's almost impossible to imagine the significance of this discovery. The statues made the covers of magazines; they made guest stints in Rome and Florence, where they were met with almost Beatles-level interest, and appeared on stamps. But despite pressure to move them to a locale with more resources (and visitors, for that matter), residents demanded that they remain in the region where they were found. The bronze statues of Riace are an important heirloom that may date to the Hellenic age, and for the Calabrese, a true cultural treasure that showcases an important step in the region's turbulent history.

So now Warrior A and B, as they are called, have their home in Reggio di Calabria's Museo Nazionale Archeologico, sitting on antiseismic platforms in a microclimate-controlled room. On a recent visit, the statues were in their full glory, real enough that you could almost reach out and touch them—much like their discovery that fateful sunny summer day. ■

ABOVE: The town of Riace gained instant fame when two ancient statues were discovered offshore. OPPOSITE: On display at Reggio di Calabria's Museo Nazionale Archeologico, the bronzes are considered to be among Italy's most revelatory works of art history.

Frances's Favorites

In Your Glass

Robust food calls for strong-armed wines. Stay close to the geography in Calabria, and you'll find good surprises. The regional winemakers have a high awareness of *biologico,* organic practices.

Librandi is a leading vineyard, and any bottle with that name on it is likely to be a good choice. While I liked the Gravello, a blend of *gaglioppo,* the local grape, with cabernet sauvignon, I loved Cirò Rosso Classico Superiore, 90 percent *gaglioppo.* Other top vineyards: Roberto Ceraudo (especially Grisara red) and I Greco. Owned by seven brothers, it makes a fine Masino that has been amply awarded by Gambero Rosso's *Italian Wines,* a guide I rely on. ∎

Stay close to the geography in Calabria, and you'll find good surprises. The regional winemakers have a high awareness of *biologico,* organic practices.

ABOVE: Barrels of Librandi wine, one of Calabria's most respected producers for vintages like Cirò OPPOSITE: At ristorante La Lamia in Tropea, diners tuck in to local dishes paired with local wines.

The beach of San Nicola Arcella near Calabria's Arco Magno, one of a series of pretty spots near Cosenza

The Calabrian Coast: In the Footsteps of Odysseus

Unlike such beach areas as Sicily and Puglia, Calabria has stayed off the radar for most American visitors (unless they are in the area searching for the roots of an Italian relative and have a few extra days to spare). And while it's true that the infrastructure may be patchier in terms of tourist services and less English is spoken compared with some other regions, this is the perfect destination for intrepid travelers who want to experience a truly authentic part of the country. It's also home to some of Italy's most exquisite beaches, with gentle turquoise water and white sand.

Start your beach tour at the castle and town of **Le Castella,** reportedly one of the castles where Odysseus was held prisoner and a spot that today seems much more a playground than a jail. The sun-bleached 13th-century fortress, in fact, almost looks like a large sand castle sitting on a promontory stretching out into transparent water. Underneath the structure sit the little beaches that make excellent hideaways on a sunny day. Book a meal at **La Scogliera** for a plate of *linguini alle vongole* (clams) and an excellent sea view, or grab a glass of wine or gelato at **Il Pescatore,** where enormous windows offer a vista of the castle in one direction and the beach in the other.

Close to the cape's lighthouse, a series of beaches line the white-gray granite curves along the **Capo Vaticano** coast, with a mixture of both public options and *stabilimenti* (beach clubs) where you can rent a sun bed and umbrella for about $12 a day. The water here is some of the most pristine in Italy.

Scilla, a village of pastel-colored homes, is also the mythical site where six of Odysseus's crew members met their end in the jaws of a six-headed monster. **Ruffo Castle** here deserves a visit before you head to the wide sand beach below for a swim. After sunbathing, make tracks to **Bleu de Toi** for a romantic setting and fresh-from-the-water sea urchins (as well as other delightful fish dishes).

The town of **San Nicola Arcella,** overlooking the Gulf of Policastro, provides another coastal treasure for Italian insiders, with a cliffside position sur- rounded by olive trees and primrose flowers that bloom in spring between the rocks. In the area close to the village, little beaches are tucked into the caves, and a watchtower at the ancient village's front provides a photo op on the water. Close to the border of Basilicata, this area is beloved by scuba divers for its variety of fish sightings, much like a seaside aquarium.

Pizzo, an easy day trip from Tropea, has two main attractions: the **Chiesetta di Piedigrotta,** a 17th-century church in a cave of soft rock right outside town, and its *tartufo di Pizzo,* a not-to-be-missed chocolate and hazelnut gelato best sampled at the **Bar Gelateria Ercole** in the Piazza della Repubblica. Afterward, meander the narrow streets of its old historic center, and visit the **Castle Murat,** where Napoleon's brother-in-law was executed. The town has gone through many incarnations: a refuge for Basilian monks fleeing persecution, a tuna-fishing hub, and now a seaside retreat with a gentle pace. ∎

> Le Castella is reportedly one of the castles where Odysseus was held prisoner and a spot that today seems much more a playground than a jail. The sun-bleached fortress almost looks like a large sand castle.

CLOCKWISE FROM LEFT: Le Castella, an Aragonese castle on the island of Capo Rizzuto; the colorful buildings of Calabria's Scilla, where some of Odysseus's crew lost their lives in the jaws of a monster; the picturesque harbor and beach of Pizzo

Chapter Nineteen
SICILY

Cervantes observed that translating a book from the original is like seeing the other side of a tapestry. When I read that, I thought of Sicily: How apt for this island that seems like its own country. Italian, but turned over. Stitches and patterns become obscured by the tangled warp and woof of colorful threads. • Is this the most complicated island in the world? The largest in the Mediterranean, Sicily juts far into

forever-active sea routes of trade and conquests. Phoenicians, Greeks, Arabs, Byzantines, Romans, Saracens, Jews, Normans, pirates—every major power and two-bit marauder once had their way with this desirable piece of real estate.

Throughout history, a tough place to grow up—but what a heritage of clashing and enriching cultures! At the sites of Agrigento, Selinunte, Segesta, and Syracuse, the majestic Greek temples and ruins rival those of their home country. Meanwhile, a strong Arab heritage pervades in everything from architecture and gardens to fishing traditions, language, and cuisine. And the last flowering of the baroque overtook the southeast after the earthquake of 1793, inspiring the construction of over-the-top fantasy towns Noto, Ragusa, and Modica. Above all, Mount Etna, at 10,925 feet (3,330 m), is the island's EKG, perpetually about to blow (or not). The mythic volcano must be at the heart of Sicilian fatalism and the strong impetus to enjoy the moment.

This year, I will take my fifth trip to Sicily. So I know Sicily well? Not a chance. Though I've seen most top sights, I'm anticipating Salina, one of the seductive Aeolian Islands, and also the windy island of Pantelleria with its fragrant *moscato passito* dessert wine. I've long wanted to see the fourth-century mosaics at Villa Romana del Casale, an elaborate Roman palace near the town of Piazza Armerina; the depic-

tions of sporty girls in bikinis are unique in archaic art. And I would love to try the Anna Tasca Lanza cooking classes, housed in an old villa near Vallelunga in the rural interior. There, you work outside, spreading end-of-summer tomatoes to dry into that essential ingredient called *estratto,* which gives local food its depth of flavor.

But by now, I have particular places I want to revisit: Marzamemi's movie-set piazza on a summer night; baroque Scicli, surely the prettiest small town on the island; and the Occhipinti vineyards near Vittorio, where two creative sisters, Arianna and Fausta, make lush wines and welcome guests at their country inn, Il Baglio. On my last visit, Catania

WHAT YOU NEED TO KNOW...

- **BEST TIME TO VISIT:** April to June for spring temperatures and less of a crowd; September and October for the still balmy days and cultural pursuits. For island adventures, stick to May, June, September, and October, which feature warm temperatures without the Italian and Northern European masses.

- **TOP SPOTS:** Palermo, Syracuse, Noto, Ragusa, Catania, Aeolian Islands, Mount Etna

- **GETTING THERE:** There are four main airports on the island, but most carriers fly into Catania and Palermo. Low-cost airlines like Ryanair also offer service to Trapani and Comiso.

Sicily's Anna Tasca Lanza, one of Italy's most famous cooking schools

Is this the most complicated island in the world? The largest in the Mediterranean, Sicily juts far into forever-active sea routes of trade and conquests.

caught me by surprise. I expected a rowdy port town, possibly dicey, but I found a *centro* of dignified buildings constructed with gray lava stone—Etna rules the view—along with elegant parks, a narrow street lined with excellent small restaurants, and two boisterous outdoor markets. Catania's heart beats to an old-world vibe—especially at the fish market, where but for the clothes fishermen wear, you could be in medieval Sicily.

Of other marvelous sites I have seen, there's Taormina. Decadent and heart-wrenchingly beautiful, this is the place for the romance of the island: a beguiling golden tiara of a town, whose semitropical garden overlooks the coast. Yes, stop and gasp.

I stayed at San Domenico Palace Hotel, a former monastery that retains a sense of silence, but with more luxury than the former pious residents enjoyed. I walked into town early and soon felt like a regular in my favorite café. I bought six antique platters, extravagantly expensive, depicting the same types of fish appearing on our plates at dinner. Hanging in my kitchen now, they always remind me of a rainy morning, the ancient man wrapping them in newspaper and telling me I would always remember Taormina. Another time when

A bird's-eye view from Madonna della Rocca church down to Taormina

I sailed out, a rosy afternoon light fell like a veil over the town. The old Greek spirits still linger in the air.

If Taormina exists in calm, rarefied air, Palermo represents the opposite: gritty, cacophonous, and one of the most stimulating places in Europe. The market of La Vucciria (from French Norman's *boucherie,* butcher's shop) explodes with color—fiery peppers, *tarocchi* (blood oranges), dripping lambs, fish of every fin, heaps of shiny eggplants, and those intense tomatoes grown in volcanic soil. Smells of guts and lemons, sage bundles, and shrimp. Raucous sellers, aggressive shoppers, chefs trailed by their helpers, mystified tourists. If you visit the market on your first morning, you're properly introduced to Palermo.

A second introduction might happen at one of Palermo's many pastry shops, such as Pasticceria Capello or Casa Stagnitta in the *centro storico,* historic center. Marvelous to see, and the heaviest sweetness to taste: *frutta martorana,* marzipan replicas of fruits and vegetables in all the colors of a crayon box. The grande dame of cakes, *cassata,* with ingredients that have come down the ages from the Arabs. So pretty all the extravagant candied fruit, nuts, and citrus, bedecking a sponge cake with fresh sheep ricotta filling. The glass cases run riot with the sumptuous cannoli that make you understand *The Godfather* thug's famous line: "Leave the gun. Take the cannoli."

Loitering in cafés may be one of the best ways to absorb Palermo. Try Caffè Opera near the Teatro Massimo or, inside the theater, the Caffè Morettino, all velvet and gilt. Making coffee in Sicily is an art form. You're served barely a tablespoon of dark liquid topped with a perfect *crema:* most galvanizing to the body.

Visit, of course, the Palermo Cathedral, with Norman and Arab heritages, and the Palatine Chapel, where the dazzling gold makes you take out your sunglasses. All the starred sights in your guidebook are musts.

Palermo has two opera houses! That's what I love about Italy: The arts run through history as strongly as upheavals,

The Mercato del Capo is a dizzying display of local vegetables and fruit in Palermo.

invasions, wars. The 19th-century Teatro Massimo is one of the largest opera houses in Europe. Of the same era, Politeama Garibaldi is just as splendid. The season for opera, ballet, symphony, and other performances lasts all year, except for August when Sicily enters a coma of heat.

Palermo offers many hotel options, but why not stay at the historic Grand Hotel Villa Igiea? Request a renovated room (some are quite dated) with a sea view; then you'll be at home in this brash, alluring place.

Driving away from the hotel and headed for the medieval hill town of Erice and the temples at Selinunte and Segesta, we became hopelessly lost. When a motorcycle roared up beside us at a stoplight, I asked the leather-clad driver for directions. He shouted, "Follow me," and we careered through bumper-car traffic, made three lanes out of two, swerved and sped behind the maniac until he pointed to an exit and veered away. We beeped. *Grazie.*

We made it to Erice and found the pastry shop of Maria Grammatica, famous for her cannoli. Sitting in the car with big slices of her almond and lemon tart, I said to Ed, "Add it to your résumé. You drove in Palermo."

A favorite place is Ortigia, meaning "quail," aka *città vecchia,* historic center of the city of Syracuse, known for its Greek amphitheater, acropolis, catacombs, and many other remains. Ortigia is a small pastel-colored island: a gem of intimate piazzas, fountains, winding walks along the sea, enticing pastry shops and restaurants. A soprano could step out any minute onto one of the flowery balconies.

The duomo, Santa Maria del Pilar, mirrors local history. Eighth-century B.C. structures have been found at the lowest excavations. Around 480 B.C., a temple to Athena was built by a victorious warrior. When Byzantium ruled, they left their traces on the building, as did the Arab, Norman, and Spanish successors. Twenty-four columns from the original temple's 36 miraculously remain.

Ancient as it is, Piazza del Duomo is one of Italy's most felicitous places to enjoy the present. Order an almond granita at a café, sit and watch the light change on the baroque facade of the cathedral and on the piazza's other sun-catcher church, Santa Lucia alla Badia. The air is limpid, the sky a glazed blue dome. Music drifts down from an upstairs window. We are allowed such pleasures! How lucky. Quintessential Sicily: right here.

The beautiful main square of Marzamemi, still a fishing village, is the perfect setting for a destination wedding or special occasion meal.

Insider's Guide

Marzamemi: Simple Seaside Pleasures

Marzamemi. Say that name to a foreigner and you might get a blank stare in return. But to Italian insiders who travel to Sicily—and the island is increasingly on the favored list due to its mix of natural beauty, ancient ruins, and new destinations—the place elicits a sigh of love and an exclamation of worry that its secret is getting out.

Once a fishing village (an occupation that remains a mainstay here), Marzamemi features a central piazza anchored by the home of the family that once owned the town's tuna-

processing facility, one of the most important tuna warehouses in the region. Today, the sun-drenched, sea-bleached main square draws visitors to the cafés around its periphery, offering views of whitewashed fishing homes with colorful doors (available for rent), small streets that lead to the sea, and painted fishing boats. It's one of the most romantic settings in all of Italy.

At seafood restaurants like **Cortile Arabo,** tables sit on a wooden deck overlooking the waterfront, offering local dishes like a simple ravioli with the sweet local tomatoes called

pachino (these come with their own DOC and are grown in salty soil nearby). Also on the docket is home-made bread made from different antique flours sourced in the area and simple, fresh seafood including grilled octopus. Nearby, **Taverna La Cialoma** has an equally stunning setting, with standouts like fresh anchovies topped with strawberries or a carpaccio of red shrimp. Pair them with wines from all over the island.

The owners of **Liccamuciula** have created a shop that features a café (with excellent desserts and freshly baked goodies like cakes and bread), along with books and a bar and restaurant—think of it as Marzamemi's answer to a concept store. Despite its name, **il tuo Gelato 2** is the spot for ice cream, including a spectacular pistachio option (look for the Bronte DOC). To enjoy the full effect, do as townsfolk do, try it for breakfast inside a sliced brioche and succumb to a food coma on a beach nearby.

Featuring more than 10 miles (16 km) of hiking trails and pristine seafront, **Vendicari Nature Reserve** is also an oasis for the herons, flamingos, and storks that roost here. The atmospheric tuna factory provides a picturesque reminder of what made this area its fortune before tourism arrived. It's also home to one of Italy's most famous nude gay beaches: **Il Marianelli.**

If you prefer more of a club scene, drive to the **Agua Beach Resort** in San Lorenzo, which offers a chic bar and restaurant, a gift shop with barely-there bikinis and more demure cover-ups, along with a gentle swimming beach.

Feeling adventurous? Organize a boat launch from the local port through the Sikelia Sail tour company and explore the southernmost part of Sicily, past **Isola delle Corrente,** where the Ionian and Mediterranean seas meet (and where a lighthouse from the mid-19th century stands in decay). Swimming here reveals just how pristine the water remains at this celebrated meeting point, and the captain is full of local lore.

If you are looking to stay in Marzamemi, options through the local agency range from simple former fishermen's homes (which are perfectly comfortable and a stone's throw from the piazza) to small bed-and-breakfasts like the newly restored **Il Borghetta** run by two sisters and with a rooftop terrace with views of nearby beaches. ∎

> To Italian insiders who travel to Sicily, the name Marzamemi elicits a sigh of love and an exclamation of worry that its secret is getting out.

CLOCKWISE FROM LEFT: A freshly baked cake topped with raspberries at Marzamemi's Liccamuciula, which doubles as a store; San Lorenzo beach is also home to the Agua Beach Resort with a restaurant by the sea; fishing boats bob in Marzamemi's harbor.

In the Know

Etna Slopes: The Oenophile Playground

Volcanic soil. Arid, windswept slopes. Varying elevations with completely different terroirs. Temperatures that change on a dime. To the uninitiated, this terrain might not seem practical for creating stellar vintages. But happily, some of Italy's most inventive wine masters have risen to the challenge—and over the past few decades, the wines of Mount Etna have gained a reputation as some of the country's most exciting and innovative offerings.

But this new renaissance is not the beginning of this region's great wine tradition. *Ma scherzi!* (Are you kidding!) Grapes have grown around Mount Etna since before humans inhabited the area, and as early as the eighth century B.C., Greek settlers began developing new techniques of viticulture here. The region continued to grow into the 19th and early 20th centuries until mass emigration and an epidemic of grapevine-destroying insects erased many improvements in quality. Etna wines became mostly associated with unmemorable carafe offerings.

Today, that's all changing as boutique producers from the island, along with famous heavyweights from Piedmont and Tuscany, are reinventing, resuscitating, and experimenting here. Winemakers like Tuscany's innovative producer Andrea Franchetti arrived early, producing not only an excellent white, Passopisciaro, but also exciting new reds made at varying altitudes. Franchetti was a visionary for under-standing the enormous potential in vineyards that had lain fallow for many years, and in the gentle walled terraces that had collapsed under eruptions and inclement weather.

Most of the white wines on Etna are centered around the *carricante,* a little-known and little-appreciated grape that producers admire for its mineral-rich notes. Winemakers call the touch of saltiness that characterizes them a product of the Mediterranean's saline winds that gust over the slopes. Producer Graci's Etna Bianco is a superb model of this type of wine, and at less than $30, a relative bargain for the quality. The dryness and full flavor go well with the food of the nearby sea: dishes like *bottarga* and spaghetti, freshly caught tuna, and *ricci,* the urchins that can be cracked open and eaten immediately.

The phenomenal reds have showcased the *nerello mascalese,* a grape once associated with the vast, but not very good, offerings that Sicily sent overseas—in a whole new way. In the past two decades, mixing it with the varietal *nerello cappuccino,* producers have tamed the sweetness and made it one of the most beloved exports from the island. The Tenuta di Terre Nere Etna Rosso provides a good sample of this new approach, featuring a blend of acidity with just a suggestion of sweetness. Tenuta delle Terre Nere's owner, Marco de Grazia, used to export wines from Piedmont and Tuscany to the United States. But now he makes his own wines here, a testament to the Etna region's appeal.

Etna-watchers are also excited to see what Gaja, one of Piedmont's great producers, will bring to the table. After purchasing a 51-acre (21 ha) property with Graci, he has just joined the Etna party—and insiders can't wait to see the results. ∎

ABOVE: Mount Etna's volcanic terrain has tempted winemakers to try their hand there. OPPOSITE: Producer Andrea Franchetti makes a delicious white wine, Passopisciaro, as well as red wines.

On the island of Salina in the Aeolians, Hotel Signum is a highlight with its sun yellow painted walls and destination restaurant.

Insider's Guide

Aeolian Islands: Sicily's Superstars

These seven exquisite islands have seemingly been transplanted from paradise right into the Tyrrhenian Sea. Designated a UNESCO-protected site, this archipelago has many fewer tourists than spots like Capri or the Amalfi Coast, and offers a low-key but stylish vibe, as well as a crystal clear sea for swimming and fishing that turns moody when the winds rise. These are just a few of the reasons that the Aeolian Islands remain one of Italy's best getaways.

Each of the archipelago's residents has its own distinct character. **Salina,** the green lush island that provided the setting for the wonderful film *Il Postino,* is arguably its most beautiful. Two extinct volcanoes create a craggy panorama that falls back down into lush fields, vineyards, and to the sea. Malvasia grapes are key ingredients for the island's signature white wine, and capers that bloom on wild bushes often reappear in seafood dishes alongside plump, sun-ripened tomatoes. Most of the island has been designated a national park, making it a secluded hiking destination. Rent a scooter and circumvent the periphery, stopping in towns like **Santa Maria Salina** and **Malfa.** Regulars bed down at **Hotel Signum,** where the restaurant is a destination in and of itself. Host owners Michele and Clara Caruso have become an Italian model for showcasing local and seasonal ingredients, including salads of local fennel and just caught fish baked in the oven with tomatoes and olives. **Capofaro** has become the island's boutique option, with a pool overlooking the sea, a chic bar, and wine and olive oil produced on-site. Anchored by the island's lighthouse, it offers elegant views of Stromboli and Panarea. Finally, don't miss a signature granita at **Da Alfredo** in Lingua, where the icy beverage provides the perfect antidote for a scorching summer day.

Stylish Italians choose **Panarea** for their summer getaway, with the **Hotel Raya** as the magnet for the jet set, royalty (Prince William is a fan), and fashion editors from Milan. After hours, the hotel morphs into a lounge-nightclub. But off-season, the island slips into more languorous rhythms, with swims off secret coves and hikes to **Punta Milazzese** as the quiet pastimes on hand.

For island voyagers looking for even more isolation, **Filicudi** is a favorite. Concentrate your itinerary on **Pecorini A Mare,** where **La Lidalina** offers daybeds and umbrellas along with stunning sea views. And don't miss lunch at **La Sirena,** where fishermen pull up with their latest catch. (The spot also rents out guest rooms, but they are quite minimal.)

Stromboli was the setting for the eponymous Roberto Rossellino 1950 film starring Ingrid Bergman, and the island, with its celebrated volcano, has remained a star ever since. (These days, it only occasionally erupts, but it

does provide a nighttime fireworks show often attended by sailors who bring their vessels alongside to watch the spectacle.) If you're looking for a closer view, **Vulcano** is the preferred viewing spot (it's a leisurely two-hour walk up to the peak from Porto di Ponente), but most visitors come for baths in Vulcano's sulfur waters. And the tiny island of **Alicudi** has some of the most limpid water of all the Aeolian choices, and the aquarium-like conditions make it a scuba diver's dream. If **Lipari** is on your itinerary, stop in at **Il Pirata** for platters of fresh fish overlooking the port. ▪

This archipelago has far fewer tourists than Capri or the Amalfi Coast and offers a low-key but stylish vibe—as well as a crystal clear sea for swimming.

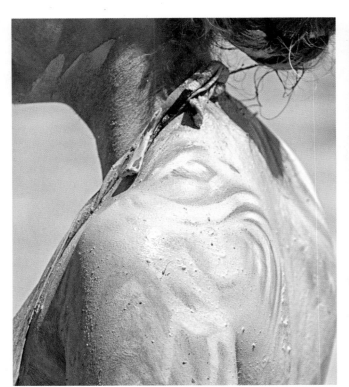

CLOCKWISE FROM LEFT: Vulcano's volcanic mud is known for its health and beauty benefits; a swimmer goes deep in Panarea's blue sea; the town of Stromboli on the island of the same name looks particularly photogenic at sunrise.

Best Of
Palermo: Sicily's Heartbeat

From its dilapidated palazzi to art deco gems, jam-packed alleys to tucked-away churches, Palermo remains one of Italy's most intriguing cities, with a new focus on modern art and revitalization of urban gems. Some quintessential spots to enjoy its various incarnations:

Dust to Dust: Sicilians are very aware of mortality, and at the surreal Catacombe dei Cappuccini, where more than 8,000 bodies have been preserved underground, it's easy to understand why locals revel in the present moment.

Noble Aperitivo: The home to a former aristocrat, Villa Igiea is one of Palermo's grande dame hotels. Have a cocktail at its old-school bar and take in the lush gardens.

Ancient Grandeur: The 12th-century duomo is one of Italy's most dazzling creations—a mix of Byzantine and Greek mosaics, lovingly carved columns, and, yes, a 65-foot-high (20 m) mosaic of Jesus.

Whet Your Beak: At Enoteca Picone, filled with Sicilian vintages both famous and lesser known, get an education in why this is one of Italy's most exciting new wine regions. Enoteca Buonivini (literally, "good wines") has a charming courtyard to sample wines by the glass alongside a plate of local cheese or a bigger plate of pasta with *bottarga* and clams.

The Contemporary View: At Sicily's Museum of Contemporary Art, modern paintings and cutting-edge installations sit against a 17th-century palace backdrop.

Mafioso Pursuits: Yes, the Mafia is still a part of Sicilian life, though many institutions have tried to stamp it out. The No Mafia tour includes the courthouse, where many of the top bosses have been tried, as well as the businesses determined not to make *pizzo* (payments), or Mafia protection money. To gain an even deeper understanding, consider adding a trip to the anti-Mafia museum in the nearby town of—yes—Corleone.

Foodie Institution: The iconic Antica Focacceria San Francesco is worth a visit not only for its *arancini* (fried rice balls) but also for its people-watching.

Night on the Town: At the Vespa Café, between Teatro Massimo and Teatro dei Pupi, images of the iconic Italian *motorino* accompany a nightcap or pre-dinner cocktail.

Leafy Oasis: To escape Palermo's chaos, head to the city's Orto Botanico. These botanical gardens have massive ficus trees, citrus groves, and all manner of local flora and fauna.

Culture Club: The city's Teatro Massimo puts on quite the show, from its ornate decor to its program of opera and ballet. Get dressed up and join local residents at the cultural heart of the city. It's one of Europe's largest opera houses, and the six-tiered art nouveau showcase will charm even those who aren't too keen on arias.

Sweet Retreat: Ilardo, a quick walk from the Piazza Santo Spirito, draws locals and gelato fiends for its mint chocolate, while Pasticceria Alba offers up cannoli, marzipan, and all manner of other sweet Sicilian treats.

Weekend Getaway: Close to Palermo, but decidedly more laid-back, the Egadi Islands are still a well-kept secret. Just off the coast from Trapani, the archipelago has three islands: Favignana (the biggest and most popular), Levanzo (with its magical Grotta del Genovese), and Marettimo (the most isolated of the three). Still mostly off the tourist radar, they have beautiful beaches, deserted coves, and plenty of secluded mountain tracks. Rent a villa through an agency like the Thinking Traveller, or book a room at a bed-and-breakfast like Dimora dell'Olivastro on Favignana. ▪

Palazzo Riso, the 17th-century backdrop for Palermo's contemporary art museum

Frances's Favorites

Leonardo Sciascia and More

Strangely complementing Giuseppe Tomasi di Lampedusa, the quirky author Leonardo Sciascia is also the opposite of the author of *The Leopard*. Born in the "dead village," as he called it, of Racalmuto in 1921, he overlapped with the life of the aristocratic Lampedusa. But Sciascia didn't look back into the Sicilian past for understanding; he looked at his own time.

Sicilian Uncles, four stories, probed the gullible, often wry, ironic streaks running through the local Sicilian character. But then Sciascia broke the silence around the forbidden subject: the Mafia. Although he was an educated man, he had a dark peasant distrust of everyone, especially Mafia informers, as well as a brilliant perception into the workings of the big crime bosses.

His wariness gives his detective novels a raspy edge. Thrillers, yes, but also literary: The spare words and details are honed. So along with *The Leopard,* slip a couple of these in your bag: *The Day of the Owl* (also a film), *One Way or Another, The Wine-Dark Sea, Salt on the Wound.*

And here, three other writers of a lighter heart who will help create the perfect trip to Sicily:

Andrea Camilleri's Inspector Montalbano detective novels, which are also the basis of a popular television series filmed around Scicli. The wry detective is a gourmet as well as a sleuth. In the Scicli area, there's a Montalbano trail to follow.

Mario Giordano's *Auntie Poldi and the Sicilian Lions* and *Auntie Poldi and the Fruits of the Lord* give us an unlikely detective: a German woman who returned to her relatives' Sicilian village for retirement. A hearty wine drinker, she embroils herself in local mischief.

Daphne Phelps's *A House in Sicily* chronicles her life in not just any house but "the most beautiful house in Sicily." After the inheritance from her uncle in 1947, she arrives and begins an enchanted, if chaotic, life. ∎

> ## Sciascia's wariness gives his detective novels a raspy edge. Thrillers, yes, but also literary.

ABOVE: The town of Racalmuto, birthplace of Sicilian author Leonardo Sciascia **OPPOSITE:** The astute and politically conscious works by Sciascia include thrilling detective novels scrutinizing political corruption and the Mafia.

The ornate ceiling painting of Chiesa di San Giovanni Evangelista in the hill town of Ragusa is only one of the church's baroque highlights.

Baroque Towns: From Noto to Ragusa

Ask a Sicilian for his or her choice of a dream destination, and **Noto** is sure to top the list. Greeks, Romans, Arabs, and Normans all made their home here over the millennia, but it was after the 1693 earthquake that the film set–worthy town was rebuilt in the style that came to be known as Sicilian Baroque. Now protected as a UNESCO World Heritage site, its sun-dappled streets wind past grand palazzi and honey-toned churches to spill into the main piazza where, sadly, part of the limestone cathedral collapsed in 1996.

The fact that Noto and its sister towns are a mere stone's throw away from beautiful beaches and an easy drive to bigger towns like **Catania** and **Syracuse** only adds to their appeal.

Entrepreneurs and lovers of the area have reinvested here. **Seven Rooms Villa Dorata,** for example, was once a prince's residence (there are a great number of nobles in Sicily). Today, Cristina Summa, a former Turin resident who used to summer in the area as a child, has turned it into a small hotel. Keeping the local tiles, frescoes, and soaring ceilings

of the original baroque palazzo, she has also added luxe touches including custom beds and one-of-a-kind bathrooms. Just outside town, legendary designer Jacques Garcia has restored two villas available for rent: a complete refurbishment that retains their former grandeur, complemented by his own personal library and art collection. These new spots, alongside institutions like the 100-plus-year-old **Caffè Sicilia** (an almond milk granita is unforgettable), have given the town fresh relevance. Among the restaurants, make sure to try **Crocif-**

isso for dishes like *casarecce alla palermitana* (pasta with wild fennel and sardines), as well as **Manna,** where *arancini,* stuffed rice balls, have been reworked as a dessert instead of an appetizer.

Noto's neighboring towns are just as appealing. Medieval meets baroque in **Modica,** famous for its exquisite dark chocolate as well as its architecture. You can sample the cocoa gold at **Antica Dolceria Bonajuto.**

Ragusa Ibla, the older part of Ragusa, seems plucked from a fairy tale with its layered duomo and baroque palaces that sit on the side of a romantic ravine. You will be treated to a stunning view of Ragusa Ilba and its famous church steeples if you descend from the newer part of the town, Ragusa Superiore. **Al Duomo** showcases the food of Ciccio Sultano, arguably one of Italy's best chefs, with specialties that include a cuttlefish carbonara and a lasagna with blue lobster, shrimp, and calamari. Leave room for a gelato at the appropriately named **Gelati Divini** nearby, where unusual flavors include cherry tomato and olive oil. In 2019, **a.d. 1768 Boutique Hotel** made its debut just behind Ragusa Ibla's showstopper of a duomo. As the name suggests, the building was constructed in the 18th century; its original frescoes, tiled floors, and a rooftop garden have been flawlessly restored. For lovely walks and tours of the region and throughout the rest of Sicily, book a trip through Anita Iaconangelo at Italian Connection tours; her love for the area shows. ▪

Ask a Sicilian for a dream destination, and Noto is sure to top the list. Greeks, Romans, Arabs, and Normans all made their home here over the millennia. Sun-dappled streets wind past grand palazzi and honey-toned churches.

CLOCKWISE FROM LEFT: Chef Ciccio Sultano's Al Duomo restaurant in Ragusa Ibla is one of Sicily's best; don't miss a stroll in the beautiful old town of Ragusa Ibla; Noto's cathedral is its centerpiece, despite having to be rebuilt following an earthquake.

Frances's Favorites
Literary Sicily

For maximum enjoyment, before you go to Sicily, read and see *Il Gattopardo* (*The Leopard*), both book and film. Giuseppe Tomasi di Lampedusa's epic story takes place in 19th-century Sicily at a crucial moment: the waning of the Bourbon Kingdom of Two Sicilies and the Risorgimento, the unification of Italy.

Prince Don Fabrizio Salina, modeled on Lampedusa's great-grandfather, is a larger-than-life aristocrat and one of the most unforgettable characters in fiction. So vivid and convincing is Lampedusa's prince that I feel as though I actually know him. The rampant leopard emblazoned on his family's ancient *stemma,* coat of arms, *is* the monumental character Don Fabrizio. Towering and fierce, he takes what he wants, often leaving his family quaking. But even the prince knows his kind is going, and he's wise enough to say, "If you want everything to remain as it is, it will be necessary for everything to change."

Without becoming didactic, Lampedusa shows a panoply of characters, his estate Donnafugata, and the prince's musings and marriage, revealing through them glimpses into what formed Sicily's culture clashes, fatalism, sensuousness, and violence. His faithful wife, mother of his seven children, calls out to the saints and Madonna at the moment of orgasm. He escapes into a more relaxing relationship in the dark streets of Palermo.

The Luchino Visconti film (1963) runs long and lavish, with countless painterly images of feasts and balls; even the wallpaper's silk birds seem alive. The prose style of the book is deliciously indulgent, like much of the baroque architecture of Sicily.

In addition to fine portrayals of its historical background, intense sense of the seared land, and depictions of the baroque social hierarchy, Lampedusa's novel is often intricate and ironic. As an intense admirer of the island's cuisine, I love his descriptions of the dinners, especially the desserts. One of the most memorable scenes in the novel is the sensuous list of sweets that adorn the table at a ball. On more ordinary occasions, Don Fabrizio enjoys his favorite rum jelly for dessert. It arrives at the table "rather frightening at first sight, shaped like a tower with bastion and battlements and smooth, slippery walls impossible to scale, garrisoned by red and green cherries and pistachio nuts." Then he describes its "transparent and quivering flanks" where a spoon plunges with astounding ease. Sexy! He takes his jelly with a glass of Marsala. ■

Giuseppe Tomasi di Lampedusa's epic story takes place in 19th-century Sicily at a crucial moment: the unification of Italy.

ABOVE: The exquisite castle of Donnafugata outside Ragusa was the home of Giuseppe Tomasi di Lampedusa in the 19th century and the backdrop to his book *Il Gattopardo* (*The Leopard*). **OPPOSITE:** A scene from the 1963 film of *The Leopard* starring Burt Lancaster and Claudia Cardinale

In the Know

Local Flavors: From Arabs to Normans (and of course, Nonnas)

Constant invasion by other countries may not have been much fun for natives, but we have these interlopers to thank for Sicily's diverse flavors. Ingredients like raisins, nutmeg, and saffron came from the Arabs who made their home here during the 10th and 11th centuries, while Norman rule featured a meat-rich diet. Greek colonists were responsible for the pistachio and olives that are a mainstay of the island, while North African settlers imported the delicious couscous that is another Sicilian standout.

Of course, the island has always had its own plentiful bounty, like tuna and swordfish. Fat, juicy eggplants became the foundation for the *caponata* (eggplant with tomato sauce, capers, pine nuts, and raisins) that's both salty and sweet; spaghetti is the backdrop for *ricci* (fresh urchin) and *bottarga* (salt-cured tuna roe), while *pasta alla Norma* showcases fried eggplant and salted ricotta using short pasta. *Pasta con le sarde,* with sardines, pine nuts, fennel, and raisins, is a Palermo specialty. And Sicily's answer to pesto comes with ground-up pistachios. In this region, street food was popular way before the current global craze. *Arancini,* deeply fried rice balls, are a favorite. For those who enjoy their innards, *pane con la milza,* a sandwich with pig's spleen, is another market food staple. Unlike spots in Tuscany where bread is almost an afterthought, here the *pane* is diverse and uses flours that have been preserved through the centuries. *Sfincione,* a deep pizza pie topped with onions and cheese, is a hearty alternative to Naples's slimmer version.

Desserts here are an island adventure all their own. Who can beat a cannoli with sweet ricotta inside fried dough? For sweet tooths, *cassata,* a sponge cake with almond paste, candied fruit, and sweetened ricotta, is a dessert that comes from the invading Arabs.

While many markets in the north of Italy have sadly become the site for cheap clothing and made-in-China products, Sicily's markets are a destination in their own right. **La Pescheria,** Catania's fish market behind the Piazza del Duomo, is one of the most theatrical. Its tables, laden with prawns, sea urchin, octopus, eel, clams, mussels, and fresh tuna and swordfish, are a sight to behold as fishmongers call out their wares with operatic flair. Although the market is open from 7 a.m. to 2 p.m., plan to arrive super early for the best catch. In Palermo, **La Vucciria** brings you back to another time—not surprising, as the market was founded more than 700 years ago. It opens at 4 a.m., but most intrepid shoppers arrive around 6 a.m. to haggle over fish or a crate of Sicilian blood oranges. Don't miss a glass of cold beer alongside housewives and chefs; it will improve your bargaining game. At **Ballarò** open-air market, join the boisterous fishmongers and start your day with *panelle,* fritters made out of chickpeas. ∎

ABOVE: The display case at Pasticceria Savia in Catania includes such Sicilian savories such as *arancini*, fried rice balls. OPPOSITE: Don't miss cannoli stuffed with sweet ricotta cream.

Hot Spot
Ortigia

I t's almost predictable: A newbie heads to the small island of Ortigia and returns with the dream of buying a house there. After all, who could resist the winding streets with now unlived-in palazzi with "for sale" signs, romantically dilapidated baroque churches, or 18th-century town houses? Although the main city of **Syracuse** was badly bombed in World War II, the romantic port of Ortigia remains almost unchanged, with sea walls looking out onto the moody water and winding backstreets.

The historic market near Via Trento and its surrounding side streets is the spot to start your immersion. Here, jaunty vendors sell violet sea urchins and snacks like fried whitebait or fresh oysters. Don't miss eating at **Caseificio Borderi,** where a line snakes out the door for Andrea Borderi's famous sandwiches piled high with unforgettable mortadella, all types of cheese, and a top secret pesto concoction best paired with an ice-cold beer, regardless of the hour. **Fratelli Burgio** is a one-stop shop for delicious Sicilian essentials. Pick up cheese, salami, and wine for a picnic (after a food porn shot) or sit at an outdoor table.

Restaurants in town tend to come and go (much like the tourist season itself), but the stalwart **Don Camillo** keeps up the foodie standard with traditional Sicilian fare beneath its vaulted ceilings. At **Ristorante Regina Lucia,** inventive seafood is served on a lovely terrace facing the Piazza Duomo. Residents also head to the stylish **Area M** for an *aperitivo* or dinner with a view over the port and harbor.

For wonderful lotions and potions, Italians always bulk up at Ortigia: soaps, candles, bath products, and perfumes using local ingredients like almond oil and Sicilian jasmine are favorites.

For more cultural pursuits, make sure to stop in at the **Temple of Apollo,** dating back to the sixth century B.C., and the cathedral, which also sits on the ruins of a Greek temple. Or wander through the **Neapolis Archaeological Park,** where the theater still offers up the plays of legendary artists like Euripides among fragrant lemon and olive groves. ▪

The Ear of Dionysius in Syracuse's archaeological park

In the Know
Where to Stay in Sicily

From grandes dames to boutique, Sicily's options run the gamut of hospitality.

Country House Villadorata: This former winery set within acres of olive trees and vineyards has been transformed into an eight-room boutique hotel close to the baroque town of Noto. Featuring a freshwater pool and large guest rooms with private balconies, its sleek design, eco-approach to energy, and beautiful views have made it an insider favorite.

Monaci delle Terre Nere: Close to the vineyards of Etna and an easy drive to Taormina, this hotel seamlessly mixes its original architecture—think rough stone floors and an original olive press—with contemporary pieces from such designers as Philippe Starck and B&B Italia. The homespun charm, alongside a true attention to detail, is nothing short of magical.

Verdura Resort: Not far from Agrigento, this luxe resort has its own beachfront destination spa, golf course, kids' club, and restaurants. But if you're seeking a more authentic Sicilian spot, this might feel too compounded.

Eremo della Giubiliana: Once occupied by the Knights of Malta, this medieval convent has been reinvented as a boutique hotel outside Ragusa. With an extensive wine cellar and pretty pool, one can explore the surrounding towns or just stay put for days.

Metropole Taormina: This small designer hotel in Taormina has large rooms in a crisp white palette—many with views of the sea—and an ideal location right off the town's main drag.

BB22: Behind a crumbling but romantic piazza, this bed-and-breakfast is one of Palermo's special hideaways for good reason. The property also has apartments for rent and offers amenities like boat rides.

Casa Talía: Milanese architect Marco Giunta fell in love with Modica and set out to showcase it for like-minded visitors. Nine rooms in the heart of town come with one-of-a-kind antique tile floors and balconies overlooking gardens bursting with fig and plum trees, as well as pristine views of the baroque gem.

Dimora delle Balze: It's pretty much a bucolic dream: only 11 rooms in a 19th-century *masseria* with 60 acres (24 ha) of citrus groves and gardens to lose yourself in. Add in a beautiful saltwater pool, views of Noto, and interlocking courtyards for reading or having a glass of wine. No wonder the property has so many fans.

Susafa: Set within a sizable estate in the quiet interior of the island, this working farm has 13 guest rooms with a bar and restaurant focusing on local and seasonal ingredients in the former granary and a pool with panoramic views over the valley. Best of all is its feeling of complete seclusion and peace. ▪

ABOVE: A view over Modica from the terraces of Casa Talía hotel. OPPOSITE: Rocco Forte's Verdura Resort has a golf course, restaurants, and a destination spa among the amenities.

Frances's Favorites

In Your Glass

No other region's wine creds have soared like Sicily's. Quantity over quality was the old motto; no more. According to Gambero Rosso's *Italian Wines,* DOC annual production is up to 10 million bottles, whereas six years ago DOC scarcely hit half a million. We wine lovers might now agree with Gabriel García Márquez: "Going to Sicily is better than going to the moon."

Lavishly pour Arianna Occhipinti's Il Frappato, and you'll get a taste of how complex and winning Sicilian wines can be.

Also stellar: Feudo Maccari Nero d'Avola Saia, grown near Marzamemi in hot southern vineyards blessed with sea breezes. Visit the vineyard, by appointment, and taste the syrah called Maharis, and the limpid white Grillo, made from the local grape.

Nero d'Avola, indigenous grape, fills most of the bottles in Sicily. It can be supple and plummy or more upright with a tannic bite. In my wine racks are plenty of the ubiquitous Planetas, some blended with a hint of merlot. Planeta is a good go-to name with assurance of quality.

Big mama Mount Etna, gift and terror for the island, spews forth top wines, as well as outstanding toma-toes. I admire the Cusumano wines, especially their Alta Mora Etna Bianco and their Nero d'Avola Sàgana vintages. Most of Etna's many vineyards can be visited by appointment—and, of course, it's possible to ship home a few cases of what takes your fancy.

Many a feast at my house ends with the dessert wine Ben Ryé Donnafugata Passito di Pantelleria. There are many other excellent *moscato passitos* from this lovely, windy island, including Carlo Pellegrino's Nes and Duca di Salaparuta di Pantelleria Florio. Bring out the lemon ricotta tart and pour this liquid poem for friends. ∎

We wine lovers might now agree with Gabriel García Márquez:
"Going to Sicily is better than going to the moon."

ABOVE: The vineyards of Planeta in Trapani. The producer has many wineries around the island and is one of its most well known labels. OPPOSITE: Passito, a pleasant dessert wine, comes from Sicilian spots like the island of Pantelleria.

Ben Ryé

PASSITO DI PANTELLERIA
DENOMINAZIONE DI ORIGINE CONTROLLATA

FUG

Chapter Twenty

SARDINIA

Light on the water. Everywhere I look along this almost thousand-mile (1,609 km) coastline, light is what I will remember. Rays clear down to the white sandy bottom. Pebbles shimmering like opals. Sun glancing along the surface of soft waves, sea colors shifting from transparent aquamarine to slate, all the way out to the finely drawn ink line of the horizon. On this island, the largest in the Mediterranean except

for Sicily, you're never far from the scent of the sea.

Sardinia's beaches are legendary. What's best in many areas is to hire a boat—easy in most harbors or through your hotel—and nip into coves where a tiny crescent of sand will be all yours. Even driving around the coast, it's natural to pull over and take a private swim. With a cold bottle of *vermentino*, some *semi-stagionata* (semi-aged) pecorino, *salume,* and a loaf of bread baked that morning, you'll be set for a memorable day.

With this kind of beauty, it's no wonder Sardinia is all about beaches—from the Maddalena Islands in the north to the fancy Costa Smeralda with yachts and gated *villagi* (tourists' villages) and all along the coasts. Notable to visit are the beautiful Spiaggia di Tuerredda in Teulada, Porto Giunco at Villasimius, Cala Goloritzé Baunei at Ogliastra, Lu Impostu San Teodoro near Olbia, the vast dunes and golden sands at La Piscinas, and the far-south island of San Pietro.

As you drive around Sardinia, your attention swerves from the next stunning beach to the hilly, rocky interior, studded with *nuraghi*, which look like rocky terrain but are actually Bronze Age structures—mostly collapsed towers—dating from 1800 B.C. to 500 B.C. Around 7,000 of these ancient sites remain. A later archaeological site is Nora, a Phoenician, then Roman, town located near Pula. The evocative ruins sit right on the coast, confirming that even in ancient

times, everyone loved to be on the sea. The spa remnants remain—cold pool and hot pool. Drains for sewage. A theater that once was tented. All this attesting to a high level of comfort enjoyed by the residents.

The interior of Sardinia—rough and covered in *maqui,* the mixed scented, scrubby plants such as juniper, lentisk, and myrtle—offers hikers, or day-trekkers like me, a spectacular terrain of precipitous mountains, waterfalls, wild horses, albino donkeys, oak and cork forests, pink flamingos, and abandoned mining sites now known as "industrial archaeology." I was startled at how quickly the mines and their settlements have receded into history and appear to be a couple of hundred years old, even though many of the copper, silver, and other minerals were quarried well into the

WHAT YOU NEED TO KNOW...

- **BEST TIME TO VISIT:** Late April to mid-June, September to mid-October. Skip July and August, when the area experiences an influx of summer travelers from other parts of Italy and hotel prices increase.

- **TOP SPOTS:** La Cinta beach, La Maddalena, Valle della Luna/ Capo Testa, Castelsardo, Alghero, Stintino, Isola dell'Asinara, Bosa, Tharros, Piscinas, Buggerru, Chia, Isola di San Pietro, Golfo di Orosei, Nuoro

- **GETTING THERE:** Fly into Olbia, Cagliari, or Alghero. If you arrive by ferry, you'll dock at the ports of Olbia or Cagliari.

Along Sardinia's northeast coast are the solitary coves and beautiful natural landscapes of Costa Smeralda.

In small villages all over Sardinia, you're likely to hear Sardo spoken.
Not a dialect, it's an actual language close to the roots of Latin.

20th century. Sardinia has wisely conserved its land: Thirteen extensive parks and reserves lure you from the beaches.

In small villages all over Sardinia, you're likely to hear Sardo (also called Sardu) spoken. Not a dialect, it's an actual language close to the roots of Latin, with some Arab and Spanish influences thrown in. Speaking Italian doesn't help you comprehend. And within Sardo there are regional variations; not even natives always can understand each other.

Recently I was in Santadi. I visited only to taste the wines of the same name but by luck happened to overhear four women gathered around a doorway. They were chatting, all four at once, in their version of Sardo. I heard a lot of flutters and clunks, rolling r's, and sometimes shrill high notes. The house was the color of a ripe persimmon, and the sunset

reflected on their faces. It was one of those moments when as a traveler you turn invisible and just observe. The voices seemed to come from an ancient past, and I hung there, in a suspended moment that burst only when a man roared up on a huge motorcycle.

My favorite town in Sardinia is Cagliari, the capital. Start your trip here because of the Museo Archeologico Nazionale, the major museum of the region. All the artifacts from the *nuraghi* and other sites from the complicated history of this desirable island are gathered there. After a couple of hours among them, you understand the framework of the culture. I was stunned at the beauty of the aesthetic jewelry, votives, figures of warriors the size of toy soldiers, exquisitely rendered bronze animals, and menacing limestone men. I was particularly entranced by a mysterious recumbent male whose body is entwined with a snake. How charged with life the molds for decorating bread, and the household pots and colanders! When you're heading to the museum entrance, let's hope the outdoor escalator is working. Otherwise, it's a heart-thumping climb. Fortunately, at the top, taxis are plentiful.

And I found many other reasons to love Cagliari: purple jacaranda trees lining the boulevard, the pretty Poetto Beach on the Gulf of Angels, cicadas screeching in the heart of town. We sampled that Sardinian specialty *culurgiones* at Fork, under towering trees at an outdoor table. The pasta is filled with potatoes and cheese and scented with pennyroyal, a minty herb otherwise used traditionally to cause spontaneous abortion. This capital city invites strolling among narrow lanes; along the way you'll find old palazzi with balconies erupting with bougainvillea and historic cafés for sitting in the sun with a lemon granita. We found a plethora of good restaurants where dinner ends with sips of *mirto*, the *digestivo* made from myrtle berries.

Wait. I said Cagliari is my favorite town. But I also love Carloforte, a village with a tropical vibe way, way southwest on the island of San Pietro. We drove onto the ferry at Portos-

Boats in the port of Sant'Antioco, Sardinia

Nuraghe Ruiu, one of the hundreds of ancient structures dotting the inland farmland of Sardinia

cuso and leaned on the rail with cappuccinos as we churned the almost 5.5 miles (9 km) to the island. As we pulled into port, I knew from the pastel buildings and the giant ficus trees that I would be captivated.

Carloforte is the only town on the island; the rest of the 20-square-mile (52 sq km) terrain is amazingly undeveloped. Here's where you feel a sense of discovery. Turn-off signs direct you to beaches and coastal walks, all pristine— and when I was there in September, blissfully empty. Here, walk on a beach with no footprints.

Carloforte doesn't look like a Sardinian town, and for good reason. It was settled by Ligurians who brought along their taste for excellent foccacia—and for tall gold, pistachio, faded blue, tallow, and cream-colored houses. The outdoor restaurants have bright red, yellow, and green tables and chairs. Color is the delight of the town, plus deep shade, and a low-key vibe of tranquillity.

What's on the menu? Tuna! This is one of the places famous for the historic rituals when boats align, nets are cast, and huge quantities of the prized fish are trapped and bludgeoned. A blood sport, it seems; they say the sea turns red. Not appetizing. Still, at a side-street trattoria on a warm night, the waiter joking and the wine flowing, you forget the tuna drama and enjoy the ambience.

Food is blissfully simple; a sautéed fish will be topped with a mound of finely chopped celery, tomatoes, and onions. Luscious and full, Sardus Pater's Is Solus is the red wine to order; it's from just across the water on the neighboring island of Sant'Antioco.

The harbor bobs with working boats and pleasure crafts— and everywhere you turn, the sea. The esplanade along the water invites strolling. Flowery doorways on intricate back-streets inspire me to Google real estate sites. Wouldn't it be nice to sit out on your own balcony and watch the flow of life on this still undeveloped island off an island? Prediction: In 10 years, this place will be prime real estate.

Driving is easy in Sardinia. You need a car to explore the whole island— although finding that beach you've dreamed of at home in January might be all you need to see during a week of deep renewal.

L'Altra Isola shows off artisanal wares from Sardinia in Alghero's old town.

Alghero and Environs: Sardinia's Perfect Corner

On the northwest corner of Sardinia, Alghero, with its spectacularly preserved historic center, winding cobblestoned streets, and authentic café culture, makes the perfect base from which to explore the coastline nearby—but is also a destination in and of itself.

The town highlight remains the beautiful promenade along the sea that once also served as a lookout point for marauding pirates and possible invaders but is now the preferred *passeggiata* (evening stroll Italian style) route, for its enviable sunset position. In addition to the sea views and harbor vistas, some of the best seafood in town is to be had at spots like **Angedras,** particularly good for its grilled whole fish like *orata* and *spigola*. The charming backstreets behind the seafront are dotted with cute cafés and excellent, well-priced restaurants including **La Botteghina.** With an intimate roof terrace and such dishes as the pizza Sarda, a Sardinian take on pizza (a flatter version with toppings like ricotta, mint, and fava beans), this is a place you may want to try more than once.

Food shops in Alghero are stuffed with Sardinian goodies: **La Bottega di Tommy,** for example, is a must for picnic supplies and items to take home. Try the beloved Sardinian wines made from *cannonau* grapes, which showcase the Italian sister to the Spanish *garnacha* grape; pecorino (a tangier flavor to its Tuscan relative); and a tantalizing mix of salami and other cured meats.

Stop in **Azul** for chic bikinis, notebooks, jewelry, and small "Made in Italy" brands. **L'Anfora** is the spot for an Aperol spritz, filled with well-heeled local residents. **Al Cafferino** is where Alghero's residents congregate for the perfect espresso and pastries like *ciambella* (Italy's take on a doughnut).

There are a number of good options for lodging in the city. The most upscale is the **Villa Mosca,** housed in a beautifully restored art nouveau structure with nine rooms and expansive views over the sea. For a less elaborate choice, try **Aigua,** a collection of six apartments owned and designed by a local architect, Emanuele Maganuco, who is full of tips for what to see and excursions to take.

Alghero is also a great launchpad for trips to the beaches around Stintino: **La Pelosa,** one of the most beautiful beaches in Italy, if not all of Europe, and the **Asinara,** a must for nature and history buffs. Formerly a First World War POW camp for Austrian and Hungarian prisoners, many of whom died of tuberculosis and cholera, it then became a high-security prison for Mafiosi, among others. The memorabilia in the former prison with nudie posters, soccer cards, a barber's shop, and exercise yard are a study in convict pastimes; one can't help but find it a pretty idyllic spot, even considering confinement. In 1997 the island became a national park; today, its sole residents are wild donkeys (including a white albino breed), Anglo-Arab horses, wild boar, and nimble goats. Tour the preserve and its pristine beaches by jeep, bike, or foot.

From Alghero, head down the coast for a stop in **Bosa.** Located on the north bank of the Temo River, it's filled with cheerfully painted houses and restaurants set along the water. Also stop by **Tharros,** the ancient Phoenician settlement on the sea founded in the eighth century B.C. that was a Nuragic settlement, a civilization particular to Sardinia, from the Bronze Age. You can still see the Corinthian columns, and the view over the sea is sublime. ▪

Alghero is a great launchpad for trips to the beaches around Stintino—including La Pelosa, one of the most beautiful beaches in Italy, if not all of Europe.

CLOCKWISE FROM LEFT: A hipster enjoys a café chat in the vibrant town of Alghero in Sardinia; the church of Madonna del Carmine in the city of Bosa; classic cars like the Fiat 850 are a frequent sight in lost-in-time Sardinia.

Hot Spot
La Maddalena

Close to Costa Smeralda and Porto Cervo, the pre-ferred stomping grounds for celebrities and VIPs, is a much more accessible and tranquil paradise. Made up of seven main islands and smaller islets off the northeast coast, the national park is full of white-sand beaches, deserted coves, and rugged pink-stone pathways reaching some of the most beautiful sea in Italy. The spot was formerly a naval base and the final home of Italian hero Giuseppe Garibaldi, but in the past few years, it has lost its military reputation and become a model for eco and sus-tainable tourism in the region. Connected to the mainland by a 20-minute ferry ride from Palau, La Maddalena town and port is the anchor for excursions. The pretty fishing vil-lage offers seafood restaurants, sailboats, and bars that come alive in the summer.

Swimming here feels like being in a tropical aquarium, with water so translucent that you can see the sand and marine life beneath you without even wearing a mask. Only the island of **Caprera** (once Garibaldi's home and now a museum) is accessible by bridge. For the other islands, you will need to charter a boat from the La Maddalena quay. Among the most picturesque beaches are **Cala Soraya, Cala Conneri,** and **Spiaggia di Cala Corsara** on **Spargi. Cala Trin-ita** is the easiest to access on the main island and boasts shallow water that is perfect for families. Boating aficiona-dos can rent vessels from La Maddalena's port or reserve them in advance through services like Charming Sardinia.

The island of **Budelli,** also known as the "pink paradise" for the crushed pink coral that makes up its beaches, is lovely by boat—though, sadly, visitors have been banned from the beach of **Spiaggia Rosa** because tourists were stealing the stunning sand. Luckily the **Spiaggia di Cavalieri** beach nearby is a knockout.

Options for accommodation here are limited, but in addi-tion to going the Airbnb route, try **Grand Hotel Ma & Ma** or **La Casitta,** a former shepherd's house that's been reimag-ined as a Sardinian getaway. ◾

Gallura in the archipelago of La Maddalena, a national park in Sardinia

Best Of
Sardinia's Beaches

Famous throughout Italy and the world, Sardinia is known for its spectacular beaches, with powder-white sand and an aqua sea perfect for snorkeling. Some of the most ravishing spots are accessible only by boat and hiking, which adds to their allure.

La Pelosa: Close to the town of Stintino, this gorgeous mile-long beach sits close to a Catalan-Aragonese watchtower. You can walk up to your knees in the ocean for what seems like miles. Just be aware that as with many other beaches on the island, the secret's out in high season; the shoulder seasons offer a more secluded experience.

Gennargentu National Park: Composed of five sand beaches on the Gulf of Orosei, this is a wilder section of the coast, backed by pine forest and limestone formations favored by adventurous rock climbers. Hike an hour on an old mule trail to get to highlights.

La Cinta: Close to the town of San Teodoro, this bay shore exemplifies the calm water and white-sand beaches on this side of the island. Don't miss the *fritto misto* at the adjacent Agua beach restaurant and an expedition to Stagno San Teodoro, a bird sanctuary.

Forlo Beach Club: Italy's beach clubs are part of the country's social network. They rent daybeds and umbrellas, offer delicious food, and provide a seaside nexus for the same families every summer. Forlo exemplifies the model, and the small but secluded cove is an excellent swimming spot. Stay for sunset when Aperol spritzes are served while a DJ spins.

Cala Brandinchi: This turquoise water and talcum-sand beach has been dubbed "Little Tahiti"—and for good reason. You'll be transported to a whole new world.

Buggerru: In addition to having a name that's fun to say, Buggerru has towering red dunes that demonstrate the diversity of the beaches on this relatively small island. Here it's huge rosy-colored massifs of sand that drop to a green sea—a real contrast to the turquoise and white models of Sardinia.

Spiaggia di Piscinas: Much wilder than its counterparts on the eastern coast (one finds complete isolation and hardly a hotel en route down the coast), this miles-long stretch of sand is home to rolling waves perfect for surfers and the Le Dune hotel, one of the island's only resorts. The Costa Verde, as the region is called, requires intrepid driving on video game–like curves, but the views are worth the adrenaline.

Archipelago di La Maddalena: Home to a number of Sardinia's finest white-sand beaches (see Cala Conneri, and Cala dei Corsari on Spargi), this jewel in Sardinia's crown is a national park that is best explored by boat.

Valle della Luna: Near Santa Teresa Gallura's Capo Testa, the enormous rock boulders here look otherworldly as they spill into an emerald sea. Come summer, the spot is a magnet for boho-hippie types who like to camp here.

Chia: Ideal for families, thanks to its powder-white sand and gentle sea, this enchanting coastal area may be crowded—but the lack of solitude is more than made up for in attendant services. Don't miss Spiaggia Su Portu to the east and Spiaggia Sa Colonia to the west.

Spiaggia del Principe: Come high season, VIPs and celebrities hit the Costa Smeralda by boat, each seemingly more blinged out than the last. In many ways the island's international reputation began with Persia's celebrated Aga Khan family—and indeed, this beautiful arc is named for Prince Karim, aka "principe." ◾

The solitary beach of Cala Luna is shielded by steep cliffs favored by rock climbers.

In the Know

Where to Stay in Sardinia

Compared with other parts of the country like Puglia or Tuscany, the Sardinia hotel scene has yet to fully blossom. Nonetheless, a number of properties are worth a stay:

La Petra Segreta: Near Porto Cervo and close to some of the area's best beaches to the north and south, this 24-room boutique hotel is nicely positioned in the hills above Costa Smeralda, near the charming town of San Pantaleo. Even if you don't bed down here, try Il Fuoco Sacro, one of the hotel's two restaurants, where perfectly grilled fish and meat speak to the island's tradition of roasting on an open fire.

Hotel La Coluccia: An excellent base for exploring the archipelago of La Maddalena, this photogenic modern structure on the water is one of the best examples of boutique-chic on the island.

Villa Mosca: A close stroll to Alghero, one of Sardinia's most atmospheric cities, this chic, nine-room hotel is housed in a beautiful art deco villa with spectacular views over the sea.

Cala di Volpe: It may be billed as a Mediterranean fishing village concept, but the layout is more VIP than blue collar, with an Olympic-size saltwater pool, 18-hole golf course, and luxury yachts—with a price tag to match.

Su Gologone: This innovative resort is located in the interior of the island, which offers a completely different atmosphere than the coastline does: rugged mountains, seldom visited villages, and archaeological treasures galore. One of the best and only launchpads to these highlights, this hotel is an off-the-beaten-track destination that's worth visiting. Its restaurant, Nido del Pane, hosts open-pit meat-roasting parties once a week and excellent rustic Sardinian cooking every night.

Le Dune Piscinas: Located on its own remote stretch of dune-backed beach (hence the name), this resort in Piscinas is worth the trek for its spectacular location and restaurant. Rooms could do with an update, but the prices are reasonable for the setting.

Forte Village: If you have kids in tow, this resort on the sea provides an almost Disney-like menu of activities, with a supervised children's club, water park, and bowling alley among the plentiful options. ■

OPPOSITE: Hotel Cala di Volpe in Costa Smeralda is one of Sardinia's best known hotels. ABOVE: Outside of Alghero's historic center, the Villa Mosca has been transformed into a boutique hideaway.

Frances's Favorites

In Your Glass

The major grape of Sardinia is *cannonau.* Once assumed to be of Spanish origin, the vines are now believed by researchers to be indigenous to the island. Also widely known as *grenache,* it's replete with antioxidants and other components. Not that you drink wine as an artery cleanser, but per capita Sardinia has more people older than 100—and the longest living men—than anywhere else in the world—and they probably started with sips of wine at age four. As in the rest of Italy, wine is food, and is enjoyed as naturally as water. A glass or two (or three), a hunk of pecorino, some seafood, and there you have daily life on the Mediterranean diet. (Sardinians also love long-roasted pork, lamb ragù, and rich pastas, none of which make it onto that particular list.)

Cannonau has a silky body, not weighted with tannins. Some say the wines taste of wild herbs and salt air. I taste blackberry and a darker, earthy note. Sardinia, formerly not a major player on the Italian wine scene, is fast changing that status, and cannonau leads the pack. The grape often is blended with cabernet sauvignon, which lends heft and body, or with tannic *carignano,* a grape that achieves its best in the southwestern corner of Sardinia. When I was in that area, I became a big fan of the voluptuous Santadi wines, especially Rocca Rubia and Terre Brune. Other respected vineyards of particular interest:

Soletta, Sardus Pater, Argiolas, and Sella & Mosca.

Among crisp-and-chilly whites, Sardinia excels with *vermentino* and *vernaccia* grapes. The island's only DOCG designation (more difficult to achieve than DOC) is Vermentino di Gallura. Made by many, the quality of what I tasted was uniformly delightful. I especially loved the *vermentinos* of Sella &

Mosca and Jankara. This sprightly, oh-so-drinkable wine seems made for sipping under the Sardinian sun.

Check restaurant wine lists for the DOC designation, for assurance of quality. The shock to an American (or a Tuscan) is the prices of these fantastic wines; in restaurants, most are around $15 a bottle. Go for the top, usually under $30. *Salute!* ∎

> Cannonau has a silky body, not weighted with tannins.
> Some say the wines taste of wild herbs and salt air.
> I taste blackberry and a darker, earthy note.

ABOVE: **Working the vineyards near Sardinia's Nurra** OPPOSITE: **Isara produces one of the island's delicious *cannonau* wines.**

A sweeping view of Cagliari, a bustling port town that is also home to one of the island's universities

Cagliari: The University City

This sprawling port city is the island's most populous, offering a vibrant and atmospheric old town, an excellent university, a wealth of art and history, plus a cosmopolitan feeling with all the boats coming and going. Don't be put off by the surrounding sprawl; you will be spending most of your visit in the vibrant historic center that sits above the port itself.

In the neighborhood of **Castello,** the anchor of Cagliari's medieval area, stop in at **Su Tzilleri e Su Doge,** a little restaurant in a tiny, colorful piazza overlooking the marshes in the far distance. The owner, Claudio, is obsessed with finding the best local products and showcasing traditional recipes from all over the island, so expect to sample new ingredients and dishes. Try the linguini with shrimp from Teulada and mountain mushrooms. Bookish types will want to check out the **Sala Settecentesca,** from 1764, one of the most beautiful libraries in all of Italy.

Find it hidden inside one of the university's main buildings. But the highlight of the neighborhood may well be its fortified castle. At the **Bastione,** the city's watchtowers and walls are blindingly white (a welcome landmark if you get lost) but afford incredible views all the way to the Sella del Diavolo waterfront.

Directly underneath the Castello is the **Galleria d'Arte Comunale,** located in the lovely Giardini Pubblici (designed by Ubaldo Badas). Check out its discreet collection of Sardinian art and recently opened gallery in a cave carved into the soft stone, *tufo.* There is a whole world of underground Cagliari built into its stone foundations, and this is one of the easiest places to experience it (as well as enjoy temporary contemporary art shows).

Down from the Castello is the neighborhood **Villanova,** with boutiques and narrow alleyways with typical Cagliari architecture with its townhouses and more modest buildings. **Bar Florio** is a great place for an evening drink, and the **Caffè degli Spiriti** is the best spot

for night owls, a nightclub that draws DJs and holidaying party mavens.

The **Marina,** the port, has tucked-away alleyways and a port-side feel. You'll find a mix of cheap souvenir shops and nice cafés here. There are also multiple Sardinian sweet shops, as well as a store selling traditional Sardinian suits (black velvet is a must). Keep an eye out for **Galinanoa,** one of the better shops for Sardinian crafts.

Also take a stroll on **Poetto,** Cagliari's sandy city beach. It has a new boardwalk dotted with cafés and is generally packed from June to

August. And don't miss **Forma,** a fantastic cheese shop that also features enticing *aperitivi.*

For architecture buffs, the city's Roman amphitheater deserves a visit in the northwest part of the city. Afterward, you can ponder the collection at the **Museo Archeologico Nazionale,** with its vast collection of Greek and Roman artifacts, as well as indigenous Sardinian findings.

Local markets are always a draw on the island; Cagliari's **San Benedetto** on Via Tiziano is full of the island's seafood booty. ▪

A NAME TO KNOW: PRETZIADA

Want to impress your design friends with your insider knowledge? Drop the name Pretziada Collective.

THE BRAINCHILD OF MILANESE ARTIST Ivano Atzori and Californian set designer Kyre Chenven, the design program and online store aims to bring the best of Sardinia—and particularly, the best of Sardinian artisanal design—to the world stage (the couple have set up their workshop close to Cagliari). With that mission in mind, the duo have scoured the island to find its most prime handblown ceramics, the rugged cowboy boots that Sardinian riders wear as they herd sheep, and handmade textiles that have been passed down by weavers for generations. They have even made their own fireplace accessories, from poker to tongs, as an homage to Sardinians' love of the open fire: an island essential for everything from heating the house to cooking.

But to call them retailers doesn't do them justice: "We host international creatives for residencies with local artisans, and serve as cultural interpreters for journalists or interior designers who want to understand the island and its traditions," explains Chenven.

In a time of mass production, the collective's determination to highlight the *pretziada* ("precious" in Sardinian) of a small island in Italy is compelling—and worth the look.

Pretziada has brought wares from Sardinia onto an international stage.

Frances's Favorites
On Your Plate

These are must-try favorites from the robust, intensely flavorful, and simple Sardinian kitchen:

Rock lobster from around Alghero, grilled and served with saffron-tinted *fregola*, a semolina pasta shaped like big bread crumbs. *Fregola* is similar to couscous in its uses. Scented with saffron, it is typically tossed with grilled shrimp, vegetables, or chicken, as well as lobster.

Bottarga, dried and salted fish roe, usually gray mullet or tuna, grated over just grilled fish. The flavor connotes the essence of the sea. Trendy as *bottarga* is, actually it's an ancient taste, invented no doubt to preserve food on the high seas with no land in sight.

Malloreddus, Sardinia's soul food, is saffron-infused semolina gnocchi. This is fun to make. Little cylinders are formed into a shell shape with your thumb, then pressed with fork tines to form ridges that hold the sauce. Sardinian households own a special board for imprinting ridges into the dough. Long-simmered tomato sauce with sausage, or lamb ragù, or simply grated pecorino and olive oil do justice to this substantial yet delicate pasta. The name, which sounds like an illness involving a bad red rash, means "bull" (from *malloro*) or possibly "little morsel" (from *malleolus*, in Latin). The dish is loved all over the island. Although visitors revel in seafood, the cuisine of Sardinia leans inland, among the sheep and goat flocks, not the dangerous coast, where invaders constantly lurked.

Cassola, a soupy casserole of fish, octopus, tomatoes, and wine, thickened with slices of bread.

Porchetta, suckling pig slow-roasted over a wood fire until meltingly tender. The skin crackles, and the herb stuffing is pungent. The best versions can be found at outdoor market stands, with the meat jammed into a hard roll.

Carasau, also called *carta di musica*, is as thin as a sheet of music. The flat cracker bread is typically served with antipasti or as a snack from the *panificio*, the bread store. It's toasty and crunchy with sea salt. ∎

ABOVE: A fragrant *zuppa di pesce* (seafood soup) OPPOSITE: The making of the traditional pasta called *malloreddus*

Authors Frances Mayes (LEFT) and Ondine Cohane in the garden of La Bandita Townhouse in Pienza

ABOUT THE AUTHORS

FRANCES MAYES'S most recent books are *See You in the Piazza: New Places to Discover in Italy* and a novel, *Women in Sunlight.* Her first Italian memoir, *Under the Tuscan Sun,* remained on the *New York Times* best seller list for two and a half years and was a wide-release film. It was followed by other international best sellers, *Bella Tuscany, Every Day in Tuscany,* and *A Year in the World.* With her husband, Edward Mayes, she published *The Tuscan Sun Cookbook* and two photo texts, *In Tuscany* and *Bringing Tuscany Home.* She has written a southern memoir, *Under Magnolia;* the novel *Swan;* the textbook *The Discovery of Poetry;* and six books of poetry. Her books have been translated into 54 languages. She lives in Cortona, Italy, and Hillsborough, North Carolina.

ONDINE COHANE is a contributing editor at *Condé Nast Traveler* and a frequent writer for the *New York Times* travel section, as well as the *London Telegraph* and other international publications. In 2006, she moved to the Renaissance village of Pienza in southern Tuscany, where she designed and co-founded two boutique hotels: La Bandita Countryhouse and La Bandita Townhouse. She has appeared on *Condé Nast Traveler's Insider Guide,* airing on PBS, as well as *Good Morning America* and the *Today* show. She runs marathons for organizations like Mexico's Entreamigos and loves teaching English at Pienza's school. Now at work on a memoir, she lives with her son in the UNESCO-protected Val d'Orcia region.

ACKNOWLEDGMENTS

Ondine and Frances are grateful to the team at National Geographic who brought so much enthusiasm to this project. Our publisher, Lisa Thomas, and our editor, Hilary Black, inspired us throughout. Moriah Petty, our project editor, kept us on the mark and put together the complex combination of our stories. Our thanks to Elisa Gibson for designing; Moira Haney and Whitney Tressel for photo editing; to researchers Chris Barsanti and Katharine Shaw; to Daneen Goodwin and Ann Day, who handled marketing and publicity; and to Allyson Johnson for guidance. We are grateful to the many photographers whose work graces these pages. Andrea Wyner shot our authors' portrait and many more.

FRANCES: I'd like to thank Amy Alipio and George Stone for publishing a longer version of "Calabria" in National Geographic *Traveler*. I'm grateful to Fulvio Di Rosa for his excellent recommendations in Courmayeur and to Robert Draper for letting us tap into his vast knowledge of Friuli wines. Intrepid Sheryl Turping shared her Dolomite adventures. To my agent, Peter Ginsberg, and the whole staff at Curtis Brown Ltd., you are the best of the best! *Grazie mille,* Steven Barclay Agency, for such amazing speaking engagements.

Cin-cin, Kathy McCabe, for all the good times we had producing her PBS *Dream of Italy* show in Cortona. It's now out in the world. Another toast to Rita Braver and Alan Gold for bringing CBS's *Sunday Morning* to Bramasole.

How many people did I meet along the way? Hundreds. I can't express how generous and hospitable they were! Chefs ready to share, everyone ready to advise, pop a cork, joke, or help change a tire—what memories. I thank them all.

Ed, my husband, and my grandson William are the best travelers I know. We had fun everywhere because of their energy and *andiamo* attitudes. *Grazie.*

And Ondine, indefatigable, funny, and ready to go! *Amiche per sempre!*

ONDINE: First and foremost, thank you, Frances, for inviting me to this project. I learned so much more about this beautiful country and gained a mentor, and very close friend, in the process. I am so grateful to the many people who traveled with me: Alison Sager, Jonathon Dominic Spada, Philip Robinson, Laura Laureto, Matt Tyraneur, Annie Ojile, Katja Meier, and Alexandra Anza, to name just a few. My beloved son, Jacopo, always helps me discover this country more deeply—the little blondie with the Tuscan accent. Thank you, *amore!* I am also thankful to my editor, Melinda Stevens, at *Condé Nast Traveler* and to Amy Virshup and Lynda Richardson at the *New York Times,* for allowing me time to focus solely on this project. Thank you to the mentors who helped me become a writer: Aimee Bell, Eric Pooley, Clive Irving, Danielle Mattoon, Alex Postman, among others. Many thanks, dear friends Joanna Hershon, Marzena Korzeniowska, Sanjiv Desai, Charlotte Bavasso, Lauren Shenkman, Natalia Savignano, the Barlow family, Elizabeth Shenkman, Paolo Kastelec, Sidaya Sherwood, Amedeo Rosignoli, Viola Fabianelli, Tonje Kristiansen, Phillip Trenchard, and Sarah Bernard and the staff and guests of La Bandita (especially Chefs David and Bertie, who feed me so well). Along with my sister, Candida, they helped me navigate writing my first book and this new chapter of my life. *Grazie.*

ILLUSTRATIONS CREDITS

Cover: (UP LE), Andrea Wyner; (UP CTR), Pete Goding/SIME/eStock Photo; (UP RT), Ana Zaragoza/Getty Images; (LO), Karen Deakin/robertharding.com.
Back cover: ClickAlps/mauritius images GmbH/Alamy Stock Photo.

2-3, Susanne Kremer/Huber Images/eStock Photo; 4-5, Ben Pipe; 8, Piero M. Bianchi/Getty Images; 10-11, Chiara Salvadori/Getty Images; 12 (UP LE), Andrea Wyner; 12 (UP RT), Andrea Wyner; 12 (LO LE), L'Alimentare Gastronomia con Cucina/Nale Michela; 12 (LO RT), Maremagnum/Getty Images; 14, Roberto Moiola/robertharding.com; 16, SFM ITALY E/Alamy Stock Photo; 17, Andreas Strauss/LOOK-foto/Getty Images; 18-19, Ulla Lohmann/National Geographic Image Collection; 20-21, Ian.CuiYi/Getty Images; 22, Andrea Wyner; 23, Andrea Wyner; 24, Sandro Santioli/Alamy Stock Photo; 25, Courtesy of Elena Walch; 26, Andrea Wyner; 27, Hans-Bernhard Huber/laif/Redux; 28, Frank Fell/robertharding.com; 30, Andrea Wyner; 31, beppeverge/Getty Images; 32, Andrea Wyner; 33, Courtesy of Dante Rivetti; 34, Davide Guidolin/Alamy Stock Photo; 35, Jörg Modrow/laif/Redux; 36-7, Marco Brivio/Getty Images; 38, Andrea Wyner; 39, Franz Marc Frei/LOOK-foto/Getty Images; 40, Cenz07/Shutterstock.com; 41, Dagmar Schwelle/laif/Redux; 42-3, Andrea Wyner; 44, Vittoriano Rastelli/Corbis via Getty Images; 45, Fototeca Storica Nazionale/Getty Images; 46, DEA/G. Gnemmi/Getty Images; 47, DEA/G. De Giorgi/Getty Images; 48, Dario Fusaro/MARKA/Alamy Stock Photo; 50, Andrea Wyner; 51, Andrea Wyner; 52, Andrea Wyner; 53 (LE), Andrea Wyner; 53 (UP RT), Robert Haidinger/laif/Redux; 53 (LO RT), Andrea Wyner; 54, Alberto Bernasconi/laif/Redux; 55, Alberto Bernasconi/laif/Redux; 56, Gunnar Knechtel/laif/Redux; 57, Andrea Wyner; 58, Robert Haidinger/laif/Redux; 59, Courtesy The Yard Milano; 60, Vincent/CuboImages/robertharding.com; 61, StockFood/Jean-Francois Rivière; 62, Andrea Wyner; 63, Isabella De Maddalena/LUZ/Redux; 64, Ben Petcharapiracht/Shutterstock; 65, Andrea Wyner; 66, Loren Irving/age fotostock/robertharding.com; 67, Matteo Carassale/SIME/eStock Photo; 68, ClickAlps/mauritius images GmbH/Alamy Stock Photo; 69, trabantos/Shutterstock; 70, Steven Rothfeld; 72, Andrea Wyner; 73, Sebastian Wasek/robertharding.com; 74, Bisual Studio/Stocksy; 75, Vittorio Zunino Celotto/Getty Images; 76, Chris Sorensen/Gallery Stock; 77, Andrea Wyner; 78, Guido Baviera/SIME/eStock Photo; 79 (LE), Franco Cogoli/SIME/eStock Photo; 79 (UP RT), Peter Ptschelinzew/Getty Images; 79 (LO RT), Guido Baviera/SIME/eStock Photo; 80, Arcangelo Piai/SIME/SOPA Collection/Offset; 81, Sandra Raccanello/SIME/eStock Photo; 82, Andrea Wyner; 83, Courtesy of Aman; 84-5, Matteo Carassale/SIME/eStock Photo; 86, Stefano Renier/SIME/eStock Photo; 87 (LE), Andrea Wyner; 87 (UP RT), Matteo Carassale/SIME/eStock Photo; 87 (LO RT), Cedric Angeles/Intersection Photos; 88, Johanna Huber/SIME/eStock Photo; 89, Gabriele Croppi/SIME/eStock Photo; 90, Lisa Linder/SIME/eStock Photo; 91, Andrea Wyner; 92, Andrea Wyner; 94, René Mattes/hemis.fr/Alamy Stock Photo; 95, Jon Arnold/Getty Images; 96, Joakim Lloyd Raboff/Westend61/Offset; 97, Whitney Tressel; 98, Simone Anne/Stocksy; 99, Nicolas van Ryk/VISUM/Redux; 100-101, Andrea Wyner; 102, Al Hurley; 103, Dominique Faget/AFP/Getty Images; 104-5, Owen Franken/Getty Images; 106, Davide Carlo Cenadelli/SIME/eStock Photo; 107, Maremagnum/Getty Images; 108, Oleh_Slobodeniuk/Getty Images; 109, Andrea Wyner; 110, Massimo Siragusa/Agence VU/Redux; 112, Sofie Delauw/Getty Images; 113, JLPfeifer/Westend61/Offset; 114, milosk50/

Adobe Stock; 115 (LE), Ellen Rooney/robertharding.com; 115 (UP RT), Gianni Cipriano/The New York Times/Redux; 115 (LO RT), Sam Burton/Stocksy; 116, Roberto Manzotti/SIME/eStock Photo; 117, Pier Marco Tacca/Getty Images; 118, Andrés Benitez/Westend61/Offset; 119, Francesco Riccardo Iacomino/Getty Images; 120, Markus Kirchgessner/laif/Redux; 121, Massimo Ripani/SIME/eStock Photo; 122-3, Luca Da Ros/SIME/eStock Photo; 124, Elena de las Heras/robertharding.com; 126, Stefano Scata/SIME/eStock Photo; 127, Franco Cogoli/SIME/eStock Photo; 128, Stefano Renier/SIME/eStock Photo; 129 (LE), Franco Cogoli/SIME/eStock Photo; 129 (UP RT), Toni Anzenberger/Anzenberger/Redux; 129 (LO RT), Toni Anzenberger/Anzenberger/Redux; 130, Franco Cogoli/SIME/eStock Photo; 131, Federica Cattaruzzi/SIME/eStock Photo; 132, Imagno/Getty Images; 133, Rick Pushinsky/eyevine/Redux; 134-5, Riccardo Lombardo/REDA&CO/UIG via Getty Images; 136, Colin Dutton/SIME/eStock Photo; 137, Colin Dutton/SIME/eStock Photo; 138-9, Marco Secchi/Getty Images; 140, Nico Tondini/robertharding.com; 142, Thomas Linkel/laif/Redux; 143, Christian Kober/robertharding.com; 144, Christian Kober/robertharding.com; 145, Matteo Carassale/SIME/eStock Photo; 146, Franco Cogoli/SIME/eStock Photo; 147, Markus Kirchgessner/laif/Redux; 148, Aiace Bazzana/Les Crêtes; 149, Massimo Ripani/SOPA/eStock Photo; 150, Davide Erbetta/SIME/eStock Photo; 151, Colin Dutton/SIME/eStock Photo; 152-3, Nave Orgad/SIME/eStock Photo; 154 (UP LE), Francesco Riccardo Iacomino/Getty Images; 154 (UP RT), Andrea Wyner; 154 (LO LE), Andrea Wyner; 154 (LO RT), Andrea Wyner; 156, Andrea Wyner; 158, Gary Yeowell/Getty Images; 159, Steven Rothfeld; 160, Pietro Paolini/TerraProject/contrasto/Redux; 161, Giulio Andreini/MARKA/Alamy Stock Photo; 162, Andrea Wyner; 163, Massimo Borchi/SIME/eStock Photo; 164, Andrea Wyner; 165, Andrea Wyner; 166, Federico Magonio/Alamy Stock Photo; 167, Christina Anzenberger-Fink & Toni Anzenberger/Anzenberger/Redux; 168, Daniel Schoenen/robertharding.com; 169 (LE), Christina Anzenberger-Fink & Toni Anzenberger/Anzenberger/Redux; 169 (UP RT), Franz Marc Frei/robertharding.com; 169 (LO RT), Michele Borzoni/TerraProject/contrasto/Redux; 170, Nico Tondini/robertharding.com; 171, Massimo Ripani/SIME/eStock Photo; 172, Andrea Wyner; 173, Andrea Wyner; 174, Alexander Brookshaw - Brookshaw&Gorelli; 175, Christina Anzenberger-Fink & Toni Anzenberger/Anzenberger/Redux; 176, Stefano Cellai/SIME/eStock Photo; 179, Nathalie Krag, Courtesy of La Bandita; 180-81, Andrea Wyner; 182, Anika Buessemeier/laif/Redux; 184, Giorgio Filippini/SIME/eStock Photo; 185, e55evu/Getty Images; 186, Markus Lange/robertharding.com; 187, Toni Anzenberger/Anzenberger/Redux; 188-9, Toni Anzenberger/Anzenberger/Redux; 190, Stefano Dal Pozzolo/contrasto/Redux; 191, Frieder Blickle/laif/Redux; 192, Olaf Gunnarsson/Shutterstock; 193, argalis/Getty Images; 194 (UP), Flavio Vallenari/Getty Images; 194 (LO), Stefan Huwiler/imageBROKER/Alamy Stock Photo; 195, Maurizio Rellini/SIME/eStock Photo; 196, Doco Dalfiano/robertharding.com; 197, Colin Dutton/SIME/eStock Photo; 198, Westend61/Lorenzo Mattei/Getty Images; 199, Westend61/Lorenzo Mattei/Getty Images; 200, Tonino Conti/MARKA/Alamy Stock Photo; 201 (LE), Artwork by Piotr Uklaski, Photo courtesy Il Giardino dei Lauri; 201 (UP RT), Artwork by Ugo Rondinone, Photo by Ornella Tiberi, courtesy Il Giardino dei Lauri; 201 (LO RT), Courtesy Palazzo Lucarini; 202, Andrea Wyner; 204, Holger Burmeister/Alamy Stock Photo; 205, Massimo Ripani/SIME/eStock Photo; 206, Giuseppe Greco/SIME/eStock Photo; 207, Courtesy of Scooteroma; 208, Andrea Wyner; 209, Andrea Wyner; 210, Gianni Cipriano/The New York Times/Redux; 211, Chris Warde-Jones/The New York Times/Redux; 212, Andrea Wyner;

INDEX

ALWAYS ITALY

Since 1888, the National Geographic Society has funded more than 13,000 research, exploration, and preservation projects around the world. National Geographic Partners distributes a portion of the funds it receives from your purchase to National Geographic Society to support programs including the conservation of animals and their habitats.

National Geographic Partners
1145 17th Street NW
Washington, DC 20036-4688 USA

Get closer to National Geographic explorers and photographers, and connect with our global community. Join us today at nationalgeographic.com/join

For rights or permissions inquiries, please contact National Geographic Books Subsidiary Rights: bookrights@natgeo.com

Library of Congress Cataloging-in-Publication Data
Names: Mayes, Frances, author. | National Geographic Society (U.S.)
Title: Always Italy : an illustrated grand tour / Frances Mayes, with Ondine Cohane.
Description: Washington, DC : National Geographic, 2020. | Includes indexes.
Identifiers: LCCN 2019030816 | ISBN 9781426220913 (Hardcover)
Subjects: LCSH: Mayes, Frances--Travel--Italy. | Italy--Pictorial works. | Italy--Description and travel.
Classification: LCC DG430.2 .M395 2020 | DDC 914.504/9312092--dc23
LC record available at https://lccn.loc.gov/2019030816

Printed in Italy

19/EV/1